## DATE DUE

| | |
|---|---|
| MAY 3 0 1997 | |
| JUN 1 8 1997 | |
| FEB 2 7 2002 | |
| JUN - 6 2002 | |
| OCT - 7 2003 | |
| | |
| | |
| | |
| | |
| | |
| | |
| | |
| | |
| | |
| | |
| | |
| | |
| | |
| | |

BRODART                          Cat. No. 23-221

# BLACK MOUNTAIN

for Hannah and Megan

# BLACK MOUNTAIN

## LAND, CLASS AND POWER
## IN THE EASTERN ORANGE FREE STATE,
## 1880s TO 1980s

**COLIN MURRAY**

SMITHSONIAN INSTITUTION PRESS
Washington, D.C.

First published in the United States
by Smithsonian Institution Press

Photoset in Linotron Plantin
by Redwood Press, Melksham, Wiltshire and
printed in Great Britain by
Redwood Press

Library of Congress Catalog Number 92–60159
ISBN 1–56098–227–6

# CONTENTS

# FIGURES

# PHOTOGRAPHS

The photographs which appear between pages 203–204 are attributed on pages 324–5.

# PREFACE

The work that went into this book began by accident in March 1980 in an obscure rural slum in South Africa. For me, the project resembled the assembly of a vast and complex jigsaw without a preview of the final picture. The pieces of the jigsaw were gathered, slowly and haphazardly, over a period of more than ten years. Even as I write this preface, the last item to go to the publisher, I still pursue odd pieces, loose ends. In this sense, of course, the work will never be completed. Many people helped me to find the pieces or to discern their place in an emerging pattern. I should like to thank them here.

Above all, I am indebted to those whom I encountered in Onverwacht in 1980 and who committed their indignation and resilience and humour and parts of their life stories, unwittingly sometimes, to my field diaries. Together, their stories led me to ask the questions which ultimately shaped this book. I am also indebted to many other people, in Thaba Nchu and elsewhere, whose experience and goodwill gave me raw material. The endnotes for each chapter specifically attribute much of this material and also identify the other sources, published and unpublished, that I have used. Other debts should be explicitly acknowledged here.

Many people gave me hospitality and help of various kinds. In Thaba Nchu itself, I have to thank particularly Raphael Mothe and Peter Brislin and other priests of the Catholic mission; Walter Gill and his family, of the Methodist church; and Lawrence and Dorothy Hall, of the Presbyterian church. Throughout the 1980s, Eunice Sebotha gave me sharp and seasoned guidance to the intricate affairs of the Barolong elite. Sam Bairstow's generous bar gave me access to the hardly less intricate affairs of the English-speaking farming families south of Tweespruit. David Ambrose, in Lesotho, gave me the benefit of his unrivalled knowledge of sources for the region, ranging from old newspapers to modern maps. He and Sumitra Talukdar were also warm hosts on several occasions, as were John and Judy Gay of the Transformation Resource Centre in Maseru. For their hospitality, friendship and assistance, I want to thank Joan and Tony McGregor, outside Johannesburg; and Connie and Mollie Anderson, outside Bloemfontein. John and Pam Parr, near Thaba Phatshwa, introduced me to the 'Coloured' village there and also kindly put me up. John and Jill Moffett, on their farm near Gumtree (eastern Orange Free State), helped me with my enquiries on the Newberry family; and David Boddam-Whetham, of Cathcart (eastern Cape), whom I never met, wrote at length with his reminiscences of three generations of that family.

Janet Tomkins worked for me in Bloemfontein and with me in Pretoria. Her special quality of attending to fine detail turned a potentially tedious trawl of transfer deeds and mortgage bonds into a mine of fascinating information. Laurine Platzky, who co-ordinated the Surplus People Project, offered tireless support to me over many years. Karen Legge pursued particular sources for me in the Botswana National Archives, Gaborone. Andy Manson obtained copies of land transactions registered in Mmabatho (Bophuthatswana). Kevin Shillington and Brian Willan responded generously to my several impositions on their expertise. John Parkington in Cape Town, David Scogings in Durban and Glen Mills in Bloemfontein enabled me to obtain aerial photographs of Thaba Nchu and Onverwacht/Botshabelo. Tim Couzens in Johannesburg made contact with the daughter of a Milner settler on my behalf. William Beinart, Mark Beittel and Diana Wylie made separate exploratory forays for me in the Union Archives in Pretoria. Andrew Spiegel carried out one inter-view for me in Cape Town, pursued a number of enquiries on my behalf and managed my precarious finances in South Africa for more than a decade.

For help with documentary evidence in Britain and South Africa, I should like particularly to thank Anna Cunningham, Curator of Manuscripts of the library of the University of the Witwatersrand; Annica Van Gylswyk of the Documentation Centre for African Studies, University of South Africa; Michael Berning, Cory Librarian, Rhodes University; and Anne Rowland, of the Sydney Jones Library, University of Liverpool. I also acknowledge the help of staff at the library of the School of Oriental and African Studies, London; Rhodes House, Oxford; the Public Record Office, London; the Orange Free State Archives, Bloemfontein; the Union Archives, Pretoria; the Deeds Registry and the offices of the Surveyor-General and the Master of the Supreme Court, Bloemfontein.

Several people translated documents for me from Setswana or Afrikaans or Dutch into English: Catharine Thupayagale, William Beinart, Reinier Holst, Joan McGregor, John Sharp, Marij van Helmond and Emanuel Kreike. I remember also the intensive sessions of 'school' work we undertook in 1980 outside the Bakane homestead in Ha Motšoane, Leribe district, Lesotho, transcribing and translating interviews from Onverwacht recorded in Sesotho. Mmapuleng Moetsuoa Bakane, in her inimitably caustic manner, contributed most to that task.

I am grateful to the Directors of the Southern African Research Program at Yale University, who invited me to spend the Fall semester of 1988 in New Haven as a Fellow of the Program. It was indeed a haven for writing. For company and conversation in that period, I especially thank Diana Wylie, William Beinart and Dunbar Moodie.

I acknowledge small grants of financial support for this work from the British Academy (twice); the Twenty-Seven Foundation; and the Research Fund of the Liverpool Institute of Higher Education.

For reading the manuscript, in whole or in part, and giving me valuable comment, I thank William Beinart, Diana Wylie, John Peel and Pepe Roberts. Paul Smith drew most of the maps; Sandra Mather drew the rest and also composed the genealogies, mysteriously, on the Apple in the drawing office of the Geography Department, University of Liverpool. Ian Qualtrough prepared the photographs.

For their support and enthusiasm over the years, I should like to thank John Peel, Sandy Robertson and Francis Wilson. I am very grateful for all the help I received. I take sole responsibility for the way in which I have fitted the pieces of the jigsaw together.

Colin Murray
Liverpool
May 1991

# NOTE ON CONVENTIONS

For convenience I have followed official usage in the Orange Free State and in South Africa in respect of units of land measurement and of currency. Farm sizes were expressed in morgen until the 1960s and in hectares thereafter. The conversion factor is 1 morgen (10,000 square yards) = 0.836 hectares = 2.067 acres; or 1 hectare (10,000 square metres) = 1.196 morgen = 2.471 acres.

Similarly, I have expressed land prices etc. in pounds sterling until 1961, when the Union became the Republic, and in South African rands thereafter. The rate of exchange was £1 = R2 until devaluation of the pound in 1967, and fluctuated through the 1970s and 1980s. The value of the rand declined sharply in the 1980s against many other currencies; it was worth US $1.30 in January 1980 and $0.43 in January 1988.

Quitrent tenure is a form of long-term occupation of land, subject to a small annual payment of rent to the government, depending on the quality of the land occupied.

I have retained the prefixes used by Africans to distinguish the people of the eastern Orange Free State, collectively (Basotho, Barolong) and individually (Mosotho, Morolong), from their language and culture (Sesotho, Serolong). My inconsistent use of particular orthographies in the text reflects the variations of habit and preference that are commonly found between different languages or dialects and between speakers of the same language from different regions. In any case, orthographical conventions themselves changed over time. For example, *pitso* (public assembly), a word common to Sesotho and Serolong, was also written *pico* in Serolong; and the name Bogatsu appears in some sources as Bogacu. I have used some words familiar in Serolong or Sesotho or Afrikaans: their meaning is explained in the text at the point they first appear. Casspirs and hippoes are armoured trucks that were sent into black townships during the States of Emergency of the 1980s.

# ABBREVIATIONS

| | |
|---|---|
| AAC | All-African Convention |
| AME | African Methodist Episcopal Church |
| ANC (in text) | African National Congress |
| ANC (in notes) | Assistant/Additional Native Commissioner |
| BAC | Bantu Affairs Commissioner |
| BAD | Bantu Administration and Development |
| BNDC | Bophuthatswana National Development Corporation |
| BPA | Barolong Progressive Association |
| BSSA | British Settlement of South Africa |
| CBAC | Chief Bantu Affairs Commissioner |
| CNC | Chief Native Commissioner |
| FA | Farmers' Association |
| GG | Government Garage |
| ICU | Industrial and Commercial Workers' Union of Africa |
| IDP | Industrial Development Point |
| JP | Justice of the Peace |
| MP | Member of Parliament |
| NAC | Native Affairs Commission |
| NAD | Native Affairs Department |
| NC | Native Commissioner |
| NCAR | National Committee Against Removals |
| NEC | Native Economic Commission 1930–32 |
| NP | National Party |
| OFS | Orange Free State |
| ORC | Orange River Colony |
| RC | Resident Commissioner |
| RM | Resident Magistrate |
| RSC | Regional Services Council |
| SADT | South African Development Trust (see SANT) |
| SAIRR | South African Institute of Race Relations |
| SANAC | South African Native Affairs Commission 1903–5 |
| SANT | South African Native Trust (see SADT) |
| SAP | South African Party |
| SNA | Secretary for Native Affairs |
| SPP | Surplus People Project |

STK          South African Development Trust Corporation
TBVC        Transkei, Bophuthatswana, Venda, Ciskei [the four 'in-dependent' Bantustans]
TTA          Tswana Territorial Authority

# INTRODUCTION

# A STUDY OF ONE DISTRICT

You can see more land and less scenery in the Free State than in any country in the world

Leonard Flemming
*A Fool on the Veld* (1916), pp. 3–4

August 1983. A slow passage by train across the parched winter veld. From the eastern border to the western border of the (old) Thaba Nchu district, the journey from Westminster to Sannahspos begins and ends, so to speak, at the turn of the century. The distance is only 70 km but the train takes nearly two hours: time to call up the shadows of the past, to pick out the landmarks of the present and to stir the entrails of the future. In his fondly satirical remark on the absence of scenery in the Free State, Leonard Flemming was unfair to this eastern corner of it. The landscape here is one of hazy grandeur, dominated by Thaba Nchu, Black Mountain (see Figure I.1).

The train left Bethlehem, in the north-eastern Orange Free State (OFS), at 0900 hours. Flanked by groves of eucalyptus, in the dry heat of mid-day, the line curves through the modern districts of Fouriesburg, Ficksburg, Clocolan and Ladybrand. These are the fertile wheat and maize lands of the Conquered Territory, taken by the OFS republic from the Basotho of Chief Moshoeshoe in the second Sotho-Boer war of 1865–8 (Chapter 1). On the eastern horizon are the jagged outlines of the Maluti mountain range in Lesotho. After Modderpoort and Marseilles, the junction for the short line to Maseru, the train pauses at the Westminster halt. This was named after 'Bendor', the second Duke of Westminster, who bought the surrounding land at the end of the South African war (Chapter 2). The splendid stables of his estate, designed by the architect Herbert Baker, still contain the saddles and bridles of forgotten Derby winners.

The train now enters the (old) Thaba Nchu district, the territory that belonged for half a century, from 1833 to 1884, to a political community of Seleka Barolong, ruled by Chief Moroka (Chapter 1). In a straight line to the south-east, on the Leeuw river, lie the grand sandstone ruins of the Newberry mill. Built in the early 1890s with Kimberley diamond money, the mill flourished on the grain boom in the OFS which followed the discovery of gold in the Transvaal in 1886 (Chapter 1). Hard by the railway line, to the north, lies the lovely homestead of Goschen. It was built in the 1920s for G.J. Van Riet, one of the local lawyers who assisted Barolong landowners to part with their farms (Chapters 3 and 4).

Passing the Tweespruit Agricultural School to the south, and the Catholic mission where the Flemish painter and priest, Frans Claerhout, has lived and worked for many years, the train stops with a ponderous hiss of brakes at Tweespruit station. It is besieged there by a disorderly cohort of hungry children, who scrabble for cigarettes and five-cent pieces tossed casually from the 'white' carriages by youthful conscripts bound for the defence of white supremacy. The grain silos which tower above the village declare its modern function as a service centre for white commercial farmers, themselves besieged in the 1980s by drought and debt, inflation and high interest rates. In the heyday of the Milner settlers (Chapter 2), Tweespruit was a small outpost of empire: cricket, bowls, tennis and—above all—alcohol. In the guerilla phase of the South African war, the open undulating country to the south was studded with Lord Kitchener's blockhouses. Between the two World Wars, it was the terrain of two 'Potato Kings'—Daniel McPherson and Jacob Boris Lurie, arch-rivals, the one an Irishman, the other a Lithuanian Jew (Chapters 3 and 7).

Further south, in the shimmer of the afternoon sun, looms the distant bulk of Thaba Phatshwa, described in 1836 by the French missionary, Thomas Arbousset, as 'one of the most beautiful mountains of the country'. Below it is the farm which belonged to Ellen Kuzwayo's grandfather, Jeremiah Makgothi, and which she fondly remembered in her autobiography, *Call Me Woman*. The farm was dismembered by his children's debts, and emerged in the era of apartheid, incongruously, as a small 'Coloured' reserve (Chapter 7). In the opposite direction, to the north of Tweespruit, wrapped around Moroto hill, are the farms which comprised the Setlogelo family estate. The northern boundary of the estate is the lovely 'ridge of cannibals' known in Serolong as Rakhoi and in Afrikaans as the Mensvre.tersberg. Like many other Barolong landowners, the Setlogelos lost most of their land in the 1920s and the 1930s; but their descendants were ubiquitous within the local state at Thaba Nchu in the 1980s (Chapters 3 and 5).

The train moves on across Egypte farm. This farm was divided amongst the sixteen heirs of the Barolong chief, Tshipinare, after his murder in 1884 and the annexation of his country by the OFS (Chapter 1). Most of the heirs rapidly sold their titles to Cornelis Van der Wath, the first OFS-appointed *landdrost* (magistrate) of the district. Close to the railway line, a fenced family graveyard reserves a small spot of eternity for some of Van der Wath's descendants. Beyond it, a shady clump of trees marks the boundary of the (new) district of Thaba Nchu, a part of Bophuthatswana, the otherwise distant Tswana Bantustan. The train pauses at Waghorn siding, below Mohono hill. Here and there, on adjoining fragments of black-owned land, are clusters of makeshift huts—a transient refuge for people forced off white-owned farms throughout the eastern OFS in the 1970s and early 1980s (Chapter 6). Most of these huts were cleared by the Bophuthatswana authorities towards the end of 1983.

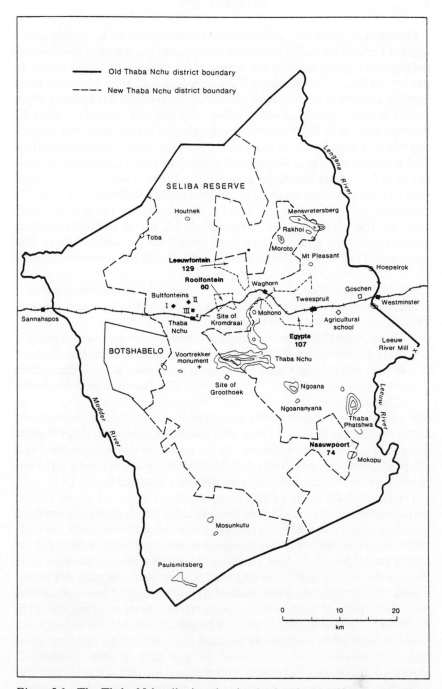

*Figure I.1* The Thaba Nchu district, showing landmarks identified in the railway journey from Westminster to Sannahspos.

Skirting a dry river bed, and crossing an open grazing area, the train passes south of Leeuwfontein, the Ramagaga family farm; and traverses Rooifontein, the Matsheka family farm, on the eastern edge of the Thaba Nchu reserve. In the late 1930s, Elisha Maimane Ramagaga and Kali John Matsheka led a populist movement known as the Barolong Progressive Association, which sought to recover lost land and to subvert the established chief (Chapter 4). Entering the Thaba Nchu reserve, the train passes the old Mokwena location and follows a wide kink in the line before reaching Thaba Nchu station. This kink embraces the site of Kromdraai, a dense sprawl of corrugated sheeting and mud-brick huts which was home in the 1970s to nearly 40,000 'illegal squatters' who were not welcome in the 'land of the Barolong' (Chapter 6). By December 1979 Kromdraai was razed to the ground and the squatters were expelled. The site adjoins that of Bultfontein III, one of a series of legalised slums which were established on land owned by the South African Development Trust on the western border of the Thaba Nchu reserve (Chapter 5).

It is 1650 hours. While the train rests at Thaba Nchu station, there is time to gaze southwards at the mountain that gave the district its name. In September 1913, in Solomon Plaatje's account:

> Thaba Ncho Hill in the background, always visible for scores of miles in every direction, towered high above the surrounding landscape. Its stony slopes covered with a light mist from peak to base, it stood like a silent witness to the outraged treaty between the Barolong and the Boers. (Chapter 3)

Below its western shoulder stands a monument to the arrival of the Voortrekkers in the summer of 1836–7. They were hospitably received by Chief Moroka (Chapter 1). Behind the mountain, to the south, lie the ruins of the Trust village of Groothoek, which was destroyed in 1982, a century and a half later, to make way for a game park and a luxury hotel (Chapter 5).

The train sets off again, puffing slowly past the Bultfontein slums. Clearly visible on the northern horizon is the long ridge which marks the southern boundary of the old Seliba reserve. Here was concentrated, from the early 1940s, three decades of popular resistance to the 'betterment' schemes of the central state (Chapter 5). Late afternoon shadows lengthen as the train pulls through the narrow gap of Israelspoort. To the south, outside Bophuthatswana, the westering sun glints on a vast array of corrugated iron roofs. This is Botshabelo: place of refuge for the Kromdraai squatters; dumping ground in the 1980s for several hundred thousand people squeezed off white farms and removed from urban locations all over the OFS; test site for the strategy of 'orderly urbanisation' which replaced the pass laws in 1986 (Chapter 6). Morning and evening, Monday to Saturday, a thick pall of dust hangs over Botshabelo as more than one hundred yellow commuter buses ply the route to and from Bloemfontein, the provincial capital, 60 km distant. Somewhere else in South Africa, the proprietors of Jakaranda Transport count the profits they extract from this waste of oil and human energy sponsored by the state.

The train bends around the contour of the Sepane stream. In the brief twilight of a winter evening, it clanks across the Modder river bridge, the western boundary of the (old) Thaba Nchu district. The journey through Moroka's territory is done. At Sannahspos, a graveyard and a small museum commemorate the ambush of a British force in March 1900 by the Boer general, Christiaan De Wet (Chapter 2).

This book is a detailed study of the (old) Thaba Nchu district over a period of one hundred years, from the 1880s to the 1980s.[1] It offers a spotlight of parochial intensity on the struggles of many of the people, black and white, who have made their lives in this part of the eastern OFS. In many respects, the Thaba Nchu district was typical of the mixed arable and pastoral districts of the southern highveld region which Tim Keegan explored in his pioneering work on agrarian transformations in the late nineteenth and early twentieth centuries.[2] Chapter 2 of this book, in particular, exemplifies a major part of Keegan's argument. It shows how the new South African state intervened in the countryside, with vigour and consistency and a large imperial loan, both to promote the capitalisation of white commercial farming and to subvert a semi-independent black peasantry.

In other respects, however, the Thaba Nchu district has a quite distinctive history. First, it was the only district in the OFS in which Africans held freehold title to land. Second, it contained two of the three small African reserves in the OFS. Third, reduced to little more than one-third of its original size, it emerged in the 1970s as part of 'independent' Bophuthatswana. Thus it became a Tswana enclave in the heart of a region where the language of power was Afrikaans and the first language of most of the inhabitants was Sesotho. All these features give the story of Thaba Nchu a peculiar interest and complexity.

The genesis of this project was the rumours I heard in March 1980 of a huge new slum half-way between Bloemfontein, the provincial capital of the OFS, and Maseru, the capital of Lesotho. Neither its name—ironically, after the farm Onverwacht ('Unexpected')—nor its precise location were then known to me or to the members of the Surplus People Project, based in Cape Town, which was about to undertake a comprehensive national survey of forced relocation. I had carried out a study of migrant labour from Lesotho in the early 1970s. In 1980, from an academic base in Liverpool, I returned to Lesotho for several months to investigate the effects of changes in mine labour recruitment which had taken place in the mid-1970s and which became known in the literature as 'internalisation' and 'stabilisation'. Two effects were obvious: sharply increased inequality of earnings, and spiralling youth unemployment.[3]

The 'discovery' of the new slum, however, entirely changed the direction of my work. Onverwacht was already a vast untidy sprawl of shacks and tents, which contained about a hundred thousand people. The site was 12 km south-west of Thaba Nchu town, from where it could be reached by rutted track. It could not, of course, be found on any map. I had two reactions, both intense: of shock and curiosity. From my old village base in Lesotho, I visited Onverwacht warily but repeatedly, and recorded the anger and frustration of some of the people who had been dumped there in poverty and squalor. They were harassed under the pass laws if they sought work in Bloemfontein. Their children were exposed to cold and hunger on the open veld.

I gathered case studies of the experiences of individual households over the previous ten or fifteen years. The question then arose of how to write up this material. As I probed the details, I grew convinced that they had to be understood as the outcomes not only of the routine brutalities of the central state but also of the particular complexities of the history of the region. The Kromdraai refugees, for example, told hair-raising stories of the violence inflicted upon them, but not by the South African police. Their terror—fresh in their minds at the time—was of 'MaYB', the Bophuthatswana police, who had made their lives a misery on the squatter site by the railway line in Thaba Nchu from which they had been removed in the second half of 1979. I had therefore to explain *why* these people, most of whom were Basotho, were not welcome in the 'land of the Barolong'. What land? To whom did it belong? Why? Each partial answer spawned a fresh tangle of further questions.

My planned research in Lesotho had already been overtaken by the urgency, as I saw it in 1980, of an investigation of mass relocation to two prime dumping grounds in the Orange Free State: the new slum of Onverwacht, described above, which later became known as Botshabelo; and the tiny South Sotho Bantustan of Qwaqwa, on the border of Lesotho, Natal and the OFS.[4] As I explored the labyrinth of struggles over land in the eastern OFS as a whole, the focus of this study both contracted in space and deepened in time. It became a study of major themes in the history of the Thaba Nchu district, strictly and narrowly construed as the territory of Chief Moroka's Barolong that was annexed by the OFS in 1884.

The geographical range contracted and the temporal perspective deepened because, in groping for an adequate framework of analysis, I found it necessary to root a study of forced relocation in regional history as well as in macro political economy. In 1984, at a Harvard workshop on 'households' in Africa, I was impressed by the insouciance of method and philosophy with which researchers at the Fernand Braudel Center at Binghampton (New York State) sought to relate their understanding of Southern African 'households' to changes in the 'world economy' through time. By contrast, I found it sufficiently difficult, empirically and analytically, to try to relate the experiences of households in the slum of Onverwacht to changes in the regional economy of the eastern OFS.[5] As the work slowly progressed, I found that even one district was too large and complex a unit of study for me to arrive at any easy generalisations.

There were other circumstances that impelled a severe practical modesty of aspiration. Firstly, my prime commitment was to rearing my two daughters in Liverpool (England), half a world away from Thaba Nchu. They are duly acknowledged at the front of this book. Secondly, throughout the 1980s, the decade of my preoccupation with this project, my visits to South Africa for fieldwork and archival research were clandestine in the sense that my visa exemption status, as a British citizen, had been withdrawn and I could not obtain a visa. For purposes of entry into South Africa, I could only use one border post with Lesotho, and that was subject to the tyranny of chance. Apart from the series of forays to Onverwacht in 1980 which I have described above, fieldwork for this project was irregular and haphazard, confined to brief and intensive visits of ten days in December 1981, three weeks in August–September 1983, three weeks in June–July 1986 and two weeks in August 1989. Fast work and trust were only possible because of the effective fluency in Sesotho that I had acquired through previous and very different experience of fieldwork in Lesotho.

Inevitably, these circumstances precluded many possibilities of direct investigation. I was unable to interview officials, for example, either of the South African state or of Bophuthatswana. In any case I had a merely rudimentary knowledge of Afrikaans, the language of the 'master race'. I was seldom able to interview people who lived in Trust villages because their headmen, fearful of official retribution, would not approve even casual conversation with a foreigner without papers. I am also acutely conscious of a lack of depth of oral evidence from the Barolong elite. This is attributable partly to the low profile that I had to assume and partly to their striking propensity to guard their own secrets, though not necessarily those of others. By contrast, I found that the inhabitants of Onverwacht/Botshabelo, devoid of property and power, talked freely about their lives and their problems. Infused with bitterness and humour and passion, they were much better informants than the Barolong elite.

For me, the intellectual fascination of the project was two-fold. In the first place, I had the opportunity and the challenge of connecting obscure and often esoteric archival evidence with contemporary oral history. Prime sources of documentary evidence, all in Bloemfontein, were the Free State Archives Depot, the Deeds Registry, and the records of the Master of the Supreme Court. Transfer deeds, mortgage bonds and estate papers together yielded invaluable material on the habits of the propertied classes, black and white: their marriages and divorces and family disputes, their testamentary dispositions, their proliferating debts and the wrangles of their lawyers. It was clear from the beginning that members of landowning families, black or white, would be identified in this book by their own names; otherwise they would be arbitrarily 'cut off' from their own family histories.

Two problems arose from this. One was the acute sensitivity of reputations. Inevitably, some passages in this book will cause offence. I can only offer the assurance that my intention throughout has been to illustrate social process and not to impugn or to malign individuals. I would also hope that any private offence will be outweighed by a sense of curiosity about the ancestors which would have been wholly deflated if I had changed people's names. The other problem was one of differential anonymity. I had originally intended to 'protect' from being identified those victims of forced relocation and other members of the 'under-classes', in the broadest sense, who talked freely of their experiences. On reflection, however, I have decided not to use pseudonyms at all. People who do not leave records in dusty archival repositories also have pride in their family histories. Why should I gratuitously preclude them from speaking in their own names here? Anthropologists and other intellectuals who disguise their oral sources also reduce their own accountability. Where, indeed, should I have drawn the line between the use of real names and the adoption of pseudonyms: between the propertied and the unpropertied classes, between the powerful and the powerless, between the literate (some of whom might read this book) and the illiterate (who will not)? I hope that, in avoiding pseudonymous attributions, I have abused no confidences.

The second intellectual stimulation of writing this book was the sheer diversity of experience encountered within easy range to the north and the south of the railway line described above. The history of Thaba Nchu that I have tried to write is not the preserve of any ethnic or racial group or of any local faction. Specifically, it is not the history of the Seleka Barolong who settled in the territory in 1833, lost it to the OFS in 1884 and partially regained it through the 'independence' of Bophuthatswana in 1977. The Barolong elite is strongly represented in these pages; yet its local political pre-eminence has been contested for a hundred years by a dissident faction with a very different consciousness of the historical record (see Chapter 4). Again, this book is not the history of the Milner settlers whose descendants inter-married through several generations and remained custodians of the Tweespruit tradition of expansive hospitality. In the 1980s they comprised some of the 'oldest' white families in the district; but they had barely an inkling of a past in which an African chief had ruled their land.

Recovery of these diverse traditions does not imply endorsement of any one of them. Indeed, as a succession of more or less tenuous claims to the land, each one places another in perspective, like ripples from stones tossed into a pond. As the Conclusion makes clear, there is neither a single nor a simple answer to the question: whose land? Any attempt to answer it has to accommodate the stark fact that the majority of the people who were living in the (old) Thaba Nchu district in the 1980s had no roots in the district. Chapter 6 explains why

this was so. The implication, however, is an important one. The history of
Thaba Nchu cannot be reduced to the engagement between one 'system' and
another 'system': that of pre-capitalist African society on the one hand and that
of western industrial capitalism on the other hand.[6] In the first place, such a
paradigm does scant justice to the complexity of the struggles outlined in this
study. In the second place, it exaggerates the integrity both of social structure
and of cultural experience, as if all Barolong belonged to one 'society' or all
Afrikaners shared the same world view. I was already deeply sceptical of the
search for any 'essences' of social structure or of culture. The writing of this
book reinforced that scepticism.

Similarly, there is neither a single nor a simple answer to the question which
dominated debates on the agrarian question in South Africa in the 1980s: when
and how did the transition to capitalist agriculture take place?[7] In a review of
this controversial terrain in 1990, Helen Bradford concluded, firstly, that the
driving force of transformation in agriculture was capital from outside;
secondly, that the process by which labour power became a commodity was
one of protracted struggle and regionally variable outcome; and, thirdly, that
these outcomes were critically influenced by diverse forms of state intervention.[8] The present study of Thaba Nchu fully vindicates these points but
also demonstrates significant variability of outcome *within* one district over
time. As I show in the analysis which follows, much of this variability of
outcome derived from the fact of African landownership, a feature unique
within the OFS.

Nevertheless, large historical trends are clearly discernible. This book about
one district contains all the important themes of the political economy of the
rural highveld of South Africa in the late nineteenth and the twentieth centuries. Africans were dispossessed of most of their land, in this case more by
the pen than by the gun. The countryside was ravaged by one of Lord Milner's
lofty imperial visions, and then repaired by another. White farmers were
launched by a 'progressive' state on a trajectory of capital accumulation. Black
peasants' livelihoods were destroyed by that same racist state. Under mounting
structural pressure, exacerbated by the great depression of the 1930s, Africans
became migrants in town or labour tenants and wage labourers in the white-
owned countryside.

In the African reserves, meanwhile, from the 1940s onwards, the central
state intervened heavily in the rural economy and imposed an oppressive
bureaucratic superstructure. The apartheid regime tightened in the 1950s; a
surge of capital intensification swept across white farms in the 1960s; and
hundreds of thousands of people were removed to the Bantustans in the
following decades. These became places of hunger and over-crowding and
joblessness and vicious inter-ethnic strife. In myriad ways, resistance to the
machinations of the central state was inverted and displaced. Popular anger
was turned against the Bantustan autocracies. In the 1980s, particularly, it was

also turned against black local authorities in 'white' South Africa. They were rickety structures of municipal oppression set up by Pretoria in the name of limited black self-government outside the Bantustans.

At the end of 1990, with the emergence of a 'new' South Africa in prospect, it is clear that the formal rigidities of racial discrimination have shifted to a significant degree. It is equally clear that the underlying structural problems of extreme inequality, intractable violence and acute poverty and unemployment will not swiftly dissolve.[9]

# 1

# 'DUST AND ASHES':
# THE COLLAPSE OF AN AFRICAN POLITY

They sowed the wind but don't believe in reaping the whirlwind.

John Daniel
Methodist missionary, Thaba Nchu
CLHR, MS 15 620, circuit report 1880

Tho' men's minds were not very easy, yet it was not imagined for a moment that a rough, strong and violent wind was rising which would in no long time scatter us to all the points of the compass like the down of some scotch thistle.

George Mitchell
Anglican missionary, Thaba Nchu
USPG, E35A, report 30 September 1880

Two prophetic comments, by rival observers, on the 'eating up' by Chief Tshipinare of the principal supporters of his enemy, Samuel Lehulere, in the first phase of the Barolong civil war.

In December 1874, in the middle of an oppressively hot summer, the historian James Anthony Froude took a short break from a controversial and partly clandestine mission in South Africa. On behalf of his friend Lord Carnarvon, the British Colonial Secretary, he was investigating the political obstacles to federation of the various states in the region. From Bloemfontein, the capital of the OFS republic, Froude visited Thaba Nchu for two days, and found a town of '1,500 beehive huts, thatched with reeds, each surrounded by a stone wall. Swarms of children were playing in the sunshine'. The old chief Moroka, who ruled over the territory, Froude described as a 'relic of another age'; he was 'handsomely dressed in leopard-skins, and walking slowly with a knob-stick'. By contrast, Moroka was attended by a 'middle-aged thick-set man, dressed in a Methodist parson's cast-off suit of clothes', who was almost certainly the chief's adopted son Tshipinare.[1]

Three years later, in 1877, Anthony Trollope—retired British post official, prolific novelist and restless veteran of several colonial tours—likewise briefly enjoyed the hospitality of the Methodist missionary at Thaba Nchu. He estimated that 6,000 people lived in the town, which he described as 'one of the most interesting places in South Africa'. Moroka he found querulous and gouty, wearing an old skin cloak and 'a most iniquitous slouch hat'; whereas Tshipinare, who obviously had much executive authority, was 'a well built man, six feet high, broad in the shoulders, and with the gait of a European'. He

wore 'a watch and chain at his waistcoat, a round flat-topped hat, and cord
trowsers, and was quite clean'. Tshipinare also had a large iron double bed-
stead which Trollope was sure had come from 'Mr Heal's establishment' in
London's Tottenham Court Road.[2]

These two vignettes reflect the transient curiosity of travellers from Europe
about a place which appears both in their own memoirs and on contemporary
maps as a geographical and political anomaly. Through the 1870s and the early
1880s, Thaba Nchu was an independent African chiefdom entirely surrounded
by a Boer republic which was constitutionally committed to white political
supremacy and exclusively white landownership. The chiefdom had been
decisively drawn into the new regional economy whose core was the rapidly
developing Diamond Fields at Kimberley. But it retained a quaintly dignified
autonomy, in which the routines of traditional authority were exercised without political threat to the Boer republic which surrounded it. It is striking that
both Froude and Trollope identified the distinctive blend of the old and the
new by reference to the incongruities of style and dress between Moroka and
Tshipinare.

Thaba Nchu in the 1870s comprised more than 1,200 square miles of
valuable arable and pasture land. It adjoined the 'Conquered Territory' taken
by the OFS republic from the Basotho of Moshoeshoe during the second
Sotho–Boer war of 1865–8 (see Figure 1.1). The population of Thaba Nchu
was about 12,000 to 15,000, distributed between the town itself and outlying
villages. The majority of the people were Seleka Barolong. They identified
themselves as members of a political community which had been founded in
the region north of the Vaal river in the late eighteenth century by Seleka, one
of the sons of Tau, the last chief of all the Barolong. Under circumstances
described below, the Seleka Barolong migrated to Thaba Nchu in the early
1830s, and they formed the core of Moroka's chiefdom through the middle
decades of the nineteenth century. They spoke Serolong, which is classified by
comparative linguists as a dialect of the Tswana language cluster of the Sotho
group of the South-eastern zone of Bantu languages.[3]

The staple diet at Thaba Nchu was sorghum porridge, but the people also
cultivated maize, wheat, beans, pumpkins, melons and a variety of sugar-cane.
Such a concentrated population was, as Trollope remarked, vulnerable to
famine, and the inhabitants of Thaba Nchu frequently had to import grain
from Basutoland. They were also vulnerable to the rapid inflationary pressures
which rippled outwards from the Diamond Fields. In response, they sold
increasing quantities of sheep's wool; some found employment at Kimberley
itself; others earned a living as transport-riders; and it was common for
Moroka's subjects to take annual or seasonal contracts as labourers on white-
owned farms in adjoining districts of the Free State. Contemporary observers
noted a significant shift in the sexual division of labour in this period. The
widespread introduction of ox-drawn ploughs induced men to assume prime

responsibility for ploughing; whereas women continued to carry out most other agricultural tasks.[4]

Livestock—mainly cattle, sheep and horses—were usually kept at a grazing camp in one of the outlying parts of the Barolong territory, so that many households either maintained two homes, alternating seasonally between them, or divided their members between town and country in a pattern similar to that found in modern Botswana. Corresponding to this pattern, Moroka's authority, exercised through councillors and a hierarchy of subordinate chiefs and headmen, was subject to a structural tension that is familiar in the historical record of Sotho-Tswana social formations. On the one hand, a strong chief enforced a regime of political centralisation. On the other hand, pressures towards residential dispersal reflected the exigencies of arable and pastoral resource management in a relatively arid environment.[5]

As Trollope predicted, the 1870s were the twilight years of the Barolong chiefdom at Thaba Nchu. In 1884, the territory was annexed by the OFS and its political independence was dissolved. I explore the reasons for this in the following two sections of this chapter, which are concerned with the developing tensions of the 1870s and the civil war of the early 1880s. I then examine in some detail the land dispositions made in 1885, for they hold the key to an analysis of processes of social differentiation in the district over the next hundred years. The most important element of these dispositions was the granting of freehold titles to senior members of the Barolong political elite. Nearly two-thirds of the land granted in this way was rapidly alienated to whites in the late 1880s and early 1890s. The final section of this chapter investigates the causes and the consequences of land loss on this scale.

## TWILIGHT OF SELF-RULE

In the mid-eighteenth century the Barolong—the people of the kudu (*tholo*)—occupied land between the Molopo and the Vaal rivers (the northern Cape and the south-western Transvaal), under their last great warrior chief, Tau. His death in about 1760 precipitated a process of political fission from which emerged a number of independent communities identified by reference to the names of four of his sons: Ratlou, Tshidi, Seleka and Rapulana. Some further subdivisions took place. In the 1820s, all these communities were caught up in the chronic insecurities of the upheaval on the highveld known to the Sotho-Tswana people as the *difaqane*. The Seleka Barolong established temporary headquarters first at Maquassi (south of Wolmaransstad) and then at Motlhana-wa-Pitse (Platberg) on the Vaal river (Figure 1.1). There they were joined by clusters of other refugees. By December 1833, the population had swelled to approximately 12,000 people, about two-thirds of whom were Seleka Barolong, under their chief Moroka. Together with the other refugees and three Wesleyan missionaries, the entire community migrated southwards from the Vaal in search of a more secure place to settle in the region west of the

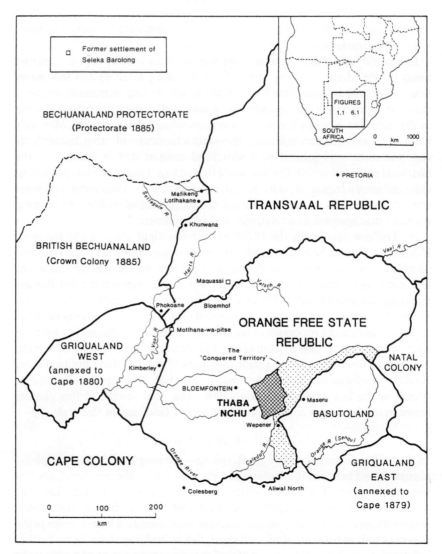

*Figure 1.1* The southern highveld, early 1880s.

Mohokare (Caledon) river. An advance expedition earlier in the year had already negotiated first with Moseme, the headman of a group of Bataung living near Thaba Nchu, and then with his political overlord Moshoeshoe, principal chief of the Basotho. Most of the immigrants settled at Thaba Nchu itself, where they built a new town at the foot of the mountain to the north-west. As evoked by Silas Modiri Molema, Chief Moroka's biographer, Thaba Nchu 'towered . . . before the newcomers, with its mantle of bush and shrub, forming a dark visage at once serene, sombre and sublime . . .'.[6]

At the time of the immigrants' arrival, some animals were handed over by Moroka to Moshoeshoe: according to one document, 'seven young oxen, one heifer, two sheep and one goat'; according to another, nine cattle and seventeen sheep and goats. The transaction which these animals represented was fraught with ambivalence. In later years, Moroka interpreted it as an act of friendly neighbourliness; Moshoeshoe consistently construed it as *peho*, specific recognition by the Barolong of his own political sovereignty; whereas, in the extravagant language of the documents drawn up at the time by the Wesleyan missionaries, Moshoeshoe thereby 'granted, bargained and sold' to them 'all that spacious country designated Thaba Nchu'.[7]

Similar 'clouds of misunderstanding' hung over the other refugee settlements, much smaller than Thaba Nchu, which were established by the Wesleyan missionaries at the same time in the region north and west of the Mohokare (Caledon) river. A small group of Griqua was intermittently based at Lesowane, south-west of Hlohlolwane (Clocolan). About a thousand Kora, under Jan Taaibosch, settled first at Mpokwane and later, after his death in 1836, at Merumetsho, on the slopes of the Korannaberg. A third group, Carolus Baatje's Newlanders, settled at Platberg, on the southern side of a large escarpment near the later town of Ladybrand.[8] In the aftermath of the *difaqane*, Moshoeshoe nominally claimed all of the territory occupied by the Barolong at Thaba Nchu and by the other outlying Wesleyan communities. It is clear, however, that the boundaries of his effective political sovereignty ebbed and flowed with shifting circumstances. Accordingly, the 'correct' interpretation of the land transactions made always depended more on prevailing political realities than on the meaning of the formal embellishments inscribed in the Wesleyan records.

The balance of power in the region was vitally affected by the intrusion of white settlers with guns. In 1836 and 1837, several parties of Voortrekkers converged on Thaba Nchu, where they were hospitably received by Moroka. They set up temporary laagers on the western shoulder of the mountain at a place which became known as Morokashoek. Standing near this place, at the narrow Victoria Nek, a monument commemorates their passage in the following terms:

'Here the laagers of Potgieter, Maritz and other Voortrekkers encamped from November 1836 to April 1837. Here, too, the first Voortrekker government was inaugurated. Across this "neck of jogging waggon wheels" (Rakgokgo) the treks proceeded northwards'.

Notoriously, Moroka assisted the Voortrekkers in their confrontations first with the Matebele of Moselekatse (Mzilikazi) and second with the Basotho of Moshoeshoe. This well-documented historical fact was the foundation of a potently misleading myth of ethnic amity between the Afrikaners and the Barolong of Thaba Nchu, which has been repeatedly used and abused by both their ruling elites. Much more than a century later, for example, this myth of inter-ethnic amity became the central theme in the ideological construction of the local state as part of the Bophuthatswana Bantustan, a process analysed in detail in Chapter 5.

In the years that followed the turmoil of the *difaqane*, however, Moroka's people were not merely pawns in a larger conflict between Moshoeshoe's chiefdom and encroaching white settlers. There were many other players on the stage, each engaged in an almost unremitting struggle for survival and independence. Such struggles were commonly expressed in the raiding and counter-raiding of livestock, the dominant currency of political control over land and people. During these years, Moroka's Barolong were inevitably caught up in local conflicts whose intensity varied with distance from Moshoeshoe's stronghold of Thaba Bosiu and with the volatility of regional alliances.[9]

In 1848, British forces were despatched from the Cape Colony in a brief and unsuccessful bid to resolve these conflicts over land in the country north of the Orange River. During the period of the Orange River Sovereignty, between 1848 and 1854, Chief Moroka entered a tenuous alliance with the British Resident, Major Henry Warden. The Warden Line of 1849 endorsed a definite allocation of territory for the Barolong; but Moroka's people also suffered repeated depradations of livestock, and by December 1852 the chief's support was reduced to a thousand followers only. Nevertheless, after the collapse of the Sovereignty and British withdrawal in 1854, Moroka became effectively politically independent and was recognised as such by the Afrikaner republic of the OFS which then came into existence.[10]

The Barolong territory emerged from the second Sotho–Boer war of 1865–8 as an isolated enclave within the OFS. It was cut off from Moshoeshoe's reach by a broad swathe of very good arable land known as the 'Conquered Territory', which was appropriated by the OFS and became subject to white settlement (see Figure 1.1). The boundaries of Basutoland were defined by the Treaty of Aliwal North of 1869, and Moshoeshoe died in March 1870. From this time onwards, conflicts over access to land in the eastern OFS took a different form. Dispossessed of direct entitlement to land there, the Basotho occupied it and farmed it but were forced over the following decades to come to terms with the fact of white ownership of it.

Surrounded by the OFS, the political independence of the Barolong territory of Thaba Nchu was highly tenuous through the 1870s, and this was perhaps inevitably reflected in the erosion of Moroka's internal authority. The evidence of his weakening political grip may be found in at least two waves of emigration from Thaba Nchu, in 1875 and 1878; a significant movement of residential decentralisation within the territory; and incipient conflict over succession to the chieftainship. These several discontents were associated with, but not determined by, inter-denominational rivalries between the Methodist and the Anglican missions which developed into strong antagonism and distrust.

The Keate award of 1871, an attempt to arbitrate land disputes in the wake of the discovery of diamonds in Griqualand West, nominally opened up an area for Barolong settlement between the Harts and the Vaal rivers that was free from Transvaal suzerainty. In submitting evidence to the Bloemhof court of arbitration which preceded Keate's award, Moroka had claimed a substantial territory in the region, by virtue of its occupation before the *difaqane* by his ancestor Tau and his father Sefunelo. He made the claim on account of his anxiety about the long-term security of a political community surrounded by the Free State. Ironically, however, the partial success of Moroka's claim at Bloemhof undermined his position at Thaba Nchu. For one of his long-standing enemies, Matlabe, a chief of the Rapulana Barolong, used the Keate award to instigate a movement from Thaba Nchu to the area north of the Vaal.

Matlabe had originally sought refuge with Moroka at Thaba Nchu in 1835, but left in 1841 with a section of his people to settle on the Mooi river in the south-western Transvaal. Thirty years later, now an old man but still of a notoriously fiery temperament, Matlabe returned to Thaba Nchu to encourage the remaining Rapulana Barolong to leave. Moroka resented his interference, because the loss of followers implied the weakening of his own political authority and stimulated rumours amongst the Free State Boers that he himself was planning to leave Thaba Nchu. He therefore refused to allow the Rapulana Barolong to go, and was only persuaded to do so by President Brand of the OFS after an open conflict had taken place in February 1874. Finally, in 1875, a large group of people left Thaba Nchu under Motuba, a brother of Matlabe, with at least thirty wagons and all their livestock. They settled at the old Tshidi Barolong town of Lotlhakane, south-west of Mafikeng, at the headwaters of a tributary of the Molopo river. In due course they were drawn into the Bechuanaland wars of 1881–4.[11]

Another group left Thaba Nchu in 1878: the Molotswana section of the Bakwena under their old chief Letlojana and his son Petrus Malefo. Initially they scattered on white farms in the Potchefstroom district (western Transvaal), but were then settled by Reverend Timothy Cresswell, a former missionary at Thaba Nchu, on a farm called Uitkyk, near Ventersdorp.[12] Such movements of secession were clearly not precluded by strong ties of affinity between the various communities at Thaba Nchu. One of Tshipinare's wives, for example, was a daughter of Petrus Malefo; another daughter was married to Tshipinare's son and heir Robert Tawana, and became the mother of Albert Setlogelo who, many years later, succeeded to the chieftainship at Thaba Nchu.[13]

Moroka's restrictions on the issue of passes, in order to prevent his people from leaving Thaba Nchu, provoked the irritation of white farmers on his borders who were accustomed to drawing seasonal labour from the Barolong territory and who also, it appears, encouraged the secession movements on the grounds that they would open up Thaba Nchu for white settlement. As the OFS economy revived in the diamond boom of the 1870s, the farmers agitated for the Volksraad to take steps to limit 'squatting', which implied tighter control on the movements of Africans. Moroka found that his own authority to issue passes for the movement of his people out of Thaba Nchu was being over-ridden by the OFS field-cornets' application of different conditions. This led to considerable friction as Moroka found he had less and less control over the employment of his people on the farms. In the face of his disapproval of the dispersal of his people, some of them acquired passes for farm employment and then used these to trek north of the Vaal. There were also constant complaints, on both sides of the OFS/Thaba Nchu border, over stock theft and the assessment of damages. President Brand exercised a growing administrative discretion over individual cases which arose out of such conflict. The OFS also wished Moroka to take joint action to eradicate the prickly cocklebur (*Xanthium spinosum*), which damaged wool.[14] While diplomatic relations remained formally correct between President Brand and Chief Moroka, many Free State burghers perceived an independent African chiefdom in the heart of white republican territory as a glaring anomaly. The question for them was when and how it would be incorporated, not whether or not it would be.

In the second half of the decade, a significant movement of decentralisation took place. The Wesleyans reported that many people who had for years resided in the town itself were moving into the country districts, and large villages were being formed in many places along the border. Their reasons were resentment at the arbitrariness of Moroka's rule and a series of economic setbacks—drought, poor harvests and rapid inflation. Such decentralisation was commonly associated, in Sotho-Tswana social formations, with a weakening of political authority at the centre. In the particular circumstances of Thaba Nchu, it also induced more disputes across the border with white farmers, over passes and stock theft. In 1877 partial crop failure was followed by severe drought, which inevitably affected the mood of the people. The Anglican missionary George Mitchell diagnosed widespread 'indifference and apathy'. He attributed this malaise to the easy procurement of Cape brandy, 'the drought and heat which are drying up everything', and some new and apparently fatal forms of sickness and disease 'which have kept some of our people away for months from church'.[15]

On the socio-economic circumstances of the Barolong community during these years, the first-hand reports of the Wesleyan and the Anglican missionaries often corroborate one another. On spiritual matters, the special prerogative of the missionaries, their relationship was one of intense mutual antagonism. This antagonism arose out of the historical conflict between the established Anglican church and the Wesleyan Methodists in Britain, whence it was transposed to the somewhat stony ground of the southern highveld of South Africa. Moroka and Tshipinare, however, had small sympathy with differences of style and dogma within the Christian proselytising effort. The strategic balance they sought was influenced more by the wider political affiliations of the missionaries, particularly those of the Anglicans. The question arises, therefore, of the extent to which internal political divisions coincided with divisions of religious adherence.

The Wesleyans had been closely associated with the ruling Barolong elite for more than fifty years. James Cameron, for example, who was at Thaba Nchu through the 1840s, was a notoriously 'political' missionary who was alleged to have persuaded Moroka to identify himself with the British Resident Henry Warden's confrontation with Moshoeshoe in 1852. Wesleyan mission families such as the Camerons and the Allisons had not only served for years as diplomatic intermediaries on behalf of Moroka's Barolong and the other communities which found themselves sandwiched between Moshoeshoe's Basotho and the encroaching Boers. They were also well connected with Free State notables. Joseph Allison, James Cameron's brother-in-law, was Warden's clerk, and later became OFS Government Secretary. In the period before the second Sotho-Boer war, as acting President, he was described as 'Moshoeshoe's main adversary in Bloemfontein'.[16] In the next generation, in 1883, John Allison Cameron became Tshipinare's resident magistrate at Thaba Nchu.

Sir George Grey, Governor at the Cape from 1854 to 1861, had encouraged Moroka to send his sons to school. Tshabadira and Richard Maramantsi, two of the chief's sons by Tshipinare's mother, Nkhabele (see Figure 1.2), went to Salem in Grahamstown under the Wesleyan William Shaw. Samuel Lehulere and George Morwagabuse went to Zonnebloem College in Cape Town. Tshabadira's son Michael and Tshipinare's sons Robert Tawana, Joel, John Phetogane and Morokanyana went to Lovedale in the eastern Cape. Their respective institutional affiliations clearly reflected Moroka's anxiety to sustain diverse political connections. When Grey was recalled to England in 1861, he was accompanied by Samuel Lehulere, who attended St Augustine's School in Canterbury for some years. On his return in 1865, Samuel Lehulere introduced an Anglican missionary to Thaba Nchu, George Mitchell, a friend and class-mate from Canterbury. Mitchell was received without enthusiasm by the Wesleyans. Samuel's 'chief reason for introducing a rival sect', as sourly expressed by Silas Modiri Molema, Moroka's biographer, 'was to supplant Tshipinare, his cousin'.[17]

Molema's reference is to a dispute over the succession to the chieftainship which quietly festered during the 1870s but only came to a head after Moroka's death in 1880. The details of this dispute are immensely complex and are elaborated in the next section of this chapter. Meanwhile it is clear that at least part of Moroka's motive for encouraging an Anglican mission at Thaba Nchu was the political link he expected to develop thereby with the British government, since his relations were strained at the time both with the Free State and with the Basotho. Initially, however, the Anglican mission did not flourish, and Mitchell was withdrawn. He was replaced in 1868 by a number of High Church Anglican monks who taught the Barolong Gregorian chants before they moved to Modderpoort the following year, leaving William Crisp in charge of the Anglican mission. A little later, George Mitchell returned to Thaba Nchu.[18]

Both Anglicans and Wesleyans, in competition with one another, rapidly expanded their activities through the 1870s. Anglican converts increased from 35 to about 500 between 1870 and 1876. By 1879, the Wesleyans had 975 members, 362 prospective members 'on trial', 30 local preachers and 43 leaders. Thaba Nchu was by far the largest of the Bloemfontein circuits. Tshipinare's rival Samuel Lehulere was elected an Anglican church warden in 1878, one of a series of incidents which, Mitchell discovered, provoked Moroka's 'resentment and illwill' towards the Anglicans in that year.[19] Thus there were close alignments, respectively of the Wesleyan ministers with the political establishment at Thaba Nchu and of the Anglican missionaries, above all George Mitchell himself, with Samuel's later bid to engage the influence of the British government on his behalf. But it is also clear, from evidence below relating to the political loyalties of the ordinary members of both churches, that the lines of political cleavage within Thaba Nchu were not determined by the gathering surge of inter-denominational rivalry in the 1870s.

There is evidence, then, of Moroka's crumbling authority, of some internal dissent and of a degree of external threat. Two years of drought were accompanied by partial crop failure in 1878 and 1879. Despite such 'trial and adversity', John Daniel, the Wesleyan missionary at Thaba Nchu, was able to look around him at the end of 1879 in a mood of insular relief: 'While so many of the South African native tribes have been involved in war with its manifold evils, our people have been preserved in peace'.[20] The defeated Hlubi chief, Langalibalele, was in exile in Cape Town. Cetshwayo of the Zulu had joined him there, after his success against the British army at Isandlhwana in January and his defeat at Ulundi in July. The Phuthi chief Moorosi had recently been killed on his mountain retreat in southern Basutoland, after a long siege by the Cape Mounted Rifles from March to November 1879. Meanwhile, the power of the Pedi paramountcy, which threatened British hegemony in the

Transvaal, was effectively broken by the storming of the Maroteng stronghold in November 1879 and the capture of Chief Sekhukhune. A series of revolts against the Cape Colonial government had also taken place in the Transkei region. By contrast, Daniel reflected, Chief Moroka's Barolong at Thaba Nchu remained the only independent African political community 'in all this part of South Africa'.[21] Nevertheless, Moroka was fast losing his grip. The harpies were gathering, in the form of land-hungry Boers and white traders and speculators.

African communities throughout southern Africa had been variously drawn into the developing capitalist economy of the region. On the highveld alone, the Pedi were long-distance migrant labourers to Port Elizabeth, Natal and Kimberley long before they were politically subdued. With their wages, they bought guns to defend their independence. The Basotho did likewise, and also, in the early 1870s, developed a vigorous peasant economy in the lowlands of the Mohokare river valley, based on the export of wheat to the burgeoning diamond mines. Elsewhere, some Tlhaping of Griqualand West, the Kimberley hinterland, prospered for much of the 1870s through an effective monopoly on the transport by ox-wagon of fuel wood, thatching grass and other products required by the mines.[22]

So long as these communities retained their political independence, internally differentiated as they were, they were able to influence the terms on which they engaged with the larger political economy. But political conquest inevitably intensified their economic subordination, through the imposition of hut tax, the widespread expropriation of lands and the seizure of livestock. John Daniel was thankful that Moroka refused to join what white public opinion at the time—fractious, volatile and ill-informed as it was—identified as a conspiracy to launch a general uprising against white rule. Moroka was therefore 'likely to die as he has lived, in cordial friendship with the English nation'.[23]

## 'TRIALS OF NO ORDINARY KIND': CIVIL WAR AND ANNEXATION, 1880–4

The old chief died on 8 April 1880. A meeting of councillors was held on 13 April, at which Tshipinare was declared chief of the Barolong. The meeting was attended by the rival claimant, Samuel Lehulere, and one of his strongest supporters, his cousin Bogatsu. Samuel argued for a public assembly (*pitso*) to appoint a successor to Moroka, and then sought to invoke on his own behalf the support of Chief Letsie of the Basotho and that of other Barolong chiefs— Moswete of the Ratlou branch and Motuba of the Rapulana branch. Tshipinare procrastinated over calling an assembly and President Brand of the OFS confirmed his recognition of Tshipinare on the grounds that he had been *de facto* ruler in Moroka's last years and also that Moroka had told him Tshipinare should succeed. A violent confrontation took place on 31 May in the chief's courtyard (*kgotla*), threatening wider political conflict. Tension in the region was already high because of the Cape Prime Minister Sprigg's misguided attempt to extend the Disarmament Act to Basutoland, which was under Cape administration at the time. Brand offered initially to mediate between Tshipinare and Samuel and, failing that, to arbitrate. Reluctantly, Samuel accepted, and hearings for this purpose took place in June and July 1880.[24]

The succession dispute at Thaba Nchu is a classic case of the kind of factional rivalry generated in Sotho-Tswana social formations by the institutions of polygyny, the levirate and cousin marriage. The fullest published source on the genealogical inter-connections of the Barolong ruling elite is Molema's biography of Moroka, from which source Figure 1.2 is primarily drawn. It should be emphasised, however, that some of the marital and other connections which the diagram illustrates were subject to detailed argument at the time. The genealogy represents, therefore, a map of the disputed terrain rather than a definitively accurate account of family relationships.

Tshipinare's mother Nkhabele was the widow of Tlale, second son of Chief Tawana of the Tshidi Barolong, who was killed in 1832. She had previously been betrothed to the eldest son Seetsela, killed in 1818. Nkhabele joined the Seleka Barolong at Motlhana-wa-Pitse on the Vaal river as a refugee, with two children—Moutloatsi and Tshipinare. Her eldest child, Setlogelo, had been captured by the Matebele. He reappears in Chapter 3 below. At Motlhana-wa-Pitse, before the move to Thaba Nchu, Nkhabele soon became Moroka's second wife, and Tshipinare grew up in Moroka's family as the chief's adopted son. He emerged in Moroka's later years as effective ruler of Thaba Nchu, and was thus in a strong position at Moroka's death to assume the reins of office. His Tshidi origin, however, was held against him by many at Thaba Nchu. What right had he to the chieftainship of the Seleka Barolong?

On the face of the matter, Samuel Lehulere had the better genealogical claim to succeed, although contemporaries found him a man of 'inferior caste of mind and body' and 'irascible, implacable and obstinate in temperament'. Moroka's eldest son in his first wife's house, Tau, had died in boyhood without an heir. Tau's younger brother Sefunelo also predeceased Moroka, leaving a son, Motlhware. Molema states that, 'about 1872', Moroka indicated at a ceremonial feast that Motlhware was his successor. He was not at that time living at Thaba Nchu, however, but with his mother, a daughter of Chief Sechele of the Bakwena. Tshipinare brought Motlhware to Thaba Nchu in 1877 and Moroka arranged for him to marry one of Tshipinare's daughters, Majang. Motlhware died without issue in February 1879, only four months after his marriage, as a result of a fall from a horse.[25] His widow Majang was taken over in the levirate by her cousin, Michael Tshabadira, another grandson of Chief Moroka. By strict custom, then, any future son of Majang by Michael Tshabadira would be 'raised for Motlhware' and thereby entitled to succeed Moroka. In 1880, however, Samuel Lehulere was the only surviving adult

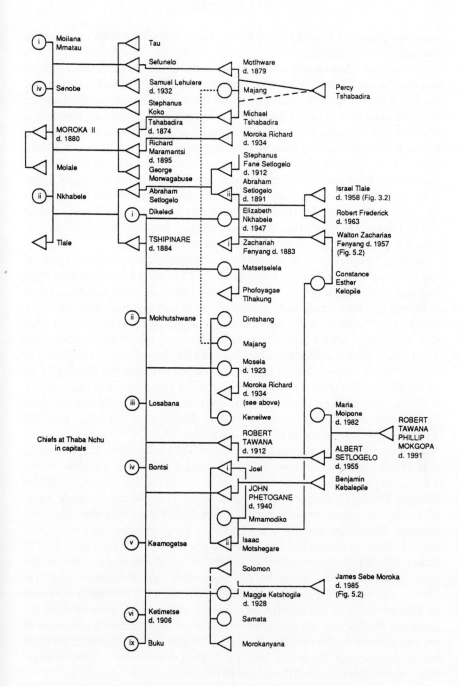

*Figure 1.2*  Partial Moroka genealogy.

male descendant of Moroka's first house, and it was on those grounds that he claimed the chieftainship.[26]

At least two other rumours clouded the issue. One was that Samuel himself was not the son of Moroka but of a 'Korana petty chief' who had accompanied the Barolong to Thaba Nchu. A hint to this effect was allegedly inscribed in the name Moroka gave to one of his sons by Nkhabele, Morwagabuse, meaning 'a Bushman (or Korana) shall not rule'. Molema advised his readers to judge for themselves by comparing Samuel's photograph in his book with that of Moroka. It is curious that, one hundred years after these events, two of Molema's readers who have themselves contributed significantly to the secondary literature drew opposite conclusions from this exercise. Janet Wales decided that 'the picture of Samuel certainly suggests that he was not a pure Rolong'; while Watson found the resemblance between Samuel and Moroka 'striking, and thus it is probable that the rumour was just that'.[27]

Molema's explicit invocation of this rumour has the implicit effect of endorsing the suspicion of Samuel's illegitimacy. This would be consistent with Molema's own genealogical proximity to the Tshidi Barolong chieftainship at Mafikeng and his own association with the Wesleyan mission's position as the established church both at Thaba Nchu and at Mafikeng. If the rumour were true, this might explain Moroka's recorded desire to secure the succession for Tshipinare, but it would not weaken Samuel's claim to succeed by reference to Sotho-Tswana custom, for his legitimacy derived not from the identity of his physical father but from the validity of his mother's marriage. For this reason it is not surprising to find that much time was taken up at Brand's hearings with the question of whether Samuel's mother Moilana, or Mmatau, was still married to Moroka at the time Samuei was born.[28]

The second rumour was one introduced by Tshipinare himself, to the effect that Motlhware was his own son, conceived by Sefunelo's widow whom Tshipinare had taken over in the levirate. In support of this suggestion, Wales invokes Trollope's account of his visit in 1877, in which he made some otherwise obscure observations about a potential dispute over the succession between Tshipinare and his son. This may be interpreted as a deliberate tactical effort on the part of Tshipinare to confuse the evidence presented to Brand relating to the primacy or otherwise of Motlhware's claim to the succession. Curiously, however, the suggestion that Tshipinare was Motlhware's father is supported by the Anglican missionary Mitchell's reference in January 1879 to an attempt by Moroka the previous year to have his grandson Motlhware, 'the heir apparent', married in church to 'a half-sister of his', Motlhware's—presumably Majang, a daughter of Tshipinare in his third house. Neither the Wesleyans nor the Anglicans approved of this arrangement, so the chief married them himself.[29]

Irrespective of the truth of Tshipinare's claim in this respect, the irony of it endures into the twentieth century history of the dispute. Percy Tshabadira, son of Majang by Michael Tshabadira and 'raised for' Motlhware, was a grandson of Tshipinare through his mother Majang and also, through his father Michael Tshabadira, a grandson of Tshipinare's half-brother Tshabadira (see Figure 1.2). He was therefore much closer to Tshipinare by 'blood', in the English idiom, than he was to Samuel. After Samuel's death in 1932, however, Percy Tshabadira inherited his exiled chieftainship in the Tati district of Botswana (see Chapter 3) through his own putative legitimacy as son of Motlhware and grandson of Samuel's brother Sefunelo. Yet Motlhware also may have been much closer to Tshipinare by 'blood' than he was to Samuel. Percy Tshabadira made an unsuccessful bid for the chieftainship at Thaba Nchu in the late 1930s, against the incumbent official representative of Tshipinare's line. This abortive renewal of the old dispute is described in detail in Chapter 4.

Brand's arbitration confirmed Tshipinare in office in July 1880. His decision was ignored by Samuel Lehulere, who remained in the territory and actively fomented discontent. In response, Tshipinare organised a police force which included several white mercenaries. Despite a public demonstration of reconciliation in mid-August, Tshipinare ordered twelve of Samuel's leading supporters to leave Thaba Nchu. This order provoked another violent confrontation. On 27 August Tshipinare's police moved to arrest four of these men at a funeral; shots were fired, with some fatalities. The following morning, Saturday 28 August, a battle took place at Bogatsu's homestead in Thaba Nchu town. Altogether about twenty men were killed, and many wounded. The missionaries' reports to their respective London headquarters were typically partisan. John Daniel wrote that 'a party of Sepinare's police while engaged in carrying out the orders of the chief were wantonly fired upon by the malcontents and a general action was brought on between them and the party of order'. George Mitchell, for his part, explained that the police had carried out a ruthless attack on defenceless people whose only fault was that they had supported Samuel's cause. Tshipinare ordered Mitchell to leave the territory immediately, on the grounds, as Mitchell himself admitted, that he had been 'a great deal mixed up in the political troubles'. Samuel, Bogatsu and a number of other rebels fled to Bloemfontein, and their property was confiscated. The atmosphere thereafter was extremely tense and bitter. 'The whole tribe', Daniel wrote later, 'has been split into two antagonistic factions burning with hatred towards each other'.[30]

The substance of this antagonism must be understood with reference to the wider political circumstances in which the dispute took place. Tshipinare was directly associated with, and indeed largely responsible for, what some of the people had experienced as the arbitrary and oppressive rule of Moroka's last years. Opposition to his succession and support for Samuel Lehulere was drawn, as Tshipinare acknowledged, 'from those whom Moroka had had to keep down by force'. Samuel's supporters included remnant groups of

Bakwena whom Tshipinare apparently intended to drive out of the country; Basotho who had settled in Moroka's territory and were always a potential source of disaffection, in the light of Moshoeshoe's former claim to the territory and Moroka's support for the Free State in the second Sotho-Boer war; and the Bataung chief Moletsane's son, Monyake, who was living in the north-east of the territory and who 'had always given trouble'. Samuel also had external allies in Moswete of the Ratlou Barolong and Motuba of the Rapulana Barolong, who were engaged at the time in a struggle of their own with the Tshidi Barolong chief, Montshiwa, over lands at the headwaters of the Molopo river, far to the north of Thaba Nchu. Tshipinare's identity as a Tshidi Morolong himself was therefore a sufficient affront to disqualify him, in their view, from title to the Seleka Barolong chieftainship.

Tshipinare, on the other hand, had the support of Moroka's headmen and councillors and of President Brand of the OFS. Brand committed himself unequivocally to recognition of Tshipinare but did not, on the whole, translate that nominal support into practical measures against Samuel's disruptive activities on the borders of the territory, which repeatedly scared and demoralised loyal Barolong at Thaba Nchu. Both Tshipinare and Brand were acutely sensitive to the rapidly developing confrontation between the Cape government and the Basotho over the extension of the Disarmament Act to Basutoland in mid-1880. Brand could not be confident, given the long history of conflict between the Boers and the Basotho over land in the eastern OFS, that the Basotho chiefs would not be drawn into the dispute at Thaba Nchu on Samuel's side; nor indeed, given British annexation of the Transvaal in 1877, that the British government would not intervene in the OFS if this local conflict were allowed to get out of hand. Brand was therefore primarily concerned to dampen the potential conflagration between Tshipinare and Samuel and also to suppress agitation by his own more fidgety burghers, who perceived at last, in the succession dispute at Thaba Nchu, an opportunity to take over Moroka's territory. Some of these farmers actively colluded with Samuel by providing places of ready refuge on the borders of Thaba Nchu and by making it easy for them to pass at will through adjoining districts of the Free State.[31]

These, then, were the wider circumstances of the dispute towards the end of 1880. The year was one of 'trials of no ordinary kind, which threatened at one time to overtake us, if not utterly to destroy our cause'. Daniel reported that five of his agents, fifteen class leaders and more than half of the ordinary members were 'misled' by the rebels. Many people fled from the country: 140 Wesleyan church members permanently, and 75 members temporarily to the neighbouring farms. By January 1881, the Anglicans had lost one third of their 163 communicants, who were probably Samuel's supporters. The leaders of the Wesleyan and Anglican missions were clearly identified with the respective political factions: in his reports and letters, John Daniel repeatedly referred to

Tshipinare's as 'the party of order' and Samuel's as 'the malcontents'; whereas George Mitchell was banished because of his active support for Samuel Lehulere. This action was directed against Mitchell personally, however, and not against the Anglican church. The rank and file memberships of both the Wesleyan and the Anglican communities were divided in their political allegiances, as the figures above make clear. The demoralising effects of the civil war were sharply exacerbated by almost total crop failure and the closure, as a result of the Gun War, of the grain trade from Basutoland on which the Barolong normally relied. Famine prices prevailed, 'at 300 per cent above usual rates'. As a result, many people were forced out of the territory to find employment on neighbouring farms in order to feed their families.[32]

In his private letters to London, John Daniel reported in some detail on political defections which were probably judged too embarrassing to be listed in his annual reports. David Mosifane, for example, took part in the rebellion and was 'afraid or unwilling' to return. Mosifane was the Methodist agent at Strachan, one of the new circuits which had been formed in response to the dispersal of the population to the outlying rural areas in the late 1870s. Simon Moroantsi 'lost his status' at Daggafontein for the same reason. The agent at Thaba Phatshwa was sufficiently indiscreet to preach a sermon of violent indignation against Tshipinare. He 'ran off' to the Free State in fear of the consequences of this being reported to the chief. The dispute also divided families. Johannes Makgothi, trained at Healdtown in the eastern Cape, had been a Methodist preacher for eleven years and an evangelist for six. He was imprisoned and fined by Tshipinare for active sympathy with the rebels, and as a result 'found that his influence for good in the country had gone'. He left Thaba Nchu, presumably with his family, and took up mission work at Colesberg (Cape).[33] His brother Stephanus Makoloi Makgothi, by contrast, remained behind and received a substantial land grant from Tshipinare when the chief had the country surveyed in 1882. His descendants were numerous and influential in Thaba Nchu in the 1980s: part of the Makgothi family history is elaborated in depth in Chapter 7.

Tshipinare imposed heavy fines on rebels implicated with Samuel. By August 1881, only fifteen months after his accession to office, he had three times levied a general poll tax of £1 per adult man, to meet the costs of the civil war. This was a heavy burden in a period of repeated crop failure, general economic depression and continuing political insecurity. The Methodists were pressing Tshipinare at the time to raise funds for a Moroka Memorial Institution, but the chief was sensitive to the consequences of further financial imposition on the loyalties of the people, and could not take any initiative of this kind while the political situation remained so volatile. Meanwhile the (Anglican) Bishop of Bloemfontein had returned from a visit to England with some £17,000 for his mission, and sent a 'very flattering letter of salutation "a la Episcopal" to the Chief, accompanied by a valuable present!!'. Daniel frankly confessed his jealousy of the Anglican material advantage.[34] The Methodists, by contrast, having no cash, could only dig more deeply into their spiritual resources.

Daniel estimated in October 1882 that 'not less than one third' of the people had left Thaba Nchu for the Free State and other parts. Many had settled on neighbouring white farms, where 'under the influence and direction of Samuel they keep up a constant agitation ... Every now and then a scare is got up in this way and scores of people fly off to the Free State with their stock'. Those who remained behind were thoroughly demoralised and in a constant state of ferment. Many hundreds of known sympathisers with Samuel remained in the country. Their activities were regarded with suspicion and distrust by the chief, so that 'a want of confidence is felt which produces a most unhappy state of affairs'. These people were bitterly resentful of what they regarded as Tshipinare's abuse of power.[35]

During 1882, politically insecure and with his administration's finances in considerable disarray, Tshipinare took steps to 'secure the ground right by title to the country'. He employed the OFS government surveyor, Bourdillon, to make 'a regular trigonometrical survey of the whole country into farms, differing in extent, which will be vested in trustees who will be furnished with charts and title deeds'. It is difficult to determine, in retrospect, whether Tshipinare's intention was to 'secure the ground right' primarily against a take-over and consequent redistribution of land by Samuel, or against the consequences of possible annexation by the OFS. At least one sceptical commentator discerned in Tshipinare's action a blatant attempt to buy the political loyalty not only of senior Barolong but also of strategically placed whites upon whom he came to depend increasingly during the protracted crisis of confidence in his rule. Moroka's biographer, however, insisted that the land grants Tshipinare made to his sons, half-brothers, petty chiefs and councillors were meant to be inalienable, unsaleable and indivisible outside the Barolong tribe. After Tshipinare's death, surveyor Bourdillon told the Gregorowski commission of enquiry that the chief 'frequently discussed with him the detriment and disadvantages attending the alienation of land'.[36] On balance, it would appear that Tshipinare's intention was to secure the administrative rights of his political subordinates through legal titles which would reduce boundary conflicts and protect their interests against a change of regime, but which could not be alienated.

Lacking confidence in traditional processes of consultation with his people, Tshipinare sought to transform his administration 'from above', by appointing trusted whites to salaried positions. John Allison Cameron was appointed in July 1883 as magistrate at a salary of £1,200 per annum; the attorney Carl Christian Mathey, who was also a member of the Volksraad Executive Council, became 'general executive' of the Barolong; and, in September 1883, Tshipinare appointed Pieter Raaff, son of N.P.C. Raaff of Bloemfontein, as commandant of his defence force. Tshipinare also concluded a Treaty of Alliance with the OFS in August 1883. These salaried appointments were a heavy drain on the limited resources of the Barolong state. Tshipinare therefore borrowed substantial sums of money from the National Bank, from Cornelis Van der Wath, a Bloemfontein attorney, and from Charles Newberry of Prynnsberg, Clocolan, who was now John Daniel's son-in-law. Tshipinare was heavily in debt when he died, and argument took place afterwards whether the debts should be charged to his private estate or to the OFS government, which had to assume responsibility for the public finances of the Barolong state. In either case, in effect, some of the farms surveyed by Bourdillon in 1882 and 1883 were mortgaged against the services of these white officers, who were amongst the beneficiaries of land grants made after annexation of the territory by the OFS.[37]

The economic circumstances were not propitious. Tshipinare had already levied a series of onerous taxes. The people were exhausted and demoralised. Three drought years followed one after the other in the early 1880s, and virtually no crops were reaped. It was a time of general economic recession, following a glut at the Kimberley diamond mines. The year 1883 was remembered by an OFS surveyor, Gustav Baumann, as:

> the worst year I had ever experienced. All was calamity. The finding of diamonds in 1869 had pulled us out of the rut of ruin; now the collapse of 1882 was dragging us into the mire of financial despair. There was no money in the land; farmers got next to nothing for their produce. I had to take oxen, sheep and mealies in payment for the work I did.[38]

The expenses of the Thaba Nchu land survey were considerable. In 1882, furthermore, owing to the spread of smallpox, Tshipinare had to prohibit transport-riding, an alternative source of income for some of the people. There were constant rumours of impending invasion by Samuel's forces. Twice during 1883, Daniel observed, the whole country 'was thrown into confusion and alarm', at a time of acute uncertainty over the political future of Basutoland.[39] The view from the other mission house was similarly gloomy:

> Sheep and oxen have died by thousands. The corn has either perished in the seed, or been withered as soon as it has sprung up. Another trial has been the presence of smallpox in our neighbourhood . . . carried from the Diamond Fields to Basutoland. The effect of all this and especially of the drought has been to create a despondent and unsettled spirit. It has even been difficult for ourselves to strike off the restless temper which has a very general demoralising influence.[40]

Many of the Free State farmers, meanwhile, were happy to stimulate dissension at Thaba Nchu in the hopes of a land grab, following the unfortunate precedent of the Bechuanaland wars in which white mercenaries were recruited by opposing sides in return for promises of land. Apparently the pass law, administered by the OFS to control the movement of Africans, was a

'dead letter', at any rate for Samuel's people. This implied that many farmers
at least covertly supported Samuel's claims to the chieftainship, allegedly on
the basis of promises to reward them with farms.[41] Samuel himself, having
failed to enlist the support of Hercules Robinson, Governor of the Cape, went
to England at the end of 1883 to try to invoke British government support for
his case. Assisted by the Aborigines Protection Society, he saw the Archbishop
of Canterbury and at least one sympathetic Member of Parliament, but failed
to make any impression on Colonial Office officials who, curiously in view of
the formal independence of Thaba Nchu, disclaimed any interference in the
affairs of the Orange Free State.[42] In desperation, Samuel returned to South
Africa and made final preparations for an attack on Thaba Nchu.

On the morning of Thursday 10 July 1884, the Anglican missionaries and
their families:

> were awakened about 5.30 by the sound of firing, and on going out of the
> house, found a considerable portion of the chief's part of the town on fire,
> and his own house surrounded by an attacking party. The onslaught was
> so sudden that Sepinare's followers were taken by surprise and fled. He
> himself took refuge in his house, in which with only one other man he
> defended himself with great bravery for at least 5 hours. At length the
> house was set on fire, and soon after the flames had caught the roof we
> heard a great shout, and knew that all was over.[43]

Another eye-witness account of the attack was that of Mathinya, a Mosotho
who lived on the eastern border of the territory. Tshipinare's son Joel reported
on Wednesday evening 9 July that he had heard Samuel would make an attack
early the following morning. Tshipinare apparently discounted the rumour,
having himself come from Maralleng, the eastern border area. At dawn,
however, Samuel's men came rapidly riding in from the east and rode straight
to the *kgotla*, the chief's court.

> The chief then tried to run to his house, when a voice said, 'There he
> is—fire!'. He, the chief, pointed his gun at the men who were at the Court,
> they hid themselves behind their horses, so he ran to his house, and a
> volley was fired on him, but he reached his house.

With him in the house were his ninth wife Buku, a daughter of the Tshidi
Barolong chief Montshiwa, his son Joel and Lang Jan Matsheka, variously
described as the chief's henchman, servant or nephew. When the house was set
on fire, Buku was allowed to escape; Joel also tried to leave but was wounded in
the side with an assegai; he was caught by the attacking party but his life was
spared on Bogatsu's intervention.

> The chief himself jumped out of a window and hid in a water closet
> [latrine], which had not been roofed yet. His enemies threw stones on him
> into the closet, also lighting some reeds which they threw into the closet.
> When this was done he (Tshipinare) tried to get out of the w.c. when he

was shot in the forehead and fell, and afterwards stabbed with assegais and stoned.[44]

His body was mutilated. Lang Jan Matsheka died with him. In the afternoon, one of Tshipinare's councillors, Joseph Thoto Masisi, and Michael Tshaba-dira, son of Tshipinare's half-brother Tshabadira, reached Thaba Nchu with some followers from their lands to the south. They 'fought a little and killed two of Samuel's men, and two of their men were also killed', but they could not regain possession of the town.[45]

Samuel and about 400 of his men occupied the town and were joined by a number of sympathisers. Great excitement and confusion prevailed. An 'immense volume of smoke' hung over the whole area for much of the day. John Daniel estimated later that about 200 houses in Thaba Nchu were burned by the rebels, 'by which more than a thousand of our loyal people have been deprived of their homes, household goods, clothing, money and grain'. This caused enormous bitterness.[46]

On hearing the news of Tshipinare's murder, President Brand immediately despatched some artillery and sixteen Bloemfontein volunteers to Thaba Nchu, and followed himself the next day, encamping on the Modder river. He arrived in the town on Saturday 12 July and proclaimed the annexation of Thaba Nchu to the OFS, at the same time guaranteeing that land grants made by chiefs Moroka and Tshipinare would be respected. Tshipinare had been buried that morning, with John Daniel officiating at the funeral. On the following day the President demanded that Samuel return Joel, Tshipinare's son, who was being held prisoner by the rebels, and also demanded that Samuel produce the murderers of Tshipinare. Eleven white men were alleg-edly involved in the invasion, led by Gert Pretorius of the farm Langverwacht, on the eastern border of Thaba Nchu. The white men took part in the attack on the town, but otherwise concentrated on plunder. They sacked the store of Abraham Setlogelo in the north-eastern part of the territory, stole many bundles of blankets and drove off about sixty cattle and several hundred sheep. They had earlier robbed the ammunition magazine at Ladybrand.[47]

On Brand's return to Bloemfontein on Monday 16 July, in the evening, his party encountered one of Tshipinare's missing councillors, Jacob Ngakantsi, near the Modder river.

> He was very much bruised, and nearly famished. It appears the raiders stoned him, and left him for dead, even refusing to stab him—simply pitching him out of the *kgotla*, like a dog, to linger and die in the cold. He slowly recovered, and after many days and nights exposure crept down the spruit, until a friendly hand helped him away.[48]

Jacob Ngakantsi was a big and heavy man, 'very gouty about his feet', and he did not long survive this ordeal. His heirs—two wives, each with nine children—were granted two farms in 1885: Mosheunyana 86 and Linana 132 (see Figure 1.3 and Appendix). Ngakantsi had been a close associate of Chief

Moroka for decades. Molema identified him as Moroka's cousin and as one of the original leaders of the Barolong refugees who settled at Thaba Nchu in 1833. During the second Sotho–Boer war he opposed Moroka's alliance with the Free State, and he was Moroka's representative on the diamond fields in 1871 at the time of the Keate award, when he allegedly declared war on the government of the OFS.[49]

The most worrying question from President Brand's point of view was the involvement or otherwise of Basotho in the attack on Thaba Nchu. Immediately he heard the news in Basutoland, Colonel Marshall Clarke, the Resident Commissioner, gave orders that the borders should be watched 'to maintain neutrality, disarm fugitives, and hold cattle coming from Barolong country at my disposal'. Armed men were placed along the border for this purpose, which induced a reciprocal scare on the OFS side and caused Brand to call out reinforcements for a border commando. In turn, this fuelled excitement and confusion within Basutoland. It appears that Basotho resident in the Barolong territory were involved in the attack on Thaba Nchu but not, despite the border scare, Basotho from Basutoland. Clarke abruptly rejected Samuel's request for assistance against annexation by the Free State. Meanwhile Samuel was directly in touch with Chief Letsie, who took advantage of these events to revive his own claim to the country. Thaba Nchu, he wrote to Clarke, was 'like a *mafisa*-ed cattle, that is to say, that the Chief Moshesh gave Moroka leave to live in that country, not as his own, but that he lent it to him'. Field-cornet Diederichs had taken two hostages from Bereng, Letsie's son, as security against an attack from Basutoland. This was interpreted by Clarke as provocative and officious, and it caused a minor diplomatic rumpus. Brand apologised, but retorted that Clarke's authority was unconvincing without sufficient force behind him to maintain it.[50]

Brand appointed Cornelis Van der Wath, a member of the Volksraad Executive Council, as commissioner and *landdrost* (magistrate) for the Moroka district, as it became known. No successor to Tshipinare was recognised, despite the presence of his eldest son and heir, Robert Tawana. Attorney C. Voigt from Bloemfontein was charged with winding up Tshipinare's affairs. The outstanding question in this respect was what debts should be construed as private ones, to be paid out of Tshipinare's own estate, and what debts were those of the Barolong government, to be assumed by the Orange Free State as successor to that government.[51]

Samuel surrendered on 17 July with a number of his prime supporters, and they underwent trial on 12 November 1884 for the murder of Tshipinare. They were discharged, however, on the grounds that the Free State had no jurisdiction at Thaba Nchu at the time the murder was committed. Together with nine others, Samuel was exiled from the OFS and given refuge in Basutoland by Chief Letsie, first at Korokoro and later at Sekanameng. From there Samuel continued to agitate against the injustice of annexation of Thaba Nchu by the Free State, and invoked the support of other Barolong chiefs on his behalf. He would not recognise any land grants made to any person in Barolong territory by the Free State. Rumours circulated from time to time that the Basotho would assist Samuel to recover the Thaba Nchu chieftainship.[52]

By the end of 1884, Thaba Nchu town, the 'largest settlement of its kind in South Africa', was nearly deserted, and the people were scattered among the cattle posts and villages throughout the territory. Both the Anglican and Methodist missions reported acute anxiety about the settlement of the country, pending the Volksraad's discussion of the President's commitment to respect established land rights. There had been three years of drought in a row, causing great loss of livestock, while 'corn is hardly to be had, and what little there is can only be purchased at 3 times its usual price'.[53] Famine conditions were still prevalent a year later. Crisp estimated there were only 800 people in the town and its immediately adjacent villages. During 1885, at least six thousand head of cattle died, worth £18,000. Crisp explained in February 1886 what had happened:

> At the end of August, on the very threshhold of our spring, a gentle, warm rain fell and continued for many days, such as had not been known for 30 years. The joy it caused was written on every man's face, but when it ceased, while the whole country was still soaked through, and our poor lean cattle were weakened by the rain, a severe frost succeeded by biting winds set in. The loss of stock was enormous. In the whole Free State between 30 and 40 thousand died, to which our Barolong territory certainly contributed a fifth. There followed, especially in the southern half of the land, a drought of 8 months duration.[54]

Lately, the weather had improved, promising the first proper harvest since 1882. But the territory was already being dismembered.

### LAND DISPOSITIONS

The question of what to do with the annexed territory caused the President and the Volksraad 'no small trouble'.[55] Brand had promised that 'sufficient ground' would be set aside for locations, and that the land rights recognised by Tshipinare would be respected. How much ground was sufficient and what land rights had been recognised by Tshipinare proved difficult to resolve. The legal issue was how far customary administrative authority, vested in subordinate chiefs and headmen, had been extended and converted into effective private title to particular bounded areas. And what were the rights of residents of these areas who held no title to them? The political issue was the quite fundamental one of the security of the people's access to land in the future.

There were two poles of interpretation, which from the point of view of ordinary citizens of the Barolong state represented the alternatives of the devil and the deep blue sea. If, on the one hand, most of the Barolong territory were formally defined as publicly administered rather than privately owned, there was considerable doubt whether African customary tenure would be protected by a state that represented white settler interests. If, on the other hand, full freehold titles were granted to individual African claimants, these title-holders would be extremely vulnerable to pressure to sell to white farmers and speculators. Residents of such land would be immediately subject to the prevailing political odium that white settlers attached to black 'squatters', and would feel correspondingly insecure. Hence the effort by some Barolong leaders to secure a settlement, in effect, between the two poles. One of the murdered chief's surviving half-brothers, Richard Maramantsi Moroka, petitioned the Volksraad at the beginning of the session in September 1884 that private titles recognised by Brand should be made inalienable, precisely because pressure would be brought to bear upon individual grantees if they were allowed to sell, and the land would soon pass out of their hands.[56]

Brand appointed a commission of enquiry on 4 August 1884, consisting of J.A. Prinsloo, commandant of the Bloemfontein district, attorney C. Voigt of Bloemfontein and the government surveyor E. Bourdillon. This commission reported a month later that Moroka had given his subjects 'more fixed' rights over ground than was consistent with Barolong custom in the past, and that he had issued written certificates from 1876 in respect of land grants made to individuals. Such land could not be sold during the lifetime of the chief nor, as had been confirmed by Tshipinare and his council in due course, during the lifetime of Tshipinare. The commission distinguished between grants of the right of ownership and grants of the right of supervision, and allowed only the former claims and not the latter. Thus the following claims were disallowed: that of Tshipinare's son John Phetogane to Morago 40, Kgalala 41, Bofulo 37 and Roodebult 33; that of Stephanus Koko Moroka to Patchoana 27 and Leeuwdraai 39; and that of Joseph Thoto Masisi to England 28, Commissiehoek 32 and Mokopu 38 (see Figure 1.3). These last five farms were particularly important. From the point of view of the Barolong, they comprised some of the best arable land in the district. From the point of view of the Volksraad, they were too near the Basutoland border, and any settlement allowed there had to be carefully supervised.[57]

The Prinsloo commission report, and the documents handed in with it, were submitted to another commission on 12 September 1884, consisting of five members of the Volksraad, of whom the most influential was J.G. Siebert. The Siebert commission proposed a very different interpretation of the evidence. It acknowledged that Moroka and Tshipinare had 'from time to time beaconed off small plots of ground for sub-captains and their followers', but inferred that the rights involved were only those of occupation, residence and grazing, not those of exclusive ownership. It followed that the land certificates issued were of no value. Nevertheless, in view of Brand's promise at the time of annexation, they recommended that 'to all Barolongs belonging to the tribe of Moroka and Sepinare, and to their councillors and sub-chiefs, certain grounds should be granted as their free property, in lieu of their positions as captains and sub-chiefs'. Of 152 farms surveyed by Bourdillon, they proposed to grant twenty-five to individual African claimants, six to Tshipinare's estate and nine to individual white claimants.

African claims were allowed only if Bourdillon knew the name of the man for whom he had surveyed the ground. Only one farm was granted to each claimant even if more than one farm had been surveyed in this way.[58] The commission justified its narrow interpretation with a specious reference to African custom. The land was properly vested in the person of the chief as trustee and, since the OFS government now stood in the chief's shoes, it was properly vested in the OFS state. The argument was applied selectively, however. Most white claims were to be granted and only a small proportion of African claims; while the rights of established residents, in terms of customary law, were ignored altogether.

Further onerous conditions were imposed. Title deeds had to be redeemed within six months and holders were to pay, in addition to the usual stamp duties, 1 per cent of the value of their fixed property, calculated at 10s. per morgen (the Volksraad amended this to 2 per cent); African grantees could only sell their land to white persons; and they should be subject to the provisions of the anti-squatting ordinance of 1876 which limited 'squatters' to five families per farm. In addition to the land attached to Thaba Nchu town, four more locations each of 8,000 morgen should be beaconed off, as far as possible from the Basutoland border. Otherwise, the rest of the land should revert to the OFS government and should be sold off as quickly as possible by public auction at an upset price of 12s.6d. per morgen, payable in ten equal annual instalments, interest at 6 per cent per annum being payable on the outstanding amount of the purchase price.[59]

This report was devastating to the Barolong. The first *landdrost*, Cornelis Van der Wath, observed that the people would rather move to Basutoland than accept such a settlement.[60] The debates in the Volksraad of 18 September 1884 failed to resolve the outstanding questions and many matters were left to the Executive Council to implement. Brand felt inhibited from taking action on the report because of rumours that the Basotho would attack the Free State in order to recover their land at Thaba Nchu. There was in any case sufficient divergence of opinion in the Volksraad, and sufficient uncertainty about the evidence of claims, that it was decided to refer the whole matter to a court. Judge Rheinhold Gregorowski was appointed on 20 May 1885 to enquire into all the land claims submitted to the Prinsloo commission and to make final judgements on them. Brand told the Volksraad that, if the judge could not accept a claim on the strength of the Prinsloo commission minutes, he would be required to hear further evidence from the Barolong. He also explained that the census of the annexed territory that had been carried out in August 1884 had revealed that more land was needed than had been recommended by the

Siebert commission. John Cameron had found 3,054 Barolong males aged 18 or over, 3,672 Barolong females and 554 Basotho, implying a total population of at least 12,000. Between them, they owned 9,506 trek oxen, 25,983 breeding stock, 8,031 horses and over 200,000 sheep and goats.[61]

Gregorowski drew up two reports, A and B, completed respectively on 25 May and 16 June 1885. The one preceded his hearing of further evidence from the Barolong. The other followed this further evidence, which was taken at Thaba Nchu from 2 June 1885. In Report A he acknowledged that Moroka had introduced a system of individual titles into the territory, in order to reduce the number of boundary disputes; the land was divided and beaconed off and certificates were issued, which were called in by Tshipinare at the time of Bourdillon's survey in 1882, to be replaced by new charts and certificates after the completion of the survey. Such certificates were issued both to white grantees and to Africans, but Gregorowski concluded that 'the sub-chiefs have not the same absolute right of ownership as the white persons', because sub-chiefs did not have the power to drive people off the land. 'A farm thus obtained by a sub-chief must be considered as having been obtained for his people and as being subject to a servitude in their favour, and consequently such properties could not be disposed of'. People had to pay taxes to the head chief and render labour service in ploughing, etc. to their own sub-chief. Under the changed conditions, Gregorowski advised that a sum of money should be paid to the sub-chiefs in lieu of those services. The substance of this report was, then, that the land grants should be formally confirmed but that grantees should not have the right to alienate or mortgage their property.[62]

After he had heard further evidence at Thaba Nchu, Judge Gregorowski changed his mind about the nature of the titles granted by Moroka and Tshipinare.

> In the last years of Moroka's reign, and principally during Sepinare's government, a great change took place regarding rights over ground in the Barolong territory, owing to the introduction of personal rights in ground, which were previously unknown. The intention of Sepinare appears to have been to introduce into his country the customs of civilised people, and consequently he had the land surveyed and made into farms and issued titles.[63]

Only one of the land certificates, in respect of Na'neng (the area surveyed by Bourdillon as the two farms Egypt 107 and Eden 96), survived the fire which destroyed Tshipinare's house on 10 July 1884. It had been given to John Daniel's son-in-law, Charles Newberry of Prynnsberg, Clocolan, as security for a loan to the chief of £2,000. Gregorowski noted that it was framed in the same terms as the grants made to white persons; and he attached considerable weight to the evidence of John Cameron, Tshipinare's magistrate, and that of John Daniel, the Wesleyan missionary, to the effect that 'the owners of farms had the full rights of ownership', including that of eviction of residents. He concluded that the holders of ground rights under Tshipinare had the full right to evict others but not the right to alienate or encumber that land. Nevertheless President Brand had committed the OFS in his proclamation of 29 July 1884 to allowing those resident on 12 July 1884 to remain in their locations or to have other ground made available to them. Gregorowski therefore recommended that farm owners be required to retain the established locations on their farms.[64] In respect of inheritance of property, the 'customs of civilised people', to which Gregorowski referred in the quotation above, embraced the principles of Roman-Dutch law.

Of the 152 farms surveyed or identified by Bourdillon, Gregorowski listed 15 farms to be granted to whites, three to the mission societies, and 95 to individual Africans. The remaining 39 farms were reserved for the OFS government (Figure 1.3). The white grantees (Figure 1.4) included trusted friends of Tshipinare or political 'insiders': the lawyer C.C. Mathey, members of the Daniel and Cameron families, the Raaffs father and son. Some of them were owed substantial sums of money by the Barolong state at the time of the chief's death. The African grantees (Figure 1.5) were overwhelmingly close kin or prominent political associates of the dead chief. Tshipinare's own estate received seven farms; his sixteen heirs—two surviving widows, six sons and eight daughters—were granted about thirty farms between them; other members of Tshipinare's family and his collateral kin who were Moroka's descendants received fourteen farms, and those of his councillors who do not appear on the genealogy in Figure 1.2 received at least another dozen.

A further commission of the Volksraad was appointed to draw up regulations for the issue of titles and to decide what to do with the government land. The commission recommended that no African should be allowed to sell his farm for five years, and confirmed Gregorowski's stipulation that existing locations should be allowed to remain. The rights of residents in this respect were protected by a servitude against the titles granted. Two reserves were set aside for Africans out of the government land (see Figure 1.3): Thaba Nchu itself (8,043 morgen); and seven farms in the northern area which had originally been Samuel's administrative responsibility and which now formed the distinctive horseshoe shape of the Seliba reserve (17,689 morgen). The Volksraad debated these provisions and confirmed them, except that it extended the period of inalienability of private land from five to fifteen years. On the expiry of this period, sales could only take place to whites. In addition, Africans could not lease their land for periods exceeding six months. All these arrangements were published in a Government Notice on 30 June 1885.[65] The areas of each category of land disposed in this way, and the respective percentages of the Moroka territory that they represented, are shown in the table attached to Figure 1.3.

One exception was made immediately, however, in respect of the inalienability clause. The President was authorised to arrange sales of land from

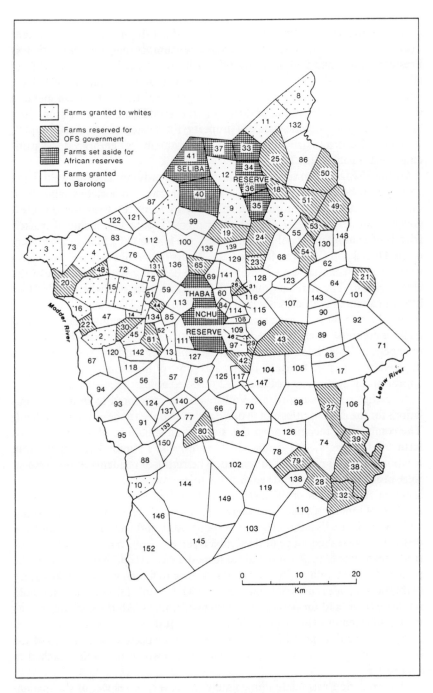

*Figure 1.3*   Thaba Nchu: the Gregorowski land dispositions, 1885.

## The Thaba Nchu Land Register: Original Farms, 1886

| Farm | No. | Note | | Farm | No. | Note |
|---|---|---|---|---|---|---|
| Vogelstruiskooi | 1 | ! | | Wildebeestspruit | 77 | |
| Travalgar | 2 | ! | | Brandkop | 78 | |
| Waterval | 3 | ! | | Salisbury | 79 | * |
| Kirkintilloch | 4 | ! | | Gladstone | 80 | * |
| Rakhoi | 5 | ! | | Lesaka | 81 | * |
| Boichoko | 6 | ! | | Tweefontein | 82 | |
| Sepane | 7 | ! | | Sterkfontein | 83 | |
| Boesmanskop | 8 | ! | | Fonteinhoek | 84 | |
| Chubani | 9 | ! | | Roodekop | 85 | |
| Rietpoort | 10 | WMC | | Mosheunyana | 86 | |
| Mokolobane | 11 | ! | | Jacobsrust | 87 | |
| New York | 12 | ! | | Ramoporoma | 88 | |
| Tabale | 13 | AC | | Lovedale | 89 | |
| Israelspoort | 14 | ! | | Tweespruit | 90 | |
| Thipa | 15 | ! | | Mooifontein | 91 | |
| Mameno | 16 | ! | | Rapuiskop | 92 | |
| Wonderkop | 17 | | | Bultfontein | 93 | |
| Sechoara | 18 | * | | Grysfontein | 94 | |
| Zoetlaagte | 19 | * | | Papfontein | 95 | |
| Likhatlong | 20 | * | | Eden | 96 | |
| Hoepelrok | 21 | * | | Koele | 97 | |
| Ramalitse | 22 | * | | Ngoanyana | 98 | |
| Maltanyana | 23 | * | | Houtnek | 99 | |
| Khumo | 24 | * | | Ratabane | 100 | |
| Golimo | 25 | * | | Goschen | 101 | |
| Schurvekop | 26 | * | | Gamabetoe | 102 | |
| Patchoana | 27 | * | | Vaalbank | 103 | |
| England | 28 | * | | Ngoana | 104 | |
| Wilgeboomnek | 29 | * | | Springhaannek | 105 | |
| Vaalkraal | 30 | * | | Thaba Patchoa | 106 | |
| Palmietspruit | 31 | * | | Egypte | 107 | |
| Commissiehoek | 32 | * | | Eenzaam | 108 | |
| Roodebult | 33 | SR | | Many Waters | 109 | |
| Kgamo | 34 | SR | | Klipfontein | 110 | |
| Seliba | 35 | SR | | Seroalo | 111 | |
| Tala | 36 | SR | | Toba | 112 | |
| Bofulo | 37 | SR | | Bultfontein | 113 | |
| Morago | 40 | SR | | Middelerf | 114 | |
| Kgalala | 41 | SR | | Bittervlei | 115 | |
| Mokopu | 38 | * | | Walhoek | 116 | |
| Leeuwdraai | 39 | * | | Dakpoort | 117 | |
| Mooihoek | 42 | * | | Mooiplaats | 118 | |
| Alexandria | 43 | * | | Rietfontein | 119 | |
| Palafala | 44 | * | | Kromdraai | 120 | |
| Parana | 45 | ! | | Wilgeboomspruit | 121 | |
| The Willows | 46 | WMC | | Rooderand | 122 | |
| Ramahutshe | 47 | + | | Paardenvlei | 123 | |
| Malika | 48 | * | | Commissiedrift | 124 | |
| Phokoane | 49 | * | | Groothoek | 125 | |
| Mafeteng | 50 | * | | Schuinsekop | 126 | |
| Mensvretersberg | 51 | * | | Victoria | 127 | |
| Bonolo | 52 | | | Meloendrift | 128 | |
| Lokoala | 53 | * | | Leeuwfontein | 129 | |
| Mount Pleasant | 54 | * | | Eliasfontein | 130 | |
| Somerset | 55 | | | Feloana | 131 | * |
| Zamenloop | 56 | | | Linana | 132 | |
| Khabanyana | 57 | | | Nogaspost | 133 | |
| Morokashoek | 58 | | | Sebata | 134 | |
| Liboba | 59 | | | Paradys | 135 | |
| Rooifontein | 60 | | | Makoto | 136 | |
| Moseia | 61 | | | Roodewal | 137 | |
| Diphering | 62 | | | Klein Geluk | 138 | |
| Andriesfontein | 63 | | | Vlakspruit | 139 | |
| Maseru | 64 | | | Brakfontein | 140 | |
| Abrahamskraal | 65 | * | | Tafelkop | 141 | |
| Vaalkop | 66 | | | Enkelboom | 142 | |
| Palmietfontein | 67 | | | Walspruit | 143 | |
| Moroto | 68 | | | Daggafontein | 144 | |
| Groenheuvel | 69 | | | Boven Logageng | 145 | |
| Goede Hoop | 70 | | | Onder Logageng | 146 | |
| Brakfontein | 71 | | | Bastardspoort | 147 | |
| Bloemspruit | 72 | | | Lima | 148 | |
| Langbewoond | 73 | | | Tlogo ea Moroa | 149 | |
| Naauwpoort | 74 | | | Kopjeskraal | 150 | |
| Potsane | 75 | | | Moroyane | 152 | |
| Ngakantsispoort | 76 | | | | | |

| Summary disposition: | Area in morgen | Percentage |
|---|---|---|
| Farms granted to Africans | 245,288 | 66 |
| Farms granted to whites | 39,750 | 11 |
| Farms reserved for OFS govt. | 58,686 | 16 |
| Two African reserves | 25,732 | 7 |
| TOTAL | 369,456 | 100 |

KEY:
! granted to whites; * reserved for OFS government; AC granted to the Anglican Church; WMC granted to the Wesleyan Methodist Church; SR government farms comprising the Seliba Reserve (the government farm comprising the Thaba Nchu Reserve was not listed in the register); + Ramahutshe 47 was initially registered in the name of the OFS government but was granted to the Goronyane family in 1889 (and therefore appears on the map as an African-owned farm). All other farms were granted to individual Africans in 1886.

Tshipinare's estate that were sufficient to cover the chief's private debts. The debts that were traced comprised several thousand pounds, of which attorney Voigt concluded that only £300 should be construed as debts owed by Tshipinare personally, as opposed to debts owed by the Barolong state. Despite this, in view of the sale of three farms from Tshipinare's private estate in December 1885, which realised £3,545, it seems likely that President Brand interpreted the discretion granted to him by the Volksraad in this matter as allowing the Barolong public debt to be met posthumously from the resources of the murdered chief himself.[66]

## THE AFTERMATH: RELOCATION, ALIENATION, SPECULATION

The Barolong resident on government farms, apart from those set aside as reserves, were supposed to move off them by 20 August 1885. None had moved to the reserves by that date; some had gone to Basutoland or dispersed to other parts of the OFS; while others remained on the government farms. Fourteen of these farms—fewer than half the number nominally available— were leased to whites on 1 September 1885. Brand did not complete the process at this time, in order to avoid the obloquy of forced evictions. By the end of the year, however, 'some hundreds of families' had left for Basutoland and other parts of the Free State. Ominously, reported the Wesleyans, 'when the measures now in progress are carried out some of our circuits will be virtually depopulated'.[67]

The Volksraad session of May 1886 confirmed the arrangements previously made, rejecting Brand's suggestion that the government farms in the south-eastern block around Thaba Phatshwa (see Figure 1.3) should be made into another reserve. Fifteen further farms were advertised for hire on 16 July for a period of ten years. The people were instructed to move by 6 July, but were extremely reluctant to do so. This time, removals were enforced. Daniel reported at the end of 1886 that seventeen farms—making a total of thirty-one—had been disposed of during the year through lease to whites, and that 'several thousand Barolong have been evicted from homes which they have occupied in some instances for more than 30 years'. Some of them had gone to Basutoland and other districts of the Free State, while others had sought refuge throughout the territory on farms held by African grantees. The people had been greatly impoverished by the loss of their houses and gardens, having already suffered severe losses of livestock and grain as a result of the three years' drought from 1882 to 1884. Many households had no trek oxen left to plough their lands. Worse, the poll tax levied on all males between the ages of 18 and 70 was imposed at double the rate demanded from Africans in the rest of the OFS.[68]

The rights of the African grantees were recognised, but under onerous conditions. They had to redeem their titles at the rate of 1 per cent on an 'excessive valuation' of 10s. per morgen, in addition to government dues,

*Figure 1.4* Farms granted to whites

| No | Farm | Grantee | Remarks |
|---|---|---|---|
| 1 | Vogelstruiskooi | Carl Christian Mathey | attorney; member of Volksraad Executive Council; 'general executive' of the Barolong |
| 2 | Travalgar | John Nelson | carpenter, Thaba Nchu |
| 3 | Waterval | James John Allison | ? a son of Joseph Allison, former OFS government secretary |
| 4 | Kirkintilloch | Estate Arthur William Cameron | son of James Cameron; son-in-law of John Daniel; stalwart Wesleyan; died 1883 |
| 5 | Rakhoi | Mary Ann Daniel | daughter of Thomas Hezekiah Sephton II; wife of John Daniel |
| 6 | Boichoko | John Allison Cameron | appointed Tshipinare's magistrate, 1883 |
| 7 | Sepani | James Cameron | son of James Cameron |
| 8 | Boesmanskop | N.P.C. Raaff | old inhabitant of OFS; friend and confidant of Tshipinare; father of Pieter Raaff |
| 9 | Chubani | John Daniel | Wesleyan missionary, Thaba Nchu, 1871–1888 |
| 10 | Rietpoort | Wesleyan church | |
| 11 | Mokolobane | Pieter Raaff | appointed Tshipinare's commandant, 1883; contract specified a farm in lieu of adequate salary |
| 12 | New York | George Finlay | son-in-law of John Daniel |
| 13 | Tabale | Anglican church | chosen by William Crisp in 1882 |
| 14 | Israelspoort | Stephanus Mey | almost certainly a 'Bastard', one of Carolus Baatje's Newlanders |
| 15 | Thipa | John W. Cameron | son of John Allison Cameron |
| 16 | Mameno | C.M.Z. & J.A. Brand | Two sons of President Brand |
| 45 | Parana | Evelina Rebecca Reid | |
| 46 | The Willows | Wesleyan church | |

## Figure 1.5 Farms granted to Africans

| No | Farm | Grantee | Remarks |
|---|---|---|---|
| | | *A  Tshipinare's heirs* | |
| 56 | Zamenloop | | |
| 57 | Khabanyana | Tshipinare's | 56, 57 and 58 sold 1885 to pay the chief's debts; bought by J.A. Coetzer, stock farmer |
| 58 | Morokashoek | private estate | |
| 108 | Eenzaam | | 108 and 109 sold 1887 to G.A. Fichardt, merchant of Bloemfontein |
| 109 | Many Waters | | |
| 107 | Egypte | | 107 and 110 divided equally between Tshipinare's sixteen heirs |
| 110 | Klipfontein | | |
| 127 | Victoria | Ketimetse | sixth wife, grandmother of Dr James Sebe Moroka; died 1906 |
| 111 | Seroalo | Buku | ninth wife; daughter of Tshidi Barolong chief Montshiwa; survived Samuel's attack on 10 July 1884 |
| 112 | Toba | | |
| 113 | Bultfontein | | |
| 117 | Dikpoort | Elizabeth Nkhabele | eldest daughter and only child in senior house; married (1) to Zechariah Fenyang (d. 1883) and (2) to Abraham Setlogelo (d. 1891); one of Molema's key informants; died 1947, aged 99 |
| 118 | Mooiplaats | | |
| 119 | Rietfontein | | |
| 89 | Lovedale | | |
| 90 | Tweespruit | | |
| 91 | Mooifontein | | |
| 92 | Rapuiskop | Robert Tawana | senior son and heir, in fourth house; chief 1902–1912; 'devout follower of Bacchus' |
| 93 | Bultfontein | | |
| 94 | Grysfontein | | |
| 95 | Papfontein | | |
| 124 | Commissiedrift | Matsetselela | daughter in second house; married to Phofoyagae Tlhakung |
| 125 | Groothoek | Majang | daughter in third house; married (1) to Motlhware, heir apparent to Moroka until death in 1879; (2) to Michael Tshabadira (q.v.); (3) to Letsapa, a Ratlou Barolong chief at Setlagole; mother of Percy Tshabadira who succeeded to Samuel's chieftainship-in-exile at Ramokgwebana, Bechuanaland Protectorate |
| 17 | Wonderkop | Joel | eldest son in fifth house; survived Samuel's attack on 10 July 1884 |
| 71 | Brakfontein | | |
| 99 | Houtnek | John Phetogane | second son in fifth house; regent in Robert Tawana's absence in British Bechuanaland; appointed chief in own right 1930, died 1940; 'clerk and bottlewasher' to legal agent Diepraam; also a 'devout follower of Bacchus' |
| 100 | Ratabane | | |
| 96 | Eden | Isaac Motshegare | third son in fifth house |
| 97 | Koele | | |
| 114 | Middelerf | Maggie Ketshogile | eldest daughter in sixth house; mother of Dr James Sebe Moroka; married to Stephen Nyokong, son of John Mokitlane Nyokong, but divorced him c. 1908; died 1928 |
| 115 | Bittervlei | | |
| 116 | Walhoek | | |

| | | B Close collaterals | |
|---|---|---|---|
| 126 | Schuinekop | Samata | second daughter in sixth house; married to Shadrack Makgothi, a son of Stephanus Makoloi Makgothi, but divorced him c. 1908 |
| 101 | Goschen | Morokanyana | son in sixth house; Dr J.S. Moroka's uncle; he lost his land to G.J. Van Riet; died 1940 |
| 103 | Vaalbank | Solomon | apparently a son of Ketimetse's by a former marriage; adopted as Tshipinare's son in sixth house |

*B Close collaterals*

| | | | |
|---|---|---|---|
| 55, 68 | Somerset, Moroto | Abraham Setlogelo | younger son of Setlogelo, Tshipinare's elder brother who was recovered from Natal in 1868; councillor |
| 120, 121, 122 | Kromdraai, Wilgeboomspruit, Rooderand | Molale | Moroka's younger brother; councillor |
| 106 | Thaba Patchoa | Stephanus Koko | son in Moroka's fourth house; councillor |
| 144, 145, 146, 149 | Daggafontein, Boven Logageng, Onder Logageng, Tlogo ea Moroa | Richard Maramantsi | son of Moroka by Nkhabele, Tshipinare's half-brother; councillor and leader of opposition to OFS rule; died British Bechuanaland 1895 |
| 102 | Gamabetoe | George Morwagabuse | youngest son of Moroka by Nkhabele; councillor |
| 98, 104, 105 | Ngoanyana, Ngoana, Springhaannek | Michael Tshabadira | son of Tshabadira (d. 1874), the eldest of Moroka's sons by Nkhabele; married Tshipinare's daughter Majang (q.v.); migrated to British Bechuanaland, then to Bechuanaland Protectorate |

*C Other councillors, senior headmen, relatives, etc.*

| | | | |
|---|---|---|---|
| 86, 132 | Mosheunyana, Linana | Jacob Ngakantsi | close political associate of Moroka, and also his ? cousin; councillor; stoned during Samuel's attack on 10 July 1884 and died shortly afterwards |
| 60 | Rooifontein | Estate Lang Jan Matsheka | died with Tshipinare on 10 July 1884; one son, Kali John Matsheka, was chairman of the Barolong Progressive Association in 1930s |
| 62, 64 | Diphering, Maseru | John Mokitlane Nyokong | senior representative of Motlatla branch of Bafokeng at Thaba Nchu; councillor; member of Tsala syndicate, etc.; died 1930 |
| 47, 66, 67 | Ramahutshe, Vaalkop, Palmietfontein | Joel David Goronyane | Methodist minister; councillor; leader of Tsala syndicate, Becoana Mutual Improvement Association, etc.; died 1926 |
| 70 | Geede Hoop | Stephanus Makoloi Makgothi | councillor; father of Jeremiah Makgothi; died 1916 |
| 73, 74 | Langbewoond, Naauwpoort | Joseph Thoto Masisi | father of Moses Masisi; councillor; died 1903 |
| 78 | Brandkop | Hermanus Keikelame | son of 'friend' and original follower of Moroka; died 1905 |
| 87 | Jacobsrust | Tlage | full sister of Moroka; married to 'Old' Ngakantsi, uncle of Moroka |
| 135 | Paradys | Timothy Mosela Seiphemo | a prominent headman; died 1916 |
| 152 | Moroyane | 'Ou Mooi' | councillor; probably the chief Mui, representative of a branch of the Ratlou Barolong at Thaba Nchu; firmly loyal both to Moroka and to Tshipinare |

Note: This list of beneficiaries is incomplete: it shows 64 of the total of 95 farms granted to Africans. However, these farms comprise substantially more than two-thirds of the land granted in this way, and all the most influential grantees are identified here (see Figure 1.2). The farm numbers are those of the first Thaba Nchu Land Register (see Figure 1.3), and may therefore be traced in a way that corresponds with the numbers in the modern Thaba Nchu registers.

surveying expenses, etc., all this under penalty of forfeiture if not redeemed within one year from June 1885. 'This has proved a fearful drain', the Wesleyans reported, 'on the resources of the people. In many cases they have had to sacrifice their stock to raise the money, and in others to borrow at ruinous rates of interest'. In the light of this pressure, and the absence of a chief at Thaba Nchu, the process of decentralisation accelerated, since people could neither afford to maintain two homes nor had any political incentive to do so. As a result, the Wesleyan day school at Thaba Nchu was closed. Despite this, the Wesleyans were trying to open an advanced school and had recruited a 'competent native teacher' for this purpose—almost certainly Jeremiah Makgothi, one of the sons of Stephanus Makoloi Makgothi of the farm Goede Hoop 70. The mission was extremely short of money, however, since contributions had sharply fallen off.[69]

The African grantees' administrative authority had collapsed; and they were under immediate financial pressure to redeem their titles. Meanwhile, there was a considerable influx of refugees on to their lands from the government farms, who brought their own livestock and in some cases, apparently, expected the owners to carry out all improvements at their own expense. All these factors made the question of the relations between grantees and residents both difficult and controversial. Leading Barolong—Richard Maramantsi, Robert Tawana, Joel, Joseph Masisi, Joel Goronyane and Abraham Setlogelo, 'representing the landed interests', appealed to the President through John Daniel not to regulate the relations between landowners and occupiers of the villages on their farms. Many residents were relatives and personal friends of the landowners; arrangements for grazing and cultivation were made for 'mutual benefit'; there was no danger of residents being evicted, 'as the owners would regard it as a calamity were the occupants to leave their farms'; landowners wished 'to have as many people as possible on their places even at the risk of overstocking the farm'. They feared that framing alien regulations would disturb the minds of the people and raise suspicion and distrust.[70] Nevertheless, so many quarrels broke out that the new *landdrost*, Johannes Marthinus De Wet, appealed in October 1885 and again in December 1886 for regulations to be drawn up. After further delay, detailed regulations were published in September 1887.

These regulations prescribed that the owners of livestock should pay 5s. per fifty head of small stock, 9d. per head of cattle and 1s. for a horse to the owner of the farm; and that the owner of the farm should make available at least two morgen of arable lands to each head of a family who wished to cultivate, while one fifth of the crops reaped should be given to the owner, who should provide the seed. Subject to agreement between the parties, payment for grazing and arable land could be made in the form of labour services to the owner, especially connected with ploughing, weeding and harvesting. These arrangements were to apply only where no other contractual agreement had been made. The above share-cropping contract, if at all widespread in practice, suggests a balance of power in favour of the tenant and against the landowner. It doubtless reflected the absence of sanctions either of a formal kind, in that *bona fide* residents in 1884 were protected by the servitude against the grantees' titles; or of an informal kind, in that it would have been invidious and unjust for the grantees to evict from their land refugees who had been expelled from the government farms.[71]

Before these regulations were published, however, several of the leading grantees had already petitioned the Volksraad to lift the restrictions on sale. Richard Maramantsi's petition was heard at the beginning of the Volksraad session of May 1887. He had resisted the alienation of land, he had complained about other aspects of the land settlement, and he had specifically requested the OFS government not to frame special regulations governing the mutual obligations of landowners and residents. It appears that the Volksraad was happy to be rid of an articulate spokesman for the Barolong, who from its point of view was a 'trouble-maker'. So he was allowed to sell his land, provided that he released his title deeds and left the state with his followers, or that he left enough land for those who remained. A similar petition from Michael Tshaba-dira was granted on 2 June 1887. These precedents effectively broke the non-alienation clause. Thereafter, provided landowners guaranteed that they and their followers would leave the state or leave enough land for their followers to occupy, permission was granted for them to sell their lands. While many more people left the territory in the wake of such land sales, others were returning to Thaba Nchu 'who for years have resided in outposts'.[72]

Two key questions arise at this point. What happened to these emigrants? And what happened to their land at Thaba Nchu? The answer to the first question is that many went to British Bechuanaland and later to the Bechuanaland Protectorate. British Bechuanaland, the territory south of the Molopo river, had been declared a Crown Colony in September 1885. The land settlement of 1886 in that region set aside as reserves or locations what the administration regarded as sufficient land for the Barolong and Batlhaping communities there; it conceded the land claims made by white mercenaries or speculators within the short-lived Stellaland republic, now incorporated within British Bechuanaland; and it otherwise left the bulk of the territory as unsurveyed Crown lands potentially available for sale to white colonists.[73] The new administration anticipated that its expenses would be met largely by the sale of Crown lands. To its considerable chagrin, however, the income from such sales in 1886–7 was only £855. The news of a move to the area by leaders of the Seleka Barolong from Thaba Nchu therefore came as a welcome relief to the Administrator, Sidney Shippard. At the end of September 1887 he reported that:

> an extensive purchase of vacant Crown land near Setlagole has recently been made by Messrs. Dunell, Ebden & Co. of Port Elizabeth, on behalf

of Richard Moroka and the Barolongs of Thaba Nchu, who are about to
leave the Orange Free State and migrate *en masse* to this country. This
movement, which appears to have afforded much satisfaction to Mont-
sioa, furnishes a remarkable proof of the estimation in which the Natives
hold the privilege of living under Her Majesty's rule.[74]

More to the point, this movement helped Shippard to balance a precarious
budget.

In February 1888, Shippard noted that the Setlagole reserve was now
surrounded on all sides by farms which belonged either to whites or to the
'Moroka Barolongs' of Thaba Nchu. Richard Maramantsi and Michael Tshabadira settled with their followers in a large block of land which straddled the
Malibane tributary of the Setlagole river. Eleven farms in the western part of
this block, falling within the former republic of Stellaland, were bought by
Richard Maramantsi from the large Port Elizabeth firm of Dunell, Ebden &
Co., in whose favour the land had been mortgaged.[75] These farms had
been granted to Charles Daly, an unscrupulous trader at Bloemhof who was
promised land in return for ammunition supplied to mercenaries during the
Bechuanaland wars of 1881–4. The eastern part of the block was a large
unsurveyed piece of Crown land which Michael Tshabadira bought from the
same Port Elizabeth firm, acting this time as agents for the British Bechuanaland administration.[76]

In the late winter of 1889, Michael Tshabadira was building his settlement at
Malibane, 'a beautiful place, with plenty of trees'. Reverend Henry Bevan, of
the Phokoane Anglican mission, stayed with them for three weeks and recorded his pleasure at renewing his acquaintance with some of his old flock:

> Michael was under me years ago as a schoolboy at Thaba Nchu, and it was
> a great pleasure to be with him again and to teach his two dear little boys,
> the second of whom will, I hope, one day be a clergyman.

There was a total of thirty-two in the congregation at St. Martin's church there,
and they sang beautifully, as they had been taught at Thaba Nchu.[77]

The settlement did not, however, last long. Michael Tshabadira borrowed
£2,000 from Henry Lamb in 1892, sold his farm to Lamb in 1893 and trekked
northwards to the Bechuanaland Protectorate. In due course, one of his two
'dear little boys', Percy Tshabadira, succeeded to the chieftainship of the
exiled Samuel Lehulere Moroka at Ramokgwebana in the Tati district, north-
east of Francistown. Richard Maramantsi died in British Bechuanaland in
1895, and his estate of eleven farms was bequeathed to his sons. By this time
Robert Tawana, Tshipinare's eldest son and heir, who was granted seven
farms in the Moroka district under the Gregorowski settlement (see Figure
1.5), had also emigrated to the Setlagole region after selling his lands at Thaba
Nchu. Molema wrote of Robert Tawana in a disconcertingly trenchant
manner: 'fear, hesitancy and diffidence took possession of his mind ... the
unrest and discord in the tribe became exaggerated in his timid mind ...

[he] therefore sold his farm[s] and ignominiously left his town, his tribe and troth for Bechuanaland'. In 1894, for £1,500, he bought two properties in British Bechuanaland, together comprising 4,000 morgen, from Owen Robert Dunell. This land was also on the Setlagole river, adjacent to the farms that belonged to Richard Maramantsi and Michael Tshabadira. Molema's suggestion that Robert Tawana's mind was disturbed is implicitly endorsed by the facts that the transaction was carried out in his name by Joseph Thoto Masisi, as legally-appointed curator of his affairs, and that Robert Tawana was entitled to the usufruct only and had no power to alienate the land. Robert Tawana returned to Thaba Nchu after the South African war and assumed the chieftainship, a mere shadow of its former self. He was, according to Molema, 'gigantic in physical proportions, suave and calm in manner', and otherwise unremarkable except for his 'devotion to Bacchus'. When he died in 1912, his only fixed asset was the small farm Nonen (604 morgen) in British Bechuanaland, now part of the northern Cape province. His heir, Albert Setlogelo, who became chief at Thaba Nchu in 1942, was entitled to one twenty-fourth share of Nonen. He was, in effect, indigent.[78]

Richard Maramantsi, Michael Tshabadira and Robert Tawana were the largest individual landowners in the Moroka district who sold all their land there in the years following annexation. But many others also lost their land. By the early 1890s, more than 60 per cent of the land granted to individual Africans in 1885 had been alienated to white ownership. This land included all the farms belonging to five of Tshipinare's six sons, his most senior surviving half-brother Richard Maramantsi, his senior half-nephew Michael Tshabadira, and his ninth wife Buku. The lands retained by members of Tshipinare's family were the farms granted to his nephew Abraham Setlogelo, his other surviving widow Ketimetse, his daughters Elizabeth Nkhabele, Matsetselela, Maggie and Samata, and one of his junior sons, Morokanyana (see Figure 1.2).[79]

Three reasons may be suggested for land alienation on this scale. Firstly, the prominent grantees, as well as the ordinary people, were profoundly demoralised by Free State rule. The Barolong chieftainship was effectively destroyed, much of the land was directly appropriated by the OFS, and the people were dispersed. Secondly, the landowners were unable to farm successfully. They faced immediate financial problems in redeeming their titles. They had experienced severe losses of livestock and many must have lacked the capital resources to engage in agriculture directly even when the depression of the early and middle 1880s was lifted by the gold boom. The form of share-cropping contract suggested by the Moroka regulations of 1887 favoured the share-cropper rather than the landowner. In addition, some of the landowners undoubtedly felt a strong sense of obligation towards their people, who in any case had a significant degree of immunity from eviction on account of the servitudes attached to the land titles. The irony is that the relative security of the resident tenants was subverted by the departure of the landowners.

Thirdly, in the light of the above circumstances, it is likely that the back-wash of speculative capital which swept over the district in the immediate aftermath of the discovery of gold proved an overwhelming incentive to the senior Barolong notables to realise their assets in the short term and to try to establish a better life elsewhere. No less than 75 per cent of the produce sold on the Rand in 1888 came from the OFS, much of it across the border from Basutoland.[80] Millers, traders and speculators in the Conquered Territory were principal beneficiaries of this boom: notably James Robertson, Charles Newberry, and the firm of D. & D.H. Fraser, based at Liphiring in Basuto-land and later at Wepener in the OFS. On a much smaller scale, traders in Thaba Nchu and Ladybrand took advantage of the indebtedness of Barolong landowners to extend mortgages to cover these debts and then to foreclose them. The activities of land speculators in the Moroka district—above all Robertson and Newberry—must be understood in terms of the boom in the grain trade from Basutoland which followed the discovery of gold on the Witwatersrand; and of the opportunities for investment which arose out of profits made at the Kimberley diamond mines. This was a very common pattern, and some biographical illustration is therefore appropriate for com-parative purposes.[81]

James Robertson emigrated from Scotland to South Africa in 1854, with his three brothers and sister. He established the mill at Jammerberg Drift, near Wepener, in 1869, which by the 1890s dominated the grain trade from Basuto-land through the Conquered Territory. He built an entirely new plant in 1890 with a capacity of 600 bags a day; in 1896, 163,000 bags of grain were transported from these mills, three-quarters of it by Barolong from Thaba Nchu. In 1900, when Robertson gave evidence to the Land Settlement Com-mission, the firm of J. and T. Robertson owned about 10,000 morgen of land, consisting of farms in the Kroonstad and Boshof districts and two in the Moroka district.[82]

His land transactions in the Moroka district, however, were undertaken on a very much larger scale than is implied by this summary of his position in 1900. In November 1887 he bought all of Michael Tshabadira's farms in the east of the district—Ngoanyana 98, Ngoana 104, Springhaannek 105 and Groothoek 125, which last was registered in the name of Tshabadira's wife Majang—for £6,162. In the following month he bought Richard Maramantsi's extensive estates in the south-west—Daggafontein 144, Boven Logageng 145, Onder Logageng 146 and Tlogo ea Moroa 149—for £10,380. He sold all these farms to Charles Newberry in June 1888 for £24,262.3s. Two other farms— Wonderkop 17 and Kopjeskraal 150—he also sold to Newberry in 1889 at a substantial profit. Later, in 1892, he bought Mooifontein 91 and Papfontein 95 from Robert Tawana, Tshipinare's heir, after which the latter left the district for British Bechuanaland.[83]

Charles Newberry and his elder brother John were immigrant carpenters and builders who arrived in Natal in the early 1860s. After five or six years of persistent work at the Kimberley diamond diggings in the 1870s, they held eight full claims and their joint estate was worth about £25,000. As the process of company amalgamation gathered pace, the brothers added their claims to those of the Kimberley Central Diamond Mining Company, in which their joint shareholding in March 1881 was £71,660.[84] Charles built an impressive estate at Prynnsberg in the Clocolan district and invested in land on a large scale, initially in the Moroka district and later in Gordonia in the northern Cape. John built the mill at Leeuwrivier in the early 1890s, which was the largest of its kind in the Free State. Both brothers pioneered extensive tree plantations, John Newberry on part of Brakfontein 71 adjoining the Newberry dam at the Leeuwrivier mills, and Charles Newberry on Ngoanyana 98 and at Prynnsberg. Charles imported black wildebeest and herds of other antelopes to the Prynnsberg estate.[85]

Charles Newberry did take some time off his remorseless dedication to building his fortune at Kimberley. In the late 1870s he was invited to visit Thaba Nchu by a friend at Kimberley, Tom Daniel, the eldest son of the Wesleyan missionary, John Daniel. He met there Tom's sister Libby (Elizabeth Mary), who was born in 1858. He:

> soon saw that she was the sort of girl I admired and I quickly made up my mind to ask her to marry me. I returned to Kimberley, but came again a few weeks later. I waited for over a year before the wedding was brought off, but most of that time I spent at Thaba Nchu.[86]

They built the estate at Prynnsberg, and Charles Newberry was persuaded by his father-in-law John Daniel, against his own better judgement, to lend Tshipinare £2,000 shortly before the latter's death in 1884. Over a year later, in July 1885, just after the details of the land dispositions were published, Newberry sought President Brand's personal intervention to assist him to recover the debt, as security for which he held Tshipinare's certificate of title to the farm Na'neng (Eden 96 and Egypte 107).[87] It is probable that this part of Tshipinare's debt was discharged by the sale of three farms—Zamenloop 56, Khabanyana 57 and Morokashoek 58—from his private estate to a farmer, L.J. Coetzer, for £3,545 in December 1885.[88] It is also probable that Newberry had impressed his anxiety for repayment of this sum of £2,000 upon his father-in-law, for it was Daniel's evidence to Gregorowski in June 1885 that partly persuaded the judge to change his mind over the inalienability of the titles granted by Tshipinare. Clearly the certificate of title to Na'neng was worthless to Newberry unless such titles could be realised in the market place.

The final question that arises in respect of the 1890s is how, in view of the rapid alienation of land described above, the transfers of ownership from black to white affected existing servitudes. The severe 'anti-squatting' legislation passed by the OFS in 1881 and 1895 nominally precluded more than five black families from living on a white-owned farm. A contradiction of principle arose at the moment of sale from black owner to white owner: many residents retained their servitude rights but were potentially subject to harassment as 'squatters'. In practice, it appears, the contradiction of principle was resolved in a number of ways. Firstly, the anti-squatting legislation was not effectively enforced in the 1880s and 1890s, and Keegan notes little response to it in the arable districts of the Conquered Territory. Secondly, a commission of enquiry appointed in 1890 to investigate 'squatters' in the Moroka district specifically recommended that the regulations should only be applied over and above the people qualified under the servitude to reside in the district. There was, however, sufficient uncertainty about the legal position, and sufficient threat of harassment at least by smaller white landowners in the district, that the Government Secretary found it necessary to confirm explicitly in 1899 that the servitudes that protected *bona fide* residents from eviction were not connected with the nominal fifteen-year non-alienation clause originally inscribed in the conditions of grant. The servitudes, in other words, only expired with the lives of the holders.[89]

The Newberry estates, representative of the large holdings of absentee landlords, afforded some respite from the pressure of population in the reserves and on African-owned farms which was of prime concern to the 1890 commission of enquiry. These estates embraced not only the eight farms purchased from James Robertson in the transaction described above, but also Wonderkop 17, Lovedale 89, Eden 96 (together with a small portion of Egypte 107) and Kopjeskraal 150 (see Figure 1.3). Some of the titles had been transferred free of servitudes, implying that no indigenous residents remained. Ngoanyana 98, whose particular history is explored in detail in Chapter 7, was one of these. But many heads of families did not wish to leave the farms with Michael Tshabadira and Richard Maramantsi, and a list of their names was passed to James Robertson. Thus some 'insiders' remained.

It seems clear, however, that the Newberry estates also provided access to land for people who were, in varying degrees, 'outsiders'. In the first place, many Barolong and Basotho who belonged to the district had been displaced from government farms leased to whites after 1885. Some of these 'spilled over' from the two reserves set aside for African occupation under the terms of the Gregorowski land dispositions. The 1890 commission of enquiry reported that 'there are already many Kaffirs, who are entitled to reside on locations, but who are hiring ground from Newberry and other owners'. In the second place, despite their servitude rights which nominally survived the sale of African-owned land to whites, 'natives resident on farms sold in the district could have matters made so unpleasant for them by the owners, that they would rather waive their rights and simply reside with persons of their own tribe on farms such as Newberry's, where they would not be daily interfered with'. In the third place, the same commission of enquiry found that 573 heads of families had *entered* the district after the annexation—mainly Barolong and Basotho but also a number of Mfengu and Batlhaping and other minorities. Most of them had no right to reside in the reserves or on African-owned farms, and at least some of them were able to pursue a semi-independent livelihood on the Newberry estates. More than ten years after the 1890 commission's report, Newberry's agent, Harry Hanger, recalled that Newberry had never taken any steps to find out how many people living on his land did not have servitude rights or were otherwise not entitled to live there.[90]

In summary, from the evidence available, a number of inferences may be drawn about population movements in the 1880s and 1890s. Firstly, a significant exodus took place from Thaba Nchu before the annexation in 1884, as both 'loyal' and 'rebel' Barolong fled from the ravages of civil war; and after the annexation, as people were squeezed off farms appropriated by the OFS government, and prominent African grantees sold up to white speculators and left for British Bechuanaland with some of their followers. Secondly, a significant internal redistribution of population took place in the late 1880s, as people evicted from government farms sought refuge in the two African reserves, which rapidly became congested, and on the remaining black-owned farms. Thirdly, a number of 'loyal' refugees from Basutoland settled in Thaba Nchu during and after the Gun War in the early 1880s; and a later substantial drift took place into the district of people who found share-cropping opportunities on the large Newberry estates and unrestricted grazing and arable land on the black-owned farms.

These swirling currents of regional stress towards the close of the nineteenth century were overtaken by the tidal waves of dislocation that swept across the highveld as a result of the South African war (1899–1902). The following chapter examines this upheaval and its aftermath in the Thaba Nchu district.

# 2

# IMPERIAL INTERVENTION:
# THE LAND SETTLERS

If we don't get a railway we don't live. That's the plain English of it.

James Robertson
14 November 1900
BPP, Cd. 627, p. 234

It is a story of twenty years' work, quite alone, endeavouring to get one
thousand acres of virgin land to my way of thinking ... like trying to
change the shape of the Rock of Gibraltar with a pen-knife.

Leonard Flemming
*The Call of the Veld* (1924), p. x

The South African war brought in its wake new strains into the district, in
three senses: a distinctive strain of 'blood', that of British settlers introduced
into the former Boer republics; the muscular strain of wrenching 'virgin land'
to their way of thinking; and the strain of intensified competition between
Boers, British and Africans. Lord Kitchener's devastation of the countryside
was Lord Milner's opportunity for its reconstruction. The experiment of Land
Settlement was one of Milner's most ambitious schemes of social engineering.
In the Orange River Colony (ORC), several hundred settlers 'of British stock'
were placed on the land by means of a large loan from the imperial treasury in
London. Many of them were concentrated in the Thaba Nchu district, where
they encountered every scourge of South African agriculture: drought, locusts, shortage of labour and abundance of debt. The British settlers also
encountered Boer resentment of the terms on which the new colonial state
favoured their enterprise, and African resentment of their intrusion into lands
formerly occupied by black share-croppers.

The settlers' self-image was that of intrepid pioneers who wrestled with a
harsh environment: as Leonard Flemming put it, 'like trying to change the
shape of the Rock of Gibraltar with a pen-knife'. Some succeeded. Others
failed. Success—where it occurred—was hard-won. The critical issue for
judgement is both a fine one, in respect of weighing the evidence in the
balance; and a fundamental one, in respect of understanding South African
agricultural development in the past, the present and the future. How far was
the eventual success of some white farmers attributable to individuals' initiative and endeavour? How far was it predicated on generous and systematic state
support? How far was it attained on the backs of and at the expense of the
remnants of an African share-cropping peasantry? These are the questions

which lie behind the story of Land Settlement in Thaba Nchu. They arise partly out of Keegan's analysis of the capitalisation of white agriculture; and partly out of the contrast of perspective implied in the quotations from James Robertson and Leonard Flemming above.

## SCORCHED EARTH

British troops entered Bloemfontein on 13 March 1900, and in May the Boer republic of the OFS was incorporated within the empire under its new name of the Orange River Colony. But the war continued in the countryside for another two relentless years. Small and mobile Boer commandos harassed the much larger and more cumbersome units of the British army, capturing supplies, cutting communications and drawing sustenance from a largely sympathetic white populace. The superficial triumphs of Lord Roberts' command—the entry into the two republican capitals of Bloemfontein and Pretoria—gave way to a grim and bitter struggle for control of the rural hinterlands. Different methods were required. Lord Kitchener's strategy was to lay the countryside to waste. The inhabitants were removed to sites along the lines of rail which became known as concentration camps. Lands were ravaged, farm buildings burned and livestock appropriated or destroyed. Both along the lines of rail and beyond them, the British army constructed an elaborate grid system of forts, and later of blockhouses, designed to contain the Boer guerillas. Simultaneously ruthless and protracted, the devastation of the countryside was Kitchener's method of winning the guerilla phase of the war. Both black and white populations of the ORC were severely dislocated by his 'scorched earth' campaign and its corollary, the concentration camps.[1]

The Thaba Nchu district was the scene of several engagements in this extended guerilla phase of the war. The earliest and best-known of these episodes was the battle at Sannahspos on 31 March 1900. Sannahspos was a small pumping station on the Modder river, the western border of the Thaba Nchu district, that was vital to Bloemfontein's water supply. There, in tactical but blundering retreat from Thaba Nchu to Bloemfontein, General Broadwood's force of 1,700 men was neatly ambushed by Christiaan De Wet between the Koringspruit and the Modder.

Other skirmishes and forays took place elsewhere in the district—at Israelspoort, and around the town of Thaba Nchu itself. At the end of April 1900, attempting to join Roberts' main army for the march on Pretoria, two brigades under Lieutenant-General Ian Hamilton were held up by groups of Boers who defended the heights of Toba and Houtnek, in the low range of hills which encircles Thaba Nchu to the north. Towards the end of 1900, De Wet's guerilla force broke through the narrow Springhaannek in the east of the district, on its way to capture the village of Dewetsdorp, near which De Wet himself had spent his childhood. The following month, in mid-December, the Boers forced their way back northwards, again at Springhaannek, through a

defensive cordon of British garrisons between Thaba Nchu itself and the
northern shoulder of Thaba Phatshwa. De Wet was to make one more raid
through the district. At the end of January 1901, he crossed the cordon at
Israelspoort in the west, between Sannahspos and Thaba Nchu, in a brief
attempt to invade the Cape Colony. Blockhouses were only constructed across
the district a year later, between December 1901 and January 1902.[2]

During 1901, fifteen concentration camps were formed for whites in the
ORC. By November of that year, they contained 45,083 people. Initially,
camps for Africans grew up alongside those for whites, although some developed separately outside garrison towns. In August 1901 a separate Native
Refugee Department for the ORC was formed, which took over responsibility
for 22,713 Africans from the parallel Burgher Camp Administration. New sites
were selected for the African camps along the line of rail north of Bloemfontein, in order to ensure security within range of the blockhouse system. The
main policy objectives of the new arrangement were that concentrated Africans
should be self-sufficient in food supplies and should also provide the army with
labour. By December 1901 there were twenty-six African camps in the ORC,
with a total of 46,000 people. This figure included refugee camps established at
Thaba Nchu and near Harrismith, where there were existing concentrations of
Africans. By the end of the war there were thirty-one African refugee camps,
with a population of 60,604; and some 12–15,000 refugees from the eastern
districts of the OFS/ORC had temporarily settled in Basutoland. There was an
appalling death rate in the African camps in the ORC, reaching 436 per
thousand per annum in December 1901. The overwhelming majority of the
victims were children. The main causes of death were gross over-crowding,
extremely insanitary conditions, inadequate shelter and poor diet.[3]

From February 1901 onwards, whites and Africans were brought in from
every outlying part of the Thaba Nchu district. In December 1901 the African
refugee camp at Thaba Nchu contained 131 men, 194 women and 1,346
children, a total of 1,671 people, compared with 287 in September 1901. But
the local population—estimated at about 16,000 in 1901—swelled with many
more refugees than were accommodated in the camp. These refugees included
displaced African landowners, their resident tenants and black tenants from
white-owned farms. A protected area was identified, within which the refugees
were directed to cultivate grain, forage and potatoes. The Native Refugee
Department reserved the right to buy surplus production, which was to be
used to supply the African concentration camps and to sell to other military
departments.[4] This experiment was relatively successful, but many of the
refugees from the southern half of the district suffered disastrous losses of
livestock. A Boer raid into the protected area in February 1902, for example,
carried off 590 cattle, thirty-two horses and 6,625 sheep and goats. A month
later, a visitor reported that small groups of Boers were constantly trying to
break through the line of blockhouses to steal cattle or to carry messages.[5]

At the time the death rate in African refugee camps in the ORC reached its peak, in December 1901, an ORC government commission of enquiry reported in detail on the conditions of land tenure in the Thaba Nchu district and on the leasing of government farms. The commission found itself quite unable to determine who had rights of residence on privately-owned farms:

> Owing to the unrest caused by the war and to recent military operations the native question in that part of the country is in a state of hopeless confusion. Natives have in some cases been compulsorily taken off the farms occupied by them and cannot now be traced, while in other cases they have left the farms voluntarily and gone to reside on others owing to the insecurity of their position.[6]

Irrespective of the chaotic conditions arising out of the war, some of the evidence received, while potentially valuable, is extremely difficult to interpret in the form in which it was recorded. Chief Tshipinare's eldest daughter, Elizabeth Nkhabele Fenyang, for example, one of the principal beneficiaries of the Gregorowski land dispositions of 1885, reported on her three farms— Dakpoort 117, Mooiplaats 118 and Rietfontein 119—as follows:

> I do not know how many natives live on the farm Dakpoort, but I have a list of all the names, but left it at Rietfontein. A lot of natives were living on the farm when Moroka was annexed. Later on, I hired several other natives, with the consent of the Government. I had a certificate of consent, but left it at the farm Rietfontein when I fled on account of the war. There were 70 men, heads of families, living on Rietfontein, and, together with Dakpoort, there were in all 110 men, heads of families. There were only eight heads of families living on Rietfontein at the beginning, the rest were all hired, and when I left were still on the farm. They could stay there as long as we agreed, but could leave when they pleased. I have paid quitrent on all three farms.[7]

John Cameron's census of August 1884 confirms that eight adult men and seven adult women were then resident at Rietfontein, but that may not have been the only settlement on this particular property. Dakpoort is not identified in Cameron's list of settlements.[8] Elizabeth Nkhabele did not specify at what date seventy heads of families were living on Rietfontein, and presumably forty on Dakpoort. The date was potentially vital, however, because the servitude rights of residents depended on whether or not they had lived on the property since 1884.

Joseph Thoto Masisi gave clearer evidence to the same commission of enquiry, but some of it was probably misinterpreted or mis-translated. His apparent claim, for example, that he had lived on his farm Thaba Patchoa 106 ever since the annexation is almost certainly untrue, since he only acquired the property in 1891 (see Chapter 7). At one time, he said, there were about 200 Basotho living on Thaba Patchoa, but most went to Basutoland after the declaration of war, leaving about fifty by the end of 1901. About forty families had original servitude rights, of which only ten remained. Cameron's census recorded more than 500 Barolong adults and 140 Basotho resident at Thaba Patchoa in August 1884, overwhelmingly the highest population for any one settlement at that time. Masisi's figures, by contrast, probably relate to the early 1890s, after many of these people had returned to Basutoland or dispersed elsewhere (see Chapter 7). As for Joseph Thoto Masisi's other property, Naauwpoort 74, where his son Moses Masisi lived, there had been about twenty original servitude holders, most of whom were still there, and about five other families had also lived on the farm before the declaration of war.[9]

Most of the other African landowners, and all the white landowners, declared very many fewer residents or potential servitude holders to the 1901 commission, the majority of whom had been dispersed by the time the evidence was taken. The commission's task was made more difficult, however, by the striking consistency with which landowners, both black and white, confused the original fifteen-year non-alienation clause with the residential servitudes which were in many cases attached to their land titles. They stated either that they did not know of such servitude rights; or that they did not know who did and who did not have such rights; or, most commonly, that such rights lapsed after fifteen years and the landowners were then free to evict people if they wished to do so. Confusion on the part of the landowners as to the correct legal position was probably deliberate misconstruction. The OFS State Attorney had delivered an apparently unequivocal opinion, publicised by a Government Notice of July 1899, that Africans who were living on farms when the title deeds were issued were entitled to remain there for their lifetimes, irrespective of whether or not the farms had been sold to other owners.[10] However, the commission's investigation was undertaken at a point in time when the notional period of fifteen years from the date of grant had just elapsed, and under circumstances in which the majority of people had been displaced from the farms which they occupied before the war. For both reasons, therefore—the landowners' wilful misinterpretation of the legal position and the severe dislocation caused by the war—the onus of proving residence rights was thrown on to those who wished to assert them.

The commission also took evidence from white *bywoners* who had rented government farms before the war. In order to preclude access to this land by established farmers or by land speculators, Chapter LXI of the OFS Law Book had been modified by Law No. 18 of 1895, which required lessees of government farms to be burghers who were not property owners and who had resided ten years in the state. They also had to occupy the farms personally and were not allowed to sublet. By November 1901, when the commission investigated the condition of these leases, many lessees were prisoners of war in Ceylon or Simonstown (Cape); their families had been taken into the concentration camps; and in most cases rent and quitrent had not been paid for two years. Imprisoned or dispersed and to a greater or lesser degree destitute, the lessees were seldom in any position to resume the leases even if they wished to do so. Accordingly, the commission recommended that most leases be cancelled without compensation from the government.[11] Two farms are examined here to illustrate the particular circumstances of these *bywoners*.

The farm England 28, in the south-eastern corner of the district (see Figure 1.3), was subdivided into five lots, all leased for ten years from 7 July 1896. Lot A was leased to Jan Frederik Labuschagne, who lived there with his family until the outbreak of the war, when he joined a commando. Rent of £27 was due for 1901 and quitrent for two years. He wished to maintain the lease. In 1903, after the war had ended, he and his family were said to be 'in very poor circumstances' by an official investigating alleged distress amongst Boers. Lot B was leased to Roelof Marthinus Brits, who at the end of 1901 was a prisoner of war in Ceylon and owed two years' rent at £27 per annum and two years' quitrent. Lot C was leased to Walter Glynn, who had paid his rent and occupied the land until February 1901 but, on the bringing in of the population, had gone to Basutoland. He wished to keep on the lease. Lot D was leased to Stephanus Daniel Weber. He never occupied it but subleased without permission to Schalk Willem Van der Merwe, who in 1901 was a prisoner of war in Ceylon. Weber was in arrears with rent and quitrent. Lot E was leased to Daniel Benjamin Lombaard, who lived on it for two years but then subleased without permission to Josiah Michael Steyn, who lived on the farm until the outbreak of war. Two years' rent and quitrent were owed and neither Lombaard nor Steyn could afford to pay. Lombaard told the commission that he wanted 'nothing more to do with the farm'.[12]

The farm Khumo 24, to the north-east of Thaba Nchu (Figure 1.3), was divided into three lots, all leased for ten years from September 1895. Lot A was leased to Johannes Marthinus Dippenaar who occupied the farm until May 1900 when he went on commando. In 1901 he was a prisoner of war at Bloemfontein. His wife Cornelia was brought in to the Thaba Nchu concentration camp in February 1901. Two years' rent and quitrent were due, which they could not afford to pay. Dippenaar wished to keep up the lease. Lot B was leased to Thomas Benjamin Dry, who was a prisoner of war in Simonstown in 1901. His wife Josina and their children were brought in to Thaba Nchu concentration camp in February 1901. They wished to maintain the lease but owed two years' rent and quitrent and could not pay the arrears. In February 1903 Dry was living in a hut on a farm adjoining Abrahamskraal 65. Lot C was leased to Martha Bezuidenhout who occupied it until she was brought in to the concentration camp in July or August 1901. She had been supported by her son who had, however, died two years previously, and she could not pay the outstanding rent.[13]

Only Labuschagne and Glynn, out of these eight lessees, were judged to have sufficiently fulfilled their conditions of lease up to the outbreak of war to deserve sympathetic consideration from the new colonial state in their applications to renew their leases of government land. Of seventy-two such applicants, Harry Hanger, erstwhile agent of the Newberry estates, who was employed after the war as the Thaba Nchu agent of the Land Settlement Board, recommended that fifty-six had no claim at all. The remaining sixteen, who were entitled to some consideration, were not allowed to take up the same land as they had rented before the war, but it was decided that they could be considered on the same basis as other applicants for settlement on government farms after the war.[14] In this way, in this district, the war accelerated the demise of a stratum of white *bywoners* who were quite unable to recover a foothold on the land.

### RECONSTRUCTION OF THE COUNTRYSIDE

This, then, was the background of chaos and dislocation against which His Majesty's High Commissioner at the Cape, and Administrator of the Transvaal, launched his Land Settlement scheme. One of Lord Milner's immediate priorities was to establish ex-soldiers of British stock on the land in the two new colonies of the Transvaal and the Orange River. He set out the argument in a series of precisely eloquent despatches to Chamberlain, Secretary of State for the Colonies, in December 1901 and January 1902. 'The principal consideration', he wrote, 'is the necessity of avoiding a sharp contrast and antagonism in the character and sentiments of the population between the country districts and the towns'. The political objective of Land Settlement was, then, to 'dilute the Dutch influence' in the countryside and to 'consolidate South African sentiment in the general interests of the Empire'. Its economic objective was to introduce a 'progressive' farming element into a 'backward' countryside. Milner anticipated no shortage of demand from settlers of British stock, in which category he included colonists from the Cape and Natal, Australia, New Zealand and Canada as well as people 'from the mother country'.[15]

The greatest obstacle to this project, before the end of the war, was the shortage of sufficient land in appropriate parts of the two new colonies for the proper concentration of such settlers. As Milner observed, the introduction of a few isolated settlers into an otherwise hostile environment would be worse than useless. The scheme of Land Settlement had therefore to be undertaken on a large scale. It required land of very good quality and settlers who had a strong commitment to farming as a livelihood and, preferably, some capital of their own.[16]

An enquiry into the feasibility of the enterprise, under H.O. Arnold-Forster, had been appointed in August 1900 and reported in November 1900. The commission undertook a series of exhaustive interviews with prominent and long-established English-speaking residents: for example, Sir Godfrey Lagden, Basutoland High Commissioner, David Scott, who had farmed for thirty-one years in the Ladybrand district, and James Robertson, miller and grain merchant of Jammerberg Drift, near Wepener, whose earlier speculative activities in the Moroka territory were described in Chapter 1. As a result of this enquiry, the Conquered Territory of the eastern ORC was identified as the most promising area for such a settlement scheme, in terms of the quality of land and the adequacy of water supplies. The commission particularly investigated the government farms in the Moroka territory which had been inherited from the late OFS and which, being on the edge of the Conquered Territory, represented the most attractive possibility. They comprised by far the largest concentration of government land in the ORC—83,000 morgen out of 271,000 morgen altogether surveyed.[17] Only 59,000 morgen of the 83,000 morgen were available for Land Settlement, the balance comprising the Thaba Nchu and Seliba African reserves.

The eventual concentration of the ORC Land Settlement project in the Thaba Nchu district was secured by the purchase in October 1901, for £90,891.5s., of two large blocks (45,446 morgen) of the Newberry estates. These blocks comprised the following farms: Ngoanyana 98, Ngoana 104, Springhaannek 105, Groothoek 125, Daggafontein 144, Onder Logageng 145, Boven Logageng 146, Tlogo ea Moroa 149 and Kopjeskraal 150 (see Figure 1.3). The sale was negotiated on Charles Newberry's behalf by his agent, J.A. Sugden, since Newberry and his family were living at the time with his brother John Newberry in Whyteleafe, Surrey (England), at a safe distance from the war. In March 1902, the government also acquired James Robertson's two remaining farms in the district—Papfontein 95 and Mooifontein 91, together 5,386 morgen—at the same price of £2 per morgen. Over this short period, then, and combined with other purchases on a much smaller scale, land available to the ORC administration in the Thaba Nchu district for the purposes of Land Settlement nearly doubled from about 59,000 morgen to about 115,000 morgen—almost one third of the whole district.[18]

The first settlements introduced were provisional ones, arranged in order to take advantage of the 1901 ploughing season but before detailed plans for Land Settlement had been approved. Responsibility for their administration was vested in the ORC Land Settlement Board which was constituted in October 1901, with Major K. Apthorp, of the Royal Irish Regiment, as its indefatigable secretary. By April 1902, seventeen provisional settlers, almost all ex-soldiers, were placed on two adjoining farms in the east of the district which had been part of the Newberry estates: Sergeant Holliday's party of four men on Springhaannek 105; and, on Ngoanyana 98, Sergeant-Major Langbridge's party of seven men from the South African Constabulary and Imperial Yeomanry, Corporal Ward's party of five, and one J. Ingram.[19] Langbridge's group occupied the ruined farmhouse on Ngoanyana 98, not far from an extensive tree plantation established by Newberry before the war. They were living 'in a queer sort of discomfort . . . There is very little roof and no window panes or sashes, but the most gaping holes are filled with sandbags. . . '.[20] Six of these provisional settlers, without capital of their own, were judged in due course to have qualified themselves by their industry and enterprise to be incorporated in the permanent Land Settlement scheme initiated later in 1902.

Meanwhile another group of provisional settlers was established by the Land Settlement Board on government farms in the district, under the auspices of Colonel Thomas Hill, on behalf of the Scottish Sharpshooters' Association. An agreement was drawn up in December 1901 with Hamilton Goold-Adams, then Deputy Administrator (later Lieutenant Governor) of the ORC, by which men recruited by Hill would occupy the farm Likhatlong 20 on the western boundary of the district, at the junction of the Sepane and Modder rivers. No rent was payable; a daily advance of 5s. per man in occupation would be paid by the ORC government, together with rations from the military outpost at Sannahspos; and up to 5,000 sheep and 100 head of mixed cattle would be introduced. The syndicate would provide 100 suitable men. This agreement was subsequently extended, so that by April 1902 thirty-five of Colonel Hill's men were in occupation of the following government farms: Likhatlong 20, Vaalkraal 30, Mameno 16, Lesaka 81, Ngoana 104, Alexandria 43, Mooihoek 43 and Groothoek 125 (see Figure 1.3).[21]

In the months after the signing of the peace treaty in June 1902, further negotiations took place between the ORC government, the Colonial Office in London and Colonel Hill's lawyers. Hill's plans now embraced a quite separate block of land in the Heilbron district of the ORC. In Britain, Hill himself was trying to launch a new company, the British Settlement of South Africa Ltd. (BSSA), with a stronger capital base of £200,000. After much delay and protracted correspondence, the new company was launched in March 1903. Under the new arrangements, however, in the light of the BSSA's prime commitment to land in the Heilbron district, and official doubt about the adequacy of the company's capital base, the ten farms of the Thaba Nchu block which were occupied by its men became a subsidiary commitment. They suffered a very bad season in 1902–3 owing to drought and frost. Eventually, the BSSA withdrew from the Thaba Nchu district, in a parlous financial condition after a series of bad seasons, and the few surviving settlers who had been set up under its auspices were transferred directly to the embrace of the Land Settlement Board. Interestingly, Colonel Hill's local manager, W.A.L. Brotherston, had specifically rejected the common expedient of share-cropping with Africans, on the grounds that 'the Directors of this Company desire to employ as much white labour as the land will sustain'; and that a better system of farming, where capital resources were available, was to set aside a portion of the farm for intensive cultivation.[22]

The terms on which the Land Settlement Board allocated farms to prospective settlers were fully elaborated in a despatch from Milner to Chamberlain in May 1902. Farms could be taken either on lease for five years, renewable for a further five or ten years, or under a thirty years' purchase scheme. If taken on lease, the rent would be equal to 5 per cent of the government valuation of the farm, payable half-yearly. If taken under the purchase scheme, the farm would be paid for by sixty half-yearly instalments, the total amount payable annually being 5.75 per cent of the purchase price. Of this amount 4 per cent was interest on the outstanding balance of the debt, and 1.75 per cent was committed to redemption, so that the debt was extinguished after thirty years. On a farm valued at £1,000, for example, the total annual payment would be £57.10s., payable in advance in two half-yearly instalments. The first instalment, however, would not fall due until the settler had been in occupation of the farm for twelve months. After five years' occupation, the settler could pay off the whole amount outstanding and acquire the freehold. In the meantime the government would make advances for permanent improvements and for the purchase of stock or implements, or for any other approved purpose, up to the amount invested by the settler, but not exceeding half of the value of the farm. These advances were repayable with 5 per cent interest by twenty half-yearly instalments.[23]

The Board emphasised that a working capital of at least £1 per morgen was necessary to start farming on this basis, and carefully selected applicants according to this criterion as well as that of an enterprising and energetic disposition. There were 5,482 applications for Land Settlement in the ORC up to 30 June 1903. Of those applicants for whom the information was recorded, 600 had no capital; 1,699 had between £5 and £500; 925 between £500 and £1,000; and a small minority had more than £1,000. The demand for farms greatly exceeded the number available under the Land Settlement scheme. Throughout the colony, at this date, there were 451 heads of families settled on separate holdings under the scheme, and twenty-nine men on land allotted to the BSSA. Of this total, 277 settlers were from 'Home and Overseas' (i.e. Britain, Canada, Australia, etc.), 160 were South African Colonials (Cape, Natal), and forty-three were Dutch.[24]

There was, by this time, a separate privately-sponsored land settlement scheme, on the edge of the Thaba Nchu district. Milner persuaded 'Bendor', the young Duke of Westminster who had been his aide-de-camp in 1899, to invest in a block of land which lay astride the boundary of the district with the Conquered Territory to the east. In March 1903 the Land Settlement Board bought on the Duke's behalf, for £31,699.2s.8d., a total of 7,879 morgen of land, comprising the original farm Rapuiskop 92 within the Thaba Nchu district and six adjoining farms outside the district.[25] The Duke visited his new estate in October 1903, reported the *African Review*, whose readers were probably familiar with the pedigrees of the three thoroughbred racehorses which accompanied him on the *Walmer Castle*. The *Review* explained that settlers would be selected from the Duke's own Eaton estate in Cheshire (England): 'Young blood is needed, and settlers' sweethearts will be brought out; while even Colonists' sisters will not be objected to if they will marry in the district'.[26]

The Westminster estate lay astride the new Modderpoort railway from Bloemfontein and Thaba Nchu. Its construction was a major, if transient, source of employment for otherwise indigent whites. One settler reported 2,000 Boers on the railway at Tweespruit in July 1903, living in tents with their families and working for 4s. a day.[27] The next stop to the east was the Westminster halt. Ironically, this was built on the site of the farm Langverwacht, from which the principal white conspirator on Samuel's behalf, Gert Pretorius, had launched his raid on Thaba Nchu in July 1884, and to which he and the other white conspirators retreated after stealing Abraham Setlogelo's livestock and merchandise (see Chapter 1).[28] Westminster railway halt was a hive of activity in 1904.

> Building material and farm implements are being unloaded and carried to the different parts of the estate; steam diggers are at work close by, preparing the ground for the settlers; here and there in the rolling plain picturesque farmhouses and outbuildings of grey stone are to be seen, and in the background is the long wall of the Basuto hills. Few more attractive spots could have been chosen in which to make a new home for Englishmen.[29]

The architect Herbert Baker was engaged to design a splendid sandstone mansion on the hill above the railway halt. Completed towards the end of 1904, it became known as the 'Big House'. Stables were also conceived and built on a grand scale, to accommodate some of the prize horses associated with the Duke's name in England. Apart from the 'home farm', the estate was divided up into eighteen farms of roughly 400 morgen. These farms, many of whose names as well as whose new tenants were drawn from the Cheshire estate, were occupied from 1904 on the basis of a tithe system. The estate supplied implements, livestock, seed and paid labour. The farm was worked by the tenant, and the estate took one-third of net profits. The Duke of Westminster himself made an initial grant of £100 to each new settler, and guaranteed a living allowance of £5 per month until the end of June 1905.

The tithe system was not a success, however, probably because it proved difficult to administer to the satisfaction of all parties. Many of the early tenants left and settled elsewhere in South Africa. Some of the farms were leased thereafter on a direct rental basis of between £90 and £110 per annum, and a purchase scheme was introduced after the First World War, by which the tenants could buy their farms on payment of one-third of the valuation in cash, with the balance on mortgage at an interest rate of 4 per cent per annum and 1 per cent redemption.[30] After a few early visits and lavish capital expenditure, the Duke of Westminster himself lost interest in his South African estate, which by the 1980s retained only the 'home farms' of Belgrave and Eaton. Ownership passed from 'Bendor' to his daughter Lady Mary Grosvenor, who had no heir, and from her to a Trust. Despite the fragmentation of the original estate, Westminster kept its distinctive social character. Finding themselves in the heart of a colonial wilderness, the early settlers nurtured Milner's imperial tradition and passed it on with self-conscious zeal to their descendants. In the early 1980s, a pack of beagles was still kept at the kennels of the 'Big House'. The title to the dukedom, however, passed to another branch of the Grosvenor family.

## EXPERIENCES OF LAND SETTLEMENT: THE EARLY YEARS

Leonard Flemming was born in Australia in 1880. As a boy on a large sheep farm in New South Wales, he grew up with an intense ambition to become a farmer himself. His father was a theatrical manager who took the young Flemming first to London, where he had a few years of haphazard education, and then, at the age of fifteen, to South Africa. He worked on two farms in the eastern Cape, respectively on the Kei river and near Queenstown, where he went into partnership on a rented sheep farm. He served in the Whittlesea commando in the Colonial Defence Force during the South African war, and his partner heard in mid-1902 of the opportunity to take up land 'on very advantageous terms' under the Milner Settlement scheme. They gathered their livestock and possessions and set off for the ORC in November 1902. The expedition consisted of Flemming and three other aspirant white settlers, thirty Africans, two wagons, each pulled by sixteen oxen, about 3,000 sheep, 500 head of cattle, twenty horses and three dogs. 'The procession took up about one and a half miles of road'. After an arduous journey of two months, they reached their destination in January 1903. Flemming's three companions—Peat, Ross and Clarke—were allocated farms in the Daggafontein block in the south-west of the Thaba Nchu district. He was allocated Geluk 110, a farm of 460 morgen on the southern edge of the district, east of Dewetsdorp.[31]

Before the South African war, as a government farm, Geluk had been leased to G.D. Kotze at £21 per annum. It had good summer grazing but 'indifferent' winter veld, and very little shelter for stock in winter. Water was scarce. Kotze had erected a mud-brick house, an outhouse, a stable and a stone kraal. He went on commando during the war and by November 1901 he owed two years' rent. Geluk was deserted. When Flemming arrived on the farm in January 1903 he found only a tumbled-down mud hut. The conditions were rough and desolate. 'I was now on my piece of land, dumped down in the middle of a bare, barren expanse, with only my wagon for a house, and two native boys the only other human beings in all my little world'. Flemming had brought up 100 sheep, six oxen, two cows, about £7 in cash and a few odd implements—working capital that was quite insufficient to start farming under these conditions. He estimated that he needed at least 'ten miles of fencing (£500), four hundred sheep (£500), twelve cows (£100), sixteen oxen (£240), a double-furrow plough (£15), a grain drill (£45), harrows (£20), mower (£30), cultivators, etc. (£30)'. Over the years he was greatly handicapped by this lack of working capital. It meant selling a few head of precious livestock in order to pay wages and odd bills. It meant waiting many years to obtain implements and stock which he might have bought in one week if only cash had been available. The Land Settlement Board advanced him £75, so he bought a piano and a new plough. The piano was a 'godsend' in his lonely hours.[32]

Flemming set to work on this bare patch of veld with energy and determination. With three or four African labourers, he ploughed thirty acres of land, built a dam, a stable and a mud-brick house and began fencing paddocks for the livestock. It was a daily life of unremitting toil, requiring great patience and offering few glimpses of potential reward. By November 1903 the first wheat crop was growing well. Then disaster struck.

> There in the distance is that sight that for a fraction of a second seems to chill the heart. You stand motionless. In that far-away distance, and ever so far away on the horizon, you see a long, faint cloud, for all the world like dust—a thin, faint, unbroken line from left to right; perhaps fifty miles long, very faint, but just enough to make the sharp outlines of the hills a little less distinct than usual. It is a locust swarm . . .[33]

In ten minutes the locusts reduced his flourishing green acres to 'the most utter desolation'. They destroyed the entire wheat crop of the district. Flemming recorded tersely in his diary, 'Locusts for two whole days—place eaten bare'. It was a massive setback, the first of many.

In later years, diverting his creative talents after the day's farm work, Flemming established a reputation as a writer whose light satirical style in verse and short stories expressed the desperate importunities of the early years of Land Settlement and, more generally, of farming as a profession in South Africa. With sincerity and passion and a sharp, ironic humour, he described the unpredictability of the seasons, the sundry afflictions of livestock, the devastation of drought and crop pests, the contortions necessary to evade creditors, the unreliability of labour. In his writing, indeed, the local Africans fulfil all the stereotypes required to vindicate the settlers' strong sense of racial superiority. They broke ploughs, they wanted their wages paid, they stole sheep. But without complaint they also indulged Flemming's own eccentricities, such as the need for cricket practice.[34] Flemming's verse and stories have amused three generations of South Africans. For more than forty years, however, apart from occasional visits abroad, he remained alone on the veld. In 1929, on a visit to Britain, he briefly married a young Australian singer, but the union did not last and he had no heir. When he died in 1946, Geluk was taken over as pastureland by the Van den Berg family of neighbouring Karreelaagte. A small stone cairn marks his grave on the top of the quiet *kopje* which overlooks his life's endeavour. In 1989, the ruins of his brick and stone farmhouse were barely visible in the shady groves of fir and eucalyptus which he had planted on his 'bare, barren expanse'. Apart from his books, those trees are his proper memorial.

Elsewhere in the Thaba Nchu district, one of the earliest provisional settlers was Sergeant-Major Ernest Langbridge. As one of six ex-soldiers without capital who was incorporated formally into the Land Settlement scheme, he was allocated Essex 219, a 451-morgen subdivision of the original large farm Ngoanyana 98. He was born in 1874. His father was a clergyman who was posted for some years in Montevideo and Lima, so that Ernest and the other children grew up partly in South America. The family was English but had strong Irish connections, and Ernest attended Trinity College, Dublin. He and his younger brother Frank both came to South Africa during the war, Ernest accompanying horses imported for the army from the Argentine to Cape Town. He served from February 1900 successively in Kitchener's Horse, Rimington's Guides and the South African Constabulary.[35]

At the end of January 1903 Ernest Langbridge was host to E.F. Knight, correspondent of *The Morning Post*, who undertook an extensive journey through South Africa at that time to explore social and economic conditions in the immediate aftermath of the war. Knight drove by Cape cart from Sannahspos to Thaba Nchu 'across a parched land, dry and dusty after the long drought, past many grim blockhouses and roofless farmhouses'. To the east of Thaba Nchu, a 'straggling little village lying under the isolated mountain of the same name', he encountered:

> a country of very different aspect to the dreary plain I had left behind me. In the valley bottoms broad stretches of vivid fresh green marked the fields of mealies and kaffir corn. I also saw great fields of ripening oats on both sides, and the yellow stubble showed where the wheat had already been harvested. Here and there was a solitary mud hut or tent, the temporary homes of the soldier-settler who had purchased a farm from the Land Settlement Board.[36]

Knight found Langbridge sharing a nine-roomed ruin with two Irish settlers—almost certainly his immediate neighbours to the south, Daniel McPherson and Jimmy Nelson, who were respectively allocated Ngoanyana 98 (rest) and Knowsley 287. By comparison with the mud huts or tents of other new settlers, this was substantial accommodation. The ruin, already described by Amy Wilson on her visit in March 1902, was the 'remains of an old Dutch farmhouse standing on the property . . . for British troops have torn off roof, doors and window sashes, leaving, however, the main door, which is riddled with shells and bullets'.[37] Like Amy Wilson before him, Knight commented with enthusiasm on Newberry's extensive plantation of firs, bluegums (eucalyptus) and oaks which lay near the farmhouse. The bones of De Wet's horses were still to be seen scattered in the valley below, from the occasion when he forced his way through Springhaannek on 14 December 1901.

Langbridge's first year was remarkably successful, despite a poor maize crop: his vegetables sold at famine prices; a first wheat crop did well, as did his oats and potatoes; and he had some thriving sheep and cattle. Knight observed that:

> a few Kaffir families are squatted on his land in accordance with the local custom. These natives have the right to graze their cattle and plough on his farm, and in return give him a percentage of their crops and supply paid labour on the farm and in the house.[38]

Langbridge also kept a small store on the farm where he bartered cloth and household goods for grain and sold, apparently, more liquor than anything else.[39] He married and had two children. The elder, Evelyn, born in 1905, recalled eighty years later how:

> swarms of white ants ate through everything except tin boxes; clothes, boots and books were soon covered in green mould and now and again a plague of locusts would demolish every leaf, so [it was] a constant fight against Nature, and the fleas, my mother once said she caught 40 on the hem of her gown.[40]

Nature eventually won this particular battle. Ernest Langbridge resigned his farm in 1910 and the family went to England. He served in the army throughout the First World War, and was killed by a buzz-bomb in the London blitz of 1940. His brother Frank remained in South Africa as a teacher, where he died in 1927. In due course Frank's daughter Marge married Sam Bairstow of the farm Jevington 276, who introduced a summer fallow wheat revolution in the Tweespruit district after the Second World War.[41]

Jevington 276 adjoins Heathfield 264. Heathfield was farmed by Frederick Nicholson, who died in 1967 as the last original Milner settler in the district. Nicholson was born in 1880, the eleventh of thirteen children of a director of the Union (Castle) Steamship Co. From 1883 the family home was a thirty-room mansion at Eastmore, Isle of Wight. Fred Nicholson had a scanty education and some brief experience of farming on the Isle of Wight. In 1899 he was given a commission in the fifth battalion of the Hampshire Volunteers, who were stationed at Aldershot to replace regular troops who had been sent to South Africa under Roberts and Kitchener. The architect Herbert Baker was a cousin of the Nicholson family and it was Baker who persuaded Fred's brothers Albert and Herbert to go out to the Cape, where they came to know the Merriman family at the fruit and wine farm Schoongezicht near Stellenbosch.[42]

Fred himself arrived in Cape Town in December 1901 and spent a year working at Schoongezicht, when fruit exports were beginning to accelerate. In January 1903 he was employed to assess war damage compensation in the northern Cape under W.C. Scully—temperamental Irishman, remarkable rifle shot, Transkei magistrate and, Nicholson discovered, 'something of a writer'.[43] After eight months he returned to Schoongezicht to find that his brother Herbert had taken up a Land Settlement farm in the Thaba Nchu district of the ORC. He went straight up to Bloemfontein but found that

Herbert had since taken up a position in the Agriculture Department of the Transvaal under the newly appointed Director of Agriculture there, F.B. Smith, whom he had known at Wye College in Kent. So Fred took over Heathfield farm on his own.

At Thaba Nchu he borrowed Harry Hanger's Cape cart and drove out to the farm:

> I found myself dumped on a large grassy plain with not a fence or a tree nor a habitation, bar native huts and a couple of pondokkies [shacks] where my neighbouring settlers lived. The only open water on the farm was a pan, which was at that time dry, and a few muddy pools in a spruit where the native cattle watered.[44]

He put up a tent and dug for water at the head of the pan. Africans on the farm had all been ploughing on half-shares, and his neighbour Thorp, on Bideford 187, had collected a few bags of sorghum on his behalf. He found he could exchange these for a few livestock with which to start ploughing. His diary for this period contains a series of laconic entries to this effect: 'Bought a cow in calf for five sacks kaffir corn'; 'Bought two ewes for sack kaffir corn'; 'Bought a cow from Kafir for six bags corn. Kafirs all drunk and one of my sheep missing in evening'. These transactions enabled him to start ploughing with a single furrow plough.[45] His diary is more routinely expansive on the sporting activities of the district: cricket with the other settlers, and shooting at weekends with his friend Ken Cowper Johnson of Waterland, on the edge of the Leeuw river dam.

In June 1904, hearing from his brother Herbert about a sale at Ermelo (Transvaal), Nicholson bought a wagon, eight mules, two heavy horses and other things. He could now start ploughing with the mule span pulling a two-furrow plough and the horses a single-furrow plough. He also had some Africans cultivating for themselves on the half-share basis. The Land Settlement Board provided him and other settlers with stock, also on a share basis, recognising that livestock were necessary to balance the unpredictability and consequent financial instability of agriculture. In 1905 the government started a butter factory at Tweespruit, and thereafter Nicholson found the monthly cream cheque vital to the farm's viability.

> Our next snag was a locust plague. The worst year it came mostly from the south, and I drove on one occasion all the way to Dewetsdorp (35 miles) through them in the hopping stage. Thaba Nchu mountain did much to stop their progress but they poured up the well covered Springhaan Nek in incredible numbers. Luckily there was a good deal of grass in the veld and lands at the top of the Nek, and, labour being plentiful, we assembled a good force each evening and burnt them as soon as they were comfortably tucked into their grassy bed for the night. By this means we managed considerably to reduce the losses that we would otherwise have suffered.[46]

Apart from passing references to African 'squatters' or labourers, these accounts of the arrival of white settlers convey an impression of a barren and empty landscape in the immediate aftermath of the war. They beg the question of what had happened to the African inhabitants of the district—the former share-croppers on the Newberry estates, the residents on African-owned farms? The magistrate reported in July 1902 a 'surplus' of Africans in the district who had no place to return to. They fell into several categories: people who before the war had access to ploughing and grazing on the government farms, presumably through contractual relationships with the white *bywoners* who had rented those farms; people from private farms whose Boer owners were prisoners of war, who had acted as cattle guards and scouts for the British troops and who were precluded for that reason from returning to those farms; and people in a similar position from adjoining districts, who had been brought into Thaba Nchu by the troops for their own safety during 1901. The two reserves were already over-crowded, and in view of this the magistrate requested the use of two government farms for the temporary settlement of this 'surplus' population. His request was turned down on the grounds that the government farms were committed to applicants under the Land Settlement scheme and that the settlers were having difficulty in securing African labour.[47]

The possibility for Africans of returning to the lands they had formerly occupied was, therefore, a strictly qualified one. In June 1902, at the end of the war, the superintendent of the African refugee camp at Thaba Nchu, Robert Dickie, noted that 'a large number' of the Africans in the camp were from the Daggafontein area in the south of the district and that most of their cattle had been lost in the big raid of February 1902. He proposed that, pending the arrival of British settlers, people could return to their former lands, start ploughing as best they could and give a third share of whatever they reaped to the settlers in due course. Since the settlers would require labourers, it would be easier for them to negotiate terms with Africans who were already established on the lands in question.

Harry Hanger, the local agent of the Land Settlement Board, approved of this proposal subject to two strict and explicit conditions: firstly, that they would have to hand over a percentage of their crop to the government or to the settler; and, secondly, that they would be prepared to move from the farm should the government or the settler require it. There should be no objection to people returning to their old homes on the erstwhile Newberry estates or to African-owned farms, provided they did not 'roam about at will' and their movements were subject to obtaining passes from the farm owner or a JP or other authorised pass issuer. Hanger recommended that anyone who wished to move in to the Seliba reserve would have to establish a right to do so in terms of residence there before the war.[48]

Less than a year later, however, the Anglican missionary at St. Augustine's, Thaba Nchu, complained that 'whole villages' had practically been wiped out because former residents were either not allowed to return or were evicted by the settlers when they did return. The magistrate, Van Iddekinge, explained that nearly the whole district was one mass of dismantled villages.

> During military occupation all natives were ordered in and as a result they all dismantled their huts and used the straw etc. on huts which they erected within the protected area. A large number of these natives so removed never returned to their original farms.[49]

The same phenomenon was observed in the southern part of the district by Charles Anderson of Kelvinside, Glasgow, who had been attached to the Northumberland Fusiliers as a scripture reader during the war. He cycled through the district in February 1904. Between the local JP Edward Worringham's farm Scotland 391, south of Mokopu (Pumpkin), and Dewetsdorp, there was 'not a soul to be seen for miles and miles, and very many ruined houses which must formerly have housed a large population. What struck me greatly was the substantial character of many of these buildings'.[50] Anderson inferred that many of the African farmers had lived at a standard superior to or at least equal to that of poor whites; and that the ruins he saw represented official obstruction to the return of the people to their lands.

On his return to Britain, Anderson arranged for a question to be raised in the House of Commons in London. Was the Secretary of State for the Colonies, Lyttelton, aware:

> that many thousands of natives, a considerable number of whom had achieved positions as farmers equal or superior to many of the poorer class of whites, who were removed during the war from the Thaba Nchu, Dewetsdorp and Thaba Patchoa districts of the Orange River Colony, have not been permitted to return; and, if so, will he say whether the prevention of their repatriation has received the sanction of his Majesty's Government; and whether the natives in question, in consideration of services formerly rendered to the late Government of the Orange Free State, held a servitude over the lands formerly occupied by them.[51]

This question prompted a flurry of official investigation. Quayle Dickson, the Adviser for Native Affairs, reported that the whole matter was greatly exaggerated. Perhaps 200 or 300 heads of families were affected. The ruined houses had been destroyed by the military; many Africans had since built new houses. The question of their right to return to the lands which they had formerly occupied, and which were now occupied by the Milner settlers, was subject to legal uncertainty. The government was looking for a test case to clarify the validity of the servitudes which were attached to many of these farm titles—whether they were purely personal or to what extent they also applied to the relatives of *bona fide* servitude holders in 1884. Meanwhile, Dickson was confident that no-one who had the right to do so had been refused permission to reside in the reserves, and anyone who claimed a servitude on the farms was

given the right to reside in the reserves. With reference specifically to the area
north of Dewetsdorp, which embraced the Daggafontein farms, Dickson
pointed out that servitudes were not attached to these farms and that local
farmers and the townspeople, being short of labour, would 'welcome an
increase to the native population'. So far from evicting Africans from the
farms, he implied, they would readily incorporate them.[52]

It is possible that Anderson's impression of devastation was exaggerated, or
rather susceptible to explanation in terms less dramatic than those implied in
the parliamentary question. But Quayle Dickson's official reassurance fudged
the issue in two ways. Firstly, those who experienced shortage of labour and
were therefore happy to see an 'increase in the native population' could only
bring pressure on people to supply such labour by subverting their conditions
of existence on the former Newberry estates, that is, by directly limiting the
number of stock or by restricting direct access to the land or both. In the face of
this pressure, it is clear that many former inhabitants of the Newberry estates
chose not to return. Secondly, Quayle Dickson appeared to be indulging those
who claimed servitudes on the farms by giving them permission to reside in the
reserves. The outcome was inevitable: in so far as people returned to or
remained in the district after the war, and were not dispersed to other parts of
the ORC, they were pushed either on to Barolong-owned farms or into the
reserves, which already contained more people than nominally had the right to
reside there.

There was, of course, no shortage of people, only of labour on the terms
white farmers were prepared to offer. Africans were not, on the whole, willing
to become wage labourers on those terms. Some local witnesses to the South
African Native Affairs Commission (SANAC) in September 1904 admitted
that the district had a bad name amongst Africans for its labour relations.
Robert Dickie, for example, who was allocated the farm Daggafontein 144
(rest) by the Land Settlement Board, explained that masters and servants
frequently disagreed about the specific contractual agreements they had made;
that employers could substantially ease the labour shortage by treating workers
much less harshly; and that the new ex-Colonial settlers apparently could not
'get along with the Barolongs at all'.[53] But the large-scale loss of livestock
experienced by the former Daggafontein people in the Boer raid of February
1902 must have vitally undermined their economic independence. Indeed,
Quayle Dickson rationalised their loss in terms of changes in 'the whole system
of farming in this Colony'. Before the war, Africans could live on their
livestock. They could no longer do this. Consequently:

> of their own accord many leave the place where they were living before
> the war to live where they can cultivate or get work. Naturally it took
> the native some time after Peace to realise the new state of things, but
> now that they are realising it, they are falling in line of their own
> account.[54]

## BONES OF CONTENTION

The self-image the settlers transmitted to their descendants emphasised the rugged virtues of the frontiersman engaged in a struggle with a difficult environment. With characteristic self-mockery, Leonard Flemming evoked the romantic idiocy of chipping at the Rock of Gibraltar with a pen-knife to express the odds against success. But his metaphor does scant justice to the proper history of their enterprise, which is better expressed in James Robertson's blunt demand for a state-sponsored railway. For the settlers recognised, of course, their dependence on a sympathetic state. There were three key issues over which they were routinely concerned, in the early years of insecurity, to invoke stronger official intervention on their behalf. The first was the shortage of black labour, which meant that many settlers depended in practice on black share-croppers. The second was alleged over-valuation of their farms, which meant that many settlers felt critically over-burdened with capital repayments and loan interest through a series of very bad seasons. The third was the granting of 'Responsible Government' to the two new colonies in 1907, which the settlers regarded as a direct threat to the long-term success of their enterprise.

The Moroka Farmers' Association (FA) was formed in early 1903. About forty settlers, variously British, Australian, Canadian and Cape Colonial, attended the first meeting on 31 January at Egypt, 'a lonely farm house on a bare eminence commanding an extensive view over the undulating veldt'.[55] The original farm Egypt 107 had been part of Tshipinare's estate and was registered in 1886 in the names of his sixteen heirs. In 1903, there were four registered subdivisions: ten-sixteenths of the farm were owned by the Van der Wath family, who had long been associated with the district, and many of whom were buried there in due course; two-sixteenths (Watervlei 430) by Harry Hanger; one-sixteenth (Smaldeel 387) by Charles Newberry; while three-sixteenths were retained in equal undivided shares by three of Tshipinare's heirs, the children of his sixth wife Ketimetse—Maggie Nyokong, Samata Makgothi and Morokanyana Moroka.

The meeting was held in the wagon shed at Egypt and chaired by Cornelis Van der Wath (junior), not himself a Land Settler. He explained the objectives of forming an association: to obtain cheaper goods through co-operative purchase; to co-ordinate the sale of produce in the best markets; and to express farmers' views collectively to the government. As E.F. Knight, who attended the meeting, astutely observed, there was no collective view on the labour question which pre-occupied the settlers' minds. Indeed, there was a significant dissension of opinion. For the majority of the settlers, the system of ploughing on shares was necessary and quite clearly, in the circumstances, to their advantage:

The poorer settler cannot afford to purchase many head of cattle, but with natives on his land who plough for him with their own oxen, and who ride transport for him with their own wagons, he is enabled to bring much more of his land under cultivation than would otherwise be possible.[56] But the Cape Colonials, a large group of whom had come up from the Cathcart district with their own livestock and settled predominantly in the north-eastern part of the Thaba Nchu district, 'object to the native squatting on their land'; rather, they wanted to employ wage labour and to prohibit access by African-owned cattle. This view reflected a decisive capital advantage over the majority of their fellows.

The fact that the majority of settlers found the share-cropping system was an immediate economic necessity did not mean, however, that it was from their point of view a desirable state of affairs. A subcommittee was appointed by the Moroka FA to investigate the labour issue. Its members were Van der Wath himself; one of his brothers-in-law, Edgar James Webb, who was remembered in the Tweespruit district for having shot someone ('the Benchfield scandal') and for having bought an expensive prize bull called Admiral Beattie, which got rheumatism and had to be destroyed;[57] and S. Arnot of Alexandria 43. This subcommittee recommended that immediate steps should be taken 'to place the Native in his proper position'. Firstly, share-cropping should be abolished, since African families with their own livestock and ploughs were clearly making a living thereby and were not willing to provide labour for the land-owner, and in any case it was 'a well known fact' that the landowner did not actually receive half of the crops reaped. Rather, such families should receive one acre for themselves for every two acres ploughed for the landowner. Secondly, legislation should be passed to force Africans without capital re-sources and apparent means of livelihood to work for white landowners at uniform wage rates of 10s. per month, with casual labour employed at 1s. per day and reapers at 2s. per hundred bundles of wheat or oats. Such Africans 'are mostly to be found on government locations and kaffirs' farms, and live from charity and theft of sheep, mealies etc. from the white population'.[58]

The Moroka FA forwarded their recommendations to the government. Quayle Dickson persuaded them to leave these matters in his hands for the moment, to give him time to work on his own proposals. His own immediate concern at the time was to defuse an adverse press report and complaints made in April 1903 by G.C. Day, the Anglican missionary, to the effect that forced labour was being procured by the administration, acting through local head-men, for the construction of the railway goods shed at Bloemfontein. In retrospect, it appeared that headmen Robert Tawana Moroka (who had by this time returned to Thaba Nchu as chief), Timothy Seiphemo and two others had exceeded their authority by attempting 'to drive away all who had not a settlement under their care and even men temporarily out of employ to work at Bloemfontein'.[59] Day's complaint partly derived from the circumstances in which four families had recently been evicted from Framley 238, a subdivision of Ngoana 104, by the settler there, Allwright, on the grounds that they had too many livestock.

Resolution of the labour shortage which white farmers complained about was thus an extremely complex issue. On the one hand, they were having to compete with urban wage levels which they could not afford. On the other hand, their experience of labour shortage on the farms was not by any means a uniform one. Some farmers, as we have seen above, had enough livestock of their own to undertake direct management of ploughing operations; most did not. Some farmers had spare arable land which they could readily allocate to black share-croppers; many did not. Local Africans were well-informed about the habits of individual white farmers, and they responded accordingly. By and large, the three Farmers' Associations which were formed in the early years of Land Settlement—the Moroka, Leeuw river and Daggafontein and Dewetsdorp FAs—were dominated by relatively under-capitalised new settlers who occupied farms which averaged only 500 morgen in size in the arable areas and up to 1,000 morgen in the livestock areas. The key to the resolution of the labour shortage, as far as they were concerned, was to restrict Africans' direct access to land as tightly as possible. Hence a virulent resentment, running through the representations which the FAs made to the ORC administration, of a build-up of 'squatters' both on the larger white-owned farms and on African-owned farms. Giving evidence to the SANAC in September 1904, Alec Wilson of The Nursery 405, a subdivision of Ngoanyana 98, bluntly explained why, in his view, the settlers could not attract Africans to work for them:

> There are two reasons. One reason is that they are too well off; the other is the system of ploughing on the halves. Some farmers have got big tracts of land, and they get these Natives to plough on the halves, and the result is that those farmers who only have small holdings, like the settlers, cannot get labour unless they like to pay big wages. The Natives are asking £2 a month round there, and the farmer cannot afford to pay that.[60]

In July 1905 the Moroka FA again urged the government to enforce the anti-squatting legislation on African-owned farms. They complained that Africans who had been removed from such farms as being 'in excess of the number allowed by law have in many cases returned to their old places'. Quayle Dickson responded by issuing instructions to the Location Ranger at Thaba Nchu to enforce the anti-squatting provisions, except in respect of landowners, their relatives, and aged and sick persons. It emerged that there were people resident on African-owned farms considerably in excess of the numbers allowed under these conditions. On the farm Gamabetoe 102 (see Figure 1.3), for example, there were thirty-nine families resident in August 1905 without residential certificates; six had left and the rest were warned to leave. The Location Ranger was instructed to obtain a list from the owner, Joel Moroka, then away in Kimberley, or his representative, of everyone who had no right to remain on the farm. They were then given two days' notice. By 19 September twenty heads of families had still not left and Joel Moroka, who was clearly given little choice by the administration, authorised their arrest.[61]

The political pressure against 'squatting', then, was mounting. On the one hand, white farmers agitated for the enforcement of the law which provided for not more than five heads of families on any one farm. On the other hand, old established African residents, at least, could invoke the residential servitudes to resist such enforcement. It seems, however, that the practical validity of the servitudes was wearing thin. The government was seeking a test case. On Eden 96 (see Figure 1.3), for example, there were 60 registered servitude holders in 1906, including the original owner, Isaac Motshegare, one of Tshipinare's sons. At this time the farm was owned by Charles Newberry, who had retained it when most of his Thaba Nchu estates were sold to the ORC government in 1901. It was managed by N. Cameron, who was based at Wonderkop 17, another of Newberry's farms. Cameron evicted a number of Africans from Eden 96 in November 1906, almost certainly as a result of pressure from the Moroka FA. He was possibly vulnerable to such pressure since he was the farm manager, not the owner, and his own social networks may have been at risk; whereas Newberry, the large absentee landlord who lived at Prynnsberg, Clocolan, would not himself have taken steps to evict established residents from Eden. Cameron was careful to seek official authority for the evictions beforehand, in order to disclaim liability in the event of any charges brought against him by the evicted servitude holders.[62]

The Location Ranger took statements from the evicted Africans, using the evidence implicitly as an administrative test of the validity of the residential servitudes. Sebeco Selisho, a Morolong, was 59 years old. He was born in Thaba Nchu and had gone to live on Na'neng—the large farm surveyed by Bourdillon in 1882 as Egypte 107 and Eden 96—in about 1861. He had resided there with his family ever since. He had thirty-one cattle, ninety sheep and forty-six goats. Rakgogo Malebo, a Morolong born at Maraphogole location, Thaba Nchu, near the modern site of Motlatla, had lived on Eden since 1879. He owned twenty cattle, 159 sheep and six goats. Molosioa Monnametsi, a Morolong born in Ladybrand district, came to Eden in about 1884 and had twenty-three cattle, seven horses and six sheep.[63] They were given temporary permission to reside in the Thaba Nchu reserve, and there is no evidence that they were allowed to return to Eden. It is likely, although it was not clearly stated, that their prime offence was the independent livelihood they derived from stock ownership on a substantial scale on white-owned land.

In the circumstances, white farmers found it intolerable that wealthy Africans should be establishing what were in effect independent tenancies on white-owned land. They could not enter formal contracts to hire such land in their own names, but they could do so through a nominal white intermediary.

Thus anxiety about the threat to the labour supply represented by prosperous Africans was closely linked to anxiety about white impoverishment.

> There are very many indigent white persons who for years have been sinking in the social scale and are prepared to do anything possible to earn a livelihood as long as they are not compelled by necessity to do any manual labour. These persons act as intermediaries between the wealthy natives and the white owners of farms. They have farms in their own names, reside on them but allow the well-to-do natives to make use of the farm and in fact become servants of the native. The native is really the lessee of the farm and the white man is simply kept for the sake of appearance. They get as many natives on the farm as possible and they simply live on the proceeds of the natives' labour. This system is having a most demoralising effect . . .[64]

In due course, Act No. 42 of 1908 was passed in order to prohibit this practice. In response, in September 1908 the Becoana Mutual Improvement Association expressed its indignation against the Act, on the grounds that it interfered with rights of ownership, it would force the disposal of livestock and it would impel Africans to take refuge in already over-crowded reserves or to leave the ORC. The Act was especially resented, the Association pointed out, by the people of the Thaba Nchu district, which was originally an independent African territory and still accommodated some 25,000 Africans. In the light of vigorous and widespread opposition to the Act, and on advice from the Colonial Office, the ORC government shelved its implementation pending rationalization of policy under Union.[65]

This episode exposes the ambivalent political position of the Improvement Association. Its officers at this time were prominent Barolong landowners— Joel Goronyane, Moses Masisi, Jeremiah Makgothi, John Mokitlane Nyo-kong—who purported to represent the interests of the Barolong community of Thaba Nchu as a whole and specifically, in this case, the interests of a small class of wealthy African stock-owners who were effective lessees of white-owned land in the manner described above. The problem was that their own class interests as owners of fixed property contradicted their defence of other Africans' direct access to land. For many Barolong landowners at this time, including Goronyane and Makgothi and other members of the politically active elite such as W.Z. Fenyang, were leasing portions of their farms for repeated periods of six months at a time, as allowed by law, to white tenants.[66] The inference may be drawn that fixed rents from white tenants were more financially attractive to them than the unpredictable returns of share-cropping with black tenants. The reason for this, in turn, was that many of them had to meet regular interest payments in order to service the mortgage bonds they had taken out on their farms.

The second major bone of contention for Milner settlers was the alleged over-valuation of Land Settlement farms. A series of difficult seasons induced a considerable number of resignations, and many settlers felt there was little relationship between the real economic viability of their farms and the valuation of them by the Land Settlement Board which determined their half-yearly payments on the purchase system. The demand for a revaluation was precipitated by a slump in land values after 1904. It came from settlers of Crout's party in the north-east of the district, the Leeuw river group in the south-east and the Daggafontein and Dewetsdorp settlers in the south-west. Most of the latter, wrote Charles Ross, who had accompanied Leonard Flemming in their journey up from the eastern Cape, had arrived in late 1902 or early 1903, and had worked themselves 'to the bone', with very little to show for their efforts. Their lands were suited for livestock but not for agriculture. He felt that they were over-valued by 20 to 30 per cent for this reason.[67]

The strength of this grievance clearly varied with the balance in any particular area between livestock and agriculture and whether or not water supplies were readily available. Farms situated in areas known to contain good arable land had a higher valuation than farms situated in livestock areas; and of course the availability of water vitally affected the viability of the enterprise. A division emerged between different groups of settlers roughly along these lines. According to Tom Marriott of Liondale 311, adjacent to Thaba Patchoa in the Leeuw river area, the arable districts of 'Leeuw, Thaba East and Moroka were unanimously in favour of re-valuation'; while the stock districts—despite the letter from Ross quoted above—opposed it. The case for revaluation was vigorously taken up in London by one settler's father, R.S. Hawkins, who had visited the ORC in 1904, and who repeatedly lobbied the Colonial Office over the conditions the settlers faced.

> Anyone conversant with the sandy water supply on one of the farms in the Petitioners' district or of their hopeless condition from 3 years' drought and in the entire absence of rain, and the more or less continued insufficiency of rain and the repeated scourge of locusts ... will comprehend at once the necessity for a totally different valuation of those lands from those of the Counter-Petitioners.[68]

Hawkins pressed the particular case of settler 'XYZ', who wrote that he had his farm rent free until water was found but it would have been better if he had had water and paid rent. In that case:

> I should not have had such fearful losses with tape and wire worm, I feel sure, and should also have escaped the misery of seeing the sheep die week after week, and all the trouble and expense of dosing, etc. By rights the sheep ought to be sent right away for a change of veldt but I can't possibly leave the farm to do this. It would cost more than I could possibly scrape together. I can only hope that the disease will die slowly out.[69]

'XYZ' turned out to be Hawkins' own son, Seymer Selby Hawkins of Hillside 271, also in the Leeuw river district, on the eastern slope of the hill Mokopu

(Pumpkin). He had grown up on a large sheep farm in New Zealand but had very little education, by comparison with his father and brothers.[70]

The ORC administration consistently opposed revaluation, largely on the economic grounds of comparison with purchase on the open market and the political grounds of widespread resentment in the ORC of the alleged favourable treatment of Land Settlers by the government. Harry Hanger tartly reviewed the comparison in mid-1906 at the height of the campaign for revaluation:

A fact that all these men overlook is that they purchase the property, the Government practically lends them the whole of the purchase amount at 4 per cent. If any one of the settlers had the idea of buying a property from a private individual he would find that the seller would demand at least a third of the purchase amount in cash and the balance would have to be secured by first mortgage bearing interest at the rate of anything from 6 to ten per cent, receiving no compensation for any improvements, should he fail to comply with the conditions of purchase.[71]

Apthorp, the secretary of the Land Settlement Board, who was on leave at the time, responded with some irritation from Scarborough in Yorkshire (England) to the various complaints of the settlers. He pointed out to the Colonial Office that all land for settlement was over-subscribed. How would this be so if it were over-valued? He underlined the probity and experience of the members of the Land Settlement Board, and rejected the principle that tenants should decide all questions of tenure in place of the landlord. The Board had always tried to treat each case on its merits, but this had resulted in settlers in other districts considering that the settlers in the Thaba Nchu and other arable areas, who were a minority of the total, were being 'unduly dry-nursed and favoured by the Government'.[72]

Nearly two years later, one of the Land Board inspectors from Bloemfontein stressed the favourable comparison of the terms of Land Settlement with those of the open market:

A man buying a farm privately for say £5,000 would probably have to pay from £1,500 to £2,000 cash, and mortgage the whole farm for the remaining £3,000 at 6 per cent, and he takes all risk of the value of land rising or falling in the future. Under the Land Settlement Ordinance a settler has to pay no cash down, and pays interest at only 4 per cent on the whole amount. He practically takes no risk of the price of land falling as he can give up his farm at any time, and at the same time he has the advantage of being able to buy at the original figure if his land should at any time rise in value. In addition to this he is refunded for practically all reasonable improvements he has made during his occupation.[73]

While it rejected revaluation as a solution to the settlers' problems, the Land Settlement Board bent over backwards to ease their predicament in other ways. It carried out improvements such as water-boring at no cost to the settler. It reduced interest rates both on the purchase capital owed and on loans for equipment, fencing and livestock. It introduced livestock on a share system between the settler and the Board. In April 1906, Apthorp reported after a tour of the Thaba Nchu and Ficksburg settlers, who had experienced 'the worst of luck', that the only way to resolve their difficulties was for the government to assist them with a further issue of breeding stock on the share system, which had proved mutually beneficial, and to ensure a permanent water supply on their farms for stock and domestic purposes.[74] In the end, the issue of revaluation died a natural death, partly because of consistently sympathetic intervention of this kind, but mainly because rising land values throughout the countryside from 1908 took the wind out of the sails of those who had agitated for a general revaluation.

The issue of revaluation was nevertheless an extremely sensitive one in 1906, because the settlers' sense of economic insecurity was compounded by the political dilemma in which they found themselves. In December 1905 a Liberal government was formed in London, under Sir Henry Campbell-Bannerman, and confirmed in office in a general election in January 1906. The granting of 'Responsible Government' to the Transvaal and the ORC emerged as high on its political agenda. The Governor of the two colonies, Lord Selborne, who had succeeded Milner in 1905, forwarded a secret despatch in May 1906 to the new Secretary of State for the Colonies, Lord Elgin, concerning the consequences for the Land Settlers of the likely political ascendancy of the Orangia Unie party. By that time 635 settlers had been placed on land in the ORC under the terms of the Land Settlement Board, of whom 383 were from Britain and other colonies, 207 were South African of British descent, and forty-five were Dutch. The Lieutenant Governor, Hamilton Goold-Adams, observed that the whole experiment had been more successful in the ORC than in the Transvaal: conditions were better both for agriculture and for livestock, despite three seasons of drought, and the ORC had 'comparative immunity' from pests such as Rhodesia red water.

A section of settlers in Thaba Nchu, however, had suffered disproportionately through an exclusive devotion to wheat-farming: 'it is these cases . . . which have come chiefly into notice in the press and in the speeches of partisan orators'. Many settlers dreaded the future, 'if the support of the Government is given in a step-motherly fashion or is altogether withdrawn'. However, the only settlers who had asked for a revaluation were from Thaba Nchu, and the request was not by any means unanimous even there. Nevertheless, only one farm out of about 170 was vacant in the Thaba Nchu and adjoining districts. Selborne himself received a petition from the Thaba Nchu district on 21 June 1906. A deputation of about fifty settlers, who impressed him as 'a remarkably capable and representative set of farmers', specifically requested that the settlers should be retained under the direct control of the imperial government, until they were thoroughly established.[75]

Their anxieties were obvious ones. Under a 'Responsible Government' with a Dutch majority, the British Land Settlers could not expect sympathetic state support to the extent that they enjoyed under the ORC administration and that they would continue to require. Particularly vulnerable were settlers who had lived in the OFS or the Cape Colony before the war and had assisted the British imperial cause either through military service or employment in the intelligence department. As one settler wrote from Ficksburg:

> We hear some queer ideas from the Dutch about what they mean to do with the settlers as soon as they get a chance, and they are pretty unanimous in reckoning us Jonahs who must be got rid of before good seasons will come again, and I am not anxious to have to beg grace from any Dutch official.[76]

The Bloemfontein *Friend* was seen as a mouthpiece of Orangia Unie at the time. It published a vigorous editorial against Milner's proposal, in a letter to the *Times*, that the settlers should be retained under the Colonial Office in London after the grant of Responsible Government. In effect, it argued, this would be 'taxing Boers to settle more Britons'.[77]

The Constitution Committee visited Bloemfontein in May and June 1906, creating an 'uneasy feeling' amongst the land settlers. At the time, their energies were directed to swatting locusts, which had been playing 'sad havoc' in several districts,[78] and to lobbying for the Land Settlement Board to remain under imperial control. Several settlers appealed over the heads of the politicians and bureaucrats to the readership of the London *Times*. Marriott of Liondale 311, Butler of Glen Mokopo 249 and Horne of Thorley 408 wrote a long and impassioned appeal for support on 12 July 1906. Having served in the imperial forces in the war, they pointed out, the settlers had been granted farms by what the Boers regarded as 'direct favouritism'. They had struggled for years without success, and if handed over to a Boer-dominated Responsible Government they would be acutely vulnerable to the 'mercy and charity' of the ex-Free State burghers. Was this 'a position the average Britisher would care to see his fellow-countrymen placed in?'[79]

The settlers' agitation bore fruit, aided by sympathetic Unionist peers in the House of Lords. It was clear that the leaders of Het Volk in the Transvaal and Orangia Unie in the ORC would oppose any extension of the Land Settlement scheme. Parliamentary debate therefore concentrated on the question of whether, and how, the existing settlers' position should be protected against the political prejudice they anticipated under Responsible Government. Winston Churchill, the new Under Secretary of State at the Colonial Office, observed that, without such protection, 'a few bad years, and a rigid and severe administration would very easily sweep them all away like mushrooms before the scythe'. He proposed a separate Land Board under imperial control, to last five years from 1907, the year in which elections were held and new ministries formed in the two colonies. This proposal was carried through cabinet and inscribed in Clause 1 (a) of Article 53 of the Letters Patent. From 1908 the Crown Agents in London dealt directly with the locally constituted Land Settlement Boards in each colony, on all financial and administrative matters connected with Land Settlement.[80]

## TOWARDS CONSOLIDATION

Slowly, then, the tide turned in favour of the Land Settlers. They experienced a series of good seasons from 1907. The Colonial Office conceded the third of their principal demands, to be retained under direct imperial administration after the transfer of the ORC to Responsible Government in 1907. The Land Settlement Board refused to undertake a general revaluation of their farms, the second of their principal demands, but otherwise vigorously exerted itself to ease their immediate financial predicament. The first major issue, that of the shortage of African labour, was part of a much wider struggle between white landlords and black tenants, the complex elements of which have been charted by Keegan in his valuable study of the capitalisation of white agriculture.[81] This struggle reached its climax in the years after Union in 1910. It gave rise to the 1913 Land Act which prohibited share-cropping, and whose dramatic effects are explored in some detail in Chapter 3.

The Thaba Nchu settlers now had a railway line, from Bloemfontein to Modderpoort, running through their arable heartlands. They had the benefit of a creamery and a government experimental farm at Tweespruit, and breeding stallions were also available there. The Land Settlement Board extended its experiment of issuing livestock on shares, in order to stabilise the settlers 'independent of gambling on agriculture', since wheat was evidently too risky for them to rely on. The Board also carried out water-boring operations free of charge to the settler; supplied windpumps on the same basis; and advanced low-interest loans for fencing materials.[82]

In addition to these facilities, the terms of repayment were substantially revised in order to help the settlers establish themselves thoroughly. Apthorp invoked the circumstances of W.A. Crout of Mount Pleasant 54 to explain the significance of this in his report to the ORC administration. The farm was 620 morgen in extent, and its purchase price was £1,550, spread over thirty years. In respect of the original terms specified, Crout was paying £89.2s.6d. per annum, representing 5.75 per cent of the purchase price. He was also paying £26.0s.0d. per annum on loans of £201, repayable in half-yearly instalments with interest over ten years. Under the revised terms proposed at the end of 1906, Crout would pay £62 per annum for the farm, representing interest at 4 per cent of the purchase price, the redemption element being postponed; and £8 per annum on the loans, interest being reduced to 4 per cent and capital repayments being made in three instalments after four, seven and ten years instead of half-yearly. He would thus pay a total of £70 per annum over the next four years, instead of £115 under the old terms, a clear saving of £45 which could be invested, for example, in breeding stock. In due course, in view of the settlers' improving record of repayment, the interest rates both for purchase and for loans were dropped from 4 to 3 per cent for the financial year 1909–10, and again for 1910–11.[83]

In September 1909, Crout was able to report enthusiastically on the progress he had made. In 1907, the Board had carried out drilling operations on Mount Pleasant and installed, at no cost to himself, a 14 foot Lloyds Aermotor windmill [windpump] capable, with a good wind, of delivering 1,800 to 2,000 gallons of water an hour. The borehole was 42 feet deep and he was storing the water in an ordinary dam 100 yards long, scooped up 4 feet high. Over a period of eighteen months since the windpump was installed, Crout's farm books showed a dramatic increase in his potato yields and substantial crops of oats, wheat, barley and pumpkins. The results of this small irrigation capacity were sufficient to cover his annual rent obligation.

These results may have been exceptional, as implied in the terms in which Crout wrote to Apthorp:

> You are at liberty to show this to any man and if you cannot convince him, tell him I will be only too pleased to show him the Mill and show him the lands and also my farm book, and then if he is not convinced of course he is hopeless.

Indeed, some of the other settlers in the same part of the district, who had come up from the eastern Cape, were reported to be generally dissatisfied at this time, 'mostly worse off than when they arrived', and contemplating, if only they could recover the cost of transport, a further trek to Rhodesia. Nevertheless, Apthorp felt that Crout's experience fully vindicated the Board's policy of carrying out free improvements on behalf of the settlers, as the best method of securing their future viability.[84]

At the end of 1909, Governor Goold-Adams reviewed overall progress with some satisfaction. Of 972 settlers who had at one time or another held land under the Board, 650 were still on the land and a further 154 were still in the ORC. The present settlers had on average nearly £800 worth of livestock each. Taking into account also the value of their housing, farm implements and fencing, and allowing for an approximate average starting capital of £400 per settler, 'the conclusion must be reached that the settlers as a whole have done very well, and are far from the destitute condition some persons wish to make out'. Agitation over revaluation had come to an end, in view of rapid inflation in the market value of land which followed recovery from the economic depression of 1904–8. While there was still a significant rate of attrition—sixty-three Land Settlement farms in the ORC were vacated in the year 1909–10—the policy of issuing livestock on shares had rescued 'several hundred deserving settlers' from having to resign their holdings.[85]

On expiry of the Land Board's five-year term of office in 1912, the new Union government passed an Act giving settlers in the OFS the absolute right to a Crown grant of perpetual quitrent tenure (virtual freehold), provided they entered mortgage bonds in favour of the government to cover repayment of the balance of the purchase price of their farms. In this way, by a striking irony, most of the new settlers in the Thaba Nchu district obtained title to their farms in 1913. This was the same year that precipitated the dispossession of so many black share-croppers of their access to productive opportunities on white-owned land. The apparent coincidence reflects, of course, the differential impetus of systematic state intervention in favour of white farmers and against black farmers. In the early years of struggle, many of the settlers had been able to survive on the land at all only through relationships with black share-croppers who had built up or retained their own substantial holdings of livestock and ploughs or other capital equipment. According to several witnesses to the Beaumont Commission in 1913 (see Chapter 3), most settlers in the Thaba Nchu district still practised 'sowing on the halves'. As Keegan has shown, however, gradual consolidation of white settler enterprise implied the creeping destruction of black tenant enterprise.[86]

By 1916, shortly after they had obtained title, some of the farms occupied by Milner settlers were represented in glowing terms in Somerset Playne's survey of agricultural, industrial and commercial resources in the OFS. In the light of intensifying antagonism between white landowners and black tenant producers throughout the highveld at this time, the style in which the survey was written is one of incorrigible hyperbole. It nevertheless expresses a strong sense of optimism and dynamism which clearly prevailed in some quarters and which is attributable to the unprecedented scale and gathering momentum of state intervention in the capitalisation of white agriculture in these years. In the east of the district, for example, Branksome 185, owned by R.W. Palmer and H.R. Wise, was a subdivision of the original government farm Alexandria 43, and adjacent to two other subdivisions, Heathfield 264 and Jevington 276. Branksome had a long list of prize Illawarra shorthorns and Large Black pigs imported from Australia, as well as 500 morgen of arable lands under wheat, maize and oats.

In the south-west of the district, more suitable for pastoral than for arable use, Arthur Cockin and his brother owned Colton 195, part of the original farm Onder Logageng 146, and De Rust 208, a subdivision of Moroyane 152. They also rented another farm. Their main business was sheep-breeding, with a flock of about 4,000 Tasmanian Merinos. They kept 300 mixed cattle for dairying and slaughter. Nearby, brothers Wilfred and Maitland Brown owned the two Land Settlement farms of Oatlands 352 and The Springs 402, which they had been respectively allocated by the Board, and Daggafontein 144 (rest), which they had bought from Robert Dickie. These adjacent properties were fenced and subdivided into paddocks. The Brown Brothers also had about 4,000 Tasmanian Merino sheep. They specialised in the rearing of stud rams for sale and the export of wool to the London market through the

Dewetsdorp Wool Producers' Association. They had 80 Afrikander cattle for draught purposes and slaughter, and about 100 dairy Frieslands.[87]

In retrospect, perhaps, one vignette from Playne's survey metaphorically captures the relationship between the imperial authorities in London, the ORC state and the Land Settlers. The Board maintained about twenty-five thoroughbred stallions, 'comprising some of the best blood attainable', at its irrigation settlement of Roodepoort, north-west of Dewetsdorp. One of these, 'Red Fox', was a grandson of 'Flying Fox', the Duke of Westminster's horse which won the Derby in 1899 and which is commemorated by the weather vane on the clocktower of the stables on the Westminster estate. Playne's contributor recommended that:

> Farmers in the Free State who possess the right stamp of mares ought to avail themselves to the fullest extent of the services of such a horse, for it is impossible to over-estimate the value of a strain of blood given by an animal of courage, stamina and speed.

One settler, Charles Ross of The Cliff 413, who had come up with Leonard Flemming from the eastern Cape, kept twenty thoroughbred mares for breeding racing and polo ponies, for which there was a ready market amongst wealthy patrons of the turf. Most of these mares, registered in the South African Stud Book, were 'put to' 'Red Fox' in the 1911 season, no doubt to Charles Ross' considerable advantage.[88] The imperial seed, so to speak, was planted in the barren landscape of the eastern ORC, feather-bedded by the local state, and germinated after due struggle by individual midwives of proven quality. Thus, eventually, did some of the settlers flourish.

Appropriately, also, in the light of the prime value of good breeding stock, the Milner settlers and the Westminster settlers married one another in subsequent generations. Shaftesbury 585 was one of the farms carved out of Rapuiskop 92, the one farm belonging to the Westminster estate which lay within the original boundary of the Thaba Nchu district. G. Shaw, first tenant and later owner of Shaftesbury, suffered from tuberculosis and came to South Africa, practically an invalid, in search of a good climate. His wife had learned to make cheese before they left England. She started a cheese factory on Shaftesbury which became the farm's distinctive achievement, based on a herd of fifty Friesland cattle. In due course, in 1940, the Shaws' son Bill married Agnes, daughter of Fred Nicholson of Heathfield 264, and they took over the cheese enterprise. Initially, the elder Mrs Shaw used to deliver the cheese herself, by horse-drawn cart, to imperial troops still stationed near Tweespruit after the South African war. Later, it was supplied to such places as the Rand Club, the Durban Club and the Civil Service Club in Cape Town.[89]

For many reasons—poor seasons, the vicissitudes inherent in highveld agriculture, deficiency of capital resources, political obstacles—Milner's Land Settlement scheme proved to be unrealistically ambitious. Nevertheless, it was launched in some districts on a sufficient scale and with sufficient consistency to establish a new generation of English-speaking farmers on the land. The Thaba Nchu district is the prime example. To the extent that their enterprises survived at all, in the first place, and ultimately prospered, in the second place, the success of Land Settlement, partial as it was, is attributable in very large measure to deliberate, sustained and well-organised state support. The state was itself the principal source of easy credit in cash and kind, derived from a generous imperial loan. The state also intervened directly to overcome the perennial problems of lack of access to markets and storage facilities, seasonal cycles of glut and famine and consequent violent price fluctuations. Finally, the imperial authorities provided direct political sponsorship of the British settlers, without which they might not have survived the antagonism expressed by some of those who inherited the local state in 1907.

# 3

# VARIETIES OF DISPOSSESSION

The morning was showery. Thaba Ncho Hill in the background, always
visible for scores of miles in every direction, towered high above the
surrounding landscape. Its stony slopes covered with a light mist from
peak to base, it stood like a silent witness to the outraged treaty between
the Barolong and the Boers.

Sol Plaatje
*Native Life in South Africa* (1969), p. 14

Most Land Settlers in the Thaba Nchu district obtained title to their farms in
1913. In that sense, for them, the year was one of formal consolidation. For
many black tenants of white landowners across the arable regions of the
highveld, by contrast, the year was one of upheaval and dislocation, as the
'great dispersal' of share-croppers gathered a brutal momentum.[1] The passage
of the Natives Land Act in mid-1913 neither began nor brought to a head the
various processes of dispossession that I describe in this chapter. But it did give
them a decisive twist. It is therefore an appropriate point of departure for
analysing social and economic transformations in the district over the two
decades between the mid-1910s and the mid-1930s. The passage of the Native
Trust and Land Act of 1936, the second major piece of land segregation legislation, gave a new and complex impetus to these transformations,
which is separately analysed in Chapter 4.

The 1913 Land Act had two principal objectives. Firstly, it prohibited
share-cropping contracts between white landowners and black peasant farmers. Secondly, it required the designation of 'scheduled' areas outside which
Africans could not buy or rent land and inside which non-Africans could not
acquire rights to land. It also provided for the setting apart of 'additional' land
for African occupation in the future. As regards the impact of the Act on black
share-croppers on white-owned land, Thaba Nchu was typical of the mixed
farming districts of the eastern highveld. The local evidence is therefore
adduced with reference to two wider and closely related issues of interpretation: the statistical and the historiographical. As regards the designation of
'scheduled' and 'additional' areas, the Thaba Nchu district was quite untypical
of the OFS as a whole. It contained two of the three small African reserves in
the OFS, and also the only concentration of African landownership in the
OFS. For reasons elaborated below, these facts made the realisation of 'additional' land for African occupation both highly controversial in principle and
extremely complex in practice.

The experience of dispossession was neither uniform nor one-sided, as the following sections of this chapter seek to show. Black tenants were dispersed from white-owned land in the Thaba Nchu district, as elsewhere. Many drifted into the two small reserves, and many were absorbed into the industrial labour force either as temporary migrants from the reserves or as effectively permanent residents of the squalid townships of Bloemfontein or Kroonstad or the southern Transvaal. Some went to Basutoland; others joined an ill-fated mass exodus to Bechuanaland. Black landowners who remained in the district, for their part, were sensitive to the developing contradiction between their private interests, which required a deracialised land market, and their public obligation to the Barolong community, which required more land urgently and specifically for African occupation. Black landowners were also increasingly vulnerable to manipulation by the small town attorneys who either held their mortgage bonds directly or negotiated on their behalf with the distant corporate finance houses which dominated the private mortgage market. According to their local reputations, which endured long after their deaths, these agents often wilfully exploited the routine confusion of their clients' affairs. This issue is discussed at some length in Chapter 4, and a specific example of a Morolong landowner's exposure to unscrupulous manipulation is presented in the Appendix. Meanwhile one detailed story, of the gradual disintegration of a prominent family's landed estate over three decades, partly illustrates this vulnerability and partly illustrates the structural context of disadvantage relative to white landowners who faced a similar predicament of escalating indebtedness. Finally, I review the evidence presented to the Native Economic Commission in 1931 on the condition of the district as a whole in the depths of acute economic depression.

### BITTER WINTER: THE SHARE-CROPPERS

On the morning of Friday, 12 September 1913, a thousand Africans gathered on the racecourse at Thaba Nchu, between the railway station and the town. They came from the surrounding farms on horseback and on bicycles, in carts and wagons; 'they included evicted wanderers and native tenants under notice to leave their farms, with letters of eviction and other evidence in their pockets'; they also included refugees from other districts who were 'constantly on the move' and had hurried to Thaba Nchu to plead for shelter.[2] The reason they converged on the racecourse was to complain to Edward Dower, Secretary for Native Affairs, about their traumatic experiences as a result of the Land Act passed earlier in the year. Many black tenants faced eviction from white-owned farms and consequent loss of livestock.

Solomon Plaatje described the scene in *Native Life in South Africa* (1969), his eloquent and scathing attack on the Land Act from which the quotation at the head of this chapter is taken. Plaatje spent the months from July to September 1913 travelling throughout the OFS, from Hoopstad on the north-western border to Ladybrand on the eastern border with Basutoland. On his bicycle in the Boshof district, he met a policeman who told him, 'If ever there was a fool's errand, it is that of a Kafir trying to find a new home for his stock and family just now'. He came across a group of refugees on the border of the Boshof and Hoopstad districts, share-cropping families who had just been evicted by their landlords. Cattle were perishing on the journey, from poverty and lack of fodder; young children were vulnerable to the bitter cold of a highveld winter. One family whose baby had died was forced to bury the body in the darkness, 'amid fear and trembling, as well as the throbs of a torturing anguish, in a stolen grave, lest the proprietor of the spot, or any of his servants, should surprise them in the act'. Somewhere in the Hoopstad district, another family had continued share-cropping after the death of the husband-father. The landlord told the widow to dispose of her stock and indenture her children to him. She refused, he evicted her and set fire to her thatched hut. Plaatje encountered her on the road, her worldly effects on her head, an infant on her back, her cattle driven before her, and two adolescent children by her side, weeping bitterly.[3]

In the Ladybrand district, Plaatje was told of a case in which, like many others, an African couple had searched without success for a new home and then taken a travelling pass to go to Basutoland with their stock. They were ambushed and shot to death and their livestock stolen. One of the murderers was arrested and brought to trial but acquitted, Plaatje reported with irony, 'presumably more by the eloquence' of General Hertzog, who conducted the defence. Towards Wepener, he found that evictions were numerous, although less damaging to livestock because of the proximity of Basutoland. But that country was itself already over-crowded:

> it became abundantly clear that the influx of outsiders into Basutoland could not continue at the rate it was then proceeding without seriously complicating the land question in Basutoland, where chieftains are constantly quarrelling over small patches of arable land.

He watched groups of refugees driving their stock towards the border, 'a distressing sight'.[4]

By early September 1913, Plaatje's financial resources for the journey were exhausted, and he was invited to stay with his friend W.Z. Fenyang at Rietfontein 119, in 'the south of the Moroka district, where I saw much of the trouble'. Without hope of a positive outcome, he advised displaced tenants to lay their complaints before Edward Dower at the meeting at Thaba Nchu on 12 September. Dower was there in place of the late Minister of Native Affairs, the 'Cape liberal' J.W. Sauer, who died immediately after the passage of the Act. The speeches were interpreted by Jeremiah Makgothi, farmer and former schoolteacher, and Reverend Peter Motiyane, the local Wesleyan minister.[5]

Dower addressed the meeting for half an hour, entirely avoiding the issue which preoccupied the people. In turn, Reverend Joel Goronyane, who had

some years previously retired from his own active Wesleyan ministry, regretted Sauer's death on behalf of the Barolong and then explained to Dower: 'All
the people you see before you are frightened by the new law. They have come
here for nothing else but to hear how they are expected to live under it.'
Speaker after speaker came forward to narrate their experiences. Having
listened to this catalogue of sufferings, Dower lamely responded that not many
people had been evicted, though many were under notice of eviction; that the
Act had been misinterpreted by landlords; and that people who felt threatened
should report the circumstances to their magistrate. Nevertheless, he said, the
old practice of 'sowing on the halves' should cease after the expiry of current
contracts, since a 'raw native' always got the worst of such a partnership.
Dower advised people either to become servants—in effect, labour tenants; or
to move into the reserve [voices: 'where is the reserve?']; or to sell their animals
for cash [sensation]. Parliament would be taking further steps to settle the land
question after receiving the report of the [Beaumont] Commission appointed
in terms of the Act. Dower's advice was both evasive and unhelpful, and the
meeting broke up in 'indescribable disappointment'.[6]

Plaatje's comment on the 'outraged treaty' between the Barolong and the
Boers was a reference to the assistance rendered to the Voortrekkers and later
to the Free State government by Moroka as chief of an independent African
people (see Chapter 1). More specifically, it may be interpeted as a reference to
the betrayal of President Brand's commitment at the time of annexation in
1884 to protect the land rights of Africans in the Moroka territory. Judging
from Joel Goronyane's evidence to the Beaumont Commission in November
1913, people still felt very bitter that the land appropriated as OFS government
farms in 1885 had been granted to white settlers under the Crown Colony
regime.[7] From 'above', the settlers' security of tenure was the logical outcome
of systematic state intervention on behalf of white capitalist agriculture. From
'below', and in a deeper historical perspective, it confirmed the profound sense
of injustice which informed local Africans' resentment of the immediate
pressures of dispossession in 1913.

The magistrate of Thaba Nchu in 1913 was Major James Wege Robertson,
who was born at Cape Town in 1873. He had already had varied civil service
experience: as a Customs Office clerk in British Bechuanaland from 1891 to
1895; and clerk to the Civil Commissioners respectively of Bulawayo and
Umtali, Rhodesia, until 1899. He joined the army in 1899 and was rapidly
promoted in the Kimberley Light Horse, commanding the garrison at Koffy-
fontein, ORC, from June 1900 to September 1901. He was appointed as
magistrate of Thaba Nchu in 1904, succeeding J.F. Van Iddekinge.[8] Robertson gave evidence to the Beaumont Commission both in the form of a written
report, submitted in his official capacity on 25 September 1913, and orally as a
witness when the Commission sat in Bloemfontein on 23 and 24 October 1913.
In the first, he estimated that 'with locations dotted about on so many farms the

system of ploughing on shares is carried on on probably 90 per cent of the European farms'; in his oral evidence, he thought that the number of families in the district that would be affected by the prohibition of share-cropping would be 90 per cent. Accordingly, provision would have to be made for ground for Africans who were forced to leave the farms. Robertson recommended extension of the Seliba reserve by purchase of New York 12, already enclosed by the horse-shoe shape of the reserve, and several other farms to the east.[9]

Both of Robertson's aggregate estimates give a clear impression of the prevalence of share-cropping in the district at the time. Another witness to the Commission, attorney Gideon Jacobus Van Riet, observed that

> With very few exceptions, there are squatters, sowing on the halves, on nearly every farm in the Thaba Nchu district. They are generally people with perhaps 20 or 30 head of cattle. Very few have sheep . . . I do not think it is detrimental to the country—this sowing on the halves. If you look round the country you will see some of our settlers who, were it not for the sowing on shares, could not stand today where they are now. The natives were planting and sowing under their supervision, and where settlers were not in a position to buy cattle these natives helped a lot. It is practised by nearly every farmer in the district and by the new settlers. I have boys sowing on the halves in my service. I pay them so much, and give them lands for their services.[10]

Despite concerted state intervention on their behalf, white farmers had not yet, on the whole, been able to establish independence of black share-croppers in respect of possession and use of their own capital resources. The black-owned farms in the district were also predominantly worked on a share-cropping basis, and many were grossly over-stocked.

It is much harder to estimate the scale of evictions which took place in the period immediately following the passage of the Land Act. The available statistical evidence is haphazard, to say the least. After the Beaumont Commission report was submitted in 1916, magistrates were requested by the Select Committee on the Native Administration Bill of 1917 to report in identical terms for their districts on the effects of the 1913 Act on independent tenants. These were defined as people who gave up a portion of their crops to the owners of the land for the right of residence, grazing and cultivation. The returns made, however, were widely variant and based, it seems, on 'very rough conjectures'. The aggregate estimate for the OFS was of 5,000 families affected by the Act, i.e. 25,000 to 30,000 people, although the OFS Local Land Committee of 1918 was sceptical of this figure:

> In one district, for instance, a total of 2,000 families is given, whilst in the adjacent district of the same size, where the conditions with regard to the cultivation of land are precisely the same, only a total of 560 is given.[11]

The problem of interpreting the figure for Thaba Nchu arises out of the fact

that the category on which magistrates were asked to report was the 'approximate number of families *likely to be turned off* farms if provisions of Natives'
Land Act prohibiting sowing on shares or leasing of land etc. by Europeans to
Natives were strictly enforced'; whereas, drawing presumably on the response
to this questionnaire, the OFS Local Land Committee cited the Thaba Nchu
magistrate as reporting 'that in his district 1,050 households [approximately
5,000 people] *were driven off* farms belonging to Europeans' as a result of the
prohibition of share-cropping under the 1913 Act.[12] A crucial ambiguity
remains.

The distribution of the African population of the Thaba Nchu district was
given as follows in the statistical appendices submitted with the report of the
Beaumont Commission:

| | |
|---|---|
| reserves | 12,500 |
| black-owned farms | 4,150 |
| white-owned farms | 10,500 |

In a separate 'Minute' of 1916, relating to the history of land in Thaba Nchu,
Beaumont gave the figure of 9,350 Africans as resident on white-owned farms.
It is not clear to what exact date(s) these figures refer, respectively. If these
aggregates are accepted as approximately reliable, the magistrate's estimate of
1,050 households evicted would suggest that roughly half of the total black
population resident on white farms in the district were either displaced or
threatened with displacement as a result of the 1913 Land Act. There was
undoubtedly a significant redistribution: some people evicted from white-
owned farms drifted onto black-owned farms or into the two reserves of Seliba
and Thaba Nchu, which were already the most congested in the Union; others
left the district altogether. The Local Land Committee of 1918 estimated there
were then 15,000 people in the two reserves, but also noted of Seliba that many
adult sons were away as migrant labourers 'for two to five years' before they
returned to the reserve; and that there had been a recent substantial exodus of
290 families to Bechuanaland.[13] Their fate is described in the following
section.

Whether, with hindsight, the magistrate's estimate should be interpreted as
prospective or retrospective, there was in any case a number of other difficulties in arriving at reliable estimates of this kind at the time. Firstly, there was
uncertainty over what precise relationships between owners and workers of the
land were prohibited by the Act. For example, in view of the apparent position
that only labour rent was now allowed, were white farmers able legally to
continue to use black tenants' livestock for the cultivation of their lands?
Secondly, as Keegan has convincingly demonstrated, there was often a clear
contradiction between the collective sentiments and the private interests of
white farmers. They were capable of vociferously denouncing share-cropping
in general on the grounds that it 'made the kaffirs too rich'. Many continued to

depend on share-cropping in particular, however, since they could not manage their own farming operations without the capital resources of their black tenants.[14] Evidence given by white farmers afterwards on the impact of the Act sometimes reflected uncertainty over whether to invoke the public sentiment against share-cropping or the private interest in favour of share-cropping. Thirdly, it was difficult to distinguish consistently between 'forced' and 'voluntary' removals, a problem familiar to those who have tried to estimate the scale of removals from 'white' rural areas in recent decades (see Chapter 6). In the face of mounting structural pressures, tenants often chose to remove themselves from the domain of a harsh master without being formally evicted. This difficulty helps to explain the striking discrepancies between the figures reported from different districts in which conditions were allegedly similar.

In an important sense, of course, argument about the validity of this or that statistical aggregate is beside the point. In retrospect, as Keegan has argued, the main significance of the Act was that it subverted the bargaining position of black share-croppers. It did not eliminate share-cropping, which continued for many years after the passage of the Act in many districts of the highveld. Rather, the Act represented a decisive moment of catharsis in the intense and protracted struggle between owners and workers of the land: over shares of the crop due to the landlord; over the amount of direct labour which the landlord could command; over the balance between cash wages, if any, and the value of the tenant's access to arable and grazing ground.[15] The fundamental implication of Keegan's argument is that, despite the misery of the winter of 1913, share-croppers were gradually squeezed by the process of capital accumulation in white settler agriculture rather than suddenly squeezed by a single piece of discriminatory legislation.

## DISMAL EXODUS: THE SAMUELITES

It is unclear whether the magistrate's estimate of 1,050 households driven off the land in the Thaba Nchu district included the 290 households—comprising 1,327 people—which departed to Bechuanaland in 1916 and 1917.[16] In order to understand this exodus we need to retrace our steps somewhat and follow what happened to the exile Samuel Lehulere Moroka after his banishment from the OFS at the end of 1884. With some of his people, he remained in Basutoland until 1896; he then moved briefly to the border area between British Bechuanaland, which became part of the Cape Colony in 1895, and the South African Republic (Transvaal), where he found temporary refuge near Khunwana and at Tlhakajeng. In 1898, he entered negotiations on behalf of himself and thirty-six followers with the Tati Company, which claimed ownership of the Tati district in the north-east of the Bechuanaland Protectorate; and agreement was reached for him to settle at a place known as Matsiloje, along the lower reaches of the Ramokgwebana river, south-east of Francistown. Chief Samuel claimed that 5,000 other people would join him there.[17]

This place proved to be arid, stony and infertile. In 1904, Samuel had only 196 people with him, who owned 347 head of cattle and 684 sheep and goats. With poor and uncertain rainfall, they had not reaped their lands successfully for three seasons, and they relied mainly on transport-riding for a living. Chief Samuel appealed to Lord Milner for permission to return to Thaba Nchu, and he visited Bloemfontein and other centres in the ORC to gather followers for this purpose. He was summarily expelled by the Colonial Secretary, whose hostile attitude in 1904 was explicitly endorsed in 1907 by Fischer's ministry, after the granting of Responsible Government, although Samuel specifically disclaimed any agitation over the 'dead chieftainship' at Thaba Nchu. Brief negotiations took place in 1906 over an alternative proposal for some of his people to settle on land owned by the Lewis and Marks partnership in the Rustenburg and Marico districts of the western Transvaal. Despite enthusiastic reports by the company's agent that the Barolong were 'very quiet people, very energetic, particular with their livestock . . .', this scheme also foundered because official permission was refused. In 1908, disillusioned and impoverished, Samuel and his remaining followers were moved to a section of the newly-demarcated Native Reserve in the Tati district, in the north-eastern corner along the Ntshe river. This section of the reserve became known as the Moroka Location.[18]

In 1910, having given up any prospect of being allowed to return to Thaba Nchu, Samuel Moroka sought permission from the Bechuanaland Protectorate administration for some of his Barolong supporters from the OFS to join him in the Moroka Location of the Tati district. Permission was refused on the grounds of the shortage of land available in the reserve. The urgency of Samuel's request was amplified, however, by the passage of the 1913 Land Act, since the effects of the prohibition of share-cropping were particularly harsh, as we have seen, in the OFS. In 1915 he conceived a much more ambitious plan for the relocation of land-hungry followers from the province. The plan was to buy from the Tati Company 237,000 acres of land in the south-eastern corner of the district, around Matsiloje, for £89,000. The money was to be raised by subscription from Barolong in the OFS and elsewhere who wished to take advantage of the scheme. Every male over 21 should pay £30, in the form either of a single lump sum or of an initial sum of £10 and four subsequent annual sums of £5. The scheme was actively promoted on Samuel's behalf by four residents of Waaihoek Location, Bloemfontein, who claimed, improbably, that 20,000 people wished to go to Bechuanaland. Samuel recognised, however, that this would not be easy to organise: 'we have been separated thirty years and my people are now scattered all over the Free State, Transvaal and other parts of the Union, some living in town locations, some in reserves and others on farms'. Further, a 'great deal of ill-feeling' still existed at Thaba Nchu.[19]

The three trustees of this purchase scheme were Samuel Moroka himself;

William Mokgothu Bogacu, a grandson of the prime conspirator on Samuel's behalf in the civil strife of the early 1880s; and Reverend Walter Lack, an Anglican priest of St. Augustine's mission at Francistown. They planned an ambitious tour of towns in the OFS and southern and western Transvaal in July and August 1915, to launch the fund-raising campaign. As 'Organising Secretary', Walter Lack was energetic and practical but 'young', according to the Resident Commissioner at Mafeking, 'somewhat deficient in savoir faire, and possibly a little indiscreet'. Lack visited fourteen different places and collected more than £1,000 in subscriptions. On 27 July he was at Thaba Nchu, where he held a meeting to advertise the Moroka Land Settlement scheme. He encountered strong objections from prominent African land-owners in the district, apparently on the grounds that 'Moroka shall never have any people if they can help it' and that they needed the labour of residents on their land. The landowners threatened to evict immediately any residents who responded to Lack's overtures. People dared not risk this because it would take time to arrange transport to Bechuanaland and in the meantime there was nowhere else for them to go in the OFS, the two reserves at Thaba Nchu being already over-crowded.[20]

Nevertheless, the first twenty-five households left Thaba Nchu on 17 June 1916; and three months later Chief Samuel reported that, of 2,500 subscribers to the scheme, 536 had recently arrived at Matsiloje. Together with their families, the new settlers must have comprised a majority of the 3,300 people living there in September 1916. They brought with them 3,000 bags of grain, but most had been greatly impoverished by their subscriptions to the purchase scheme and by the heavy cost of the long railway journey from various centres in the OFS to Francistown. Worse, many of the new settlers died within the first six months of their arrival. Some succumbed to pneumonia as a result of over-crowded trains, initial exposure on the open veld and sharp changes of temperature. Otherwise, most deaths were attributable to malarial infection endemic in the new environment, resistance to which was naturally low amongst the Barolong from the OFS but whose effects were compounded by a grossly inadequate diet at Matsiloje. Infants and the elderly were particularly vulnerable.[21]

Rumours of a high death rate at Matsiloje spread back to the OFS and undermined further recruitment to the scheme; while 600 familes who had intended to travel to Bechuanaland in 1917 were prevented from doing so by official anxiety about the spread of bubonic plague from the Union. On his return to Matsiloje in the later months of 1917, Walter Lack quarrelled openly with Chief Samuel about the conditions under which the new settlers were living, inadequate arrangements for their welfare and the apparent difficulty the men experienced in getting passes for labour elsewhere. Investigating these complaints in October 1917, the local British official at Francistown found 'many people suffering from swollen feet and limbs; some of them being unable to move. I also found several children in a shockingly emaciated condition, just skin and bone . . . Moroka professed to be ignorant of the fact'. Lack resigned as a trustee of the scheme in early 1918, observing that he 'could not agree with the chief any longer in the way he rules the people', and alleging that Chief Samuel was 'under the influence of Josiah Bogacu who is the cause of the misrule'. The immediate problem was one of widespread destitution. But there was no prospect of relief. A series of droughts undermined the agricultural efforts of the community; the soil was inhospitable at best; and wild animals 'played havoc' with their livestock.[22]

By mid-1920, only £9,650 had been raised; one third of that sum had been paid to the Tati Company; one third was absorbed by expenses; and a cash balance of one third remained. The purchase scheme was abandoned, and the people became tenants of the Company, liable to pay an annual rent of £1.10s. The Company also received the remaining cash balance in return for not enforcing penalties for breach of contract. The Matsiloje settlers became steadily poorer and more depressed. As Molema expressed it, 'frowning misfortune seemed to dog their every step'. They cast around, unsuccessfully, for alternative places to settle: in 1923, in neighbouring Rhodesia; in 1926, on the Barolong farms lying north of the Molopo river in the extreme south of the Bechuanaland Protectorate. By this time, Chief Samuel himself was aged, infirm and nearly blind, and had not 'sufficient push to please a certain section of the Baralongs especially those who came up to Tati a few years ago from the OFS'. In early 1924, in frustrated response to their worsening circumstances and the failure of the land purchase scheme, a group of settlers at Matsiloje organised a deputation to Francistown to raise the possibility, once again, of a return to Thaba Nchu. They argued that the chief had been banished for forty years and had surely expiated his original offence of having tried violently to depose Tshipinare in 1884. Chief Samuel himself was too ill to attend, but the deputation was accompanied by Michael Tshabadira, Samuel's headman at Moroka Location, and William Bogacu and Michael Bogacu, two of Samuel's councillors at Matsiloje.[23]

At this point, tactics diverged. The five men who had organised the deputation decided, without Samuel's authority or the agreement of his councillors, to organise a similar committee in Bloemfontein, in order to register the names of those interested in returning to Thaba Nchu. They achieved this through a resident of Bloemfontein, J.S. Kehiloe, who was sympathetic to their objectives and who had himself come up to Matsiloje to raise the question directly with Samuel. A series of allegedly secret meetings was held in Bloemfontein, which provoked a 'commotion' between the local survivors of the officially recognised Moroka Land Settlement Fund, which had come to an end in 1920; and the newly-constituted, self-proclaimed and officially unrecognised Barolong Land Fund Committee. The whole matter was investigated in July 1924 at the kgotla at Matsiloje. Chief Samuel denied authorising any renewal of his past efforts to return to Thaba Nchu; while the dissidents took advantage of this public opportunity to air their grievances. They specifically wished to recover land at Thaba Nchu, but Chief Samuel had been unable to achieve any progress towards this end. A violent confrontation nearly took place in March 1925, when Chief Samuel fined thirty-eight 'strikers' at least one beast each and attempted to have three 'ring-leaders' banished from Matsiloje. In the end, however, the conflict was defused by default, through the continuing and intransigent refusal of the South African authorities to sanction Samuel's return to Thaba Nchu, or that of his followers, under any circumstances.[24]

In 1929, it was reported that the settlers at Matsiloje had not reaped any crops for the previous four years, and their cattle were dying in the drought. The majority of the survivors wished either to return to the OFS; or to go to the Moroka Location, which was more densely populated but also more fertile than Matsiloje, and whither Chief Samuel had himself returned. They were not allowed to do either. In 1932, they were temporarily removed from their homes by the establishment of a five-mile Foot-and-Mouth cordon along the Rhodesian border, and they had to survive on government rations. In 1932, also, 'childless, half-blind, old, wretched and poor, worn out in body and spirit, weighed down with the disappointments, misfortunes, cares and sorrows of exile', Samuel Lehulere Moroka died. By that time, many of his people were dispersed. They had drifted to other parts of the Tati district or to other districts of Bechuanaland, and some had filtered back into South Africa as urban migrants.[25] Samuel was succeeded as chief of the Moroka Location and of the Matsiloje settlement by Percy Tshabadira, son of Michael Tshabadira Moroka, who had many years before joined his uncle Samuel Moroka in exile, following his own brief sojourn in British Bechuanaland. One more forlorn effort was made, in the late 1930s, to recover the Thaba Nchu chieftainship. This is described in Chapter 4.

### HORNS OF A DILEMMA: THE BLACK LANDOWNERS

The Beaumont Commission 'scheduled' three African reserves within the OFS—Witzieshoek in the Harrismith district, and Seliba and Thaba Nchu in the Thaba Nchu district. Together they comprised 74,290 morgen, less than half of 1 per cent of the province. Beaumont also identified nineteen other fragments of land as 'additional' areas to be 'released' in due course for African occupation, amounting to 148,316 morgen. The 'additional' areas comprised, firstly, mission land and mission reserves in the Harrismith, Edenburg and Jacobsdal/Fauresmith districts; secondly, farms owned by 'Coloured' persons in the Hoopstad, Senekal, Kroonstad and Fauresmith/Jacobsdal districts; and thirdly, the surviving African-owned farms scattered throughout the Thaba Nchu district, amounting to 82,677 morgen (see Figure 3.1).[26]

These proposals were embodied in the Native Administration Bill of 1917. However, this bill met vehement opposition from white farmers and their

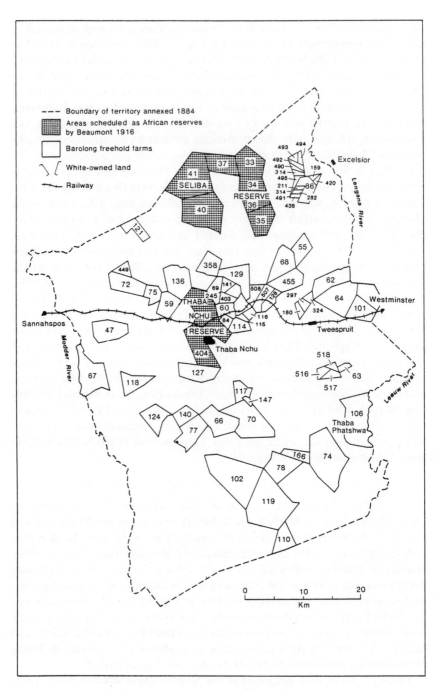

*Figure 3.1*   Thaba Nchu: African reserves and Barolong farms, 1913.

representatives in the Union Parliament, on the grounds that any extension of the existing reserves would further threaten the labour supply of farmers.[27] This opposition was particularly strong in the OFS, and the OFS Local Land Committee which was appointed to make alternative recommendations reflected the reluctance of white farming interests to make more land available for African occupation. Accordingly, it excised Beaumont's 'additional' areas from every district of the OFS other than Thaba Nchu and Harrismith. It thereby cut the total area to be 'released' from 148,316 morgen to 79,000 morgen. Apart from one small farm bordering Witzieshoek, this land was to be concentrated entirely in the Thaba Nchu district.[28]

The largest single 'additional' area identified by Beaumont consisted of a block of farms, 39,101 morgen in extent, situated on the border of the Fauresmith and Jacobsdal districts. These farms belonged to thirty-two families, the heirs of Adam Opperman. Adam Opperman was the son of Frederick Opperman, skilled smith and famous ex-slave from Graaff-Reinet in the Karoo (Cape), who had escaped from his master in the 1820s and later established a large estate near the Bethanie mission station. The Local Land Committee felt able to eliminate the 'additional' land outside Thaba Nchu on the grounds that its owners were not only not African (naturellen); they did not even qualify as 'Coloured' (kleurlingen) in a constitutional sense. Rather, they had been looked upon as burghers of the Free State, and for this reason the Committee saw no reason why their lands should be proclaimed 'additional' areas for African occupation.[29]

The recommendations for Thaba Nchu were that the fragmentary patchwork of 'additional' areas identified by Beaumont—the privately-owned farms shown in Figure 3.1—should be reduced in range and rationalised in distribution. Some white-owned land should be purchased between certain of Beaumont's 'additional' fragments, and other 'additional' fragments should be excised from the schedule of the proposed Act. Thus the Committee envisaged the formation of two consolidated blocks of land in the Thaba Nchu district, consisting together of just over 100,000 morgen. It rejected the possibility of 'neutral' areas, in which either black or white persons would be permitted to own land. It acknowledged that the Seliba reserve (17,660 morgen, 8,700 people) and the Thaba Nchu reserve (6,631 morgen, 6,250 people) were the most densely populated of all the 'scheduled' areas throughout the Union of South Africa; and that the desperate over-crowding there derived partly from the mass evictions from white farms which had taken place since 1913. Its solution to the problem was to recommend that the government should purchase many of the white-owned and African-owned farms within the boundaries specified by the Commission. These farms could then be 'thrown open for communal occupation', and this would help to relieve the acute congestion in the reserves.[30]

Pending legislative arrangements for implementing these proposals, the status of black-owned land which fell outside the two 'scheduled' reserves in the Thaba Nchu district was subject to considerable uncertainty. On the one hand, under the terms of Chapter XXXIV of the OFS Law Book, which remained in force after the passage of the 1913 Land Act, such land could not be sold or transmitted to Africans unless the prospective buyer or inheritor was shown to be a close 'blood relation' of the vendor or testator.[31] Such restrictions were in striking contrast to the nominal freedom of Africans both to purchase and to inherit land in the Cape province. In any case, however, very few Africans could afford to buy land even if the law had allowed them to. On the other hand, several witnesses to the Beaumont Commission clearly presumed that Beaumont's intention would have immediate effect, namely that black-owned farms identified as 'additional' could no longer be disposed of to whites. Black landowners were placed in an immediate dilemma. Under inherited Free State legislation, and in prevailing market conditions, they were effectively unable to sell their land to other Africans. Now, it appeared, after a generation of rapid alienation of land titles from black to white owners (see Chapter 1), they could no longer sell to whites either.

The dilemma arose out of the fact that, as the magistrate pointed out, most black landowners had their property more or less heavily mortgaged, and the bond-holders were overwhelmingly either white-controlled financial institutions or individual white investors and speculators. Only ten of the fifty-four black-owned farms in 1913 were not bonded.[32] Most owners depended on continuing access to 'white' finance capital to service their debts; and many of them also leased portions of their land to whites, as the most obvious means of ensuring a regular cash income with which to meet the interest payments on the mortgage bonds. According to Beaumont's figures, more than one-fifth of African-owned land was leased to whites in this way.[33]

Thus the immediate material interests of most black landowners in the Thaba Nchu district required the possibility in principle of selling or leasing their land to whites. In so far as this was precluded by the way the Act was locally interpreted in 1913, the Act undermined the position both of Barolong owners who could not redeem their mortgage bonds and of white bond-holders who could not realise their speculative investments. The magistrate, J.W. Robertson, expressed this effect concisely in his evidence to the Beaumont Commission:

> When existing bonds on Native farms are called up the mortgagee is in the position that he is unable to procure money from Native sources, he is prevented by law from obtaining it from Europeans, and in many instances he cannot sell as there is no Native who can purchase.[34]

The value of the land would accordingly be drastically reduced. Local attorney G.J. Van Riet gave a specific example to illustrate the point. One of his clients—probably Morokanyana Moroka, the youngest son of Chief Tshipinare—had a bond due for repayment in November 1913. 'Under this law

different financial houses will not lend the money'; he could get no assistance
from the Land Bank; he would therefore lose his farm, 'which would be a
distinct hardship'.[35] Van Riet made his own livelihood, it may be surmised,
out of the 'distinct hardship' of other people (see Appendix). As it turned out,
he bought Morokanyana's property, Goschen 101, in 1916, probably in the
wake of the latter's bankruptcy. Morokanyana had a reputation for living
beyond his means: he was, for example, the first black owner of a motorcar in
the district.[36] But the circumstances in which Morokanyana lost his land
suggest Van Riet's active collaboration in his extravagance.

The extent and the nature of black landowners' indebtedness was an acute
public embarrassment for them, because their private interest in the possibility
of selling or leasing their land to whites was in conflict with the tenor of the
advice which they otherwise urged upon the government—to extend the land
available for African purchase or occupation, and to protect it from alienation
to whites. Plaatje was indignant that Beaumont published in 1916 a 'list of
mortgaged native-owned farms in the Thaba Nchu district'.[37] But the grounds
of his indignation should be interpreted not simply in the terms that he alleged,
that publication was a violation of the privacy of individuals' financial affairs.
Rather, the issue was such a sensitive one because it brought into question the
credibility of the landowning class as spokesmen for the Barolong community
as a whole.

Several specific examples may be given here to illustrate the mortgage
indebtedness of leading landowners and their propensity to lease portions of
their land to whites. Reverend Joel Goronyane was the principal witness to the
Beaumont Commission on behalf of the Barolong. In 1916 his two properties,
Ramahutshe 47 and Vaalkop 66 (see Figure 1.3), were mortgaged respectively
for £1,200 and £850. Portions of both farms were leased to whites. Goronyane
was accompanied as a witness by John Mokitlane Nyokong, whose farms
Diphering 62 and Maseru 64 were jointly bonded for £2,250. Jeremiah Makgothi, ex-teacher, interpreter, farmer and nationalist politician, had bonds
totalling £6,000 outstanding on his farm, Thaba Patchoa 106, of which a 1,000
morgen portion was leased to his friend and near neighbour, Edward Worringham, a Land Settler and local JP (see Chapter 7). Israel Tlale Setlogelo, who
was half-brother to W.Z. Fenyang and whose circumstances are outlined in
detail below, owed £3,700 on his farm, Matlapaneng 455. Their mother,
Elizabeth Nkhabele Fenyang, had two of her three farms jointly mortgaged for
£2,600. Both were leased to whites.[38]

In these two ways, then, the black landowners' interests were vitally undermined by a segregation policy that threatened a collapse in the market value
of their property. But they felt inhibited from saying so in public. It
is not surprising, therefore, to find that it was white witnesses to the Beaumont Commission, such as Robertson the magistrate and Van Riet the
attorney, not the black landowners themselves, who expressed concern that

the implementation of the segregation policy would induce a collapse of precisely this kind. A deputation of leading black landowners met the Commission in November 1913 and presented a formal 'statement' of their demands. Within the terms of reference of the segregation policy, they asserted that, 'in order to save the Natives as a nation, land should be provided where they can develop in their own way under a capable and sympathetic administration'. The whole district of Thaba Nchu should be scheduled a 'native area' for this purpose. In submitting the formal statement, Joel Goronyane told the Commission that 'what has been read to you is the feeling of the people here. There are one or two things that require to be explained in addition'. One of these things was a request for government assistance for landowners whose property was heavily mortgaged. 'We know for certain that some natives will be pressed'. The other thing was a request that the Barolong people should be consulted over the setting aside of 'additional' lands.[39]

The first of these incidental requests was Goronyane's sole reference to the predicament of the landowners themselves. Otherwise, he insisted throughout his evidence, given at Bloemfontein on an earlier occasion, that proper provision of land should be made for black tenants under threat of eviction from white-owned farms. He carefully avoided answering the direct question: how had the Land Act affected him? 'My opinion is that the people should have been provided for. Personally it has not affected me. It is the people'. After three pages of vague and apparently deferential response to the question of how such provision could be made, Goronyane was finally goaded into claiming the recovery of the erstwhile government farms which had been granted to the Land Settlers.[40] Reading here between the lines, one may surmise that the restrained style of Goronyane's evidence had more to do with the implicit general threat to private property than with any personal inclination to defer to his white interlocutors. John Mokitlane Nyokong, for his part, was bold enough to recommend to the Commission that:

> the whole country should be divided by the main [railway] line right from Port Elizabeth up the whole way, and I think the people would be satisfied—the one to live on one side and the other on the other side.[41]

In practice, it appears that the threat to the private interests both of black landowners and white bond-holders was suspended by the failure of the Native Administration Bill of 1917 and the protracted wrangle which subsequently took place over the recommendations of the Local Land Committees of 1918.[42] For reasons elaborated in Chapter 4, these recommendations were not given legislative effect until the passage of the Trust and Land Act of 1936. Then, in the process of implementation of its provisions, the surviving black landowners were precisely impaled upon the horns of the same dilemma, the contradiction between their private interests and their public responsibilities. The implications of this contradiction are explored in detail in Chapter 4.

Meanwhile, in default of the government's commitment to purchase 'additional' land for African occupation, the Barolong landowners concentrated on the only way open to them of reconciling their private interests and their public responsibilities. They asserted the need for Africans to be allowed to buy land freely within the district as a whole. Since they knew as well as anyone that very few Africans could afford to buy land even if they were allowed by law to do so, this implied, in practice, a campaign that was even more narrowly defined: the repeal of the restrictive provisions of Chapter XXXIV of the OFS Law Book. Members of the Barolong landowning class repeatedly urged the government, to no avail, to abrogate what Plaatje called the 'oppressive chapter' that precluded transfer of black-owned land to Africans other than close blood relatives of the owner.

In due course, however, they evoked a sympathetic response from the Native Affairs Commission, which was constituted under the Native Affairs Act of 1920. Two members of the Commission, Dr A.W. Roberts and General L.A.S. Lemmer, visited the Thaba Nchu and Seliba reserves in December 1922, and made representations to the government on behalf of the leaders of the Barolong community. Three main issues were raised. Firstly, Africans should be able to buy land anywhere in the Thaba Nchu district. Secondly, it was vital for Africans to have access to a Land Bank on a similar basis to white farmers, especially 'at this time of crisis when merciless mortgagees are calling for their bonds for settlement'. Thirdly, there were specific grievances relating to over-crowding and taxation in the two reserves.[43]

In putting their case to the government, the Secretary of the Native Affairs Commission pointed out that African landownership in the Thaba Nchu district was being steadily whittled away. In 1916 there were seventy African-owned farms, comprising 82,677 morgen and bonded to the amount of £56,525. In 1922 there were ninety-one African-owned farms, comprising 73,715 morgen and bonded to the amount of £133,707. These figures indicate three clear trends: decreasing aggregate area, increasing formal subdivision of individual farms and rapidly deepening indebtedness.

> Slow but sure, here and there, every month practically—Native farms are put up for sale and only people of European descent can buy while Natives, quite capable and qualified in all other respects but that their skins are black, look on wistfully, marvelling at the awkwardness of the black man's lot in the Free State in spite of the much vaunted protection of the weaker races by the stronger according to the sacred principles of the western civilisation.[44]

The Smuts government agreed that *bona fide* Barolong—not Africans in general—should be able to buy and rent land in the Thaba Nchu district. It promised that the question of a Land Bank for Africans would receive consideration, and that the issues of over-crowding and taxation would be dealt with in separate legislation.[45] A draft bill to realise the first commitment was submitted in October 1923. Sol Plaatje returned from a period spent in

England, Canada and the United States just in time to lobby actively for the bill before Smuts' resignation as Prime Minister in April 1924 precipitated the dissolution of parliament and a general election. The Moroka Ward Land Relief Act was finally passed by the Hertzog government in September 1924.[46]

Strikingly, the Act fell short of the official commitment to allow Africans to buy and rent land in the Thaba Nchu district. It was phrased in terms of the right to sell and not the right to buy. Thus it allowed African landowners in the district to sell or lease land to *bona fide* Barolong, who would be approved as such by a local committee appointed for the purpose of vetting prospective purchasers or lessees.[47] The reason for this limitation was presumably to avoid prejudging the final determination of the 'released' areas, and in the meantime to retain administrative discretion over what land transactions were allowed. A policy decision had already been taken that the 'released' areas defined by the Local Land Committee of 1918 should be recognised administratively from 1922 as areas within which Africans could buy or rent land.[48] This decision rendered the restrictive provisions of Chapter XXXIV administratively anomalous as well as grossly inequitable. In retrospect it appears that, while the central bureaucracy in Pretoria remained impervious for years to the gross inequity, it moved relatively quickly to resolve the administrative anomaly. The resolution was only partial, however: it still left thoroughly uncertain the status of black-owned land which fell outside the 'released areas'. Within the terms of the Moroka Ward Land Relief Act, such land could now, apparently, be legally sold to other Africans. But administrative discretion to approve market transactions between Africans did not extend outside the 'released areas' themselves. While existing titles were not threatened, there remained some doubt whether they could be freely disposed to other Africans.

For several reasons, therefore, the Moroka Ward Land Relief Act itself afforded only very marginal relief. In the first place, it was narrowly conceived in terms of the right of African landowners to sell or otherwise transmit land to other Africans, not in terms of the right of Africans to buy land. Thus it did afford relief in the somewhat esoteric case of the Setlogelo nephews whose circumstances are described in detail below. In the second place, it was administratively pre-empted, in respect of the 'released' areas, by a policy decision taken two years earlier to allow Africans to acquire land in those areas. This made possible in principle investment in land from outside the district by members of the Barolong diaspora who had sufficient means to do so. Local white officials and established Barolong landowners at Thaba Nchu, however, had no wish to facilitate purchase by Barolong from outside the district who were identified as supporters of Chief Samuel. No doubt, in view of the 'commotion' at Matsiloje and Bloemfontein which arose in 1924 out of a renewed effort by those supporters to recover land at Thaba Nchu, and which was described in the previous section, the consultative committee appointed in terms of the Land Relief Act would not exercise its discretion on their behalf.

In the third place, irrespective of such discretion, hardly any Africans, from inside or outside the district, could in practice take advantage of the new local land market which the administrative decision of 1922 and the Relief Act of 1924 nominally opened up.

Indeed, the only local African who bought land from time to time over the next two decades was Dr James Sebe Moroka. He had invested in a long and expensive education in Scotland on the strength of his ownership of a half-share of the farm Victoria 126, which he had inherited from his grandmother Ketimetse, who was Tshipinare's sixth wife. The farm was leased to and managed by P.F.R. Steytler, who lent him a substantial sum of money for his medical training.[49] On his return from Edinburgh in 1918, at the age of 26, Dr Moroka established his own medical practice in Thaba Nchu, which launched him on a trajectory of private accumulation and made him the wealthiest African in the district. Giving evidence to the Native Economic Commission in 1931, Dr Moroka recalled his experience of the earlier obstacles to freedom of purchase. In one case, he was able to buy despite the statutory restriction of Chapter XXXIV of the OFS Law Book. In another case, after the repeal of the 'oppressive chapter', he was unable to buy because Pretoria refused to exercise administrative discretion in his favour.

In 1919, he wanted to buy his uncle Morokanyana Moroka's small farm, Brereton 180. This property was a one-third portion of Mooipan 324, which itself comprised three-sixteenths of Egypt 107 and had been inherited jointly by the children of Tshipinare's sixth wife, Ketimetse (see Figures 1.3 and 1.5). He was only able to buy Morokanyana's portion by arranging separate consecutive transactions through his mother Maggie Moroka, Morokanyana's elder sister, as a result of which he had to pay double transfer duty.

Nearly ten years later, in 1928, Dr Moroka wanted to buy another one-third portion, Mooipan 324 (rest), which belonged to his cousin, Alfred Benjamin Moroka. The problem was that this farm had already been sold to a neighbouring white farmer, Dr Ernest Clement Sephton Daniel, who was well known in the district as a son of the missionary John Daniel and was himself a long-time medical practitioner at Thaba Nchu. Dr Moroka had his own strings to pull, however. He appealed to the assistant magistrate, Coen Steytler, the son of his old benefactor and a 'great friend', to recommend that the government should not approve the sale. Dr Moroka argued that he should be given preference in securing possession of the farm, on the grounds that it had been part of the family lands for a long time. He also offered £12 per morgen against Daniel's £10 per morgen. Steytler did intervene on his behalf, and Dr Moroka went himself to Pretoria to see the responsible Ministers, as well as writing to the Prime Minister, General Hertzog. All to no avail. Dr Moroka learned a lesson from that experience: that it was 'not the intention of the Government to do anything to help us Natives'.[50] Both these farms, it may be noted, lay outside the 'released' areas.

## ONE ESTATE DISMEMBERED: THE SETLOGELO SAGA

Dr Moroka's shrewdly acquisitive land deals were entirely exceptional. The common pattern, as is evident from the figures cited above, was one in which family estates were more or less rapidly diminished in size, progressively subdivided on transmission to the next generation, and increasingly burdened with mortgage debt, so that portions had to be sold off from time to time to appease creditors. This very common pattern is illustrated here in detail through an account of what happened to the Setlogelo family lands in the north-east of the district from the 1910s to the late 1930s. At the beginning of this period, the family estate of two adjacent farms was still intact as an integral property. By the end of 1938, only small fragments were still owned by members of the Setlogelo family (see Figure 3.3). The whole of the rest of the original estate belonged to the South African Native Trust.[51]

Despite the emphasis here on the dismemberment of the family estate in the 'second generation', this is not in any simple sense a story of the decline of the original African landowning elite. On the one hand, rapid demographic expansion was inevitably accompanied by multiple subdivision and gradual loss of family lands. This was offset only to a small degree by consolidation of property arising out of marriages within the landowning class. Thus family antagonisms intensified as the members of the next generation found themselves at odds over dwindling material resources. On the other hand, many of the landowning elite educated their sons and daughters on the strength of the financial liquidity, transient and deceptive as it was in many ways, that they derived from bonding their landed property. Their sons and daughters took their place in due course in the ranks of the modern African elite, a process of socio-economic transformation which is illustrated in some detail in Chapter 5. I anticipate that argument here by observing that out of the ruins of the landowning class emerged the bureaucratic, professional and commercial class that dominated the (new) Thaba Nchu district (Bophuthatswana) in the 1980s. The Setlogelos, perhaps, especially epitomise this process of socio-economic transformation. The rooting in the district of the first generation was strangely haphazard, as will be seen. The second generation lost most of the family land in the manner described below. But differential access to educational opportunities, and a series of suitable marital alliances, made many members of the third and fourth generations highly influential in the affairs of this fragment of Bantustan.

Tshipinare had come to Thaba Nchu as a boy in 1833 with his mother, Nkhabele, and the other Barolong refugees. He had an elder brother, Setlogelo, who had previously been captured by the Matebele and of whom nothing more was heard for over three decades. In 1868, however, a man arrived at Thaba Nchu who claimed to be Tshipinare's elder brother. According to William Crisp, the Anglican missionary, this man gave:

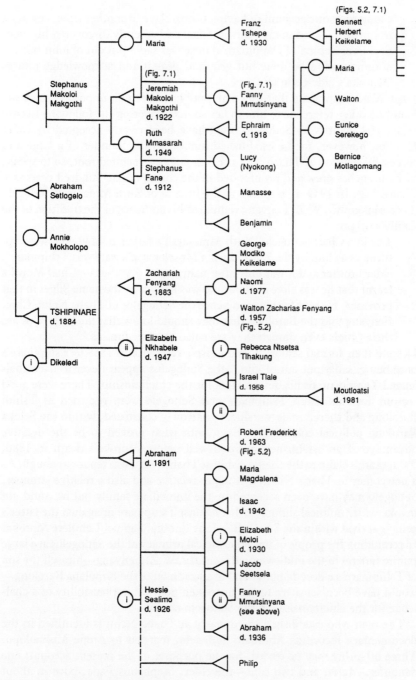

*Figure 3.2* Partial Setlogelo genealogy.

a long romantic account of having been a slave to another tribe—escaped from them—lived many years in Natal and recently discovered his identity. Poor Sepina's [Tshipinare's] nose was sadly put out of joint but . . . nothing was to be done but grin and bear it and acknowledge him as 'Moroka's eldest son'.[52]

Janet Wales comments that this man may have been an imposter, since she found no other reference to him in her sources covering the following twenty years. His identity as Setlogelo must have been clearly accepted by Chief Moroka, however, for he established himself as the founder of a large and successful dynasty at Thaba Nchu. From one transplanted root, so to speak, many branches grew and proliferated in the course of one hundred years (see Figure 3.2). In 1949, in a speech at the funeral of Ruth Mmasarah Setlogelo (born Makgothi), W.Z. Fenyang reminded his audience of the tradition of the family's origin:

The late Chief Setlogelo [Ruth Mmasarah's father-in-law] who was captured as a child by the Zulus during Moselekatse's wars was Tshipinare's elder brother and it was only after many years that the late Chief Moroka learnt that he was alive in Natal and was known by the name Silges in that province. He sent for him and hence the Setlogelos in Thaba Nchu. Chief Fenyang told the Barolong that they should know that the Setlogelos are their Chiefs even though they are ruled by their juniors.[53]

Despite their formal seniority, and Crisp's reference in 1868 to Tshipinare's nose being 'sadly put out of joint', the Setlogelos appear never to have challenged Tshipinare or his descendants for the chieftainship. There were good reasons for this. Both Tshipinare and Setlogelo were regarded as Tshidi Barolong and therefore as 'outsiders', narrowly construed, within the Seleka Barolong political community. Even with what proved to be the decisive advantage of an established position well before Moroka's death in 1880, Tshipinare's claim to the chieftainship at Thaba Nchu was tenuous enough. As a newcomer to Thaba Nchu, a stranger relative and also a relative stranger, Setlogelo may have been accepted by the immediate family but he could not invoke wider political support either against Tshipinare or against the latter's principal rival within the Seleka Barolong lineage, Samuel Lehulere Moroka. In reminding the people of the genealogical primacy of the Setlogelos at a large public funeral in the mid-twentieth century, W.Z. Fenyang—himself the son of Tshipinare's eldest daughter and of a headman of the Rapulana Barolong— would have been sensitive to the unspoken political implausibility of a challenge for the chieftainship by the Setlogelo family.

The man who established the dynasty at Thaba Nchu is identified in the documentary record as Abraham Setlogelo, married to Annie Mokholopo. Three offspring may be traced, for the purposes of the present account: one daughter, Maria; and two sons—the elder, Stephanus Fane, born in about 1848, and the younger, Abraham, born in about 1852 (see Figure 3.2). Their father must have been dead by 1885, for he does not appear as a beneficiary of the Gregorowski land dispositions made in that year, after annexation in 1884 (see Chapter 1). Stephanus Setlogelo claimed the farms Mensvretersberg 51, Lokoala 53, Mount Pleasant 54 and Somerset 55 (see Figure 1.3). Tshipinare had taken these lands from Monyake, son of the Bataung chief Moletsane, in 1880 after Monyake had joined Samuel's rebels against him, and granted them to Stephanus Setlogelo.[54] But this claim was rejected by the Siebert Commission, probably on the spurious grounds that surveyor Bourdillon could not identify the man for whom he had surveyed the farms in question. Instead, Abraham Setlogelo was granted title to the two farms of Moroto 68 and Somerset 55; while Mensvretersberg 51, Lokoala 53 and Mount Pleasant 54 became government farms. Although it appears that Stephanus Setlogelo's implicit right to Somerset 55 was recognised within the family, this quirk of judicial arbitration profoundly affected the fortunes and misfortunes of the respective descendants of Stephanus and Abraham.

Stephanus Setlogelo married Ruth Makgothi, eldest daughter of Stephanus Makoloi Makgothi, who owned the farm Goede Hoop 70. As recorded in Chapter 1, Stephanus Makoloi had remained loyal to Tshipinare while his brother Johannes, a Methodist preacher and evangelist, had sided with Samuel in 1880 and then left Thaba Nchu in disgrace. Stephanus and Ruth Setlogelo had four children: Ephraim, Lucy, Manasse and Benjamin. Abraham Setlogelo was briefly polygynous. His first wife was Hessie Sealimo, by whom he had a daughter, Maria Magdalena, and three surviving sons, Isaac, Jacob Seetsela and Abraham, the last of whom was born in 1892 after his father's death. Abraham's second wife was Elizabeth Nkhabele Fenyang, Tshipinare's eldest daughter and his own first cousin, whom he married after the death of her husband Zachariah in 1883. By her, Abraham had two sons, Israel Tlale and Robert Frederick 'Tabanie' (Tawana). Elizabeth Nkhabele maintained her own domestic establishment at the farm Rietfontein 119, in the south of the district, which was registered in her name. She had two other children: the elder was Walton Zacharias Fenyang, the pillar of the political establishment at Thaba Nchu throughout the first half of the twentieth century; the younger was Naomi, who was married in due course to George Modiko Keikelame of the neighbouring farm Brandkop 78. Abraham Setlogelo died in 1891 at the age of 39, to be long survived by both his widows, Hessie Sealimo dying in 1926 and Elizabeth Nkhabele in 1947. These genealogical intricacies are shown in Figure 3.2.

Shortly before Abraham's death, in 1890, Abraham and Hessie Setlogelo made a joint will. Under the terms of this will, the farm Moroto 68 was to pass in unequal shares of 2,000 morgen to their eldest son, Isaac, and 1,655 morgen to Abraham's elder son by Elizabeth Nkhabele, Israel Tlale. Transfer of these portions of Moroto was subject to the right of free residence for the respective full siblings of the heirs. The farm Somerset 55, which adjoined Moroto 68, and part of which lay on the steep ridge of the Mensvretersberg, was to pass in equal shares to Ephraim Setlogelo, eldest son of Stephanus, and to Franz Tshepe Setlogelo, a son of Abraham and Stephanus Setlogelo's sister Maria. The disposition of Somerset 55 was subject to a right of usufruct in favour of the surviving spouse and the right of free residence for all the children of Stephanus Setlogelo.

Moroto 68 was not formally divided according to the provisions of the will until 1911, when the two heirs Isaac and Israel had come of age (see Figure 3.3). Somerset 55, however, could not be formally transferred at all to Abraham Setlogelo's nephews Ephraim and Franz, because of the restriction in Chapter XXXIV of the OFS Law Book which precluded transfer to an African other than an immediate blood relation, as discussed in the preceding section of this chapter. Chapter XXXIV was narrowly interpreted in practice to mean a sibling or a child only, and it had been rigorously enforced by the ORC administration.

In 1910, this restriction was the subject of a direct appeal by Sol Plaatje to the newly appointed Minister of Native Affairs in the Union Government, Henry Burton. Plaatje was in a unique position. He knew the leading Barolong families at Thaba Nchu, and was a particular friend, as we have seen, of W.Z. Fenyang; his new newspaper, *Tsala ea Becoana*, was funded by a syndicate which included Fenyang, John Mokitlane Nyokong, Jeremiah Makgothi, Moses Masisi and Joel Goronyane. He had also known Henry Burton for many years, from his experience in the courts at Kimberley and Mafeking. Accordingly, Plaatje pressed Burton to introduce short amending legislation to abrogate the 'oppresssive chapter'. In this case, the effect would have been to allow transfer of title to Somerset 55 from the estate of Abraham Setlogelo to his two nephews, Ephraim and Franz.[55] It was the opening move in a long campaign, for relieving legislation was not passed until 1924, as we have seen above.

Meanwhile, a row was brewing within the Setlogelo family, which came to a head shortly before Stephanus Setlogelo's death in August 1912. It concerned the practical interpretation of Abraham and Hessie Setlogelo's joint will. From the evidence of estate papers and of attachments to transfer deeds, it is possible to reconstruct the reasons for the row along the following lines. Firstly, there was an apparent impasse over conflicting rights to Somerset 55. The farm was still registered in the name of the estate of Abraham Setlogelo. Hessie Sealimo, as his surviving widow and executrix of the will, had usufructuary rights. The children of Stephanus Setlogelo had the right of free residence and also a strong moral claim, though not a legal one, to the whole farm. The eldest of them, Ephraim, and the other nephew, Franz, were each entitled under the terms of the will to a half-share of the farm, but this entitlement could not be legally realised because of the statutory restriction described above. Under the circumstances, disputes were inevitable over the right to plough and reap on Somerset.

Secondly, in discharging her executive responsibilities, Hessie Sealimo appears to have distinguished in practice between the claims of her own children—Isaac, Jacob and Abraham—and those of their half-brothers, Israel Tlale and Robert. Thirdly, in 1872, when she was aged about seventeen, and before her marriage to Abraham Setlogelo, Hessie Sealimo had borne another son, Philip, who was not recognised as a beneficiary in Abraham and Hessie Setlogelo's joint will. It is clear that she wished, after Abraham's death, to incorporate Philip in the arrangements for the disposition of fixed property. Under the terms of the joint will, however, she was constrained from making any provision for him.

Thus the principal protagonists were Hessie Sealimo herself, her own sons Isaac and Philip (by different fathers), her co-wife's son Israel Tlale, her brother-in-law's son Ephraim and her husband's sister's son Franz Tshepe (see Figure 3.2). Conflicts over the estate reached the point where Hessie Sealimo took the family to court and an agreement had to be hammered out in Bloemfontein to resolve the problem. The terms of the agreement, signed on 9 July 1912, were that Hessie Sealimo would receive 1,500 morgen of land, consisting of 380 morgen cut from Somerset and the rest from Moroto, including the dwelling house on Moroto, in settlement of all her claims against the estate of her late husband and against other members of the family. She would also waive her rights of usufruct over the rest of Somerset. For their part, defendants Isaac, Israel Tlale, Franz and Ephraim would withdraw a Supreme Court action and waive their claims against Hessie Sealimo.[56]

This agreement clarified the respective rights of Hessie Sealimo and the defendants. Title to Somerset 55 could not be transferred into the names of Hessie Sealimo, Ephraim and Franz without a change in the law. Nevertheless, the farm was formally surveyed and subdivided, by agreement between the parties, and Ephraim and Franz occupied their respective portions. Relations between the Setlogelo cousins remained acrimonious, however. Ephraim and Isaac ploughed ground on Franz' portion, and Franz sought a court interdict against trespass by them. An interdict was refused on the grounds that Franz was prohibited by Chapter XXXIV from the necessary degree of possession implied by ownership of the land. This decision was overturned on appeal to the Supreme Court, which held that the legatees, while precluded from formal ownership, nevertheless had definite rights of possession that entitled Franz to protection against trespass by his cousins.[57]

All these proceedings proved expensive in legal costs as well as in frayed relationships. According to Sol Plaatje, both Ephraim and Franz were present at the meeting on 12 September 1913 at the Thaba Nchu racecourse, when the people were devastated by Edward Dower's remarks on the Land Act. Plaatje observed of Ephraim and Franz' predicament that:

their numerous representations to the Union authorities have only met with promises, while lawyers have taken advantage of the hitch to mulct them in more money than the land is worth. The best legal advice they have received is that they should sell their inheritances to white men.[58] Plaatje was clearly commenting on the spirit rather than the letter of that advice. Since the two men could not receive transfer of the land into their own names, it followed that they could not sell the titles to anyone.

The absurdity of the legal quagmire in which they found themselves was highlighted by Ephraim's own death in November 1918, at the age of 30. His widow, Fanny Mmutsinyana Setlogelo, was anxious to resolve the difficulties over Somerset on behalf of herself and her four minor children. This provoked another expensive counsel's opinion. On the one hand, as established in *Setlogelo v. Setlogelo* (1914), the two legatees had definite rights of possession of their respective portions of the farm, including those of occupation and usufruct, as against any other person who attempted to assert such rights. Counsel's opinion favoured a narrow and literal interpretation, for example, of the right of free residence, which in the case of Somerset 55 vested in the surviving children of Stephanus Setlogelo. Free residence should not imply any right to carry on farming operations, and therefore barely qualified the rights of possession vested in the legatees. On the other hand, the legatees did not have rights of formal ownership, and could not compel sale by Hessie Sealimo, as executrix of the joint will, in order to derive benefit by liquidation of the estate.

Further, it was not feasible for the restriction of Chapter XXXIV to be overcome by the expedient of indirect transfer from the estate of Abraham Setlogelo to his respective siblings and thence to the two nephews. The first part of such a transaction would be contrary to the terms of the will. The only alternative would be a public sale to the best advantage. In that case, however, Franz's mother and the estate of Stephanus Setlogelo would be required to compete with other potential purchasers; and, if successful, Ephraim and Franz would have to pay the market price of the land in order to receive what had been intended as a free bequest. If, instead, fictional payments were recorded between the three parties to the transaction, then no *bona fide* sales would have taken place.[59]

It was only after the passage of the Moroka Ward Land Relief Act of 1924 that title to specified subdivisions of Somerset 55 could be transferred to Ephraim's estate and to Franz Tshepe. Hessie Sealimo, meanwhile, had made a will of her own in respect of the fixed property which would be registered in her name as a result of the implementation of the 1912 agreement. Her rights in Somerset 55 were willed to her son Philip Setlogelo, who had assumed her late husband's family name but was not, under the terms of the joint will, entitled to inherit any of his land. Her rights in Moroto 68 were willed to the two other sons, Jacob Seetsela and Abraham, who had not received land in their own right. Thus, shortly before Hessie Sealimo's death in June 1926, a division of Isaac Setlogelo's 2,000 morgen portion of Moroto 68 took place, by which he

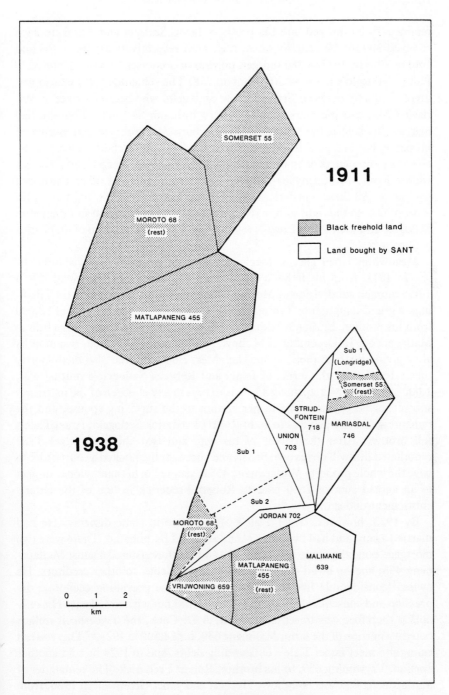

*Figure 3.3*  The disintegration of the Setlogelo family estate.

retained 1,400 morgen and his brothers Jacob Seetsela and Abraham each received 300 morgen subdivisions, registered respectively as Union 703 and Jordan 702. In 1927, a 380 morgen portion of Somerset 55 was registered in Philip Setlogelo's name as Strydfontein 718. The remainder of the farm was divided equally between Franz Tshepe Setlogelo, who became owner of Mariasdal 746, and the heirs in the estate of Ephraim Setlogelo. Ephraim had married his cousin Fanny Mmutsinyana (born Makgothi) in community of property, but had died intestate, so that his four minor children were registered as joint owners of an undivided half-share of Somerset 55 (rest), and his widow Fanny Mmutsinyana received in her own right the other undivided half-share. All these transfers, with the exception of that of Strydfontein 718, were subject to the right of free residence in favour of Manasse and Benjamin Setlogelo and their sister Lucy Nyokong, the surviving children of Stephanus Setlogelo.[60]

Meanwhile, Israel Tlale Setlogelo had experienced severe financial difficulties. In 1911, from his father's estate, he had inherited Matlapaneng 455, a 1,655 morgen subdivision of Moroto 68. He married Rebecca Ntsetsa Tlhakung, a grand-daughter of Tshipinare. In 1913 he borrowed the sum of £2,600 from his mother, Elizabeth Nkhabele Fenyang, on the strength of his title to Matlapaneng. In December 1914, however, his young wife died, two months after giving birth to their second daughter. Both children also died shortly thereafter. Under the terms of Israel and Rebecca Setlogelo's mutual will, 1,000 morgen of Matlapaneng 455 was to pass to any children of the marriage, subject to the payment of £48 per annum to the surviving spouse, and the remaining 655 morgen was to go to Robert Frederick Setlogelo, Israel Tlale's full brother. After the deaths of his wife and two children, Israel Tlale repudiated this will on his own behalf and successfully invoked a court order to have the whole property Matlapaneng 455 registered in his name alone, subject to an agreed sum of £660 paid to Robert Frederick in lieu of the latter's entitlement under the will.[61]

By 1922, however, Israel Tlale's affairs were in some disarray. He had married again, and had two sons, Moutloatsi and Bathobatho. There were two mortgage bonds, respectively of £2,500 and £600, registered against Matlapaneng 455; and he owed about £1,100 in 'loose debts' to other creditors. He owned 'considerable livestock' but, owing to the prevailing economic depression and consequent slump in prices, he did not wish to sell any. His only option therefore was to sell some land. A.D. Cock, the Tweespruit miller, bought a portion of the farm, Malimane 639, for £2,500 in 1923.[62] This was not enough to meet Israel Tlale's outstanding debts, and in 1924 he sold another portion, Vrywoning 659, to his brother, Robert Frederick. The remainder of Matlapaneng 455 was bought by Herbert and Janet Greenwell in 1926, from whom, in turn, Robert Frederick Setlogelo bought it back in 1931 when they went bankrupt. By the late 1920s, then, Israel Tlale had entirely lost his landed property in this part of the district.

There are hints in the documentary evidence that, at this time, Israel Tlale took on the role of predator within the wider family. He was well equipped to do this through his earlier official employment as court interpreter, which placed him on familiar terms with the local law agents and attorneys. After the division of his mother's estate in 1929, the two minor sons of his second marriage, Moutloatsi and Bathobatho, directly inherited a 300 morgen portion of Rietfontein 119 (Melacwana 774), a disposition which almost certainly reflected a view on the part of his mother's family as to Israel Tlale's irresponsibility both as a landowner and as a parent. Nevertheless, Israel Tlale was able to mortgage this property in 1935 in his capacity as his sons' 'father and natural guardian'; it was also bonded in 1940 by W.Z. Fenyang in his capacity as administrator of their affairs. This is *prima facie* evidence of another family dispute and of legal steps taken by their mother to protect the interests of her sons against the depradations of their father.[63]

Otherwise, Israel Tlale allegedly influenced Fanny Mmutsinyana to send her eldest son, Walton, to school in Edinburgh, Scotland, in 1928. It was of course necessary to mortgage her landed property more heavily for this purpose. Her three farms were already substantially burdened with mortgage debt (see Chapter 7). 'Fanny was very rich', her younger sister Blanche recalled, 'but she was not careful enough. She signed blank papers'. Israel Tlale and his attorney, Blanche Tsimatsima implied, may have taken advantage of Fanny's 'carelessness' to drive her into insolvency.[64] Fanny Mmutsinyana married her first husband's cousin, Jacob Seetsela Setlogelo, shortly after the death of his wife in 1930. Both were heavily in debt and, married out of community of property, Fanny Mmutsinyana was taken to court by the South African Association and forced to sell her undivided half-share of Somerset 55 (rest) in 1931 at public auction. It was bought by John Henry Faustmann, the Thaba Nchu attorney, for £340. The property was divided accordingly: Faustmann's share (Longridge, Sub 1) consisted largely of a part of the Mensvretersberg itself; the other half-share of Somerset 55 (rest) was registered in the names of each of Fanny Mmutsinyana's minor children, each title being encumbered with a bond. Being unable to meet the interest payments, the children were threatened with legal proceedings by the bond-holders. They were only rescued by the direct intervention of Bennett Herbert Keikelame, a son of W.Z. Fenyang's sister Naomi. He had married Fanny Mmutsinyana's eldest daughter, Maria; he bought the shares of her three younger siblings and the creditors were paid off in 1939.

What happened to the other subdivisions of the original farm Somerset 55, and to the remainder of Moroto 68 (see Figure 3.3)? Franz Tshepe died in 1930, and his widow Emily sold Mariasdal 746 to Faustmann in 1934. In the same year Philip Setlogelo sold Strydfontein 718 to Joseph Thoto Masisi, one of Moses Masisi's sons. Jacob Seetsela Setlogelo sold Union 703 in 1933 to Cecil Rayner Morgan, a local land speculator and stock farmer. Abraham Setlogelo died in 1936 and his property Jordan 702 was sold to the South African Native Trust (SANT) in 1938, together with Union 703 by Morgan, Strydfontein 718 by Masisi and Mariasdal 746 and Somerset Sub 1 (Longridge) by Faustmann.

Israel Tlale's half-brother, Isaac Setlogelo, had inherited Moroto 68 (rest). By the end of 1930 his affairs also were in some disarray. There were three mortgage bonds registered against the farm: £1,500 in favour of Constance Adeline Legge; and two bonds of £1,000 each in favour of J.H. Faustmann. In an application for a new bond in March 1931, his attorneys Faustmann and Paver had to justify his expenditure in order to obtain official sanction of this bond, for £400 in favour, as it happened, of J.H. Faustmann. Isaac Setlogelo had to have his farmhouse repaired; he spent £40 on reapers and other labour in December 1930; £80 interest was due by 9 February 1931 on existing bonds; he needed £20.13s.3d. for threshing of wheat on 13 February; and £30 for 'general farming expenses' on 21 February. By 1933 no fewer than five mortgage bonds had to be serviced and repaid, three of which were held by Faustmann himself, and Isaac had no prospect of meeting his liabilities. He was forced to sell the greater part of the remainder of Moroto 68, Sub 1 (Tawana, 800 morgen) to Faustmann in 1934, who in turn sold to the SANT in 1938. Isaac had to sell another portion, Sub 2 (375 morgen), directly to the SANT in 1938, so that there remained only a small portion of the original farm (225 morgen) for his five children. Isaac Setlogelo then retired to his wife's family farm, Bloemspruit 72, in the west of the district, where he died in 1942. The old dwelling house on Moroto was taken over by the SANT and used as a Methodist school for the children of the new Trust settlement on the farm. It was destroyed by a cyclone in 1943.[65]

### DISTRICT IN DEPRESSION: A CROSS EXAMINATION

In the previous section I have explored the evidence of the dissolution of one landed estate over a period of nearly three decades. In the final section of this chapter I draw on evidence submitted to the Native Economic Commission (NEC) of 1930–32 in order to examine conditions across the district in the depths of the great depression. A succinctly grim picture of impoverishment, over-crowding, land loss and social stagnation was drawn by the advocate F.A.W. Lucas, the most consistently liberal member of the Commission, in his long, dissenting 'addendum' to the main report. He relied on the evidence of three witnesses in particular: Dr J.S. Moroka and W.Z. Fenyang, both of whom have already been sufficiently introduced; and Reverend F.E. Gilks, minister of the Anglican church. Of the three Africans who appeared before the Commission at Thaba Nchu on 20 February 1931, Dr Moroka gave the most substantial evidence; Fenyang insisted on the need for more land in the

Thaba Nchu district; while Job Sedite Pule, a prominent stock-owner from the Seliba reserve, made a brief statement about over-crowding in Seliba. He was unable to contribute more because 'I came here and I have been here the whole day and there was only one language spoken [English] and that is a language which I do not understand'.[66] Two prominent members of the local white elite also gave evidence [in Afrikaans]: Gideon Jacobus Van Riet, attorney, farmer and land speculator; and his brother-in-law, Johannes Marthinus De Wet.

The evidence given to the NEC ranges widely, over poor conditions on farms, over-crowding in the reserves, the alleged inefficiency of African agriculture, the inadequacy of educational provision, official neglect and discrimination, the insidious influence of alcohol, the breakdown of 'tribal' morality and the prevalence of syphilis. The witnesses were repeatedly distracted by the almost wilful mystifications of some members of the Commission. In raising questions about addiction to customs such as witchcraft, bridewealth, chieftainship and ritual slaughter, they were groping for simple and reductionist explanations of the complex and inter-related crises which the NEC was appointed to investigate: those of rapid urbanisation, apparently irreversible de-tribalisation and rural immiseration.

Van Riet described conditions on his property of 2,600 morgen to the east of Tweespruit. It comprised the farm Goschen 101, which he had bought from Dr Moroka's maternal uncle, Morokanyana Moroka, in 1916, and much smaller adjoining portions of other farms which he had variously acquired through the 1920s. At the time he gave evidence to the NEC, Van Riet had his own law practice in Thaba Nchu but he was living at the spacious family mansion which he had built on the ridge at Goschen and which commands a fine view sweeping northwards over the lands laid out below it. He had sixteen African families on the farm, supplying thirty-two labourers. They worked throughout the year—except for fifteen days' leave—for a cash wage of 15s. to £1.5s. per month, depending on competence and reliability; and in addition they were each given half a bag of mealie meal per month. Collectively they had access to 1,000 morgen of grazing land and 100 morgen for their own cultivation. He estimated their holdings of large livestock were about forty cattle and fourteen horses. Time off during the ploughing season was allowed for the men to plough their own lands, using Van Riet's ploughs. They sowed mainly wheat, but also maize and pumpkins.[67]

Two members of the Commission—the chairman John Holloway and A.M. Mostert—pressed Van Riet to elaborate on the cost to the farmer of keeping labour on that basis. In addition to the monthly wage and the cost of the food in kind, there was the opportunity cost of alternative use of the land, which Van Riet reckoned as 6s.8d. per morgen per year, averaged out for grazing and arable land. The drift of the question seemed to be to suggest that it would be much more economical to lease the land in question, by comparison with an inefficient system of labour tenancy whose hidden costs to the farmer were much greater than the nominal cost of wages in cash and kind. Interestingly, Van Riet resisted the comparison, on the grounds that 'to get satisfaction it's necessary to do what I do here. I must give them grazing, and also land for themselves to work. It is for me necessary in order to get the trust and service of my people'. He implicitly denied that the contract was one of labour tenancy, by stressing:

> No, we don't give land in payment. That's not at all the custom. We pay them in money, and then they get certain privileges in addition to that. I pay no attention to what they cultivate and I don't count their animals.

Nevertheless, a limit was imposed on the quantity and kind of livestock allowed. Specifically, for the protection of his own breeding stock, Van Riet did not allow Africans on his farm to keep bulls.[68]

Van Riet's brother-in-law, Johannes Marthinus De Wet, who owned Seroalo 111, to the west of the Thaba Nchu reserve, explained to the NEC that white farmers in the western part of the district were unable to make so much land available to Africans as farmers in the eastern part, but it was still necessary to allow people to keep cattle, in order to maintain stability on the farm:

> If he's got nothing, then we look on him as a bird on a branch. Today he's here, tomorrow he's away. He travels around all over and doesn't stay on one place long. But if he's got something, then he stays. I've got people on my farm who've been with me for fifteen years, and they're completely satisfied to stay.[69]

Otherwise, conditions were similar, with cash wages being about £1 a month. De Wet added that he allowed people to go on leave to Bloemfontein for three or four months in the year to earn more wages. His African families kept sheep on the farm, which were subject to regular dipping. They could also get time off for sheep-shearing elsewhere or in the height of the potato season as casual day labour. It was common to operate a 'sick fund', such that when an animal died on the farm there was strict rotation of individuals' entitlement to eat some and to sell some of the meat; 15s. was taken off the proceeds of any sale and put into the fund, to pay for any medical expenses arising.[70]

The magistrate estimated that wages prevalent on white farms at this time ranged between 10s. and 25s. per month. Desertions were frequent, although an offence under the Master and Servants' Act, and this was attributable to the fact that labourers were often 'very poorly paid and fed'. 'Male labourers usually receive grazing for a number of stock and in some cases a small piece of land for cultivation'.[71] These arrangements, as elaborated by Van Riet and others, appear to fall between labour tenancy in the traditional sense—as a transaction in which labour is given in return for access to land—and full-time wage labour. Farm workers were paid in cash throughout the year; but the wages in cash and kind were quite insufficient for a livelihood and it was necessary to provide grazing and arable land in order to retain a stable work force. In this part of the eastern OFS, it appears, the transition to wage labour was more 'advanced' than in many other regions of the country such as the Transvaal, northern Natal and the northern OFS. White farmers were squeezed by declining market prices, escalating mortgage debt and the high opportunity cost of tenants' grazing and arable land. Black tenants were squeezed by stagnating real wages, intensified demands for family labour and inexorable encroachment on their allocations of grazing and arable land. As Helen Bradford has expressed it, 'Proletarianization thus hung like the sword of Damocles over the bulk of white masters and black servants alike, infusing their struggle with considerable hatred and despair'.[72]

Two comparisons recur in the evidence from Thaba Nchu that was given to the NEC. One comparison was drawn with J.B. Lurie's labour arrangements on his property of 4,000 morgen south of Tweespruit. Lurie was the 'Potato King' of the district: his enterprise was described in 1928 in the pages of a farming journal as an outstanding example of progressive agriculture. His farming operations were conducted on a massive scale: 700 oxen, fifty-six ploughs, seventy cultivators and twenty-four harrows. 'On these farms he has three large locations as in his busy season he employs up to 600 natives'.[73] Despite the fact that Lurie refused to allow African-owned cattle on his farms, Africans were attracted to work there both by the higher wages that he paid—up to 30s. or 35s. a month—and by the company of large numbers of their own people.

There was also another factor, which provoked disparaging comment from Dr Moroka in his evidence to the NEC. Most of Lurie's labourers were alleged to be women from Basutoland, more or less 'loose' in their marital and sexual commitments. Asked by the Commission why Lurie could obtain all the labour he wanted, despite not allowing people to keep stock on his land, Dr Moroka acknowledged that Lurie paid higher wages than generally applied in the district but laid more emphasis on the

> fact that, at Lurie's place, any Native can go there and get a wife any day he likes ... that is why Lurie has no difficulty ... When a woman goes to Lurie's place, she is never asked anything. She simply goes there and stays there and, as long as she can go and cart wheat or scoffle potatoes or reap mealies, no questions are ever asked of her.[74]

In these respects, no doubt, Lurie's was an exceptional place. It is also clear, from the testimony of many farm families displaced in the 1970s (see Chapter 6), that a significant influx of labour from Basutoland took place throughout the Conquered Territory and the Thaba Nchu district in the 1920s and the early 1930s. The latter period of severe drought offers a distinctive mnemonic reference point: it is recalled as the time of the Great Dust (*lerole leleholo*).

The other comparison was drawn with arrangements prevalent on African-owned farms. These lands were heavily over-stocked, the magistrate observed: 'in most cases the land is occupied by squatters who plough on the halves; there

are a few good Native farmers, but the majority simply have squatters'.[75] The
Reverend Gilks of the Anglican church described the standard of farming
generally as 'of a very low order': lands were seldom fenced or rotated,
fertilisers were not applied, and the seed used—mainly for maize, sorghum
and oats—was of an 'indifferent' class, with correspondingly poor yields.

> Almost without exception, Native farms suffer from too many so-called
> employees. The normal custom on these farms is the feudal system. Each
> employee gets grazing and a certain amount of land in lieu of payment and
> very few employees get a proper wage. Nearly all Native farms are
> overstocked with relations of the owner and employees with their cattle.
> In return for being allowed some land and grazing, these employees do a
> little work, but it is very little work indeed.[76]

In his evidence, G.J. Van Riet was also disparaging about the absence of thrift,
the failure to plan ahead or to plough deeply enough, and the consequent low
productivity. He commented, too, on what was obviously a fundamental
problem for black landowners: their inability to derive an economic rent in
cash or kind from the numerous residents on their land.[77]

Van Riet's own immediate neighbour to the north-west was John Mokitlane
Nyokong, who owned Maseru 64 and had also inherited Diphering 62 from his
half-sister, Phokoane Mokgobisi. The two farms together comprised just over
5,000 morgen and by the mid-1920s were jointly mortgaged for £10,000.
Nyokong could not meet his debts and, on Van Riet's advice, he sold several
portions of both farms in 1927 and 1928, amounting to two-fifths of the whole
property, in order to pay off the large bond. By comparison with other
members of the landed elite, Nyokong was a serious farmer, not merely a
landowner with 'squatters'. Shortly after the South African war, he had bought
a threshing machine for £1,000 but was prevented from using it except under
the supervision of a white engineer whom he could not afford to employ all the
year round. He was also a member of the Thaba Nchu syndicate which funded
Sol Plaatje's newspapers. But progressive agriculture required the displacement of an unproductive tenantry, which was incompatible with the broad
community obligations of the Barolong elite. In the period before his death in
August 1930 at the age of 85, Nyokong had 'between 70 and 80 families' on his
land. Van Riet was responsible for winding up the estate; he remarked in
February 1931 to the NEC that these families had 'lived there for a long time,
but the owner has always to help people, to get them out of difficulty. There's
always something wrong, and he must support them. He gets very little from
them'.[78]

This was the nub of the black landowners' dilemma. Most farms were more
or less heavily mortgaged. The money was used variously to invest in the
education of their sons and daughters or to consume, more or less conspicu-
ously, on a scale beyond their fragile earnings. The Reverend Gilks expressed
this trend in stark and pejorative terms: 'The trouble with them now is the

rising generation, who want motorcars and such things. . . '.[79] Few landowners invested in the capital resources that were necessary for them to engage directly and successfully in agriculture themselves. They therefore depended in part on their own off-farm income, professional or otherwise; in part on the variable and generally low returns from labour tenancy or share-cropping arrangements with Africans resident on their land; and many of them, in part, on leasing portions of their land to whites.

It was the last expedient on which they relied in order to secure a regular income from which to meet the mortgage interest payments. The magistrate reported to the NEC that no fewer than forty-three African-owned farms in the district were leased to whites. Curiously, in view of this figure, precisely forty-three 'landowners and members of the Barolong tribe' were sufficiently alarmed by one important implication of the official land segregation policy— that they would no longer be able to lease land to whites—that they signed an appeal to the Minister of Native Affairs in February 1930 not to implement this provision. Specifically, they made the point that 'the revenue derived from the leasing of such land to Natives will not cover the interest due on bonds or the costs of maintaining minor children'. For the next seven years, the Minister decided, they would continue to be allowed to lease to whites.[80]

This analysis reveals a double historical irony in the position of the surviving Barolong landowners. In the first place, as political spokesmen for the dispossessed, they argued that more land should be made available to Africans and then protected against alienation to whites. But the market value of their own farms depended precisely on the possibility of selling or leasing their land to whites. In the second place, strong social obligations towards their own relatives or towards other African tenants who were over-crowded on their land precluded the sanction of eviction and made the landowners' bargaining position very weak, so that they found it impossible in practice to exact an economic rent. This made it necessary for them to lease their land to whites, to that extent reducing the amount of land directly available to Africans.

The two reserves of Thaba Nchu and Seliba were also grossly over-crowded. 'There are so many landless natives today that the position is really alarming', W.Z. Fenyang told the NEC. 'We ask for more land because more than half the inhabitants of the reserves have no land'. For many years there had been a steady drift of people into the Thaba Nchu and Seliba reserves, despite the formal restriction of rights of residence and access to those who had a convincing claim, as followers of Chief Tshipinare, under the terms of President Brand's proclamation of 29 July 1884 (see Chapter 1). After the 1913 Land Act, in an attempt to relieve the distress of people evicted from white farms, the central government allowed temporary certificates of residence to be issued. Applications for these certificates had to be supported by the relevant reserve boards. Since their establishment in 1907, with limited local

administrative responsibilities, the reserve boards had been the only recognised form of local representation, albeit their members were nominated and
not elected.

Immigration into the two reserves continued, so that Sir William Beaumont
recognised in 1916 that Thaba Nchu and Seliba were the two most densely
populated reserve areas in the Union. The OFS Local Land Committee of 1918
endorsed this but claimed that 'almost half of the Natives found in the locations
have no right to be there', a view indignantly rejected by the Thaba Nchu
reserve board.[81] The disagreement, of course, was less about the numbers of
illegal residents than about the criteria that should be applied in practice to
regulate residence rights.

From 1918 the magistrate issued visiting passes to approved applicants,
which were renewable monthly and subject to the conditions that no livestock
should be introduced, homestead sites should not be fenced and arable land
should not be allotted to them. By November 1926, when the whole question
was officially investigated by the Native Affairs Commission, 290 such temporary certificates had been issued for the Thaba Nchu reserve and 215 for the
Seliba reserve. Holders approved by the reserve boards were then granted
permanent certificates, in an effort to rationalise prevalent insecurity, but the
government insisted on applying 'a most conservative attitude' with respect to
future admissions, in view of the acute congestion in the reserves. People
would only be admitted who could establish 'without any shadow of a doubt at
least a strong moral claim' under the terms of the 1884 Proclamation.[82]

Since 1927, many applicants had been turned down in circumstances of
hardship: for example, African landowners who had lost their farms and
looked to the reserves 'for an asylum'; the daughters of established residents
who had married outsiders with no residence rights; and 'squatters' evicted
from white farms who were often elderly and devoid of their own resources.
These last were particularly vulnerable, as prices for wool, maize, wheat and
potatoes collapsed in the late 1920s. As Dr Moroka expressed it:

> Things are getting very difficult for the farmers. Times are changing and
> the farmers in many instances cannot afford to keep on many Natives.
> Then the question arises what is to become of these Natives. The locations
> cannot keep them, the farmers are crying out and telling us that they have
> too many Natives and that they cannot keep them any longer. What is
> going to happen to these Natives? If no provision is made for them and no
> land is given to them, they will simply become criminals and they will
> roam all over the country causing endless trouble.[83]

Such hardships were compounded by the fact that the reserve boards required
a payment of 10s. per annum in respect of residence rights. If absent wage-
earners in Bloemfontein or Johannesburg or elsewhere failed to pay this sum
over a period of about ten years, they lost their entitlement. In many cases they
had been away for longer than ten years, without knowing that they had to

maintain their residence rights through regular payments to the board. Seeking ing then to return to Thaba Nchu, they were refused access to the reserves, to their distress and indignation. For this reason, in his evidence to the NEC, Dr Moroka advocated a policy of open admission to the reserves. With a secure home base there, people could go to town for wage employment with confidence that they would be able to return home and find their families in the reserves.[84]

In summary, people faced intolerable dilemmas, and a cycle of bitterness and resentment was the result. Many could no longer make a living within the district. Dispersed, therefore, to urban centres throughout the Union, they could find no security in town on account of the pass laws and the acute scarcity of urban housing. Simultaneously, under pressure of collapsing agricultural prices, African tenants or labourers were squeezed off white-owned farms which were themselves often mortgaged to the hilt. Urban wage labourers and redundant farm 'squatters' often belonged to the same families. Neither could readily find refuge in the reserves. These were the ingredients of a cauldron of discontent.

# 4

# STRUGGLES OVER LAND

We are fed up with the rule and administration of the government. We want nothing from them seeing they are against the taking over of the released areas from them. The land is ours and we are taking it . . .

The Barolong Progressive Association
1 February 1940
VAB, LTN 2/1, N1/16/5, Exhibit 'O'

In these troublous war times we are even more eager than usual to assist the government to maintain a spirit of contentedness and quiet. We are loath, sir, to evince any spirit of disgruntledness which might give unscrupulous persons occasion for pernicious propaganda . . .

The Thaba Nchu African Farmers' Association
10 July 1940
UWL, AD843, B101.19, Makgothi to Rheinallt Jones

The cauldron of discontent did not immediately boil over. Paradoxically, the embers beneath it were fanned into flame in the late 1930s by the state's belated effort to provide more land for Africans. Mainly because fragmentary patches of land survived in black ownership, the implementation of the 1936 Trust and Land Act in the Thaba Nchu district was immensely complex. The passage of the Act raised a series of fundamental questions. How much land, and whose, would be bought by the state for African occupation? How would such land be administered by the state agency concerned, the South African Native Trust? What were the implications for white farmers whose land fell within the shadow of prospective purchase by the Trust? What were the implications for black landowners, the value of whose farms was no longer protected by their potential sale to whites? How, in the circumstances, could the black elite plausibly represent the aspirations of landless people? What were the effective limits of popular struggle for access to Trust land?

After the 1913 Land Act, as shown in Chapter 3, white farmers in the OFS had vigorously resisted the extension by state purchase of land available for African occupation. When it eventually became clear, however, through the passage of the 1936 Act, that more land would be bought in this way, there ensued a discordant clamour to contrive the best advantage. Initially, some white landowners agitated to have their farms excised from the Released Areas scheduled under the Act. Later, having discovered the high prices being obtained for land sold to the South African Native Trust, the same farmers agitated to have their farms re-incorporated. Some succeeded in this endeavour, by skilful and unscrupulous manipulation of official contacts. Others failed.

Surviving black landowners, for their part, were critically undermined by the passage of the Act. Their lands already heavily mortgaged, they could not obtain new bonds in favour of whites; the Trust would not take over their existing bonds; and many were finally compelled to sell to the Trust. These sales reduced the amount of land the Trust had to buy from white landowners in order to fulfil the OFS Quota specified by the Act. Black landowners were therefore vulnerable to the charge of 'selling out' to the Trust in more than a literal sense. This fuelled the frustration of Africans both inside and outside the district who hoped to recover or to establish a foothold on the land. Accordingly, the first wave of land purchases by the Trust in 1938–9 opened up an opportunity for widespread and urgent mobilisation by a local populist movement, the Barolong Progressive Association (BPA). The BPA directed its campaign both against the local officials of the Native Affairs Department, who were responsible for administering access to Trust land; and against the Barolong political establishment, which had allegedly split and dispersed the community and betrayed the original tradition of open public access to land. Agitation over Trust land and renewal of the 'war of the chiefs' (*ntwa ya dikgosi*) were a potentially explosive combination, and the movement was harshly suppressed.

Thus the implementation of the 1936 Act exposed and sharpened diverse conflicts of interest: within the white farming community itself; between white and black landowners; within and between prominent Barolong families, whose members often belonged to opposing factions; and between white officialdom, which supported the incumbent chief at Thaba Nchu, and the disaffected heirs of the cause of Samuel Lehulere Moroka. These conflicts are explored in detail below. First, however, it will be helpful to give a brief account of the political background to the 1936 Act at the national level.

### SEGREGATION: SWAPPING THE VOTE FOR THE LAND?

The Beaumont Commission of 1916 had identified 11.16 million morgen throughout the Union as 'scheduled' (reserved) land within the terms of the 1913 Land Act, and 8.37 million morgen as 'additional' land to be 'released' for African occupation in due course.[1] Its recommendations in the latter respect were embodied in the Native Administration Bill of 1917, which fell victim to widespread protest from white farming interests. Five Local Land Committees were appointed to resolve the impasse. Their alternative recommendations, which likewise reflected the influence of the white farming lobby, cut the overall provision for areas to be 'released' for African occupation from 8.37 to 6.81 million morgen. The most drastic cuts, proportionally, were made in Natal, from 1.86 to 0.43 million morgen; and in the OFS, from 148,316 to 79,500 morgen.[2]

These revised proposals were also not implemented. They were broadly incorporated, however, in General Hertzog's Land Amendment Bill of 1926, one of the four 'Native Bills' whose tortuous passage through the Union parliament over the following decade marked the consolidation of segregation as official government policy. The four Bills were eventually reduced to two Acts passed in 1936: the Representation of Natives Act, which removed the Cape African franchise and introduced a complex and very limited form of indirect representation of Africans in the Senate; and the Native Trust and Land Act, which purported to make a 'final' settlement of the land question. These two key elements of segregation policy were closely linked, for a number of reasons that deserve elaboration.[3]

Firstly, in order to abolish the Cape African franchise, Hertzog needed broader political support than he could muster from the Nationalist/Labour coalition in parliament. On the one hand, Hertzog and other politicians derived considerable short-term electoral advantage from stoking white constituents' anxieties about the long-term endurance of white supremacy. They invoked absurd demographic projections of the 'swamping' of white voters within fifty years. Such anxieties were a striking feature of the *swart gevaar* ('black peril') election of 1929, and they were used to justify the removal of Africans from the common voters' roll. On the other hand, the non-racial qualified franchise in the Cape was constitutionally entrenched in the 1909 Act of Union, and could only be removed by a two-thirds majority in both Houses of Parliament. In order to tamper with the constitution in this way, Hertzog had to transcend his own parliamentary majority to achieve sufficient political support.

Hertzog therefore repeatedly insisted on linkage between the franchise issue and the land issue, so that he could substantiate his claim to arrive at a 'fair' resolution of the 'native question'. More land for many Africans was presented as a *quid pro quo* for the loss of a small minority's right to vote. Hertzog argued that withdrawal of the Cape African franchise could be, and would have to be, made palatable to Africans by offering alternative means of political representation and by fulfilling the state's commitment to make more land available to them. As it turned out, three of the four Bills, and Hertzog's insistence on linkage between them, were not palatable to the delegates to the fifth Native Conference which met in Pretoria in November 1926 to express African opinion on the government's proposals.[4] More important, as a political barrier to the achievement of Hertzog's objectives, was General Smuts' repeated prevarication over the 'Native Bills'. As leader of the opposition South African Party (SAP), Smuts strove to prevent his party from splitting over the 'native question'. Some SAP members from the Cape were dependent to a significant extent on African votes. Other SAP members from Natal were strongly committed to ending the Cape African franchise. Thus it took several years of complex manoeuvring through Select Committees, and some upheaval in white party politics, before the revised Bills were sufficiently palatable to the white parliament to pass into law.

The second reason for linkage was a substantive legal impediment to the implementation of segregation. The basis on which Cape Africans had acquired the right to vote was a property or income qualification. Since the 1913 Land Act formally prohibited the acquisition of land by Africans outside the areas 'scheduled' by Beaumont, it was held to interfere with the potential to qualify for voting rights in the Cape and was declared *ultra vires* in that province in 1917. So long as the Cape African franchise remained intact, therefore, numerically insignificant though it was, the segregation of land along racial lines could not be implemented in the largest province of South Africa.

Thirdly, the franchise and the land issues were closely related at the level of arguments about the political philosophy of white supremacy in South Africa. The gathering triumph of segregation implied the demise, as Saul Dubow has expressed it, of 'the universalist principles associated with mid-Victorian liberalism'.[5] The Victorian 'civilising mission' sought to promote individual property rights and, eventually, unitary citizenship on the basis of a responsible exercise of voting rights. Segregation meant a reversal of that historical tendency. It meant the erosion of any possibility, in principle, of political representation through a universal franchise. It meant drawing clear lines of demarcation on the map between 'white' and 'black' areas. It meant the assertion and protection of 'group rights' in place of individual advancement by education and merit, irrespective of race. It meant 'retribalisation', imposed 'from above' as an effort to discover and institutionalise the essential political, economic and social elements of a 'tribal' way of life, conceived as quite distinct from those of a 'civilised' way of life.

This polarisation emerged starkly out of the political conflicts over Hertzog's Bills, both inside and outside parliament. Thus George Heaton Nicholls, an SAP member and prominent segregationist from Natal, who was a prime architect of the revisions eventually incorporated in the two Acts passed in 1936, explained in 1935 that his notion of 'trusteeship' was the antithesis of unitary citizenship. Politically, trusteeship meant the marginal and indirect representation *of* Africans *by* whites. Territorially, trusteeship meant the administration of 'communal' tenure *for* Africans *by* the white supremacist state. As Davenport and Hunt have described it, the form of tenure envisaged in the 1936 Trust and Land Act was 'a variant of the communal system, a form of tenancy-at-will, with control removed now from the hands of the chief and placed in those of departmental officials'.[6]

Recent detailed analysis of the politics of this period has thrown into sharp relief a number of interesting questions concerning the historiography of segregation. For Marian Lacey, the arguments over segregation reflected an underlying structural requirement in the South African political economy for the 'super-exploitation' of African labour, above all in the mining industry and in white commercial agriculture. For Saul Dubow, the arguments over segregation revealed its ideological capacity to transcend and accommodate diverse political positions, both inside and outside the white supremacist state. From his point of view, these conflicts are not reducible in any simple or direct sense to the requirements of capital.[7]

Marian Lacey rejected the linkage between the franchise issue and the land issue as an adequate explanation either of the protracted wrangle over Hertzog's 'Native Bills' or of its outcome. Instead, she interpreted the period in terms initially of conflict and latterly of mutual accommodation between the respective demands for labour of mining capital and white farming capital. Mining capital, she argued, had an interest in extending the African reserves sufficiently to sustain them as viable bases for migrant workers. The Native Economic Commission, which reported in 1932 on the appalling environmental condition of most of the African reserves, gave important impetus to that point of view. White farming capital, by contrast, had an interest in rigorously restricting the extent of reserved land in order to retain and redistribute Africans as 'captive' cheap labour on white-owned land. Thus differences over how much land was to be 'released' for African occupation, of what kind, and on what terms, were essentially differences over whether mining capital's or white farming capital's requirements would prevail. The South African Party (SAP), representing the former, and the National Party (NP), representing the latter, sank their differences in the secret and powerful forum of the Joint Select Committee which examined and revised the 'Native Bills' from 1930 to 1935 and which reflected, in Lacey's view, an eventual consensus over how best to 'super-exploit' African labour. Hertzog and Smuts gave political expression to this sinking of their differences through the formation of a coalition government in 1933 and the fusion of the SAP and the NP in 1934 to form the United Party.[8]

Saul Dubow offered a different perspective on the fault lines within the political economy that lay behind the debate over Hertzog's 'Native Bills'. Two elements of his argument are especially relevant to this discussion. In the first place, he showed that the state was by no means monolithic or univocal in its representation of various capitalist interests. The Native Affairs Department (NAD), for example, was bureaucratically and politically weak in the early 1920s, and its relationship with both the Lands and the Justice Departments was one of active mutual hostility and suspicion. The NAD was able greatly to strengthen its position by the late 1920s by presenting itself as the protector of African interests against the rest of the white supremacist state, under the umbrella of major segregationist measures such as the Native Administration Act of 1927.

In the second place, Dubow argued that the political significance of segregationist discourse lay in its capacity to 'draw a wide range of politically interested groupings within the ambit of its ideology'.[9] The political, legal and philosophical linkage between the franchise issue and the land issue, discussed above, is fundamental to this interpretation. Dubow analysed the responses of various political interest groups outside parliament: the Non-Racial Franchise Association, which represented the remnants of the 'great tradition' of Cape liberalism; small, elite African political organisations committed to the defence of the Cape African franchise; the Joint Councils movement and the South African Institute of Race Relations, dominated by white liberals such as Howard Pim, Edgar Brookes and J.D. Rheinallt Jones; the African National Congress (ANC), under its leader of the mid-1920s, Reverend Z.R. Mahabane; and the Industrial and Commercial Workers' Union (ICU). Dubow then showed that most extra-parliamentary groupings, while expressing public opposition to the Hertzog Bills, were nevertheless drawn into pursuing political compromises which were variations, in practice, on a trade-off of land for the loss of direct political representation.[10]

Dubow's analysis, with its themes of ambivalence and confusion, makes it possible to elucidate some of the ironies and the contradictions of the drama that was played out at Thaba Nchu, on a very small part of the national stage, through the late 1930s. Many white farmers publicly opposed any extension of the Released Areas; and privately manoeuvred to have their own land incorporated within the Released Areas. Heaton Nicholls, arch-segregationist, came to investigate Thaba Nchu in late 1936 in his capacity as a member of the Native Affairs Commission. Rheinallt Jones, on the other hand, stalwart of the liberal establishment, closely advised the Barolong landowners in their initial confrontation with the NAC. Nehemiah Mogorosi Motshumi, secretary of the Thaba Nchu African Farmers' Association, served as the vital link for this purpose between Rheinallt Jones and the Barolong elite. Motshumi was son-in-law to Moses Masisi, who died in 1933 as the outstanding African farmer of his generation at Thaba Nchu.

Another of the prominent Barolong landowners, W.Z. Fenyang, 'sister's son' to the chief, was the vital link between the Barolong political establishment and local officials of the Native Affairs Department (NAD). He lost much of his own land to the South African Native Trust. The NAD, for its part, wrung its hands in simulated impotence as black landowners lost their freehold titles because of the heavy burden of mortgage debt which they had incurred; and simultaneously busied itself with taking over their land on behalf of the Trust. The NAD thus actively promoted the form of 'communal' tenure envisaged in the 1936 Act, nominally on behalf of landless Africans. When some of those same landless Africans, who were 'fed up with the rule and administration of the government', moved spontaneously to implement their own form of 'communal' tenure by occupying Trust land, the NAD prosecuted the 'agitators' concerned and relied heavily upon its local political allies, landowners such as W.Z. Fenyang, to defend the *status quo*. The Thaba Nchu

African Farmers' Association, meanwhile, an organisation mainly of surviving landowners, hastened to assert its political loyalty to the government in the 'troublous war times' of 1940.

The irony is that many of the Barolong elite, as private landowners, lost much of their land in the late 1930s to the South African Native Trust, protagonist of 'communal' tenure; that same elite, however, as political stake-holders in the process of 'retribalisation' imposed from above, offered vital collaboration and support to the central state. The local representatives of the central state committed much effort and many resources to the implement-ation of Trust schemes of 'communal' tenure, which are described in detail in Chapter 5; but could not tolerate African initiatives to take advantage of the Released Areas directly to relieve the acute congestion in the reserves.

### FIXING THE RELEASED AREAS

The Trust and Land Act of 1936 established the South African Native Trust as a state agency with wide-ranging powers to acquire and administer land 'for the settlement, support, benefit, and material and moral welfare of the natives of the Union'.[11] All land 'scheduled' in terms of the 1913 Land Act was vested in the Trust; and, through annual sums voted by parliament, the Trust was responsible for acquiring the Released Areas identified in the First Schedule to the 1936 Act. Provision was made for the acquisition of 7.25 million morgen, distributed in the following provincial Quotas: Cape, 1,616,000 morgen; Natal, 526,000 morgen; Transvaal, 5,028,000 morgen; Orange Free State, 80,000 morgen. The OFS thus had by far the smallest amount of Quota land. The Governor-General, as Trustee, delegated his powers to the Minister of Native Affairs, acting in consultation with the Native Affairs Commission (NAC). The NAC was primarily responsible for identifying areas in each province that were not defined in the First Schedule to the Act but were required to make up the respective provincial Quotas. Strict conditions con-cerning expropriation, exchange and compensation were laid down in the Act. The Trust was empowered to make detailed regulations for the administration of land for which it assumed responsibility. In addition to these arrangements, Chapter IV of the Act outlined further harsh controls, such as compulsory registration and punitive licence fees, on 'squatting' and labour tenancy on white-owned land. Chapter IV was not implemented at the time, however, in view of the difficulty of finding land for the settlement of those large numbers of Africans who would be directly affected.

The Trust and Land Act of 1936 is conventionally understood as formally extending the land available for African occupation beyond the areas 'sched-uled' under the 1913 Land Act, i.e. from about 7 per cent to about 13 per cent of the land area of South Africa. In a number of senses, however, this conventional representation should be qualified. Firstly, the provision envis-aged by Beaumont had been substantially reduced. Taking account both of revisions to the originally 'scheduled' areas, which comprised 10.41 million morgen by 1933, and of the cuts in the 'released' areas imposed by the Local Committees of 1918, the prospective 'release' of 7.25 million morgen within the terms of the 1936 Act implied an aggregate of 17.66 morgen, by comparison with Beaumont's aggregate figure of 19.53 million morgen.[12] Secondly, successive drafts of the relevant legislation took no account of the land that was already owned by Africans either inside or outside the 'released' areas and that therefore could not be construed as being made 'available' by the state. Thirdly, much white-owned land inside the 'released' areas was already fully occupied by Africans, as 'squatters' or otherwise, and could not therefore be regarded as available for settlement by other Africans even after purchase by the state nominally on their behalf.

As we have seen, the 1936 Act specified a Quota for the OFS of 80,000 morgen. With the exception of the small farm Eerstesending, adjoining the Witzieshoek reserve, all the land to be acquired in fulfilment of the Quota was in the Thaba Nchu district. The boundaries of the Released Areas identified in the First Schedule to the Act were the same boundaries as recommended by the OFS Local Land Committee of 1918.[13] They are shown in Figure 4.1. Here, as in the other provinces, the Native Affairs Commission was required to investigate the local areas specified and to make any recommendations necessary to fulfil the Quota. The NAC made its first visit to Thaba Nchu for this purpose in December 1936.

Prior to that visit, however, interested parties had already manoeuvred to impress their views on the practical determination of the Released Areas. White farmers around Thaba Nchu had formed a Vigilance Committee, which canvassed individual landowners likely to be affected as to whether they wished their land to be incorporated within or to be excised from the Released Areas. On this basis they formulated a set of proposals which they presented to the NAC as an agreed bargaining position. Prominent in the Vigilance Committee's activities were two local attorneys, Gideon Jacobus Van Riet and Eric Heath, partners of the Thaba Nchu firm of Van Riet and Heath. Van Riet himself owned a block of land in the east of the district, which embraced Goschen 101, Cloverfield 192 and a portion of Maseru 64 (see Figure 3.1); and three stock farms in the west of the district—Ngakantsispoort 76, Veepost 450 and Jacobsdeel 451—which had been part of the Ngakantsi family estate. Eric Heath became a landowner in the district, in effect, when he married Marge McPherson, second daughter of a well-known Milner settler, Daniel McPherson, whose successful farming career is outlined in Chapter 7.

There was much concern, too, amongst Barolong landowners as to the implications of the Act. But it appears from the surviving documentary record that only one of them both appreciated the infinite complexities of the position and took the time and trouble necessary to unravel them. This was Nehemiah Mogorosi Motshumi, who through his marriage to Moses Masisi's elder

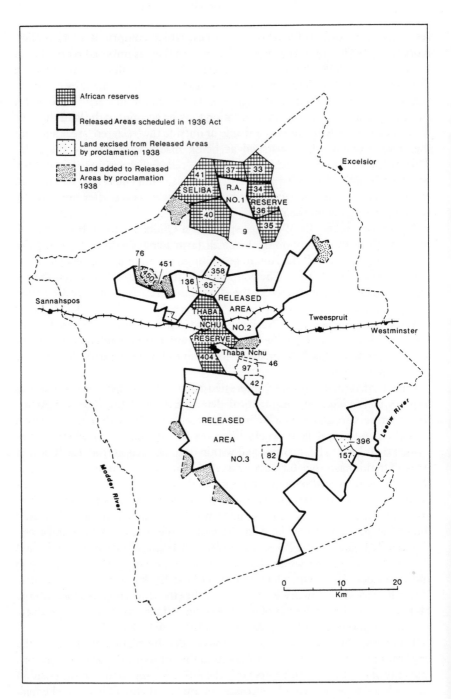

*Figure 4.1* Thaba Nchu: Released Areas, 1936, and revisions, 1938.

daughter, Maggie Magdalena, had acquired a stake on behalf of his two sons in the Masisi estate, consisting mainly of the large farm Naauwpoort 74 (see Figure 3.1). Motshumi was an interpreter-clerk in the magistrate's office at Thaba Nchu; he had been secretary of the Native Advisory Boards of the Union, and he became secretary of the Thaba Nchu African Farmers' Association when it was founded in 1937. In his involvement with the Advisory Boards, he had come to know J.D. Rheinallt Jones, with whom he now developed a substantial correspondence over Thaba Nchu land matters. Rheinallt Jones was the best-known white veteran of the Joint Councils movement, and Adviser to the South African Institute of Race Relations (SAIRR); he was also, for five years from 1937, one of two senators representing Transvaal and OFS Africans in terms of the Representation of Natives Act of 1936.[14]

His wife Edith Jones, Honorary Organiser of the Women's Section of the SAIRR, had a formidable capacity for detailed engagement with maps and statistics in order to analyse the implications of the Trust and Land Act. In September 1936, shortly after the Act came into effect, she made a series of calculations relating to the Thaba Nchu district. The Released Areas in the First Schedule to the Act comprised 79,342 morgen, leaving 658 morgen, the balance of the Quota, still to be officially defined. However, Africans owned 44,882 morgen inside the Released Areas and 11,294 morgen outside the Released Areas. The following year she conceded that these latter figures were probably too high in that 'so much of the land was heavily bonded and therefore not virtually Native at that date. It is a most important point . . .'.[15] It was a most important point because the Institute had taken legal advice on the interpretation of Section 10 of the Act and on this basis argued, successfully as it turned out (see below), that land owned by Africans prior to the commencement of the Act should not be taken into account for the purpose of meeting the Quota. By contrast, the NAC initially took the view that only 658 morgen remained to be identified for purchase by the Trust. This difference of interpretation vitally affected the acquisition of land for African occupation in the Thaba Nchu district. It was the difference between a negligible addition to the amount of land already scheduled under the 1936 Act on the one hand, and on the other hand the necessity for the NAC and the Trust to extend the Released Areas by nearly 45,000 morgen.

It was clear to Rheinallt Jones and to Motshumi, then, that the exaction of maximum benefit from the very limited provision made for land for African occupation in the OFS depended on the ability of individual Barolong landowners to retain formal title to their farms. This applied both to land inside the Released Areas, which if sold to the Trust would be lost to total morgenage legally held by Africans; and to land outside the Released Areas, which whether expropriated or exchanged for land acquired by the Trust inside the Released Areas would likewise be lost to total morgenage. In 1937 the magistrate reported that there were 117 black-owned farms in the district, ninety-seven of which were in the Released Areas. 'A large majority of these farms are bonded and a good proportion of these are, with arrears interest involved, almost up to straining point'.[16] In the light of this pressure, and of its implications for subverting the necessity to extend the Released Areas, Rheinallt Jones concentrated his own efforts on behalf of the Barolong community at Thaba Nchu on attempts to persuade the Native Affairs Department, acting through the Trust, to ease the landowners' crippling burden of indebtedness. The discovery that he could best help the landless by helping the landowners to keep their land was entirely consistent with his political philosophy. He repeatedly opposed the communalism implicit in the ideology of segregation and explicit in the notion of 'trusteeship'; he wished to encourage, instead, a progressive class of farmers with freehold rights or at least individual leasehold rights of tenure.[17]

Motshumi rightly suspected that the white landowners would present their own case to the Native Affairs Commission through lawyers who would 'naturally know how to put questions to the native witnesses in a mild catchy way'. He felt it essential, therefore, to invoke the help not only of Rheinallt Jones himself, on behalf of the Barolong, but also of a sympathetic advocate to represent them before the NAC. A decision to this effect was approved by a meeting of the African Advancement Association at Thaba Nchu, chaired by Dr James Moroka. Prominent Barolong on the Rand also took the matter very seriously: notably P. S. Merafe, a civic leader and businessman (and Ellen Kuzwayo's father, see Chapter 7), and J.J. Musi, a teacher, both of Pimville, who helped co-ordinate the arrangements. Through a Johannesburg firm of solicitors whose partners were sound Methodists and 'men of undoubted integrity', Rheinallt Jones approached 'Bram' Fischer, at that time a recently qualified advocate from a family with impeccable credentials in the political and judicial establishment.[18] His grandfather had been first Prime Minister of the ORC; his father was Judge-President Fischer of the OFS Supreme Court. Later, notoriously, 'Bram' Fischer joined the South African Communist Party.

The NAC visited Thaba Nchu on 7 December 1936. Its four members were George Heaton Nicholls, MP for Zululand (Natal); Colonel W.R. Collins, MP for Ermelo (Transvaal), sole surviving signatory of the Beaumont Commission report of 1916, and later Minister of Agriculture; General E.A. Conroy, MP for Vredefort (OFS); and J. Mould Young, chief magistrate of the Transkei (Cape). The Commissioners met a white delegation in the morning, consisting of a committee of the Thaba Nchu Farmers' Union, other white farmers and representatives of the Dutch Reformed Church and the Town Council. Its spokesman was the attorney Eric Heath. The delegation proposed the following substitution. Seventeen specified farms should be added to the Released Areas, amounting to 7,023 morgen. These were mainly peripheral fragments which reflected the individual owners' convenience in prospectively selling to the Trust. Three other farms, comprising nearly 2,000 morgen, were offered separately by their owners. Correspondingly, the white delegation proposed, twelve farms should be excised from the Released Areas, amounting to 7,700 morgen. These included Tweefontein 82, owned by P.J. Fourie; Abrahamskraal 65 and Strathearn 396, owned by Colonel W.A. Ross; Paradys 135, owned by J.M. De Wet; and several portions of the original farm Makoto 136 which belonged to one of G.J. Van Riet's daughters-in-law (see Figure 4.1). J.M. De Wet was G.J. Van Riet's nephew and worked as a clerk in the firm of Van Riet and Heath. These landowners and others expressed their anxiety that the market value of land adjacent to the Released Areas would decline and that future farming operations there would be insecure.[19]

In the afternoon and evening of the same day, the NAC met representatives of the Barolong, including Chief John Phetogane Moroka, Dr James Moroka and W.Z. Fenyang, with 'Bram' Fischer as their advocate and Rheinallt Jones as their adviser. They made the essential point that, under Section 10 of the Act, the Quota allowed for 'release' did not include land owned by Africans prior to the commencement of the Act. The NAC disputed this but promised to submit the question to the legal officers. A subsidiary legal issue arose, as to whether land acquired by an African from another African was or was not part of the Quota. Narrowly construed, it appeared that it was. In due course, in March 1937, the legal officers confirmed that land owned by Africans prior to the commencement of the Act was not to be construed as part of the Quota. They stressed that it did count towards the fulfilment of the Quota if it was sold to the Trust after the Act came into effect. They also confirmed that land acquired by an African from another African became part of the Quota, but they proposed to amend the Act in this respect because that was never the intention of the legislature.[20]

Meanwhile, however, pending the resolution of these issues, the Barolong delegation reported to the NAC in the evening of 7 December 1936 its strong disagreement with the package of substitutions presented by the white delegation, on the grounds that the seventeen farms proposed for addition were not a fair exchange in terms of quality of agricultural and pastoral land for the twelve farms proposed for excision. Nothing more was heard at Thaba Nchu until April 1937, when Rheinallt Jones was able to prise out of Douglas Smit, the Secretary for Native Affairs, a few relevant summary paragraphs from the report that the NAC submitted to the Department of Native Affairs in February 1937. These paragraphs contained something of a bombshell:

> On the following morning [8 December 1936] Dr Moroka, speaking on behalf of the Natives, informed the Commission that they would agree to the European proposed adjustment provided the farms Koele No. 97 and the Willows No. 46 were substituted for the farm Mooihoek No. 42 which was of no agricultural value. This proposal was submitted to the European representatives and agreed to by them.[21]

The Barolong representatives were shocked to hear of this alleged consensus. In response to Motshumi's investigation of the matter, Dr Moroka indignantly denied that, in conversation with Commissioner Young on the morning of 8 December 1936, he had purported to represent the Barolong. It emerged that, early on 7 December, Dr Moroka and W.Z. Fenyang had privately asked Charles Morgan, owner of Glamorgan (the two farms Koele 97 and The Willows 46), whether he was willing to have his land incorporated in the Released Areas, in substitution for Mooihoek 42 which consisted almost entirely of rugged mountain terrain. Morgan had agreed, Dr Moroka had discussed this with Commissioner Young on the morning of 8 December, and Young either mistakenly or wilfully misconstrued this personal conversation, relating only to Glamorgan, as formal endorsement of the whole package. Despite a vigorous effort by Motshumi over several months to disclaim any such 'agreement', this official sleight of hand was confirmed as unalterable by the Native Affairs Department.[22]

By November 1937, however, the 'agreement' was being actively undermined by white farmers who had changed their minds. In the wake of government valuations through the middle months of the year, they discovered that, in addition to the full value of the land and improvements, compensation at 20 per cent of that value was being paid to farmers whose land was purchased by the Trust. As Motshumi expressed it in a letter to Edith Jones:

> It is rumoured that some of the farms are fetching exorbitant prices, i.e. £10 to £14 per morgen including improvements... To our greatest surprise, since the valuation of the other European farms, this gentleman [Fourie of Tweefontein 82] has been to see the chiefs and other leading Barolong asking them to assist him so as to have his farm included again in the Scheduled Area for natives.[23]

Fourie's bid for the re-incorporation of Tweefontein 82 was successful, on the grounds—as allowed by the Trust and Land Act—that it was almost entirely surrounded by Released Area. Colonel Ross and J.M. De Wet, two of the most aggressive opponents of the whole scheme of Trust purchase in the district, now sought to have their farms included. They were not successful, and protested against the re-incorporation of Tweefontein 82 alongside the continuing exclusion of Abrahamskraal 65 and Paradys 135. G. Ingham wrote from Umbogintwini in Natal to complain about the exclusion of Mooihoek 42. The widow Salzmann of Chubani 9, partly enclosed by the Seliba reserve and adjoining Released Area No. 1, begged for her farm to be included. She had just lost her husband and she had three minor sons. 'As we're all terribly hard up it would be a blessing if the Government would take it.' She was refused. Eric Heath reported on behalf of the Vigilance Committee in September 1937 that he was receiving 'dozens of applications' to have farms incorporated in the Released Areas.[24]

Collectively, then, white farmers in the district resisted the extension of the

Released Areas, in a manner that was consistent with the parsimonious approach both of the 1918 Local Land Committee and of the NAC's initial interpretation of Section 10 of the 1936 Act. Individually, on the other hand, many white landowners scrambled to have their farms taken over by the Trust. A glaring contradiction between their public declarations and their private inclinations was resolved in due course, for some of them, by the legal officers' confirmation that land owned by Africans prior to the commencement of the 1936 Act did not comprise part of the Quota, so long as that land was not acquired by the Trust. For this judgement meant that the NAC had to identify for 'release', and the Trust had to take steps to acquire, at least 40,000 morgen of additional land to be incorporated within the Released Areas. However, the Trust's obligation in this respect was not fulfilled until the second wave of land purchase in the district in the late 1940s. The delay had critical implications for black landowners, for the overall morgenage to be acquired by the Trust from white landowners, and thence for white farmers who scrambled to have their land incorporated in the Released Areas.

The prime example of an unscrupulous scramble of this kind was attorney G.J. Van Riet's successful effort to substitute his own three farms, Ngakantsispoort 76, Jacobsdeel 451 and Veepost 450, on the northwestern border of Released Area No. 2, for Charles Morgan's farm Glamorgan (Koele 97 and The Willows 46), which lay in the lee of the mountain and across the main road to the east out of Thaba Nchu town (see Figure 4.1). Both the Van Riets and the Morgans were old established Thaba Nchu families. G.J. Van Riet's father had practised in Thaba Nchu before the South African war, and he established his own practice there as a law agent after the war. In 1896 he had married a daughter of J.M. De Wet, the second *landdrost* of Thaba Nchu. The Morgans, a family of staunch Methodists, had come up to Thaba Nchu from the eastern Cape in 1886, and bought Koele 97 shortly afterwards from Isaac Motshegare Moroka. Charlie Morgan had six sisters and seven brothers, several of whom owned land in the district. In variable combinations, they were stock inspectors, farmers and land speculators. Charlie Morgan was a client of Van Riet and Heath.[25]

Following the recommendations of the NAC in February 1937, Morgan's property Glamorgan (Koele 97 and The Willows 46) became part of Released Area No. 2. In September of that year a valuation of £12,000 was agreed for the land and improvements, and the government valuator took a three-month option on the farm. Strong opposition, however, was emerging from various quarters to the inclusion of Glamorgan in the Released Areas. The Native Commissioner, for example, objected to the inclusion of Glamorgan without consultation with the Town Council, as the effect would be practically to surround the white town of Thaba Nchu with African-occupied land. Morgan then discovered by accident that a meeting of about twenty residents was taking place on 3 November 1937, attended by General Conroy, one of the members of the NAC. He was outraged to find that the apparently clandestine purpose of this meeting was to approve the substitution of Van Riet's three farms for his own. To achieve this end, as Morgan explained afterwards, Van Riet had lobbied personally in Pretoria; he suborned the Vigilance Committee to vote in his favour; and he subsequently and unsuccessfully tried to invoke Dr Moroka's influence with the Barolong community on behalf of his scheme. The substitution of Van Riet's three farms for Glamorgan was officially confirmed in March 1938.[26]

In failing health, at the age of 77, Morgan fought a vigorous rearguard action against the exclusion of Glamorgan through a direct appeal to the Prime Minister, Hertzog, for an enquiry. There were several grounds of his appeal. Firstly, the behaviour of Van Riet, while 'ingenious', was also 'unneighbourly' and thoroughly devious. Secondly, there was an element of both 'absurdity and ungratefulness' in the objection from the Town Council to the prospect of virtual encirclement by Trust land. The Town Lands, excised from the original Thaba Nchu reserve, had been freely given to the municipality by the Barolong before the South African war. In addition, the clause in the Act which committed the government to purchase white farms surrounded by Trust land would not in practice apply in the case of Glamorgan. Finally, Morgan pointed out the inferiority of Van Riet's farms for purposes of irrigation, and the clear and repeatedly expressed preference of the Barolong for Glamorgan. Morgan made a strong case for the acquisition of his own farm. 'The place is, unquestionably, the beauty spot of the district...'; it had flourishing fruit orchards, three large dams, a profitable dairy industry and highly productive arable lands; and it was healthy for horses. He even envisaged for the future, 'as their culture advances, an Arboretum, a Botanical Garden and a Veterinary Laboratory of their own...'. His appeal fell on deaf ears. Glamorgan was excised from the Released Areas. Charlie Morgan died in August 1939, having put Koele 97 into a trust for his only grandson, then six years old.[27]

SELLING OUT: BLACK LANDOWNERS AND THE TRUST

One element of struggle over land, then, concerned which farms should and which farms should not be incorporated within the Released Areas. Another crucial element of struggle concerned the extent to which, in practice, titles to land both inside and outside the Released Areas were subverted by their owners' mortgage indebtedness to corporate financial institutions or to individual whites. As Edith Jones expressed it, how far was the approximate aggregate of 45,000 morgen owned by Africans in 1936 'not virtually Native' in this sense? Notoriously, the predicament of the owners opened up substantial opportunities for speculative investment and personal gain on the part of local attorneys. The attorney whose name recurs most frequently in the records of local land transactions in the 1930s was John Henry Faustmann, who had practised in Thaba Nchu since the South African war. His clients included, for example, several members of the Masisi and Setlogelo families, whose affairs were highly complex. But it is clear from the Bloemfontein Deeds Registry that G.J. Van Riet was also heavily involved, as a landowner and bondholder himself and as agent on behalf of other landowners and bondholders. The inference may be drawn that attorneys such as Faustmann and Van Riet represented their Barolong clients with one hand, so to speak, in their efforts to consolidate their debts and arrange further mortgages, and with the other hand called up the mortgage bonds which they held themselves or which they managed on behalf of other clients. In his evidence to the Native Economic Commission in February 1931, Van Riet spoke with the authority of more than three decades of direct involvement in such transactions:

> But the custom, the practice amongst the Africans is almost always that if they have a mortgage on their ground then they don't pay the interest and then there's one bond after another and there comes a day when he loses possession of the ground completely. That is why so many of the Africans here have lost their property as the years have gone by.[28]

The significance of this is best illustrated through detailed examples of individual cases. Walton Zacharias Fenyang has already appeared several times in the course of this story. As we have seen in Chapter 3, he was host to his friend, Solomon Plaatje, when Plaatje toured the eastern OFS to record the suffering caused by the 1913 Land Act. His mother, Elizabeth Nkhabele Fenyang, was Chief Tshipinare's daughter by his first wife and he was there-fore 'sister's son' to two of Tshipinare's sons who succeeded to the chieftain-ship: Robert Tawana, who died in 1912, and John Phetogane, who was incumbent for ten years until his death in 1940. Through the 1920s and the 1930s, alongside Dr Moroka, he was a principal spokesman for the Barolong in their representations to the central state. He was an OFS delegate at four 'Native Conferences' held annually in Pretoria between 1923 and 1926, and he gave evidence to the Native Economic Commission in 1931.

Fenyang was also a substantial landowner. His mother, Elizabeth Nkha-bele, was registered owner of three properties: Dakpoort 117, Mooiplaats 118 and Rietfontein 119 (see Figure 3.1). Dakpoort was mortgaged from 1907 onwards and the interest payments were met through the rent that accrued from leasing Dakpoort and Mooiplaats and part of Rietfontein to whites. Dakpoort and Mooiplaats were jointly mortgaged in 1912 for £2,600, in favour of the South African Mutual Assurance Society. Further mortgages were taken out and the whole of Rietfontein (6,000 morgen) was bonded for £2,000 in 1924. All of these bonds were cancelled in 1929 when a division of the estate took place between Elizabeth Nkhabele's children and grandchildren. One property, Mooiplaats 118, was then sold in two portions to whites, in order to meet the outstanding liabilities of her estate. All the subdivisions of Riet-fontein were bonded for substantial sums either immediately or very soon afterwards.[29]

In the early 1930s Fenyang held the following properties in his own name, the first three of which he had inherited as his mother's principal heir: Rapulana 776 (1,000 morgen), a subdivision of Rietfontein 119; the remaining extent of Rietfontein 119 (2,950 morgen); Dakpoort 117 (857 morgen); and Boesmanskop 799 (232 morgen), which he bought from Emily Moroka for £1,500 in 1932. In November 1933 he took out a fresh bond of £5,000 in favour of the South African Association of Cape Town, with interest at 6 per cent per annum, to cover his existing liabilities, including one bond of £2,000 in favour of John Henry Faustmann. His debts rapidly proliferated in the following years so that, by April 1937, three separate bonds were held over his properties for amounts respectively of £7,000, £5,000 and £500, with interest outstanding. The South African Association then lost patience with his inability to meet his interest payments, and threatened legal action if Fenyang did not forward the outstanding interest by return post. This threat was precipitated by the Association's anxiety about the security of its investment, in view of the fact that all Fenyang's landed property lay within Released Area No. 3 and could not therefore, after the passage of the 1936 Act, be sold to whites. In these circumstances Fenyang's attorneys, the Thaba Nchu firm of Faustmann and Paver, asked for advice from the Native Affairs Department on how to forestall legal action by the South African Association. Cecil Rayner Morgan, Charlie Morgan's younger brother, who held the bond of £7,000 over Rietfontein 119—and many other bonds over African-owned land—was also pressing for payment.[30]

Fenyang's only option was to enter negotiations with the Trust to buy as much of his land as was necessary to clear his accumulated liabilities of about £15,000. By the end of 1937, agreement had been reached. He sold 2,000 morgen of Rietfontein 119 to the Trust at £7 a morgen. He also sold 300 morgen privately to Reverend Zachariah Nyokong of Bothaville, who paid for the land by means of a loan of £1,260 from the Trust, with interest at 4 per cent per annum, representing 60 per cent of the purchase price and a first mortgage bond over the property in question. Servicing this loan, incidentally, proved a major financial headache for Zachariah Nyokong throughout the following decade. At the same time, unable to resist the importunities of reverends, as his youngest daughter recalled, Fenyang sold two other small portions of Rietfontein 119 to Reverend Jonah Simeon Litheko and his brother Hosea Litheko, members of a prominent Methodist family from Kroonstad. J.S. Litheko was treasurer of the All-African Convention (AAC) in Kroonstad at this time, and actively involved in Rheinallt Jones' election campaign in 1937. The mother of the Litheko brothers was a daughter of John Mokitlane Nyokong of Maseru 64, who died in 1930 and whose affairs were referred to by his neighbour and attorney, G.J. Van Riet, in his evidence to the Native Economic Commission (see Chapter 3). Fenyang leased the remaining portion of Rietfontein 119 to a white farmer, J.M. Lombard. Later, in 1946, he sold 500 morgen of Rapulana 776 to Dr Alfred Xuma, then president-general of the ANC.[31]

Having disposed of 2,000 morgen of Rietfontein 119 to the Trust in 1938, Fenyang arranged with the Native Affairs Department that all the residents on his own remaining portion who had lands on the portion purchased by the Trust should move to reside on the Trust portion. On taking possession of this land on behalf of the Trust in June 1939, the Agricultural Officer noted that, of eighty-three families listed as having lands on the Trust portion, thirty-one were resident on the Trust portion and fifty-two on Fenyang's private portion; but that there were a further forty-five families, presumably landless, resident on the Trust portion. All these people were instantly converted from share-croppers or tenants on privately-owned land to tenants of the Trust, paying rent on the same basis as 'squatters' on Crown Land in the Transvaal, pending the implementation of 'planning' which followed the establishment of a Trust village at Rietfontein in 1941 (see Chapter 5).[32]

The point here is that the lives of Fenyang and his close relatives followed a very different trajectory from the lives of the common people who found themselves caught up in the 'rehabilitation' and 'betterment' schemes associated with Trust villages. In 1936, Fenyang and his wife accompanied their eldest daughter to Britain, where she trained as a nurse from 1936 to 1938, and the expenses of that visit must have contributed very largely to his acute financial embarrassment of 1937. His two other daughters were trained as teachers. They inherited his surviving properties shortly before his death in 1957. W.Z. Fenyang had one full sister, Naomi, who was the widow of a neighbouring landowner, George Modiko Keikelame of Brandkop 78. One of their sons, Bennett Herbert Keikelame, became a prominent local business-man, and in the next generation one of his sons, Ephraim Keikelame, became Minister of Economic Affairs in the Bophuthatswana cabinet (see Chapter 5). Fenyang also had two half-brothers, the sons of his mother by her second husband, Abraham Setlogelo. The elder of these, Israel Tlale Setlogelo, lost his own land in circumstances described in Chapter 3. In the late 1930s he was Bloemfontein correspondent of the *Free State Advocate*, a supplement to the paper *Mochochonono*, based in Maseru (Basutoland). Israel Tlale was the father of Moutloatsi Setlogelo, who became Bophuthatswana's first Minister of Educ-ation (see Chapter 5). Israel Tlale's younger brother, Robert Frederick Setlogelo, trained as a doctor in Edinburgh (Scotland) relatively late in life, returned home in 1938 and established a medical practice in Bloemfontein.

The Setlogelo family lands, the farms Moroto 68 and Somerset 55, were in the north-east of the district (see Figures 3.1 and 3.3). In the early 1930s, Moroto 68 (rest) was owned by Isaac Setlogelo, half-brother to Israel Tlale and Robert Frederick. His experience, the particulars of which were described in Chapter 3, illustrates another aspect of the process of deepening indebtedness and eventual sale to the Trust. Trust Regulations 59, 60 and 62, passed in

terms of the Act, allowed the Trust to make loans to Africans, for the improvement of their land or the redemption of mortgage bonds, of up to 60 per cent of
the value of the land and improvements, subject to repayment by half-yearly
instalments over twenty years at an interest rate not exceeding 4.5 per cent.[33]
In 1937, in terms of these regulations, Isaac Setlogelo applied for a loan from
the Trust of £2,250 in order to pay off his outstanding debts, and a substantial
correspondence developed over this application between Faustmann and
Paver and the Native Affairs Department. The NAD refused to sanction the
loan, on the grounds that Setlogelo was not a 'reliable farmer' and he had a long
record of cumulative debt. Faustmann and Paver expressed 'alarm' on behalf
of their client that he might be forced to sell at a significantly reduced price.
They explained this alarm at length to the Native Commissioner at Thaba
Nchu:

> As far as Barolong Mortgagors are concerned, it must be pointed out that
> European Mortgagees invested money on native land in a very conserva-
> tive manner, with the result that, if the Trust wishes to see Mortgagees sue
> Mortgagors, and then compete merely with the Mortgagee for the land,
> native-owned land in this district will be sold to the Trust at figures well
> below the price at which such land could have sold at public competition
> prior to the Act coming into operation, and the native owner will be the
> loser. Prior to the Act coming into operation, the prairie value of native
> land was no different from the prairie value of European land in the same
> areas, and the value of such land was ascertained by Europeans competing
> for such land, whereas, since the Act has come into operation, the prairie
> value remains the same, but European competition, the means of raising
> the land to its true ruling value, has fallen away.[34]

It should be added that Faustmann and Paver were also alarmed on behalf of
white mortgagees:

> In view of the fact that the operation of the Native Trust and Land Act has
> deprived them of their ordinary rights to open public competition where it
> is found necessary to sell land in execution, and has limited competition to
> native purchasers, of which there are definitely none, and the Trust,
> Mortgagees, no matter how anxious they are to obtain capital sums and
> interest due to them, are loath to incur further costs in instituting actions,
> for it is problematic whether they will recover their money or be saddled
> with land in the Released Area, where all the existing European land is
> about to be acquired by the Trust.[35]

The main question of principle, then, was whether sales of black-owned land
in the Released Areas were to take place in execution or at a fixed valuation. On
the one hand, if they took place in execution, there would be negligible
competition, confined in practice to the Trust and the mortgagee, since blacks
could not afford to buy the land and whites other than the mortgagee were not
allowed to purchase land in the Released Areas, and the land would be sold to

the Trust at a price well below its value. On the other hand, if sales to the Trust took place at a fixed valuation, as in the case of white-owned farms, the sellers would receive the 'true' market value of the land.

It was becoming clear by the end of 1937 that the Trust would not exercise in practice its capacity under Regulation 60 (1) to take over mortgage bonds up to 60 per cent of the valuation of the property concerned. John Makgothi, a well-known teacher and farmer who had inherited a portion of Good Hope 70, observed that 'a number of farmers are now on the waiting list for sale to the Trust because owners have been refused help by the Trust and advised by their lawyers to sell very much against their wishes'. Again, 'we are in a much more difficult position than we were before in that bondholders are being induced by their lawyers to call up their bonds and as we have no other alternative we are compelled to sell to the Trust'.[36] Rheinallt Jones pleaded on behalf of the Barolong landowners for the Trust either to influence bondholders to stay their hand or to exercise its discretionary capacity to take over such mortgages, since any such sales would reduce the amount of land that needed to be acquired to fulfil the Quota. Douglas Smit wrote back at length, reviewing the history of policy in this matter and describing the 'thriftless and improvident behaviour' of most Barolong landowners over many years. He regretted the inability of the NAD to help in circumstances of indigency, incompetence, idleness, etc., and stressed the 'inevitability' of ultimate sale in most cases.

> It must be borne in mind in this connection that if the Trust were now to proceed to buy its full quota of land for the Orange Free State from Europeans in or adjoining the released areas and some of the Native owned farms in the released area were subsequently sold up, the Trust could not buy these farms and the Department would have to acquiesce in their being taken over by Europeans . . .[37]

There is no evidence on which to impute conspiracy on the part of the NAD to defraud black landowners. Yet the logic of its position decisively tilted the balance against them. Firstly, the demarcation of Released Areas subverted the private mortgage market and immediately intensified the financial pressure on black landowners. Secondly, the Trust's refusal to take over existing mortgages compelled ultimate sale to the Trust. This consideration itself dictated a very cautious response to individual white landowners' offers of their farms for inclusion within the Released Areas. If the Trust fulfilled the Quota through immediate purchase of white-owned land, it would be unable to buy black-owned land which subsequently came into the market. As Smit pointed out, such land would have to be sold to whites and this would imply haphazard distortion of the plan for consolidation of segregated land. If, however, the Trust took over the mortgages of black landowners, on more generous terms than they had been able to obtain in the private mortgage market, and thereby relieved the landowners from the necessity of selling their land, the Trust would still have to find and purchase enough other land to fulfil

the Quota. It is scarcely surprising that the Trust failed, except in a very few
cases, to exercise its discretionary capacity to take over existing mortgages; or
that it justified this failure by lumping almost all black landowners within the
category of the improvident and the undeserving.

The advantage from the NAD's point of view of an arrangement whereby
the Trust bided its time until black-owned farms fell into its lap, so to speak,
was obvious to the Barolong. In the first place, although land values were
generally rising in real terms in this period, the average price paid per morgen
of black-owned land was rather lower than the average price paid per morgen
of white-owned land. Purchase of black-owned land to fulfil the Quota would
incur significantly lower aggregate expenditure than purchase of white-owned
land for that purpose. In the second place, through a strategy of procrastina-
tion of the kind implied by Smit in his response to Rheinallt Jones, the NAD
could relieve itself of unwelcome political pressure from local white farmers
opposed to the extension of the Released Areas. As Rheinallt Jones pointed
out, 'the Natives are already suspicious that the bondholders have been
persuaded to press so that the additional morgenage need not be given'.[38]

Such suspicions inevitably came to rest on the local attorneys, who were the
spiders at the heart of the web. They represented both Barolong mortgagors
and white mortgagees, and they must have resolved the inevitable contradictions of professional obligation in ways that were most consistent with their
own values and aspirations and habits of social interaction. Furthermore, they
were often landowners and holders of mortgage bonds themselves. It must,
therefore, have been very easy to 'persuade bondholders to press'. From time
to time, local officials attempted to elicit sympathetic consideration from
Pretoria for the owners of heavily-mortgaged farms.[39] Nevertheless there were
reasonable grounds for suspicion of collusion between the NAD, the Trust and
the local attorneys. African suspicions along these lines were of course exacerbated by the appearance of General Conroy in November 1937, as Charlie
Morgan expressed it in another context, 'more in the character of Mr Van
Riet's delegate than as a Commissioner of the Union government'.[40]

Whether or not the suspicion of collusion was justified, a flurry of sales to the
Trust took place in 1938 of white-owned land and black-owned land inside the
Released Areas, which were amended by proclamation in August 1938 to
reflect the NAC's recommendations of 1937. As described above, many white
landowners pressed individually to have their land included in the Released
Areas, once it became clear that handsome compensation was forthcoming
from the state. Many black landowners had no option but to sell to the Trust,
as they were pressed for repayment of outstanding capital and interest by
private bondholders who no longer had confidence in the security of their
investment. By definition, such land could not be sold to whites. The NAC's
recommendations of 1937 had not yet taken account of the morgenage that had
belonged to Africans at the time of the passage of the Act. To the extent that

this land survived in black ownership after the first wave of purchase was completed in 1939, further provision had to be made in the future to fulfil the Quota. Such provision was effectively suspended, for the time being, by the outbreak of the Second World War.

A flurry of sales also took place in 1937–8 to individual whites of black-owned land outside the Released Areas. Motshumi reported to Rheinallt Jones late in 1938 that:

> many native farms in the Tweespruit area have been voluntarily sold by the owners and some have gone out of their possession through executions of judgements in court . . . Some of these natives who sold their land were able to buy land from the natives in the released area who were hard-pressed to sell in order to meet their bonds.[41]

By comparison with Edith Jones' estimate in September 1936 that Africans owned 11,294 morgen outside the Released Areas as then defined, officials estimated in March 1938 that Africans owned 6,071 morgen outside the Released Areas.[42] These lands became 'black spots', to be eliminated in due course.

It should be emphasised for comparative purposes that the rapidly proliferating indebtedness of Barolong landowners at Thaba Nchu through the 1920s and 1930s was exactly paralleled by the rapidly proliferating indebtedness of many white farmers throughout South Africa in this period. Small town attorneys were the most familiar predators. Consider Macmillan's biting commentary on the ills of South African agriculture in the late 1920s:

> The evidence is conclusive that all over the country the falling in of mortgages means that great blocks of land (and any little wealth there may be in the district) are passing into the hands, sometimes of stronger farmers, more often of the chief agricultural bankers—country store-keepers, and 'law agents' of one kind or another, in the neighbouring villages. That cute lawyers so often become the most successful farmers is testimony to the low standards of agriculture generally.[43]

Nevertheless, the position of African landowners in the 1930s was distinctive in at least three respects. First, white farmers could exert political pressure to ease their own predicament. The settlers in Thaba Nchu who had been established under Milner's Land Settlement scheme found themselves in acute financial difficulties in the early 1930s, when the 30-year period for redemption of their mortgages expired. They sent a deputation of two farmers to Pretoria who knew General Smuts personally. Both these farmers were introduced in Chapter 2. One was Leonard Flemming of the farm Geluk, near Dewetsdorp, who was also a popular writer. The other was Fred Nicholson of Heathfield, south of Tweespruit, who was well-connected through the Merrimans at the Cape. Although Smuts himself was in opposition at the time, he apparently used his influence to secure an interview with the Minister of

Lands. The result was legislation which extended the redemption date of the settlers' mortgages from 1933 to 1937.[44]

Second, African landowners had no state-subsidised sources of credit. They were entirely dependent on corporate or individual sources of finance in the private market, in which interest rates ranged from 6 to 8 per cent or more in this period. White landowners were primarily but not exclusively dependent on these sources; they could also obtain loans from the Land Bank, which charged interest at 4 or 4.5 per cent. More important was the fact that black landowners could not take advantage of the bulk buying, storage, marketing and credit facilities available to many white farmers through state-sponsored co-operative societies. Arguments about the differential impact of the pressures of dispossession on white and black landowners are therefore crucially dependent not only on the effects of segregationist legislation but also on the scale of the Land Bank's involvement in the mortgage market and on differential access to other forms of state credit.[45]

Third, the implementation of the 1936 Trust and Land Act gave a peculiar twist to the impact of market pressures on black landowners. Ironically, whereas many black and white landowners were indeed displaced by larger farmers or bankers or small town commercial predators in the way Macmillan described, many black landowners were ultimately dispossessed by the state provision, albeit minimally, grudgingly and belatedly, of land for 'communal' African occupation. In retrospect, the formal establishment of the Trust may be seen to have precipitated the final loss of many freehold titles.

### 'CRYING FOR LAND': THE BAROLONG PROGRESSIVE ASSOCIATION

The third element of the struggle over land in the 1930s, that of the common people, now remains to be investigated. The aspirations of the landless were most clearly expressed in a protracted agitation by the Barolong Progressive Association (BPA) over two issues which were closely interconnected: access to land acquired by the Trust, and refusal to acknowledge the authority of the recognised chief at Thaba Nchu. The roots of this agitation lay in the succession dispute which had paralysed the political community in the early 1880s, and which was analysed in detail in Chapter 1. Its contemporary appeal was based on a skilful capacity to give expression to widespread and fundamental grievances over shortage of land.

The first official record of the BPA appears in February 1928, when its officers asked the magistrate to register it as an association. Its then vaguely expressed purpose was to 'build a body of the Barolong tribe or co-operation. . . '. A year later, according to its secretary, Jeremiah Soldaat, its object was 'to raise money to buy ground for the Barolong Tribe and also to stand against laws and regulations which ruin out [sic] our people'.[46] Specifically, it opposed a regulation approved by the Thaba Nchu reserve board that deprived anyone who had been away for more than seven years of residence rights in the reserve. Anxiety to 'unify' the Barolong was constantly expressed in the BPA's communications with officials in this period. An apparently vague and innocuous aspiration was interpreted by the BPA, however, quite specifically within the historical framework of the annexation of Thaba Nchu, the dispersal of the Barolong people and the patterns of material differentiation that had developed within the district. Thus the BPA enquired of Pretoria in March 1929: did President Brand's proclamation of 1884 'separate the Barolong tribe into two camps—those of Chief Sepinare [Tshipinare] as one, and those of Chief Samuel as the other'; and provide only for the former to live in Thaba Nchu? 'We shall also be pleased to know what court [is] competent to judge who are desirables and who are undesirables as residents of Thaba Nchu'. Again, in July 1930, 'we wish the government to allow the Barolong children who are all over the Union contributing to the various markets for the adequate provision of the Union to be among their old parents and relatives'. The women of the BPA added their own impassioned plea 'for ourselves and for our children, who are scattered all over the industrial areas, a homely residence in the land of our fathers'.[47]

The BPA thus expressed strong anxiety about the conditions under which people from Thaba Nchu who were dispersed in urban centres of employment throughout South Africa could retain their residence rights in the reserves. As indicated in Chapter 3, the NAC was asked to investigate this issue in late 1926. People's anxiety was intensified by the government's determination, following that investigation, to enforce an extremely conservative policy over future admissions. Applicants would have to have a strong claim for consideration in terms of President Brand's proclamation of 1884, which protected the residence rights of 'followers of Chief Tshipinare'. This formula begged the question of who qualified and who did not qualify as 'followers of Chief Tshipinare' for this purpose: the descendants of all citizens of the political community at that time, or the descendants only of those people who had been demonstrably loyal to Tshipinare? The Secretary for Native Affairs sought to clarify the policy in mid-1927:

> Those Barolong who were subjects of Sepinare [Tshipinare] Moroka, had taken no part in his murder and who were not among those provided for by grant of farms . . . originally had a clear right to occupy the Reserves. These people, or their descendants, have a moral claim to reside in the Reserves now, save in so far as such claim may be regarded as having subsequently been abandoned, e.g. by prolonged absence, permanent removal to another district etc.[48]

Many people affected by this policy were obviously sceptical of its even-handed application in practice, not least because the Thaba Nchu reserve board was dominated by landowners who were, almost by definition, the descendants of members of Tshipinare's faction. The BPA was sufficiently provoked to express an important subtheme of its campaign to 'unify' the

Barolong: its defence of Samuel Lehulere Moroka's faction as the losers in the civil war and in the land dispositions that were made thereafter. In the early years of the BPA's campaign, however, this partisan political identity was submerged within the terms of a generalised desire to recover the people and the land. The people were those Barolong who had been 'lost' as a result of the disintegration of the political community in the 1880s and subsequent dispersal throughout the farming districts of the OFS and the industrial areas of the Union, or who had been displaced from white farms by the South African war and by the 1913 Land Act and were unable to gain access to the Thaba Nchu and Seliba reserves. The land was the territory of the old Chief Moroka that had been annexed by the OFS in 1884 and subsequently dismembered.

This theme, of recovering the people and the land, was most strongly articulated by Kali John Matsheka, the charismatic leader of the BPA. Many others, outside the BPA's own constituency, were also concerned with the acute shortage of land for Africans in the OFS. Some of them had national political connections. Reverend Z.R. Mahabane, for example, who was twice president-general of the ANC (1924–7, 1937–40) was an influential member of the Thaba Nchu diaspora. He made representations from Kimberley to the Minister of Native Affairs in December 1930, in which he sought to impress on the government the need to buy land in the Thaba Nchu district 'to relieve the congestion which exists in that district and in certain urban centres such as Bloemfontein'. Specifically, he suggested the government should buy seven farms between the Seliba and Thaba Nchu reserves, whose owners were apparently willing to sell. The proposal was dismissed as 'impracticable' on the grounds that land in the district 'fetches a large price' and Africans could not possibly pay back the sums involved even on the basis of their willingness, as Mahabane alleged, to be taxed for this purpose.[49]

An approximate consensus on the urgency of the problem emerged most clearly through the evidence given to the Native Economic Commission (NEC) in February 1931. The principal spokesmen for the Barolong, as on so many occasions, were W. Z. Fenyang and Dr J.S. Moroka. Fenyang pointed out, in particular, that half of the residents of the Thaba Nchu reserve had no land. Independently of Fenyang and Moroka, the BPA also submitted evidence to the NEC, expressed in a highly generalised appeal for justice. In his long addendum to the Commission's report, the advocate F.A.W. Lucas reviewed prevailing conditions in the district: many Africans had been evicted from farms as they were alienated to whites; the two reserves of Seliba and Thaba Nchu were grossly over-crowded and over-stocked, vegetation was scanty and land erosion very bad; while 'large numbers of Basuto and amaXosa have drifted into the district from time to time and have remained working on the farms'.[50]

There were two reasons, however, why a widespread consensus on the urgency of the problem could not be translated into common political action.

The first reason was that the BPA very quickly identified the two reserve boards as targets of its campaign, on the grounds that they arbitrarily excluded people with connections with the district from access to the reserves. The reserve boards were in a difficult position, for they had to deal with a rising tide of applications for residential certificates through the 1920s, but they were also constrained by official insistence on rigorous control of admission.

The second reason was that the Native Affairs Department had taken steps in the late 1920s to 'consult' the Barolong over the appointment of a chief and headmen at Thaba Nchu; and that the 'wrong' chief, from the point of view of the BPA, was appointed. Local officials had worked routinely through location headmen, appointed by the NAD on the magistrate's advice. But the chieftain- ship itself had fallen into effective abeyance after Robert Tawana Moroka's death in 1912. His only son, Albert Setlogelo Moroka, was still a boy at the time but was recognised by the government as successor to the chieftainship. His uncle, John Phetogane Moroka, and others were appointed as guardians. Albert Setlogelo was convicted of stock theft in 1922 and disqualified from office on the magistrate's authority. John Phetogane became acting chief.[51]

The Native Administration Act of 1927 represented a significant shift of policy towards 'retribalisation'. This implied a recovery and a strengthening of the powers of chiefs, and also a decisive subordination of their position to the strategic requirements of the central state.[52] In partial compensation for this, some NAD officials stressed the need for 'consultation' of the people in order to achieve legitimacy for the appointments made by the NAD. The magistrate at Thaba Nchu in 1926, T.W. Kilpin, took a dim view of this process. He warned that 'consulting the natives' would result in the selection of John Phetogane. 'He is', the magistrate confided to the Secretary for Native Affairs:

> a useless and untrustworthy fellow, at present a bottle-washer and errand boy for one of the local doctors. He lost his land years ago owing to his predeliction for strong drink and still takes more than is good for him. He has a fairly large following and would very likely get a majority over the man I want as Headman, Fenyang. You met him here—an absolutely straightforward fellow who attended the last native congress.[53]

The NAD insisted that meetings be held in the locations to determine public feeling on the matter, and John Phetogane Moroka was duly appointed as chief of the Thaba Nchu reserve in 1930. Officials were confident that this appoint- ment would forestall further agitation on behalf of Samuel Lehulere Moroka.[54]

W.Z. Fenyang, the 'absolutely straightforward fellow' preferred by the magistrate, was a generous and dedicated man who through his long life devoted his energies and abilities in many ways to public service on behalf of the Barolong community at Thaba Nchu. Through his involvement in the ANC, also, he was engaged with wider political issues. He committed sub- stantial private resources to causes in which he believed. He helped to fund Sol Plaatje's newspapers, for example, and he rescued the Moroka Missionary

Institution at Thaba Nchu from its chronic financial difficulties in the 1940s. Repeatedly, he appealed to the state authorities to find more land. Over the land issue, however, his material assets and his material liabilities drove him inexorably into a position from which he could not plausibly represent the interests of the dispossessed. Much of the land he owned was leased to whites. As described in the previous section, he was eventually forced to sell out to the Trust: literally, in that the 2,000 morgen block of Rietfontein 119 was the largest single purchase made by the Trust in 1938; and figuratively also, in that this sale reduced the total morgenage that had to be otherwise acquired to fulfil the Quota.

With hindsight, then, it is intriguing that Fenyang was allegedly involved in the founding of the BPA in about 1925. However, he withdrew along with other landowners when it became evident, firstly, that restoring the 'right' chief to Thaba Nchu would in the BPA's view imply restoring the land to administration by the chief on a communal basis; and, secondly, that the chief the BPA had in mind was not a descendant of Tshipinare but Samuel Lehulere Moroka or his heir. Thus the official appointment of John Phetogane Moroka in 1930, as chief of the Thaba Nchu reserve, served two immediate purposes: it temporarily suppressed the threat of renewal of the 'war of the chiefs'; and it clarified the divergence between the 'moderate' political establishment and the 'extreme' demands of the BPA. According to Moses Nkoane, who joined in 1929, the BPA underwent a rapid and very significant transformation from an organisation intended loosely to promote the unity and welfare of the Barolong community as a whole to an organisation intended specifically to displace the beneficiaries of the original disposition of freehold titles.[55] Hence Fenyang's later, vigorous, opposition to the BPA is unsurprising. For the moment, the point is that the linkage asserted by the BPA between its political commitment to Samuel's faction and its advocacy of a 'communal' mode of land adminis-tration drove an irrevocable wedge between the BPA and many of the landed elite, whose superior life-chances were based on the financial liquidity they derived from mortgaging their private titles.

Nevertheless, the lines of cleavage at Thaba Nchu, between the political establishment and the BPA, did not simply or directly reflect a polarisation between the landed and the landless classes. The 'war of the chiefs' divided families in the 1880s, as explained in Chapter 1; it also divided them in the 1930s. Kali John Matsheka, the president of the BPA, was the most enthusi-astic protagonist in the late 1930s of the claim of Percy Tshabadira, Samuel Lehulere Moroka's successor, to the chieftainship at Thaba Nchu; whereas his father, Lang Jan Matsheka, who died with Tshipinare during Samuel's attack on Thaba Nchu in July 1884, is described as Tshipinare's 'faithful attache'.[56] Asked to explain this apparent anomaly in 1989, Amos Tlale Matsheka, Kali John Matsheka's eldest son, observed that his grandfather's family were 'servants' of the old chief Moroka, and that one son had been 'placed' with

Tshipinare, another had been 'placed' with Samuel. Their political loyalties diverged accordingly. Amos Tlale, born in 1913, was himself named after Israel Tlale Setlogelo, who was a close personal friend of his father, Kali John Matsheka. Israel Tlale, it may be recalled, was also half-brother to W.Z. Fenyang, and the two did not get on. Elisha Maimane Ramagaga, the chairman of the BPA, quarrelled with his elder half-brother, Nehemiah Ramagaga, when the latter put pressure on him in the early 1940s, at the time of Albert Setlogelo Moroka's accession to the chieftainship, to provide cattle to help the chief to marry. In the next generation, Nehemiah's son, Moses Ramagaga, became an active member of the Barolong Tribal Authority (see Chapter 5); while his cousin, Solomon Ramolehe Ramagaga, was keen to preserve a collective memory of the BPA as an organisation that offered principled opposition to the political establishment.[57] Thus family animosities remained an integral feature of the factional divisions at Thaba Nchu.

Further, both Matsheka and Ramagaga—two of the BPA's three long-serving officers—were landowners themselves, albeit on a small and declining scale. Matsheka had power of attorney on behalf of his mother, who owned the farm Rooifontein 60 (see Figure 1.3), but was unable in 1930 to meet the outstanding mortgage interest payments,[58] and was forced to sell in 1932, to one of the local attorneys. Elisha Ramagaga inherited a portion of the farm Leeuwfontein 129; and he also had a butchery and general dealer's licence in Ratlou location in the Thaba Nchu reserve. Jeremiah Soldaat, the secretary of the BPA, owned no land but apparently ran an eating house and a general dealer's in Thaba Nchu.[59]

The leaders of the BPA were, then, marginalised landowners or small businessmen without land. But they were shrewd enough to exploit the general grievance of acute land shortage and also a specific resentment of the common practice by which Barolong landowners in debt leased their farms to whites in order to generate sufficient regular income to meet their mortgage interest payments. One implication of the land segregation policy was that this practice would be officially disallowed. Barolong landowners were so alarmed by the threatened imminence of this in 1930 that forty-three of them signed a letter imploring the Minister of Native Affairs not to implement the policy in this respect, because it would cause 'untold distress and hardship'. Especially in view of the decline in the prices of wool, maize, wheat and potatoes, leasing their land to Africans could not possibly command a rent sufficient to cover the interest due on bonds or to maintain minor children.[60] The terms of this request starkly reflect the material interests of black landowners at the time, when rather more than half of all black-owned farms were leased to whites. The circumstances of the depression exacerbated their dependence on this arrangement.

The BPA, for its part, was capable of a boldly extravagant style in its approaches to the central state. In 1933, Matsheka requested Rheinallt Jones

of the SAIRR and Bishop Walter Carey of Bloemfontein to forward a petition
to the government on behalf of the BPA, in which he put the following
sweeping demand:

> We therefore claim from the OFS Government the whole of the Barolong
> territory, with not a bit cut off. We do not want it divided, for it was never
> divided by Chief Moroka into farms and given to his sons, councillors and
> heads of the tribe. These helped to rule the people but were not em-
> powered to drive the people out of the territory nor to reduce them to a
> state of poverty.[61]

Despite the hopeless unrealism of this ambition, it appears that the BPA was
able to articulate a constituency of the dispossessed because, while the 'sons
and daughters' of Thaba Nchu were scattered on farms and in urban locations
throughout the Transvaal and OFS, they retained an active sense of their roots
in the district and a strong historical consciousness of lost independence.

The BPA was also active on the other front of its campaign. In 1935
Matsheka sponsored a visit to Thaba Nchu by Percy Tshabadira Moroka from
Bechuanaland, who had succeeded Samuel on the latter's death in 1932. Percy
Tshabadira was politely though not enthusiastically received by Chief John
Phetogane and introduced to the people. This visit was accidentally condoned
by administrative confusion between the Departments of the Interior and of
Native Affairs. The BPA held a series of meetings without the chief's approval
in 1938 and 1939, and John Phetogane complained repeatedly to officials that
his authority was being undermined. Percy Tshabadira was at Kimberley and
Bloemfontein in February 1939, following widespread fund-raising by the
BPA to facilitate his return to Thaba Nchu as chief. He was then expelled from
the OFS and returned to Bechuanaland. Matsheka attempted, nevertheless, to
arrange another visit; and the Bishop of Bloemfontein was invited to conduct a
service at Thaba Nchu in May 1939 to celebrate Percy Tshabadira's installation. This was aborted by a flurry of official action to prevent Tshabadira
from entering the Union again.[62]

While the weight of official anxiety about the resurgence of the BPA concerned the subversive implications of the attempt to supplant John Phetogane
with Percy Tshabadira, it is clear that it was the first wave of land purchases by
the Trust that opened up political space for the BPA to garner widespread
support. In view of the past dispersal of Samuel's supporters, the issue of the
chieftainship at Thaba Nchu was a relatively narrow, specialised, one. When it
was linked to the question of access to Trust land and the future administration
of Trust land, it was a potentially explosive issue. In October 1936, rumours
spread amongst Africans on white-owned farms in the district that land would
be bought for them and handed over for them to occupy. Officials put their
own gloss on Dr Moroka's report of high expectations in this respect: the result
was a certain amount of 'friction' between farmers and labourers and of
'insolence' in the attitude of the latter to the former, arising out of the prospect

that the government was providing ground for labourers who would no longer find it necessary to work for white farmers. The Assistant Native Commissioner was instructed to take every opportunity to disabuse people of this idea.[63]

Frustration mounted through 1938 and 1939 as it became clear that the Trust intended to assert tight control over residence on and use of arable and grazing land. A series of spontaneous movements on to Trust land took place, and officials responded by imposing trespass fines. Initially, the Trust insisted that only established residents were entitled to remain on a farm after transfer to its ownership. In the case of black-owned farms, these people had been predominantly share-croppers; in the case of white-owned farms, they had been predominantly wage labourers. Both categories were transformed at a stroke into tenants of the Trust. Together with the inhabitants of the two reserves, they all became subject in due course to the pressures of 'betterment', rehabilitation and the forced culling of livestock. These were the issues which dominated the rural protest movements of the 1940s and 1950s. They are examined in Chapter 5 below.

Matters came to a head with the delivery of a 'threatening' letter from the BPA to the magistrate: 'We are fed up with the rule and administration of the Government. We want nothing from them seeing they are against the taking over of the released areas from them. The land is ours and we are taking it...'.[64] Despite official warnings, the BPA leaders went ahead with a public meeting on 25 March 1940, which was attended by about 500 people and addressed by Elisha Ramagaga as chairman, Kali John Matsheka as president and Jeremiah Soldaat as secretary. The three were charged with holding an illegal meeting, in terms of Proclamation 252 of 1928, which prohibited an assembly of more than ten people without the chief's and the magistrate's permission, except for religious purposes or 'for the regulation of the domestic affairs of any particular kraal' or for official administrative purposes. They were found guilty by the magistrate at their trial on 28 May 1940. Ramagaga and Matsheka were fined £10 or one month in gaol and Soldaat £6 or three weeks in gaol.

According to a joint statement by six Barolong witnesses at the trial, Matsheka declared at the BPA meeting that the Released Areas had been bought with the money contributed to the BPA; that the 'whole district' was now available for the people's free occupation; that he would personally arrange the expulsion of the Assistant Native Commissioner, Jacobus Petrus Booysen; and that Percy Tshabadira would be coming to Thaba Nchu as chief. All these things, of course, if they were accurately reported, were wishful thinking, and reflect Matsheka's flamboyant rhetorical style. But many people wanted to believe him. Booysen told the enquiry which took place later in the year that, as a result of the meeting on 25 March, 'a large number of Natives turned their stock on to Trust land without permission'. The defendants' appeal against conviction was heard in the OFS provincial court on 4 July 1940. The key issue was whether the BPA meeting could be construed as having been confined to 'the domestic affairs of any particular kraal'. Counsel for the appellants argued that the question of succession to the chieftainship was a 'domestic affair' of the kraal of Moroka, but this argument was rejected by Judge-President Fischer on the grounds that the chieftainship was a 'national' and not a 'domestic' issue. The appeal was dismissed, and the convictions and sentences upheld. An official enquiry was held at the end of October 1940, which Matsheka refused to attend. The enquiry took evidence from local officials, the chief, Fenyang and several other 'loyal' Barolong, and two members of the BPA. Having given his evidence from his sick-bed, Chief John Phetogane Moroka died three days later, on 2 November 1940. Matsheka was deported to a remote part of the central Transvaal for eight years. Ramagaga could not be deported as he was a private landowner.[65]

The acquisition of land by the Trust was officially publicised in Bloemfontein *after* the illegal meeting of 25 March 1940. The Bloemfontein magistrate informed the local Native Administration Department that 'additional land has been acquired in the Thaba Nchu district and has been reserved primarily for the accommodation of such Barolongs, who may form part of the surplus Native population in this and other towns'. This letter was forwarded to the BPA in Batho Location, Bloemfontein, which was closely connected with the BPA at Thaba Nchu. It implicitly invited applications for accommodation on the newly-acquired land, and explicitly requested the BPA to publicise this amongst the Barolong in Bloemfontein.[66] Outside Thaba Nchu, then, officials were prepared to concede that the BPA was representative, if only informally, of the Barolong diaspora. Inside Thaba Nchu, however, they could make no such concession without undermining their own authority, partly exercised as it was through John Phetogane Moroka as the established chief. Correspondingly, at Thaba Nchu the BPA had no political means of expressing its grievances within the law. It therefore conducted its campaign outside approved channels and often in deliberate antagonism to them. Not surprisingly, its methods and style proved offensive to the official mind.

They were offensive to other minds also. Strikingly, whereas Rheinallt Jones offered detailed and sympathetic assistance to the landowners, in their particular predicament described above, he was unable to respond to the BPA's various efforts to solicit his intervention on their behalf, expressed as they were in terms that he found both vulgar and imprecise. After the trial of the BPA leaders in 1940, Kali Matsheka and Daniel Ngakantsi appealed for his help again:

> The Barolong go from place to place with their loads of trek. They have no where to settle. Some of them are granted small portions of ground where to settle, and their cattle are dying from want of grazing grounds. Some people have not been given lands where they can plough and some are

being expelled from the country. We therefore place all these into your hands.

In turn, Rheinallt Jones placed them in the hands of Assistant Native Commissioner Booysen at Thaba Nchu: 'I cannot make head or tail of their complaint. What is the position now in regard to these people?'. Booysen explained:

> The Progressive Association has been spreading news to all natives in the whole of the Free State that they have now procured the land for them, and that every native can now come and take residence in the district, and as a result of these misleading statements several natives from various parts of the OFS left the farms, and wish to take up residence on Trust farms. You will no doubt realise my difficulty in this matter . . .[67]

The BPA sought primarily to express the desperate need for land. Daniel Ngakantsi, one of its members who gave evidence in its defence to the official enquiry in October 1940, explained its objective in these terms:

> The country has been occupied by white people, I mean the District of Thaba Nchu, and we wanted to settle the Barolongs, all of them the people of Moroka, in this District, to round them up from other districts and put them here.[68]

The letters and complaints of the BPA over the years are characterised by a strong retrospective invocation of the status quo ante 1884. What were the terms on which Moroka's country was taken over by President Brand and then broken up? Was it intended to perpetuate a division within the tribe between the followers of Samuel and the followers of Tshipinare? Why was Trust-acquired land not immediately available for occupation by the people who needed land, when the whole district, not merely the 'released' areas, properly belonged to the Barolong?

The story of the Barolong Progressive Association is a small episode in a protracted and continuing struggle for a just distribution of land in South Africa. The questions it raised with such urgency reflect an intensely parochial pre-occupation with the particular history of the Seleka Barolong of Thaba Nchu. Its rhetoric of 'aggressive communalism' in the late 1930s must be interpreted specifically in relation to the perceived opportunity—with land purchase by the Trust—of reconstructing an independent polity on land recovered from the colonial state.[69] This aspiration was wholly unrealistic in practice. But the BPA's political support in the 1930s significantly transcended the boundaries of the Thaba Nchu district precisely because it touched the deepest sensitivities of two generations of the dispossessed. Their land was arbitrarily taken over and broken up. Independent peasants were turned into share-croppers at home or refugees abroad. Many found themselves rapidly proletarianized in squalid urban locations throughout the OFS and the Witwatersrand. Share-croppers on white farms, in turn, were evicted or turned into wage labourers. Years of exhaustively reasoned and reasonable 'crying for land' were brutally ignored by a state in which they had no political representation. Little wonder, perhaps, that the BPA developed a faintly millenarian style in its ill-fated confrontation with that state.

It remains difficult to judge the extent of popular support for the BPA, in the light of archival sources heavily dominated by official correspondence. As against the forty-three 'landowners and members of the Barolong tribe' who appealed to the Minister of Native Affairs in 1930 not to prohibit the leasing of black-owned land to whites, the BPA mustered forty-five signatures for its petition to the House of Assembly in 1933 to restore to the people the whole of the original Moroka territory.[70] I have been unable to trace any connection of the BPA with what Bradford refers to as a 'short-lived branch' of the Industrial and Commercial Workers' Union (ICU) at Thaba Nchu between 1926 and 1930.[71] The BPA was, however, well-organised and active in Bloemfontein and Kimberley and perhaps elsewhere, and reached the peak of its popular impact in the three-year period from 1938 to 1940. The Bloemfontein branch survived until the early 1960s, concentrating solely on the issue of the chieftainship.[72] Otherwise, the organisation was not revived after 1940, except to the extent that its activities in the late 1930s directly influenced the dissent that smouldered in the Seliba reserve, and occasionally burst into flame, throughout the 1940s and the 1950s (see Chapter 5). Even in the late 1980s, however, the subject of *ntwa ya dikgosi*, the 'war of the chiefs', remained an extremely sensitive one in the local Bophuthatswana state. The BPA's briefly effervescent campaign is the reason for that.

# 5

# THE MAKING OF A BANTUSTAN

Near this place [Thaba Nchu] I saw the most desolate village of my travels. It is called Gladstone, and is apparently a new settlement created for landless folk. Bleak and bare, with hardly a blade of grass in sight and not a tree for miles around, the miserable stone and mud huts of the Natives huddle together as if seeking to hide behind each other from the bitter winds that pierce the marrow in winter-time hereabouts.

Oliver Walker
*Kaffirs Are Lively* (1948), p. 69

Objections to the resettlement into Trust villages have been both strong and vocal. Most people, however, eventually resigned themselves to their fate and moved peacefully, some being encouraged by having their houses knocked down for them by the Government . . . In many of the villages I saw groups of demoralized-looking people living under a few pieces of corrugated iron. These were the people from Morago.

Cosmas Desmond
*The Discarded People* (1971), pp. 208, 210

Oliver Walker, a journalist, spent fifteen months in 1944–5 exploring South Africa—both remote rural areas and crowded urban slums—to record his 'backstage' impressions of daily life towards the end of the Second World War. The Native Affairs Department had commissioned his investigation for its own propaganda abroad, in order 'to present Native policy in South Africa in a true perspective'. Walker's impressions, however, did not please the Department, and he published them independently in 1948. Gladstone, which he found 'the most desolate village' of his travels, was one of the first Trust settlements established in the southern part of the Thaba Nchu district, in the early 1940s (see Figure 5.1). A generation later, Cosmas Desmond, a Franciscan priest, traversed the country for six months from March 1969, in a journey of similar distance (24,000 miles), to document the overwhelming scale of forced relocation and the devastating particulars of the experience. His revelations did not please the South African government, which imposed a banning order on him. The last chapter of his book, *The Discarded People*, published in 1971, contains an account of the experience of the people of Morago, in the erstwhile Seliba reserve. They were brutally dumped in various resettlement sites in April 1969 after they had strenuously resisted, for many years, official schemes of 'betterment' and residential concentration in Trust villages.[1]

The years between these two journeys were marked by intensive and oppressive intervention by the central state in every aspect of daily life in African rural areas. New controls were introduced on the use of arable and pastoral resources; familiar modes of livelihood were severely disrupted; people were uprooted from their homes and forced to move to planned villages; new structures of authority were created, albeit cast in a 'traditional' idiom; and the state rode roughshod over the popular protests which were directly provoked by these diverse impositions. This was the period of the making of the Bantustans.

There were four critical elements of the process. The first element was partial consolidation of the land. From the late 1930s, through the purchase of 'released' land by the South African Native Trust, small and scattered reserves were partly consolidated into larger fragments or blocks.

The second element was the enforcement of a regime of land use that was characterised by a rigidly bureaucratic system of central planning and a uniformly inadequate resource base. The state extended its control over this partly consolidated land by introducing a series of 'betterment' and rehabilit- ation schemes in the 1940s and the 1950s. These schemes were intended to improve farming practices and to stem the tide of exhaustion and erosion that had engulfed the land. In reality, however, people experienced the schemes as unjust and heavy-handed; and they often bitterly resisted them.[2]

The third element was the creation of separate 'ethno-national' structures which were supposed to accommodate the demand of black South Africans for political representation. The Bantu Authorities Act of 1951 envisaged the construction of an elaborate hierarchy of three administrative tiers throughout the African reserves. These were known as Tribal, Regional and Territorial Authorities. There emerged, at different dates in different regions, one Terri- torial Authority for each of the ten 'ethno-national' units eventually identified, none of which ever achieved territorial integrity. Chiefs, headmen and council- lors were alternately bullied and seduced into serving on these bodies, whose principal task in many areas was to impress upon their reluctant subjects the long-term collective advantages of culling their livestock, enclosing their pastures, relocating and redistributing their arable lands, and moving them- selves into planned villages. On the one hand, such collaborators often in- curred popular odium by assuming, to a significant extent, the repressive function of the central state. On the other hand, the material rewards of collaboration were greatly increased: the fledgling Bantustan bureaucracies were rapidly expanded; official salaries were deliberately inflated; and unpre- cedented opportunities for private accumulation arose out of privileged access to the 'development' resources which flowed from Pretoria in order to sustain these retroverted political structures. There emerged a class of bureaucratic accumulators who were well placed to take advantage in due course of Pre- toria's granting of political 'independence' to four of the ten Bantustans: Transkei in 1976, Bophuthatswana in 1977, Venda in 1979 and Ciskei in 1981.

Professional and commercial opportunities for upward mobility for Africans were likewise concentrated largely within the Bantustans.[3]

The fourth element was the destructive crystallisation of ethnic animosities. Access to a job, a place to stay, a pension, etc. became conditional on citizenship of one or other 'ethno-national' unit. Scarce resources were administered through the Bantustan bureaucracies. Competition for them was structured in terms of who 'belonged' and who did not 'belong' to the dominant ethnic group associated with each Bantustan. Thus the experience of general socio-economic deprivation—gross over-crowding, high unemployment and extreme poverty—was routinely transposed into experiences of specific inter-ethnic antagonism. This was the bitter harvest of Bantustan 'independence' that was reaped in blood and anger in the 1970s and 1980s. It is illustrated in Chapter 6 below.

This chapter, meanwhile, offers an analysis of the first three elements outlined above. The process of partial consolidation of land for African occupation in the Thaba Nchu district took place in two phases. The first phase, in the late 1930s (described in Chapter 4), preceded the introduction of the new settlement regime and gave rise to considerable local conflict—between landless Africans, black landowners and white farmers—over access to newly-acquired Trust land. The second phase of partial consolidation, in the late 1940s, allowed a renewed effort by the central state to 'rationalise' access to arable and grazing land.

The culling of livestock and the relocation of arable lands provoked a general rumbling of discontent, but its manifestations were unevenly distributed. On newly-acquired Trust land, the Native Affairs Department had *carte blanche* to impose conditions of settlement and was therefore able to enforce the new regime with relative ease. In the Thaba Nchu reserve, the expression of discontent was inhibited by a number of factors. Firstly, senior members of the Barolong political establishment, such as W.Z. Fenyang, were actively loyal to the government. Many of them, as private landowners, were in any case not directly affected by Trust regulations. Secondly, many people who lived in the Thaba Nchu locations, the only residential area of the reserve, were substantially dependent for a livelihood on wage employment rather than on livestock and cultivation, and were probably marginally rather than decisively impoverished by the Trust regime. Thirdly, one important aspect of the 'betterment' programmes, the concentration of people into planned Trust settlements, was not applied within the Thaba Nchu reserve. The inhabitants of the reserve were already physically concentrated in the old locations. Some were moved to Trust villages outside the reserve in the early 1960s, with their livestock; but the old locations were not otherwise disturbed in this period.

The Seliba reserve, by contrast, stoutly resisted official impositions for nearly three decades, from the early 1940s to the late 1960s. The reasons, again, are not hard to discern. Firstly, Seliba had a distinctive political

tradition: it was historically associated with the Samuelite faction; it had been
territorially disconnected from the Thaba Nchu reserve and the surviving
fragments of black-owned land, throughout the twentieth century, by a long
ridge of hills and a block of white-owned farms (see Figure 3.1); and its
inhabitants were reluctant to acknowledge the authority of the chief at Thaba
Nchu. Secondly, most households in Seliba were still substantially dependent
on land and livestock for a living, and were therefore strongly affected by the
Trust regime. Thirdly, there was a clear difference between the position of
people who, as immigrants from elsewhere, occupied Trust villages that were
established on land acquired by the Trust from white farmers; and the position
of people who, as in Seliba, were forced to build new communities on land
where they had been established for several generations. Unsurprisingly, these
people fiercely resented the arbitrary brutality of a 'betterment' scheme which
forced them to destroy their old homes. Their physical relocation was not
accomplished, for this reason, until the late 1960s.

One central theme of this chapter, then, is the chasm of mutual incomprehension and antagonism that divided reforming state officials and small farmers already on the margin of survival. On one side of the chasm, the South
African state committed itself to an ambitious and, as it turned out, misplaced
programme of social engineeering in the African reserves. On the other side of
the chasm, most small farmers wished to rear their livestock and cultivate their
lands without this heavy yoke of government regulation.

Another central theme of the chapter is the mediation of this relationship of
incomprehension and antagonism by the Barolong elite, through the chieftainship, the Barolong Tribal Authority and the Tswana Territorial Authority.
Many of the elite were drawn into the political and bureaucratic structures of
the local state which emerged in December 1977, according to the procedures
inscribed in Pretoria's strategy of separate development, as an isolated enclave
of the 'independent' Republic of Bophuthatswana. A few of the elite remained
independent of these structures. In the third section of this chapter, through
an inevitably selective and parsimonious biographical cross-section of the
Barolong elite, I analyse the interlocking trajectories of bureaucratic, professional and commercial mobility that define this local ruling class.

Finally, in a brief epilogue, I illustrate two sides of the experience of
'development' at Thaba Nchu in the 1980s: the destruction of two Trust
villages, south of the mountain, to make way for a game park and a tourist
haven in which the Bophuthatswana National Development Corporation had a
very substantial stake.

THE TRUST REGIME: FOR 'BETTERMENT' OR WORSE?

At the end of the first wave of purchase in 1938–9, the Trust had acquired
50,172 morgen of land in the Thaba Nchu district. This comprised the whole
of the Released Areas, as amended by proclamation in August 1938, except for

the surviving black-owned farms and three portions of Brakfontein 140 which were owned by the Terblans family, officially identified as 'Coloured'. A balance of nearly 30,000 morgen still had to be acquired by the Trust in order to make up the Quota of 80,000 morgen, subject to deduction of land bought privately by Africans from whites after the 1936 Act came into effect. Approximately 35,000 morgen within the Released Areas remained in private black ownership; most of it was heavily bonded and would, it was anticipated in November 1939, 'probably have to be purchased by the Trust in order to save it from falling into the hands of Europeans'.[4]

Figure 5.1 shows the distribution of the 50,172 morgen acquired by the Trust in the late 1930s. Two small fragments adjoined the Seliba reserve; a substantial block, to the south-east of Seliba, was separated from the reserve only by a narrow strip of white-owned land, part of Rakhoi 5. Three blocks of Trust land adjoined the Thaba Nchu reserve, on its north-western, eastern and southern borders. The southern block was by far the largest aggregation of Trust property. It was part of Released Area No. 3, which also contained many farms still in black ownership: for example Naauwpoort 74, which belonged to the Masisi family; several subdivisions of Good Hope 70, the Makgothi family farm; most of Vaalkop 66, which belonged to the Goronyane family; and the portions of the Fenyang family farm of Rietfontein 119 which had not been sold to the SANT. On the eastern edge of the district, following the Vigilance Committee's representations to the Native Affairs Commission, the farm Thaba Patchoa 106 had emerged as an isolated enclave, cut off from the rest of Released Area No. 3 (see Chapter 4). For this reason, it was identified as an appropriate site for the relocation of the 'Coloured' community of Carolusrus in the Seliba reserve, whose particular history is outlined in Chapter 7.

The vital questions were: who was to have access to Trust land, on what terms and for what purposes? The NAD produced its own blueprint. Early in 1939 a reclamation survey was carried out by local officials to determine the most appropriate use of Trust land. Their report was subject to detailed scrutiny and amendment by senior officials in Pretoria and by the Native Affairs Commission. The policy that emerged from this protracted exercise was that Trust farms should be used, firstly, to relieve congestion in the two established reserves and, secondly, to provide for the settlement of those Barolong whose forebears had resided in the district but who 'through force of circumstances' had been driven from the land. This latter phrase was to be construed, in practice, as referring to 'surplus Barolong Natives resident in urban areas' in the OFS.[5]

Two key restrictions are evident here. In the first place, people resident on white-owned farms were generally precluded from access to Trust land. The reason for this was the government's commitment to protecting the labour supplies of white farmers, who were experiencing acute shortages of seasonal labour at this time, if not necessarily of permanent labour. Such labour was not

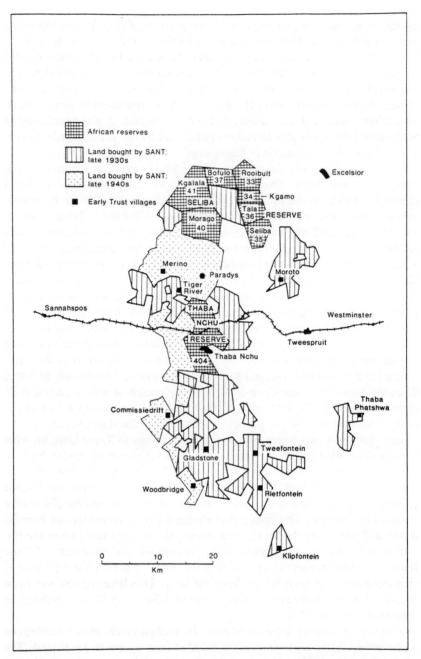

*Figure 5.1* Thaba Nchu: land bought by the South African Native Trust, late 1930s and late 1940s.

evenly distributed, and there were in any case far more 'squatters' on white-owned farms than could possibly be accommodated on Trust land at Thaba Nchu, if the anti-squatting provisions of Chapter IV of the 1936 Trust and Land Act were put into effect. In the second place, people were restricted from access to Trust land by a criterion of ethnic identity. The reason for this was not, apparently, an explicit policy commitment to 'protect' Thaba Nchu for the Barolong, although officials justified the decision by reference to the historical roots of the Barolong in the district. Rather, the documents convey the impression, although they do not state explicitly, that restriction by ethnic identity was a convenient administrative device for disqualifying the majority of half a million Africans in the OFS from competing for access to Trust land. Nevertheless, it was recognised that exceptions would have to be made to accommodate Africans other than Barolong who were displaced from towns under the Urban Areas Act of 1923.[6]

The calculations made by the reclamation committee in making its recommendations for settlement, as well as subsequent commentary by the Chief Native Commissioner (Northern Areas) and the Secretary for Native Affairs, reflect the dominance of the notion of 'carrying capacity' in official thinking at this time. Stock limitation was perceived as a fundamental condition of rehabilitation of the reserves. The argument was that the reserves were grossly over-stocked. The quality of stock was poor and would continue to deteriorate without adequate control over breeding. As a result, livestock were vulnerable to disease and unsuitable for draught purposes. The state had a responsibility to intervene in order to interrupt the vicious spiral of decline. It assumed powers to do so through Proclamation No. 31 of 1939, which provided, after 'consultation' of the people concerned, for the declaration of any area as a Betterment Area, in which livestock could be culled and the use of arable lands regulated.[7] The Thaba Nchu reserve was quickly declared a Betterment Area in terms of this proclamation.

In 1939 the Thaba Nchu reserve, 6,631 morgen in area, was estimated to hold 5,000 people and 2,330 'cattle units', from which figures the reclamation committee inferred that the people were under-stocked and the reserve was over-stocked. The people were under-stocked in the sense that, having only 0.8 cattle per taxpayer, it was impossible to plough adequately to produce their own food supplies, even if enough arable land were available. The reserve was over-stocked in the sense that available grazing was badly denuded and in that condition could only carry one beast per 10 morgen. Subject to proper regeneration of the veld, the carrying capacity of the reserve could be increased to one beast per 4.5 morgen. In order to achieve this, however, it was necessary to exercise proper control over rotation of arable lands and fencing of pastures; to extend the anti-erosion measures which had been initiated about five years previously; to repair dams and ensure appropriately-sited water supplies; and to facilitate credit for the formation of mechanical ploughing units, in order to reduce the livestock necessary for draught purposes. The committee proposed that 16,922 morgen of land be set aside as an 'adjunct' to the Thaba Nchu reserve, consisting of the three blocks of Trust-acquired land which immediately adjoined it. This would allow each taxpayer 14.5 morgen of grazing land, sufficient for 3 cattle units. As regards arable land, the weight of official opinion was that an allocation of 4 morgen per taxpayer was sufficient for the Thaba Nchu people, many of whom derived a partial livelihood at least from wage employment in Bloemfontein and in Thaba Nchu itself. It was also proposed that there should be a three-season fallow period in the use of arable lands. No one explained how this would work in practice, for it implied the need for double the original allocation.

Similar calculations were made for the Seliba reserve, which was 17,687 morgen in area and had 7,050 people and 5,118 cattle units. It contained 3.39 cattle units per taxpayer, more than three times the mean stockholding in the Thaba Nchu reserve. Judging by the estimated carrying capacity of the grazing land, Seliba was 100 per cent over-stocked, and immediate culling was therefore necessary. It was originally proposed that the whole of the Moroto block, consisting of 10,533 morgen, should be set aside as 'adjunct' land for the Seliba reserve, which would allow 4.7 to 5 cattle units per taxpayer, taking into account the needs also of the existing population on the Trust farms. This proposal was subsequently amended so that part of the Moroto block was made available to the Thaba Nchu people, and part to the Seliba people, which had the effect of producing a roughly equitable notional mean of 2.7 cattle units per taxpayer for both reserves. Arable plots of 4 morgen per taxpayer were similarly recommended for Seliba.

The NAD also laid out detailed plans for the settlement of the forty-three farms in the southern block, comprising 20,805 morgen. They contained plenty of arable land, but the limiting factor was the stock-carrying capacity of one cattle unit per 5 morgen, or 4,160 cattle units overall. Allowing an average holding per taxpayer of 2.8 cattle units, not more than for Thaba Nchu or Seliba, this implied provision of settlement for 1,400 families in addition to the eighty families already living on those Trust farms. These areas, the report noted, were 'to a great degree unoccupied'; if they were advertised as openly available, the NAD would be 'inundated' with applications from all over the OFS. Whatever the policy adopted to restrict access, 'the settlement of the farms should be carried out on an orderly and systematic basis', which meant the proper demarcation of residential sites and arable and grazing lands, with adequate provision for rotation.

The report also made detailed calculations of the rent that would be payable for the use of Trust land. It was based on the price paid for the various properties, discounting the value of improvements and the compensation element. An annual return to the Trust of 3 per cent of its capital outlay implied a rental assessment of £5,500. Since there were approximately 3,370 taxpayers in the two reserves and on the adjunct farms, the tribal levy payable for the purpose would have to be £2 per taxpayer. Taxpayers were already liable for £1 general tax and 10s. per hut per annum. In view of the onerous total liability implied, the report recommended that the annual levy per taxpayer be reduced to £1.10s. per annum in respect of the use of Trust farms.[8]

The NAD took more than a year, from early 1939 to early 1940, to produce, revise and prepare to implement these plans as official policy. Much of this work was carried out far from Thaba Nchu itself. Meanwhile those interested in working Trust land had not been idle. One constituency keen to compete for access consisted of established African farmers who had the capital resources to plough, and had been in the habit of ploughing, much larger areas of ground than the 4 morgen which individuals were allowed under the new policy. Late in 1938, the recently-formed Thaba Nchu African Farmers' Association had already been refused access to arable land on Trust farms on the grounds that 'only a small section of advanced natives' would benefit therefrom. As Secretary of the Association, Nehemiah Mogorosi Motshumi protested to Senator Rheinallt Jones against this policy of imposing uniformity by 'levelling down'. He described the constraints imposed on arable cultivation on Trust farms as 'wholesale legalised impoverishment'. The limitation to 4 morgen of arable land, for which the effective rent was 30s. per annum, would have 'disastrous effects' for men in the district who possessed more than two spans of oxen and double-furrowed ploughs and who 'must be obliged to sell their oxen and plows and be ruined instead of having their praiseworthy industry encouraged by the Government'. Rheinallt Jones agreed with Motshumi that this policy 'spells the doom of progressive farming'.[9]

A small and relatively prosperous minority of black farmers was not, however, the only constituency competing for access to Trust land. Early in 1938, of 51,000 morgen then still owned by Africans in the district, more than 11,000 morgen was leased to whites. Late in that year, by which time roughly one quarter of that 51,000 morgen had been sold to the Trust or to individual whites, the NAD decided that leases to whites of black-owned land in the Released Areas would be terminated at the end of 1939, since they were inconsistent with the policy of land segregation. Despite alleged hardship for black landowners who relied on such leases to meet the interest payments due on their mortgage bonds, no policy distinction in this respect was drawn between encumbered and unencumbered land. All such leases therefore ended on 31 December 1939. White farmers no longer had access to privately-owned land in the Released Areas.[10]

Partly for this reason, and partly because of a serious drought which exacerbated the shortage of grazing, the NAD received by early February 1940 no fewer than seventy-four representations from white farmers anxious to hire grazing on Trust farms 'not occupied by Natives with beautiful grazing going waste'. Such land was 'not occupied' by Africans because both arable and grazing facilities granted for one season in 1939 had been withdrawn, presumably to facilitate the implementation of the reclamation proposals. This left many owners of stock stranded and cultivators frustrated. The Thaba Nchu African Farmers' Association was outraged, therefore, when the government allowed three months' grazing for 1,500 cattle on Trust land to white farmers, from February 1940, at a rental of 1s. per head per month, in order to spare itself political embarrassment. The Association was not mollified by the discovery that black landowners could still lease grazing rights on a temporary basis to white farmers, since the Supreme Court had decided that lessees did not thereby acquire an 'interest in land' within the meaning of the 1913 Land Act.[11]

Anomalies were rife in the early months of 1940—precisely the period, it may be recalled, when agitation by the Barolong Progressive Association over access to Trust land was coming to a head (see Chapter 4). Within the terms of the policy of land segregation, the state had bought land for African occupation. Africans with livestock and capital resources for ploughing were prevented from using this land for arable or grazing purposes, pending official approval of the reclamation and settlement proposals. Some of the land, however, which had been reserved for winter grazing, was temporarily leased to white farmers who desperately needed grazing facilities and who could bring political pressure to bear on Pretoria that was out of all proportion to their numbers. Meanwhile the policy objective of land segregation was further breached by a legal loophole which allowed white farmers to continue to hire grazing land from black landowners, to the advantage of those landowners who could not otherwise meet their mortgage interest payments. Another policy objective, that of 'levelling down', was contradicted by the embarrassing revelation that Dr James Moroka, doctor, private landowner and wealthy owner of livestock, was grazing 800 head of cattle on Trust farms for a rental payment of 2d. per beast per month, the same rate as applied to African 'squatters' already living on those farms. This rental was quite uneconomic from the Trust's point of view, on account of the high prices paid for the Thaba Nchu farms.[12] It was also arguably unfair to those who were unable to obtain grazing for much smaller numbers of stock.

Accordingly, the NAD revised its rates so that grazing rentals for stock on land not required for the people of the Thaba Nchu reserve were the same for African owners as for white owners. This provoked another protest from the African Farmers' Association, which drew attention to 'a great deal of confusion and uncertainty' over policy. The Association objected that the sharp rise in grazing fees was a 'harsh and unsympathetic measure' in view of the recently prevalent drought, a poor season for maize and wheat and the high cost of living in wartime conditions. It was unjust to charge African landowners the same grazing fee as white farmers who were generally better off. In any case, the African landowners also had to pay the tribal levy of 30s. per annum in respect of Trust land. The Association argued that, pending settlement of the large southern block of Trust land in Released Area No. 3, they should be allowed to plough more than 4 morgen of land in what were 'the best arable farms in the district'.[13]

In view of declared official policy on and conflicting local pressures over access to Trust land, it is hardly surprising that individual applicants for land from outside Thaba Nchu received short shrift. Rheinallt Jones, as Senator, received frequent requests for help and advice from many districts of the OFS, from people with a more or less tenuous connection with Thaba Nchu. Nehemiah Gabashane, for example, appealed for help in November 1937 from Randfontein location in the western Transvaal. He was 75 years old, and he wished to spend his last few years, with his children, on 'his farm' at Thaba Nchu: 'Sir the Farm belongs to me, and I have the right of claiming it'. The farm in question was Fortuinspruit 233, a portion of the original farm Lovedale 89, which had been granted to Robert Tawana Moroka, Tshipinare's heir, in 1886. In the 1890s it was part of Charles Newberry's large estate; it was retained by the Newberry family after sale of most of the estate to the ORC government in 1901 for Land Settlement; and it was bought by J.B. Lurie in 1917 from Ernest Newberry, Charles Newberry's eldest son. Thus Fortuinspruit never formally belonged to Gabashane; but he expressed surprise when officials in Pretoria told him that 'some people were owning the farm since 1917'.

His story emerged in due course. Nehemiah Gabashane asserted that his grandfather had owned Fortuinspruit; that after the latter's death the farm had passed to his father, who joined the Wesleyan ministry; that he himself had been 'in charge' of the farm until 1904, when he visited his father at Klerksdorp (western Transvaal); that Samuel Lehulere Moroka, then on a visit to the ORC, had asked Gabashane to accompany him to Bloemfontein; that he had been expelled with Samuel and his followers from the ORC in 1904 (see Chapter 3); and that he, Nehemiah Gabashane, had been 'wandering from farm to farm ever since then' until he came to live in Randfontein location. It is probable that, for at least twenty years until 1904, Gabashane had been a principal sharecropper on Lovedale 89, and his testimony suggests a vigorous sense of rights to land which could not be suppressed merely by the superimposition of someone else's formal title. Officials had no evidence in 1938 that he would now be allowed to return to the farm, which was part of J.B. Lurie's extremely successful 'potato kingdom', briefly described in Chapter 3. In any case, Fortuinspruit 233 lay outside the Released Areas, in the heart of the Milner Settlement in the east of the district (see Chapter 2). Gabashane's request was therefore refused.[14]

Another story from the Institute of Race Relations files illustrates the extreme difficulty of finding a place for retired or redundant farm workers. E.A. Tsoai, a teacher, wrote in July 1937 from Bothaville district on behalf of his father, who had been told to 'trek' by his master. Tsoai enquired whether land was now available at Thaba Nchu for Africans to buy or rent. The application was officially rebuffed; but Tsoai persisted through 1938, 1939 and 1940 in the face of repeated refusals to accommodate his father on Trust land at Thaba Nchu.

> My father for whom I was applying was born at Theunissen. His father was born at Thaba Nchu at a certain place there called Tsoaing. He sided with Boers during great Boer war. He even got broken in the war. He was given a notice to leave the farm of his Baas at the end of August 1938. But no farmer was willing to take him . . . He is old and broken. He is 66 years of age.

Tsoaing, Tsoai's place, appears in Cameron's 1884 census of the Moroka territory, but not on any modern map. Eventually, in December 1940, in response to continuing pressure, a special concession was made to accommodate E.A. Tsoai's father and his household—but not the whole Tsoai family—on one of the Trust farms. In 1942, Rheinallt Jones received a similar appeal from Azael Tsoai, writing from Orlando Township (Johannesburg) on behalf of his father, who turned out to be a twin brother of the first old man. Azael Tsoai commented indignantly on the persistent bureaucratic refusal to accept non-Barolong at Thaba Nchu.

> Today we are being called to sacrifice for freedom for what freedom then if we are not allowed to buy land or be given residence at the reserves only that one is not Barolong. Is there any justice then? If we cannot see justice shall we get it tomorrow never? The first Native to win a military metal [sic] in this war is a native from the OFS but I am afraid unless he is a Barolong what will he get from all his services if he is not a Barolong, nothing.

Azael Tsoai's father was a labour tenant who had been 'driven away' from the farm on which he was living and forced to sell his cattle. His appeal for a place at Thaba Nchu was turned down.[15]

The reclamation and settlement proposals for Thaba Nchu were formally approved in January 1940, and the Chief Native Commissioner (Northern Areas), E.W. Lowe, was instructed to 'explain the schemes in detail to the communities or persons concerned and endeavour to obtain their acquiescence'. At the same time he should take the opportunity of persuading the people of Seliba to accept the provisions of Proclamation 31 of 1939. Should they fail to be convinced of the need to limit their livestock, the NAD 'would in their interests regretfully be compelled to introduce the provisions of the Proclamation against their wishes'. The CNC visited Thaba Nchu for this purpose in early March 1940. He reported a month later that the Thaba Nchu reserve had accepted the proposals and the Seliba reserve had rejected them, 'mainly on account of their objection to any limitation being imposed upon their stock'. In Thaba Nchu, nevertheless, there was also much 'disquiet', mainly on the part of people who had cultivated much more than 4 morgen of arable land and would fight the new limit 'tooth and nail'. In view of this disquiet, nothing was said in public about the proposal for arable lands to lie fallow after three seasons. The people of Thaba Nchu were only persuaded to accept the recommendations overall by the influence of the 'leading men of the tribe' such as W.Z. Fenyang. As for the Seliba people, they 'regard their individuality with some jealousy'; they were not subject to the influence of the 'leading men of the tribe'; and objections to the official plans came mainly from those 'of a progressive type' who had farmed on a considerable scale in the reserve. The NAD imposed an immediate punitive sanction against the Seliba people's refusal to accept the reclamation package, by withdrawing their grazing rights on Trust farms. Officials were determined to disabuse them of the impression that they could rent cultivation and grazing rights outside the reserve without accepting the 'betterment' provisions.[16]

Six Trust villages were established in the district as a result of these proposals. Two outlying settlements, Tiger River and Moroto, were created in the north-western and north-eastern portions, respectively, of the Trust land set aside as 'adjunct' to the Thaba Nchu reserve. They included a number of Xhosa families and other 'foreign natives' who had, it emerged, negotiated residence rights with white landowners prior to Trust purchase of their farms, in order specifically to be taken over with the farms when the Trust assumed responsibility for them. Four settlements—Gladstone, Tweefontein, Rietfontein and Klipfontein (see Figure 5.1)—were set up in the southern block of Released Area No. 3. These four were apparently planned to accommodate 500 families altogether. A culling operation throughout Trust-administered land was carried out in 1940. It encountered 'serious opposition' in Seliba, and did not succeed anywhere in reducing overall livestock numbers to conform with the estimated carrying capacity of one cattle unit per 8 morgen. Nevertheless, the figures reported show that one quarter of all stock units in the Seliba area and nearly one third of all stock units in the Thaba Nchu area were culled. Altogether, 28 per cent of the large stock units counted on Trust-administered land were culled, representing a massive assault on the resource base of individual households.[17]

Otherwise, the reclamation proposals were barely implemented at this time, being held in abeyance through shortage of funds and personnel until the end of the Second World War. Initially, therefore, it was the experience of the culling of livestock that epitomised the impact of 'betterment' on rural communities throughout South Africa. This experience also illustrates the absurdity and fraudulence of the official effort to 'obtain the acquiescence' of the people. Even in the early years of 'betterment', when the schemes purported to serve the long-term interests of a population still dependent on the land to a significant extent, at least two fundamental problems became quickly apparent. Firstly, the schemes were constructed on the basis of a deep official ignorance of the diverse sources of income or combinations of activities from which most reserve households actually managed daily survival. The number of large stock units notionally allowed per taxpayer or per household was derived from the estimated carrying capacity of grazing land in the relevant area and the total number of resident taxpayers or households. Likewise, the size of individual plots allowed for cultivation was derived from the amount of arable land available and the number of households which nominally shared that land. Neither limit was derived from a realistic estimate of the household resource base actually required to make an adequate living from the land. In this way, the NAD rendered itself impervious to the routine complaint of Africans across the country that no household could derive an adequate livelihood from 4 morgen of arable land and three large stock units. Proper 'consultation' of the people was therefore never seriously intended or attempted.

Secondly, resources such as livestock were in practice, of course, unequally distributed between reserve households. The implications of this for the management of pastoral and arable operations, or for the enforcement of culling, were nowhere discussed or resolved. How could culling be administered 'fairly' in these circumstances? On the one hand, culling a specified *number* of cattle units per stock-holding household had an extremely regressive impact upon the poor. On the other hand, culling a specified *proportion* of cattle units per stock-holding household provoked howls of outrage from farmers 'of a progressive type' whose co-operation was vital to the success of any 'betterment' scheme. Again, if households without stock were allowed to accumulate up to the notional mean stock-holding per household inferred from the live-stock-carrying capacity against the total number of households, this would imply the need for a disproportionately severe cull of the livestock of established stock-owning households. The problem was compounded by the continued over-stocking of privately-owned farms, over which the Trust had no direct control. Officials repeatedly impounded stock found trespassing on neighbouring Trust farms.[18]

Towards the end of the Second World War, with the operations of the Trust having been largely suspended through the war, white farmers in the district felt acutely insecure in respect of future Trust policy. The Quota had not yet been fulfilled. In 1945 over fifty white farmers, through resolutions forwarded by the Farmers' Associations, urged the NAD to clarify what additional land the Trust would purchase and when such purchase would take place. They experienced planning 'blight', as described by J.M. De Wet, an earlier active protagonist of the Vigilance Association. On the basis of his fifty-five years' residence in the district, he argued of Trust policy:

> that the acquisition of European owned ground outside the released areas in fragments, spread over the district, for occupation by natives, makes it impossible for Europeans to carry on undisturbed and profitable farming;

that it is not only a danger of total or partial isolation, constantly kept in mind, but causes a deterrent effect in the erection of necessary and reproductive improvements, on account of doubtful future enjoyment and occupation, which will ultimately reflect on the value of the farms.

This uncertainty, however, provoked conflicting responses. On the one hand, some farmers such as De Wet himself argued that no further purchases of white-owned land should take place. This argument was feasible only because promises had allegedly been made to white farmers that the Trust would acquire the balance of the Quota by buying black-owned farms in the Released Areas whose owners could not meet their mortgage interest payments. De Wet's position was supported by the 'white' municipality on the grounds that the first wave of Trust purchase had induced a depression of business confidence, an evacuation by the 'wealthier class' of white residents and a collapse of property values. On the other hand, other white farmers submitted competitive bids to the Native Affairs Commission for the inclusion of their farms in the areas to be identified for further purchase by the Trust.[19]

By this time, the Trust had acquired 53,020 morgen of land in the Thaba Nchu district. Africans had bought 1,411 morgen of land from whites. These two categories of land together comprised 54,431 morgen. The balance of the OFS Quota, 25,569 morgen, had still to be acquired. The NAC came to Thaba Nchu in March 1946 to resolve the clamour of conflicting local voices. The Thaba Nchu South Farmers' Association offered for sale to the Trust a block of farms along the south-western boundary of Released Area No. 3. Clarence Paver, of the Thaba Nchu attorneys Faustmann and Paver, offered a block of farms between the two reserves, in the north-west of the district. The 'white' municipality argued against this latter option on the grounds that white traders in Thaba Nchu would suffer from the withdrawal of the white landowners concerned. The Dutch Reformed Church also rejected the 'northern' option, on the grounds that thirty-five to forty families would be lost to its congregation. The Tweespruit Farmers' and Seed Potato Growers' Association, for its part, wanted the new 'Coloured' settlement at Thaba Patchoa to be removed.

The 'leading men of the tribe' also submitted evidence to the NAC, over the names of Chief Albert Setlogelo Moroka; his chief councillor, Isaiah Tonya Makgothi; W.Z. Fenyang; Dr J.S. Moroka, who was now a member of the Native Representative Council; and two reserve headmen. They asked the Trust to acquire all land between the Thaba Nchu reserve and the Modder river to the west, and all land between the Thaba Nchu and Seliba reserves. They based this request on Fenyang's allegation that 75 per cent of the people had insufficient land. Local officials' response was a measure of the chasm of incomprehension that prevailed. The Assistant Native Commissioner produced figures showing that, of 1,157 residential siteholders in the Thaba Nchu reserve, 235 had no land; of 1,088 siteholders in the Seliba reserve, only nineteen had no land; finally, out of 482 siteholders in the four new southern

Trust settlements of Gladstone, Tweefontein, Rietfontein and Klipfontein, only five had no land. Overall, the figures for the Released Areas and the two reserves showed that 514 out of a total of 2,727 siteholders (19 per cent) had no land. This was a different point from the one Fenyang had made: that most of the people had too little land. The carrying capacity of the land, the Barolong memorandum pointed out, was one third of the minimum requirements for a livelihood.

> Surely, Gentlemen, it does not even require argument to convince anyone that the present average of three head per householder is totally inadequate. We cannot all be 'farmers' but at least those who are entirely dependent on the land for a living should be placed in such a position that they can take their daily bread out of the soil. The African's savings bank is his stock kraal. Cattle have been through the ages our most treasured possession.

Unhappily, however, it would take a great deal more than mere argument to convince the Union government that Africans needed more land.[20]

The members of the NAC decided by a majority of four to one in favour of the purchase of a block of farms between the two reserves. Their detailed recommendations had to be revised in the light of an error in their figures discovered by Eric Heath, attorney and erstwhile secretary of the Vigilance Association. After adjustment, a list of farms was agreed which together comprised 25,514 morgen: a block between the two reserves, consisting of nearly 14,000 morgen; a block west of the old Thaba Nchu reserve, consisting of 6,320 morgen; and various farms along the western boundary of Released Area No. 3, amounting to 5,285 morgen. These arrangements left a conspicuous 'white spot' of farms virtually enclosed by the Seliba reserve and the Moroto block (see Figure 5.1); 'but all these farms are situated on the Excelsior main road and they will not in the slightest be affected ... they are not interested in selling their farms to the Trust, nor do they object to the adjoining farms being purchased ...'. The NAC noted that Africans still owned 33,981 morgen, bonded to the extent of £79,130. In order to overcome the problem of the Trust being unable, after fulfilment of the Quota, to buy black-owned farms inside the Released Areas that subsequently came on to the market, the NAC recommended that the 1936 Act be amended so that land acquired by the Trust from Africans should not be construed as Quota land. The NAC also recommended the excision of Thaba Patchoa 106 from the Released Areas, not in order to remove the newly-relocated 'Coloured' community but because its continued administration under the South African Native Trust was a clear constitutional anomaly. Accordingly, compensating land had to be bought by the Trust elsewhere in the district. This matter was not resolved until the early 1950s (see Chapter 7).[21]

Almost all of these farms recommended by the NAC were acquired by the Trust during 1948. Despite the strict limits imposed on household pastoral and arable resources, it is clear that intense pressure had already developed to exceed the residential limits imposed in the original six Trust settlements. A visiting agricultural officer observed huts 'springing up like fertilised mushrooms' at Tiger River. It turned out that 187 new residential certificates had recently been issued for the Trust villages. This relaxation of the original planning restrictions played havoc with existing demarcations of residential and arable areas. There was also a sharp increase in destitution, since the new settlers nominally had no rights to arable or grazing land. By 1949, when a committee of officials drew up a plan for the settlement of the second wave of Trust-purchased land, Gladstone had 227 families, Rietfontein-Klipfontein (jointly administered) had 169 families, Tweefontein had 162, Tiger River 120 and Moroto eighty-five. The agricultural officer warned against the consequences of uncontrolled expansion: 'we are playing with fire to merely increase the number of building sites and taking on Natives indiscriminately merely because they tell a pathetic story to the Additional Native Commissioner'.[22]

New Trust villages were recommended in the following places: Woodbridge and Commissiedrift, in the south, to accommodate the existing residents on newly-acquired Trust land and the 'surplus' from established Trust villages in Released Area No. 3; and Merino and Paradys, both close to Tiger River in the north, to accommodate existing residents on newly-acquired Trust land in that part of the district and also, if possible, landless families from the Thaba Nchu reserve (see Figure 5.1). Three farms in the north-east corner which straddled the Mensvretersberg should be transferred to the Moroto block to relieve congestion there. Two of the newly-acquired farms to the south of Seliba should be used to compensate the people of Seliba for their loss of the above three farms to the Moroto block. The other newly-acquired farms adjoining the reserve should only be available to the Seliba people for grazing purposes if they accepted the original reclamation proposals, especially the demarcation of their arable lands. The Seliba arable lands were still 'uncontrolled' in that sense, so that there was a 'mal-distribution of land and thus a shortage of grazing'.

The committee also specified appropriate methods of land use in the district, with reference to the prevailing soil structures. Arable lands should be laid on the exact contour by permanent grass strips; bushes or shrubs should be planted for protection against wind erosion; bluegum (eucalyptus) plots should be established; all arable lands should be fenced and no grazing cattle allowed into them. Maize, sorghum, cow peas and sweet potatoes were recommended as suitable crops for rotation. Wheat or other winter cereals could not be justified in view of the shortage of winter rainfall:

> To eliminate those people who are incapable of farming and who refuse to learn from the agricultural officers of the Department, and further to ensure that the Trust ground is cultivated to the best advantage of the

people as a whole, it is strongly recommended that allocations of arable allotments be made on a basis of merit only.

Accordingly, only 3 morgen of arable land should be allocated initially, and either increased or decreased according to the performance of the individual holder as assessed by agricultural demonstrators. The maximum holding should be 6 morgen.[23]

As regards grazing land, in view of serious erosion and deterioration of the veld, the committee declared that it was essential for pastures to be subdivided into camps according to veld type, and that these camps should be rotated to allow time for the recovery of the veld from over-grazing. Culling had therefore to be vigorously pursued. Emphasis should be placed on milk production through the Brown Swiss and Red Poll breeds of cattle; and draught animals should be reduced. In addition to these measures for the control of arable and pasture lands, the committee recommended that a 'rural village' should be established for people who worked in Bloemfontein and who only required a residential site in Thaba Nchu. This was the origin of the 'new' town of Selosesha, on the edge of the 'old' Thaba Nchu locations. It was not built, however, until the 1960s.

### 'THE OBSTINATE BUNCH': UNREST AT SELIBA

Throughout the 1940s, the 1950s and the 1960s the Seliba reserve was the prime site of opposition to the measures of 'betterment' and rehabilitation introduced by the authorities of the NAD on land administered by the South African Native Trust. The Seliba reserve consisted of seven farms: Morago 40, Kgalala 41, Bofulo 37, Rooibult 33, Kgamo 34, Tala 36 and Seliba 35 (Figures 1.3, 3.1 and 5.1). They were set aside in 1885, under the terms of the Gregorowski land dispositions, as one of two African reserves in the Moroka territory annexed by the OFS. The seven farms formed a distinctive horseshoe shape, and they lay beyond the northern ridge of hills which stretch from Toba in the north-west to Lokoala (the Mensvretersberg) in the north-east.

Seliba possessed a distinctive political character also. In the period before the Barolong civil war between 1880 and 1884, the area was one of Chief Moroka's cattle posts. Known as *stasie* ('station'), it was politically associated with Samuel Lehulere Moroka, the pretender to the chieftainship at Thaba Nchu. After his exile, the locations were described as bleak and barren and full of Samuel's supporters. This was hardly surprising. Seliba in particular was an obvious refuge for those of Samuel's supporters who remained in the district but sought to evade the political animosity of the land grantees, who were overwhelmingly members of Tshipinare's family or of his council (see Figure 1.5). In the ORC period, separate reserve boards were established for Thaba Nchu and Seliba, and Seliba had its own headmen. Consequently, when John Phetogane Moroka was appointed chief at Thaba Nchu in 1930, he had neither civil nor criminal jurisdiction over Seliba. At the beginning of the period discussed in this chapter, each of the seven farms, or locations, that together comprised the Seliba reserve had its own residential areas, although these varied both in number and in size. Kgalala had three separate straggling settlements, for example; Kgamo had one very small one.

The extension of the Trust regime to the reserves, and the acquisition by the Trust of farms which lay between them, implied the need to integrate the two reserves for political and administrative purposes; and the NAD accordingly took steps to extend the chief's authority over Seliba. However, there was no territorial integration until the second wave of Trust purchase was completed in 1948–9; and some people at Seliba still protested in 1956 that they did not 'know' Chief Albert Setlogelo Moroka or W.Z. Fenyang, by which they meant they did not recognise the authority of the chief at Thaba Nchu. In view of the separate provision of land defined as 'adjunct' to the two reserves after the first wave of Trust purchase was completed in 1938–9, the people of Thaba Nchu and the people of Seliba had to be consulted separately over the implement-ation of 'betterment' and rehabilitation. As we have seen, Seliba refused to co-operate with the reclamation measures: 'Natives in this reserve', a local official remarked in 1942, 'are most difficult'. They were strongly opposed to the culling of their livestock. Confrontation also took place over the cutting of the lands which was required to divide arable from grazing areas and to accommodate conservation measures such as the building of contour banks. The policy of the NAD at the time was that every holder of a residential certificate should be allotted 4 morgen of land for summer crops. Headman Andries Setouto of Seliba location allegedly told his people not to co-operate with the cutting of these 4-morgen plots when work began on this in October 1941: 'how would we manage to do the work', he asked, 'as people were opposed to it?' Having been a headman for seventeen years, Setouto was summarily dismissed in January 1942, on the grounds, as he reported the words of the Assistant Native Commissioner, 'You blooming fool you are making up the people to be against the instructions of the Government'.[24]

Setouto was untypical of the location headmen, it appears, in standing up to official authority. In any case, however, some Seliba residents proved to be more 'difficult' than others. In January 1945, Job Sedite Pule of Kgalala location complained that 157 of his sheep had died because of shortage of grazing. In response, the agricultural officer noted that he and his son and son-in-law were the largest stock owners and also 'the most undesirable people in the reserve'. In 1940, at the time of the first cull, Pule was allotted thirty-one cattle, two horses and 213 sheep. In August 1944 he had forty cattle, four horses and 364 sheep. He did not look after the sheep adequately. He deprived others of grazing. His losses were attributable to his obstinacy, a 'studied attitude of passive resistance on the part of his son' and 'complete disregard for his fellow location inhabitants who are being over-run by his stock'. He had 'practically eliminated' other stock owners. He had 'strenuously opposed' the fencing and closing of grazing camps. He refused to take advantage of local sales and 'for reasons best known to himself has preferred to allow his sheep to die rather than dispose of them'.[25]

A branch of the African National Congress (ANC) was formed in the Seliba reserve in October 1945, with Abel Kenke as chairman. Its main object in the district, in the view of the Assistant Native Commissioner at Thaba Nchu, was 'to thwart our efforts in the direction of stock limitation and stock- and veld-improvement'. Applications for meetings were refused, largely on these grounds, despite contrary advice from the Chief Native Commissioner, who noted that 'the chief and other leading men are members of the Congress already'. In 1947–8 the ANC at Seliba took up two issues in particular: the limitation of livestock and the 'Moroka Tribal Levy', the 30s. per annum for which every taxpayer was liable in order to compensate the Trust for its expensive purchase of land for African use. As a result of its imposition, allegedly without consultation:

> the annual taxation on the African has become so heavy that a good many people are already trekking to European farms, such people being usually poor people, who have not even the bare necessities of farming, but are still expected to pay this tax.[26]

The Levy was replaced in 1949 by a system of charging grazing fees related to the number of stock owned.

The Barolong establishment, meanwhile, observed recalcitrance at Seliba with some dismay. In October 1950, less than a month before the Witzieshoek rebellion came to a head, Chief Albert Setlogelo Moroka and W.Z. Fenyang requested the government to implement stock culling without delay:

> The Barolong Tribe as a whole have accepted the Betterment Scheme and a full scale rehabilitation of Native areas is long overdue; and it is desirable that the Government should take a firm stand and not dilly dally with the inhabitants of Seliba Reserve . . .

They noted that 5,000 morgen of additional land had been set aside for the Seliba people under the 1949 plan, on condition they accepted 'betterment'; if the Seliba people did not wish to use this land, it should be used to settle many others. The Assistant Native Commissioner supported this view, observing that 'residential sites arise like mushrooms everywhere'. He recommended that the 5,000 morgen should be used to settle landless families from the Trust village of Moroto and '80 landless stranded families' on the black-owned farm of Meloendrift 128. Fenyang followed up the matter in May 1951: four-fifths of the inhabitants, he claimed, having reluctantly accepted the 'betterment' scheme, were now beginning to appreciate the benefits of reclamation, and would feel aggrieved if the programme were not similarly carried through at Seliba.[27] He did not offer evidence to justify his claim.

The demarcation of arable lands in Seliba was already being enforced much more vigorously. To the NAD's exasperation, the reaction was a stubbornly consistent refusal, on the part of some residents of the reserve, to accept the newly-surveyed 6-morgen plots in substitution for their old lands. They then complained that their own lands had been appropriated and rented out to others in 6-morgen plots. The culling of livestock was also more vigorously enforced in this period. Early in 1951, a number of people from the Seliba reserve were arrested for refusal to bring their stock for culling. They spent three months without trial in Bloemfontein gaol, alongside some of the alleged 'ringleaders' from Witzieshoek. By 1953, in Morago and Kgalala locations, people had refused to pay all taxes, including grazing fees, for three years, and they were therefore subjected to a heavy police raid in the middle of that year. A series of complaints from Seliba—over taxes, grazing fees, the cutting of lands and the operation of Bantu Authorities—was transmitted through the provincial office of the ANC to William Ballinger, who represented Transvaal and OFS Africans in the Senate.[28]

Fenyang's attitude to such open flouting of authority—for he was the driving force of the chieftainship—reflected the tension at national level between the cautious conservatism of the older leadership of the ANC and the more militant populist impulse represented by the formation of the Youth League in 1944. This tension was most precisely and explicitly articulated at Thaba Nchu in the position of Dr Moroka, who was president of the ANC between 1949 and 1952. On the one hand, as a doctor, landowner and successful farmer, he was a prime representative of the educated African elite. On the other hand, as president of the ANC, he was responsible for initiating the first national Defiance Campaign in June 1952. His appeal met with a keen response from Seliba but none from the rest of the Thaba Nchu district.[29] This was the source of the strong suspicion with which officials, and some of the Barolong establishment, thereafter regarded Dr Moroka's local political interventions.

Grievances at Seliba came to a head in the early months of 1956. The spark that ignited the powder keg, as Native Commissioner C.N.J. Welman expressed it, was a change in the medium of instruction in primary schools from Sotho to Tswana, which followed the introduction of Bantu Education in the previous year. The change induced a strong backlash from Sotho-speakers. There were also significant minorities of Hlubi, Xhosa and Thembu in the district, who were concentrated in Morago location and Moroto Trust village. The Thaba Nchu School Council, a partly-elected local advisory body which was constituted in terms of the Bantu Education Act of 1953, deliberately and provocatively transferred a Xhosa-speaking teacher from the Xhosa-medium school at Morago to Kgalala school, and a non-Xhosa-speaking teacher from Kgalala to the Morago Xhosa school. The Council took this action in order to bring simmering resentments over the language issue into the open, and to secure the formal primacy of Tswana as a medium of instruction in schools throughout the district. This flare-up of the language issue confronted officials with a thorny dilemma. Either they had to repudiate, for some children and

their parents, the declared policy of mother-tongue instruction; or they would
be seen by 'law-abiding Barolong' to give way to a 'riotous and rebellious
minority'.[30]

The School Council's action reflected the anxiety felt by some of the Barolong elite over the threat to the local predominance of their language and
culture which was posed by the gradual infiltration into the district, despite
nominally tight control over residential certificates, of Basotho and various
ethnic minorities. In the years before Welman's appointment to Thaba Nchu
in 1954, such infiltration was apparently facilitated by J.S. Hlake, who had
come to Thaba Nchu from Basutoland in 1950 to work as a translator/clerk in
the local tax office. Welman alleged that Hlake had used his position to secure
tax and residential certificates for many Basotho who came to live in the Thaba
Nchu reserve. In 1956 he was a member of the Ereskuld school committee
in Thaba Nchu, and an active member of the ANC. The high-level impact of
such infiltration was symbolised, for Welman, by the fact that two of W.Z.
Fenyang's three sons-in-law were not Barolong. One of them, Paul Mahabane,
from a Sotho family background, was secretary of the School Council.[31]

The language issue was the spark. 'The spreading of the poison', Welman
observed, shifting his metaphor, 'was quick and effective'. At the annual
livestock inspection in February 1956, 172 out of 452 livestock owners in the
three locations of Seliba, Tala and Morago did not bring their animals for
culling. Welman diagnosed a pervasive restlessness not only within the Thaba
Nchu district but also outside it. He attributed this to an intensive campaign on
the part of the ANC to create unrest, 'with old, dormant grievances being
raked up and every pinprick scratched until it has become a festering open
wound'.[32] He recommended strong and immediate action against the defaulters, an 'obstinate bunch' who without exception, he alleged, were supporters
of the Samuelite faction. They were emboldened in their actions by the fact
that a successor had not yet been appointed to the late chief at Thaba Nchu,
Albert Setlogelo Moroka, who had died in April 1955. The succession dispute
is examined in the next section of this chapter.

Welman identified Isaiah Masisi Mihi, of Tala location, as the leader of the
resistance movement. Mihi was a 'cunning and clever propagandist' who did
not himself own livestock but allegedly incited others not to bring their stock
for culling. He was 'the major poison in the district', 'behind every single
problem surfacing in Seliba', and an active member of the ANC. Both he and
Joubert Toolo of Seliba location, another 'agitator', should be deported.
Others should be closely watched, including J.S. Hlake, described above;
Gladwin Nkoane, local chairman of the ANC; and Samuel Thubisi, another of
W.Z. Fenyang's sons-in-law, a teacher at the Moroka Institution who was
strongly opposed to Bantu Authorities, who openly criticised Fenyang for
allowing 'all the stupid people' to rule at Thaba Nchu, and who was 'very

thoroughly affected' by the influence of Reverend Illsley at the Moroka Institution.[33]

In March 1956, in an act of deliberate defiance of the authorities, about 200 residents of Morago, Tala and Seliba locations ploughed over the contour banks that had been built, from 1949 onwards, when 6-morgen plots were surveyed, demarcated and allocated. These people were particularly resolute and determined. Police reinforcements were sent for, and an official expedition proceeded to Morago on 17 March to negotiate a temporary truce. The people agreed to stop ploughing their old lands across the contour banks, provided the Chief Native Commissioner came to hear their grievances and that seven people arrested the previous day were released.[34]

On 27 March the Chief Native Commissioner for the Western Areas, Mr Holtzhausen, came to a public meeting at the Petra clinic, between Morago and Tala locations, which was attended by about 150 residents of the Seliba reserve and a full complement of senior police officers, members of the Special Branch and agricultural officers. Petrus Makoba of Morago expressed three complaints on behalf of the people. First, their lands were being carved up without their consent. Second, they had been told that 'selection'—apparently an official euphemism for culling—would only last for three years. Third, they wanted the old Seliba reserve board to be restored, in place of the Barolong Tribal Authority which had been established in 1953 under the Bantu Authorities Act of 1951. The reserve board used to listen to their complaints, Makoba said, whereas people could not speak at meetings of the Tribal Authority. Of these three issues, the culling of livestock provoked the most bitterness amongst the people.

> We were born here on the Reserve. We used to have between one and a hundred animals. I had 18 cattle, 25 sheep and 2 horses. That was in 1940. Today I have 2 cattle and 2 calves. The rest have been branded. I don't have a horse or a sheep left. My cart stands idle. I can't use it because my horses were also branded. I am just told to point one out and it is branded 'C'. If I prevent my cattle from being branded, the inspectors turn to the sheep. [Meeting: Yes! That is the complaint of us all!] In the course of the years my stock has gone down in numbers. In 1940 7 cows and 1 bull were culled; my sheep went down to 15 and my horses to 1. The next year two of my cattle and one horse were branded. During the following years, every year one head of cattle was branded, so that today I have just two left. I now have no sheep left. I just had to slaughter the branded sheep.[35]

Other people joined in. David Molehe of Seliba location, one of those whom Native Commissioner Welman wished to deport from the district as persistent trouble-makers, summed up the feelings of many when he said: 'We don't want our cattle to be branded. You just have to leave us alone with our chief, allow us to rule ourselves. All the people would be very happy'.

The Chief Native Commissioner could not agree. In response to the complaints, he insisted on the necessity of government intervention:

> All of us seated here would be very glad if the Government left us to do what we would like to do . . . but what would happen? We would quarrel, there would be famine, people would die, there would be droughts and our cattle would die of lack of grazing. I know this. I have done this job already for 37 years. When we left you alone, your cattle died of the effects of drought. I personally arranged for maize to be taken to Nebo, Pokwani, Nqutu and Barberton . . . They had been ploughing where they liked, their cattle had grazed where they wanted to. As a result the veld was so bare you could spot a snake creeping over the ridge. Yes!—old people and children died of hunger. [Meeting, very loudly: We want to live as we did then!!!].[36]

For his part, the Chief Agricultural Officer insisted on the necessity of strict limits on both the size of arable land allocations and the numbers of livestock allowed. He pointed out the logical impossibility, given limited land overall and a rapidly expanding human population, of the sons of the next generation each having access to the same amount of land as their father. He disputed Petrus Makoba's evidence of the drastic impact of culling on an individual's livestock holdings. He suggested that people could fatten up culled animals before selling them for between £12 and £20 a head.

The meeting broke up, inconclusively, in the rain. But the wheels of the legal machinery continued to grind. By the end of the year, about 600 successful prosecutions had taken place, for refusal to bring livestock for culling, for damage to contour banks and other works, and for cruelty to animals. The prosecutions involved 194 Africans, of whom many served terms of imprisonment of two weeks with hard labour. More than £1,000 in fines were collected. Many of those arrested were represented by the Johannesburg firm of Basner, Kagan and Millin, who were engaged by Isaiah Masisi Mihi. In addition, Joubert Toolo, as one of the principal 'agitators' identified by Welman, was found guilty of incitement under Act No. 8 of 1953. These arrests and indictments had a 'noticeable effect' in the district, and all owners of livestock brought their animals for inspection at the next culling which took place. For the time being, the trouble appeared to be over, except that Welman's campaign against tax defaulters in 1956 was undermined by repeated leaks of official information through an interpreter and a court messenger who were members of the ANC.[37]

A decisive shift of policy was imminent, however, as a result of the report of the Tomlinson Commission in 1955. This report marked a formal shift away from the presumption of a uniformly inadequate resource base for all taxpayers, and towards an explicit division of the rural population into a category of full-time farmers and a category of landless people who gained their livelihood by other means. Tomlinson also recommended the decentralisation of labour-intensive industry and the promotion of small-scale industries to ac-commodate the pools of 'surplus people' displaced from agriculture. The rationale of the new strategy was the obvious impossibility, by the mid-1950s, of a rapidly increasing reserve population being able to derive a substantial proportion of its livelihood from reserve agriculture.[38] Poor farming methods, as opposed to shortage of land, were routinely invoked to explain both declin-ing yields and absolute deficiencies of output. The logic of the diagnosis was that 'good' farmers should be encouraged and 'bad' farmers should be discouraged.

The practical implementation of Tomlinson's proposals was critically undermined both by the parsimony of the central state, which refused to provide more than a small proportion of the sum of £10 million per annum for ten years that Tomlinson estimated was required; and by the internal contra-dictions that lay at the heart of the proposals themselves. For example, 'most witnesses' to the commission proposed an annual income of £120 as an appro-priate figure for the purpose of determining the size of farming unit that would be necessary. Tomlinson calculated, however, that this would imply moving 80 per cent of reserve families from the land, the implications of which were too appalling to contemplate. He therefore invoked the results of an 'economic survey' of 111 full-time African farmers in mixed arable and pastoral regions to propose an alternative gross income of £60 per annum, half of the other figure, as a basis for the detailed planning of the reserves. As a result, the 'economic unit' adopted across the country for planning purposes was the amount of land that would notionally generate, through arable and pastoral activities, an income of £60 a year. A relevant comparison with income from wages may be derived from the fact that, in the late 1950s, many men from the Seliba reserve were employed as railway workers in Bloemfontein, where their wages were £3 or £4 a month.[39]

A detailed planning report was produced for Seliba in January 1958. Sep-arate calculations were made for the small Groblersdam irrigation scheme in the Seliba location, and for the rest of the original reserve with its attached Trust farms. The irrigation scheme should accommodate eighty-two settlers, each with 1.5 morgen allotments, 0.25 morgen residential plots and two large stock units. The total area of the scheme was thus calculated at 896 morgen, on the basis of a carrying capacity for grazing purposes of 4.5 morgen per large stock unit. The rest of the Seliba reserve with its attached Trust farms comprised 23,117 morgen, distributed between six locations: Morago, Kga-lala, Bofulo, Rooibult, Tala and Seliba. Of this total area, 5,546 morgen were judged to be suitable for dryland agriculture. An 'economic unit' in the eastern part of the Thaba Nchu district, which fell into agro-economic region B.6, was assumed to comprise 9 (6 + 3) morgen of arable land and ten large stock units, with a carrying capacity of 4.5 morgen per large stock unit and a ratio of one large stock to three small stock. Of the 9-morgen arable allocation, 3 morgen would be fallow at any one time. The assumed yield was 3.5 bags of grain per morgen, by comparison with a 1955 calculation of a prospective yield of 4.5 morgen and an actual average yield of three bags. One bag of grain was valued at £1.15s., so that the annual income notionally derived from agriculture was £36.15s. The income derived from ten large stock units, at £2.10s per unit, was £25, making a total annual income of £61.15s.[40]

On the basis of these calculations, combining the requirements for arable land and for livestock, 509 dryland 'economic units' were planned in Seliba. We have seen that eighty-two irrigated 'economic units' were planned for the Groblersdam scheme. Thus the area as a whole could accommodate 591 farming households. The document recorded a total of 1,232 families resident in Seliba in 1958, of which 563 had both land and stock; 158 had land without stock; 306 had stock without land; and 184, having neither land nor stock, were described as 'non-farming'. It was clear that less than half of Seliba's total population could be accommodated as farming households which would work the designated 'economic units'. The report recommended that two categories of households should be excluded from consideration for settlement: those which were not farming and those which had stock but were not working the land. Of the latter, 'these people on investigation have been found to be *wegwerkers* [migrants? rail workers?] and without exception are those natives who were rebellious when the land was surveyed—they still refuse from that time to take up land'. As soon as the settlement plans were implemented, then, several hundred households would have to be moved to 'a rural village' elsewhere.[41] The report did not further clarify their fate.

This planning report, which is typical of those produced not only for other Trust-administered areas in Thaba Nchu but also for Betterment Areas throughout South Africa, begged some fundamental questions about modes of livelihood in these rural areas. Firstly, as we have seen above, the annual income inscribed in the definition of an 'economic unit' was arbitrarily fixed at about half of the realistic estimates of required household income that were offered in evidence to the commission. This drastic adjustment downwards was made in order to reduce the absolute numbers and the overall proportion of people who would have to be moved from the land. The income level specified was not even adequate to meet the food component alone of the 'subsistence bundle' required by a family of five persons at the time. Further, the income level still applied for planning purposes many years after this particular report was drawn up was not, apparently, revised to take account of inflation.[42]

Secondly, there was no indication in the report of how existing inequalities of distribution both of land and of livestock would be ironed out in order to establish 'economic units' for the farming households. One immediate manifestation of such inequality was the fact that most private landowners, who resided mainly in the old locations of Thaba Nchu reserve rather than on their farms, thereby qualified for grazing and arable rights on Trust-administered land. In September 1958, such landowners had grazing rights for 242 large stock units on Trust land, which represented only a small proportion of their total livestock holdings but interfered substantially with the management of the 'economic units' that were officially envisaged. Having exhausted their own lands, alleged the Chief Agricultural Officer, the private landowners pushed their 'surplus' stock on to Trust land, and control was extremely difficult. Officials decided to revoke these 'privileges' with the implementation of the redevelopment plans in each Trust-administered area, but did not find this easy in practice.[43]

Thirdly, the division of the rural population into 'farming' and 'non-farming' households assumed no relationship through time between income derived from land and livestock and income derived from employment or other 'non-farm' activities; whereas it is clear, from the experience of successful farmers in the district, whether landowners or not, that the capacity to invest in farming was, to a significant extent, dependent on outside capital. Landowners had ready access to credit, private or institutional, above all by mortgaging their private titles; non-landowners often relied on income from wage employment either locally or outside the district to generate livestock and other capital resources necessary for farming. This glaring failure to recognise a relationship between farm and off-farm income allowed Welman to rid himself of 'the obstinate bunch' by arbitrarily and vindictively excluding from settlement in Seliba, and redistributing elsewhere, the owners of livestock who were landless in 1958 because they had consistently refused to accept 6-morgen plots.

Strikingly, a separate list was compiled of employees of the state then resident on Trust land in Thaba Nchu, most of them with land or stock or both. On that list there appeared the names of 222 men employed by the state who were residents of the six locations of Morago, Kgalala, Bofulo, Rooibult, Tala and Seliba. No fewer than 191 of them worked for South African Railways, almost all in Bloemfontein; the majority of the remaining thirty-one were teachers.[44] Three inferences may be drawn, by comparison with the figures cited above. The first is that state employment on the railway was overwhelmingly the most important source of off-farm income for residents of Seliba. The second is that there must have been significant overlap between the list of railway workers and the list of persistent 'trouble-makers' whom Welman wished to exclude from settlement as farmers. The third is that some of the railway workers themselves, moving between Bloemfontein and their rural homes, were probably the most important contacts between the networks of resistance at Seliba and the ANC organisation at provincial level.[45]

The 'trouble-makers', unsurprisingly, experienced the 1958 proposals as a further provocation. About twenty residents of Seliba came to Thaba Nchu in January 1960 to present a familiar litany of complaints through two spokesmen, Isaiah Masisi Mihi and Joseph Tanyane. The Chief Bantu Affairs

Commissioner for the OFS attended this meeting, with senior agricultural officers, the regent Maria Moipone Moroka, several members of the Tribal Authority and four headmen from the Seliba reserve. Mihi said the people had never agreed to the culling of livestock; they wanted their old lands back; and they wanted the old reserve board instead of the Tribal Authority. Tanyane, who had also been chosen as spokesman, 'but not at a meeting', explained his own experience. He used to plough about 11 morgen, and was prosperous. Then the old lands had been taken away and surveyed, but he had refused to accept a new 6-morgen plot in substitution, because it was too small. As for livestock, he used to have eleven beasts, but now only had two cows, one heifer and two horses. At the stock inspection in 1958, he reported that he had lost a calf, a young ox, which was recorded on his stock list. The following year, the calf was still missing, and the agricultural officer told him it could not be registered. He was therefore not allowed to replace it. He was still charged a grazing fee of £1.5s. in respect of that calf, and received a summons for non-payment. He was forced to pay the fee but could not get leave from his work in order to complain about the whole matter to the Bantu Affairs Commissioner at a time when this official was available.[46]

One of the senior agricultural officers responded that, if everyone were allowed as much land and stock as he wanted, 'it would be a big mess'. He could not understand their complaints, since people had refused to accept lands when they were offered. He stressed, however, that not everyone could be a farmer: 'we now try to get everyone who farms to the standard of an economic unit'. Others had to go out to work for some other means of livelihood. Two headmen then spoke up, in defence of the strategic objectives of 'betterment' and even of the limits imposed on arable holdings. 'Those who accepted 6 morgen saw many improvements. If someone works his 6 morgen properly, he can make a good living from that'. E.N. Modiakgotla, secretary of the Tribal Authority, explained that the complainants had used the wrong channels; they should have brought their complaints forward through their headmen to the chief. 'Here there is only one chief and one meeting for all the locations from Klipfontein to Rooibult. We meet only under the chief and headmen'. He was supported by Moses Ramagaga, a member of the Tribal Authority, who also owned a portion of his family farm, Leeuwfontein 129. These interventions allowed the Chief Bantu Affairs Commissioner to dismiss the complaints as insubstantial because they were improperly expressed. 'It is not a tribe that is complaining. It is individuals, perhaps two, perhaps five, perhaps ten, but not a tribe'. He advised these individuals not to 'kick a wall', for they would only stub their toes, and not to 'fan the fire', for they would get burnt themselves.[47]

It is clear from the circumstances of this meeting that the implementation of the 1958 plan met with considerable opposition in Seliba, and was subject to delay for this reason. Late in 1961 the Barolong Tribal Authority requested that replanning of Morago, Kgalala and Rooibult locations should be 'speeded up'; and specifically that preference should be given to 'surplus people' from these areas in new Trust settlements such as Ratabane that had recently been opened up. In the Seliba area as a whole, in 1963, there remained about 100 men who had refused to co-operate at all with the implementation of the 1958 plan. They would not move into new residential sites; their refusal 'hinders the development of the area'; officials wished to take legal action to force them to move and also to withdraw permission for them to maintain livestock.[48]

Meanwhile, the plans for development of a 'rural village' near the railway line, on a site adjacent to the 'old' Thaba Nchu locations, had been slowly taking shape. The proposal had originally been made in 1949, as part of the planning exercise of that year. Through the 1950s, there were arguments over the suitability of the site proposed; over the adequacy of water supplies; and over whether the proposal would not contradict the necessity to separate farmers from non-farmers within the 'old' locations themselves and to redistribute the former to outlying Trust villages. In mid-1963, the Tribal Authority urged that only Tswana should be settled in Selosesha, the name of the new township, and not Sotho or Xhosa, in order to avoid a 'most unhappy situation' in which customs would clash, the Barolong would be outnumbered and demands would be made for recognition of other languages than Setswana in schools.[49] By the late 1960s the original 'rural village' for urban workers in Bloemfontein and elsewhere had evolved into a regular township, with services such as water and electricity, in which sites could be bought by individuals. Selosesha was occupied by many of the salaried employees of the local state. It was not open to redundant farmers from Seliba or elsewhere. For them, by this time, about thirty-five Trust villages had been established, in the north and the south of the district (see Figure 6.2); and the presumption that residents of Trust villages would all be full-time farmers was finally destroyed. A generation after his journey in 1944–5, Oliver Walker would have recognised the bleak and barren aspect of most Trust villages.

Resistance at Seliba sputtered on. By 1965, forced resettlement was imminent. The Bantu Affairs Commissioner at Thaba Nchu threatened the people that all permanent residential certificates would be cancelled; those who refused to apply for new temporary certificates would be imprisoned; their homes would be destroyed by bulldozer; and their children would be driven out. Several 'strikers' were convicted in March and April 1967 of ploughing land in the grazing camps of Tala location. Agricultural officials intervened and cut down the maize stalks for silage, which provoked outrage at the loss of 2,000 bags, or forty bags, according to different versions.[50] By the end of 1967, so many criminal proceedings were outstanding, in respect of Seliba people refusing to move their homes from areas demarcated as grazing camps, or of people illegally cultivating such land, that a breakdown of administration took place between the South African Police and the Bantu Affairs Commissioner's court. Both officials and police were nearly overwhelmed, through acute shortage of manpower to pursue these proceedings, by a wave of recalcitrance in Tala, Kgalala, Morago and Seliba locations.[51]

As part of his investigation of forced relocation throughout the country, Cosmas Desmond reported the final burst of this wave of popular recalcitrance in Seliba. Twenty men were arrested on 5 December 1968 for still living in the old Morago location. Three of them were blind. They were taken to Bloemfontein to await trial and their cattle were impounded by the Bantu Affairs Commissioner. They lost the case in Bloemfontein on 11 March 1969. Lorries came to Morago on 20 April and dumped the people in Bultfontein and in various Trust villages. As 'strikers', they were forced to sell all their remaining livestock by October of that year.[52]

Desmond described the scattered tents and shacks of mud-brick and corrugated iron sheeting that in May 1969 made up Bultfontein I, about six miles north-west of Thaba Nchu town, to the left of the road past the railway station, and the beginnings of Bultfontein II, on the other side of the road. About seventy families had arrived in the first settlement:

> Some of these were previously living in the Reserve but for some reason did not qualify to be resettled in a Trust village. Others had been evicted from white farms; some had been endorsed out of towns like Welkom, and at least one from Johannesburg; a few were from the locations at Thaba Nchu and there were about six families from Morago.[53]

By the mid-1970s, the site of Bultfontein III, near the railway station and on the western edge of the old Thaba Nchu reserve, had also filled up with refugees, some displaced from Bloemfontein and other urban areas, others displaced from white farms throughout the eastern OFS. None of them had access to any other land than their residential plots. All three Bultfonteins, known locally as the 'Zones', were situated on the original farm Bultfontein 113, which had once briefly belonged to Buku, one of Tshipinare's widows (see Figures 1.3, 1.5 and 6.2), and which was bought from its white owner by the South African Native Trust in 1948. For many people, by the early 1980s, the three Bultfonteins were temporary staging posts on their inevitable passage to Onverwacht/Botshabelo, the huge rural slum whose distinctive place in the political economy of apartheid in the 1980s is analysed in Chapter 6.

### THE 'CREAM OF THE BAROLONG': AN INTERLOCKED ELITE

For eleven years, from 1954 to 1965, overseeing much of the turbulence at Seliba described above, C.N.J. Welman was responsible for Native (Bantu) Affairs at Thaba Nchu. In the streams of confidential official memoranda that he despatched to his superiors, first at Potchefstroom and then at Bloemfontein, he did not spare them the virulence of his private opinions on the personal qualities and presumed motives of assorted pretenders to the chieftainship and of dissenters and suspected agitators in the district. Welman was also capable of sweeping generalisation on the failure of the Barolong to accommodate themselves to the 'tribal' mode of behaviour required by official philosophy:

> The Barolong today are very badly detribalised, a relatively weak lot, too well-learned to do manual work, too poorly-learned to do clerical work, too civilised to be native and too uncivilised to be white, tribal as it suits them, detribalised as it suits them. The cream of the Barolong is very good, but the milk is very watery.[54]

In Welman's view, the 'cream' of the Barolong comprised two 'outstanding' men—W.Z. Fenyang and Ephraim Mojanaga—and several members of the Barolong Tribal Authority. Political loyalty to the central government was obviously a prime ingredient of this diagnosis, as were the personal virtues of sobriety and self-restraint. Fenyang was prominent in public affairs; Mojanaga was a successful farmer; both were God-fearing men and committed teetotallers.

Welman's trenchant opinions reflected, of course, the heavy bias of his official position. For that very reason, however, they are an appropriate point of departure here for analysing the diverse ways in which the Barolong elite mediated the conflict between the central state and the 'obstinate bunch' at Seliba. The chieftainship and the Tribal Authority were the most important instruments of mediation in the 1950s and the 1960s. In the first part of this section, therefore, I outline the power struggles that took place for control of these instruments of mediation. In the second part of this section, through brief profiles of six prominent men, I show, firstly, how the old landed elite was transformed into the modern bureaucratic, professional and commercial elite; secondly, how the members of this local ruling class were bound to one another through intricate connections of kinship and affinity; and, thirdly, how superior access to educational opportunities gave them occupational, marital and geographical mobility far beyond the boundaries of the district.

Chief John Phetogane Moroka's death in November 1940 created an impasse over the succession. There were two contenders: Albert Setlogelo Moroka, son and heir of Robert Tawana, who had died in 1912; and Benjamin Kebalepile Moroka, son and heir of John Phetogane (see Figure 1.2). Albert Setlogelo had been convicted of stock theft in 1922 and disqualified by the magistrate from succession to the chieftainship. John Phetogane was therefore chosen to be chief at a public assembly, and formally appointed in 1930, in order to forestall further agitation by the Samuelites (see Chapter 4). It was left unclear whether his own heir would succeed him or not. Shortly before John Phetogane's death, on the understanding that Albert Setlogelo had been officially disqualified, some of the senior members of the Barolong establishment, including W.Z. Fenyang and Dr J.S. Moroka, took steps to legitimise John Phetogane's son, Ben Kebalepile, through the payment of bridewealth cattle (*bogadi*) for the latter's mother. However, at the official enquiry which took place in March 1941, chaired by J. Mould Young, the chief magistrate of the Transkei, Fenyang and Dr Moroka took up opposed positions. It emerged that the local magistrate's disqualification of Albert Setlogelo had never been approved by the government. Fenyang and others therefore supported Albert Setlogelo, as the rightful heir of Robert Tawana; Dr Moroka championed the cause of Ben Kebalepile. The Committee unequivocally upheld the rule of primogeniture and recommended the appointment of Albert Setlogelo Moroka.[55] He married a teacher from Bloemfontein, Maria Moipone, in 1942. They had three daughters, all of whom died; and one son, Robert Tawana Phillip Mokgopa Moroka, born in 1952.[56]

Albert Setlogelo died in April 1955. He had been 'ill' for some time, a familiar official euphemism for a chronic addiction to alcohol. The authorities had to resolve a difficult situation at a sensitive time: the wrangling over the succession was renewed; resentment of Bantu Authorities and the 'betterment' programme, especially at Seliba, was a running sore for the administration; and replanning of Trust-administered land along the lines recommended by Tomlinson was imminent. The Native Commissioner, Welman, identified three factions in respect of the succession dispute: that of the ruling group, led by W.Z. Fenyang, who was also chairman of the Tribal Authority which had been constituted in 1953; that of Ben Kebalepile Moroka, led by Dr Moroka, who had recently completed a suspended sentence for his role in the national Defiance Campaign; and that of the Samuelites, strongly represented in Seliba, Kgalala and Morago locations, who wished to instal Percy Tshabadira from Bechuanaland.

Welman's task, as he saw it, was either to reconcile the first two factions or 'to build everything from scratch again'. He urged that Percy Tshabadira's claim should not be considered at all. The proper heir, Robert Mokgopa, was barely three years old. The Barolong had given 'very little respect' to Albert Setlogelo, because he had been 'appointed by whites'; and even now his widow, Maria Moipone, had to fetch her own water, a considerable indignity. Some members of the Tribal Authority favoured Ben Kebalepile, but it would be 'fatal' to appoint him, in Welman's view, because he was 'weak ... and headstrong ... and very much under the influence of Dr Moroka'. For this reason, Welman insisted, a public assemby (*pitso*) to determine the people's preference should be avoided at all costs. Welman's own choice of a steady hand on tribal affairs, that of W.Z. Fenyang, would counterbalance the 'weakness' of Ben Kebalepile and the allegedly insidious influence of Dr Moroka; but Fenyang was elderly and very frail and his death was expected at any moment.[57]

A series of complex and 'admittedly peculiar' arrangements was made to overcome these problems. Robert Mokgopa was declared successor to Albert Setlogelo; his mother, Maria Moipone Moroka, was appointed Acting Chief, or regent; W.Z. Fenyang was appointed as her deputy for all administrative purposes other than the hearing of civil and criminal cases; Ben Kebalepile was appointed as her deputy for the sole purpose of trying civil and criminal cases, since Maria Moipone as a woman had no *locus standi* for this purpose in Tswana law and custom as officially interpreted in terms of the Native Administration Act of 1927. Ben Kebalepile also retained his previous office as headman of Mokwena location. Maria Moipone and her two deputies were formally installed in March 1957.[58]

The precarious balance of power contrived by Welman was disrupted firstly by Fenyang's death in July 1957; secondly by a request from Percy Tshabadira, in Bechuanaland, to settle in Thaba Nchu with some of his followers; and thirdly by developing 'complications' in the relationship between the chieftainship and the Tribal Authority. In November 1959, having handed over his chieftainship in Bechuanaland to his son Walter Mokgosi, and having briefly visited Basutoland, Percy Tshabadira suddenly appeared in Thaba Nchu, and declared that he wished to come 'home' to die. He was 77 years old. Not generally infirm, Percy Tshabadira nevertheless had sore feet as a result of his journey, and he asked the regent, Maria Moipone, to come and greet him at the house of his cousin, Eliza Tlhakung. This was a clear reversal of conventional propriety by which visitors should present themselves to the chief, and Welman found his behaviour and his demeanour both insolent and provocative. He also insisted that there was no land available at Thaba Nchu for Percy Tshabadira to settle with his followers, and expelled him from Thaba Nchu within 24 hours.[59]

Meanwhile matters were deteriorating in the tribal administration. Ben Kebalepile had assumed the function of Chief Administrative Officer, together with the chairmanship of the Tribal (Regional) Authority. Its secretary, E.N. Modiakgotla, complained that the regent was trying to assume autocratic powers over the Authority. The regent complained that she was being kept in the dark over important decisions, and was expected to sign blank financial requisitions. Ben Kebalepile started drinking less and being more forceful, so that 'where, at first, he made a sad blunder every time he stood up to speak, he now takes fairly important decisions on his own with, for him, relatively few faux pas'. The result was a three-way split within the ruling group, a situation exploited by the 'militant pro-Samuel group' which, in 1960, Welman guessed to have the support of 30 per cent of the people, against 25 per cent for the establishment and 45 per cent who were indifferent. The regent complained at the end of that year that some of the councillors 'are making propaganda against me and are instigating all kinds of troubles for their own advantage'. She wished to replace six out of twelve members of the Tribal Authority. Welman's view was that the trouble was fomented primarily by Modiakgotla, secretary of the Authority. Welman urged his department to support the regent's bid for full recognition and her request to reconstitute the membership of the Tribal Authority.[60]

In 1964, Maria Moipone was fully accepted as a member of the Tribal
Authority, the only woman, and she represented Thaba Nchu as a delegate in
the Tswana Territorial Authority (TTA). She later joined the Democratic
Party of Bophuthatswana, formed by the Chief Minister, Lucas Mangope, and
sat in the Legislative Assembly until 1979, when her son Robert Mokgopa
succeeded her. She died in 1982. In 1964, also, following the death of Ben
Kebalepile, a new chairman and deputy regent was installed in the Tribal
(Regional) Authority: Moutloatsi Setlogelo, a nephew and protege of W.Z.
Fenyang.[61] He was also a delegate in the TTA; he became the first Minister of
Education and Culture in the Bophuthatswana cabinet, and Thaba Nchu's
most prominent and influential son. He died in 1981. His background is
explored below.

The official effort to 'retribalise' the Barolong reached a climax in 1969 with
the inauguration of a 'Moroka Memorial Day' in October of that year. It was
suggested, apparently, by the 'tribal elders' and encouraged by white officials
and by a white professor of history at the University of the OFS, J.J. Oberholster. Senior politicians and officials attended in force: the Minister of Bantu
Administration and Development, M.C. Botha; the Commissioner-General of
the Tswana, Dr Kloppers; the Administrator of the OFS; the Chief Bantu
Affairs Commissioner of the OFS; the Chief Minister of the Tswana Territorial
Authority, Lucas Mangope; two ministers from the Transkei government; and
a councillor from Witzieshoek. There were also representatives and visitors
from most of the Tswana areas of the Republic. The Master of Ceremonies
throughout was Moutloatsi Setlogelo.

Through the morning of 4 October, speeches were made by M.C. Botha and
Lucas Mangope on the theme of collaboration and mutual understanding, to
which the public response was polite and lukewarm. In the evening, a historical pageant was staged in a school sports field. African dignitaries sat on one
side of the enclosure and white villagers on the other side. A ragged torchlight
procession preceded another series of speeches. J.M. Mothibatsela, a local
historian, who was then employed at the Lobatsi Training College (Botswana),
told the story of the Seleka Barolong migration from the north. Professor
Oberholster told the story of the 'special relationship' between the Barolong
and the Boers. Finally, Dr J.S. Moroka, to the embarrassment of the whites
and the TTA dignitaries and to the spontaneous enthusiasm of the crowd of
ordinary people, pointed out that Thaba Nchu now consisted only of one third
of the territory that Chief Moroka had ruled, and that individual allocations of
land were absurdly insufficient. 'I ask you, and the white people present, can a
man live on 6 morgen of ground?'. Officials had made strenuous efforts to
exclude Dr Moroka entirely from the programme. Ripples of tension spread
through the crowd as he spoke.[62]

Through the 1950s, the 1960s and the 1970s the institutional structures
of the chieftainship, the Tribal Authority and the emergent 'republic' of

Bophuthatswana formed the public stage upon which many of the Barolong elite made their careers. The incumbents of the chieftainship in the twentieth century—those who held formal seniority within the genealogy of Tshipinare's descendants—were notoriously 'weak' men, mainly on account of their predilection for strong drink. Both senior surviving sons of Chief Tshipinare, Robert Tawana (d. 1912) and John Phetogane (d. 1940), had lost their land by the early 1890s; the former was virtually indigent on his death in 1912, and bequeathed that condition to his son, Albert Setlogelo (d. 1955). In the late 1950s, the Tribal Authority had to build a decent house for the regent, Maria Moipone, and the young heir, Robert Mokgopa, in place of the 'hovel' which they occupied.[63] Robert Mokgopa himself, also an alcoholic, died in 1991.

The 'strength' of the local ruling class, then, was rooted in the men and women of lesser rank in the genealogical hierarchy: those who retained portions of their land, and built their careers on the decisive material advantage they derived from access to mortgage finance. Few of them were successful farmers; but superior education opened up opportunities of other kinds. Brief biographies of six men are presented here in order to illustrate these diverse trajectories: Walton Zacharias Fenyang; Israel Tlale Setlogelo; Ephraim Mabilo Mojanaga; Dr James Sebe Moroka; Bennett Herbert Keikelame; and Dr Robert Frederick Setlogelo. Fenyang's life and work are perhaps the appropriate point of departure for this purpose, for three reasons. Firstly, Fenyang and Mojanaga were singled out by Welman as the two 'outstanding' men in the district, without equal in his experience. Secondly, more to the point, Fenyang was the power behind the chieftainship for three decades. Thirdly, his position in the genealogies of the elite was absolutely pivotal. While the Fenyang family at Thaba Nchu was itself demographically insignificant, W.Z. Fenyang's mother's second marriage, to Abraham Setlogelo, had the decisive effect of hingeing the Setlogelo genealogy to that of Tshipinare's descendants, so that all the men listed above, except Ephraim Mojanaga, an outsider to the district, were more or less closely related. These relationships are shown in Figure 5.2.

*Walton Zacharias Fenyang* (1877–1957) was reared devoutly in the Methodist tradition at Thaba Nchu. He barely knew his father, Zachariah Fenyang, who was a headman of the Rapulana section of the Barolong and a prominent councillor both to Chief Moroka and to Chief Tshipinare. His mother, Elizabeth Nkhabele, also known as Mmatshipinare, was Chief Tshipinare's eldest daughter. She had two children by Zachariah Fenyang (d. 1883): Walton and Naomi; and two children by Abraham Setlogelo (d. 1891): Israel Tlale and Robert Frederick (see Figure 5.2). Her two married lives were short but her own life was very long: she died at the age of 99 in September 1947, mourned by many at Thaba Nchu and elsewhere. She was a stalwart of the International Order of True Templars. She was also a prime source of oral history for Chief Moroka's biographer, S.M. Molema.[64] In the Gregorowski land dispositions, she was granted three farms: Dakpoort 117, Mooiplaats 118

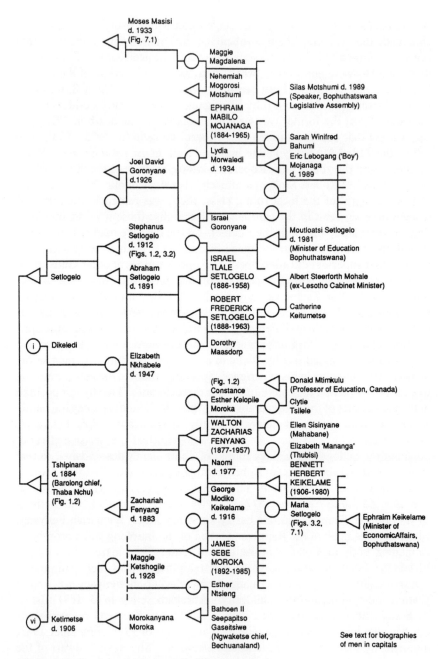

*Figure 5.2*  Partial genealogy of the Barolong elite.

and Rietfontein 119 (see Figures 1.3 and 1.5). The family retained Rietfontein when Elizabeth Nkhabele's estate was divided in 1929. By the late 1930s, however, W.Z. Fenyang was forced to sell much of the portion that he had inherited, in circumstances outlined in Chapter 4.

In 1909, Fenyang married his cousin, Constance Esther Kelopile Moroka. Her mother was Mmamodiko, who was married first to Joel, Chief John Phetogane's elder brother, and then to Isaac Motshegare, their younger brother. Fenyang was active in the ANC in the 1910s and 1920s, when he was OFS provincial president. He appears to have withdrawn from close involvement thereafter, but he retained strong influence in local politics at Thaba Nchu. Through his mother, Elizabeth Nkhabele, Fenyang was 'sister's son' to two chiefs, Robert Tawana and John Phetogane. His wife was a niece of them both. He was a first cousin of John Phetogane's successor, Albert Setlogelo (see Figure 1.2). Throughout his long career as the power behind the chieftainship, Fenyang held no official position, except that he was headman of Ratlou location for some years; he was briefly acting chief in the interregnum between the death of John Phetogane in November 1940 and the accession of Albert Setlogelo in May 1941; and even more briefly, before his own death in July 1957, he was the regent's deputy for administrative purposes. He was the one person who, in Welman's view, 'held the tribe together'; and in that sense he inherited the mantle of 'Father of the Barolong' from Reverend Joel Goronyane, who died in 1926.

Fenyang had three daughters. The eldest was Clytie Tsilele (b. 1912), also known as Morwa, who trained as a nurse in England in the late 1930s. In 1939 she married Donald Mtimkulu, a member of the ANC and a well-known educationist who became President of the African Teachers' Federation and later head of Adams College, Amanzimtoti (Natal). They left South Africa in the late 1950s and lived in Northern Rhodesia until 1965, when they separated. Don Mtimkulu spent the remainder of his professional career in the United States and Canada. Clytie Tsilele lived in Britain for some years and, from the early 1970s, she worked as matron at the women's hospital in Gaborone (Botswana). She died in 1986. The second daughter was Ellen Sisinyane (b. 1919), a teacher, who married Paul Mahabane; she was heavily in debt when she died in 1965, and her husband had to sell her portion of Rietfontein. The third daughter was Elizabeth 'Mananga' (b. 1925), who trained as a teacher and married Samuel Thubisi, a teacher at the Moroka Institution who strongly opposed Bantu Authorities. She later divorced him. In the mid-1980s she was head of a primary school in Thaba Nchu, and share-cropped her portion of Rietfontein with a white farmer. Elizabeth Thubisi herself had four daughters, two of them teachers, a third with a law degree from Witwatersrand University.

W.Z. Fenyang's half-brother, *Israel Tlale Setlogelo* (1886–1958), was introduced in Chapter 3, in a detailed account of the disintegration of the

Setlogelo family estate, as a wayward opportunist who both lost his own land and preyed upon his gullible relatives. He was a court interpreter, journalist and, in retirement, a farmer at Kleinkrans, close to the Trust village of Tiger River. His political position was either ambivalent or inconsistent. He was a close friend of Kali John Matsheka, the leader of the Barolong Progressive Association (BPA). The BPA flourished in the late 1930s in opposition to the established chief and to the Trust's exclusive control over newly-acquired land (see Chapter 4). In the 1950s, however, judging from a confidential report to the Secretary for Native Affairs, Israel Tlale appears to have served, unofficially, as the department's 'eyes and ears' in Thaba Nchu; for he drew officials' attention to the way in which ANC activists were assisting the people of Seliba who had been charged with multiple offences in 1956 to defend themselves in court. He sought specifically to discredit Dr Moroka, on the grounds that residents of Seliba had twice demonstrated at Dr Moroka's house in support of the Defiance Campaign of 1952. Welman commented to his superiors, 'Israel Setlogelo is no fool and keeps his eyes and ears wide open'. Israel Tlale was also at odds with W.Z. Fenyang, apparently because of their mother's marriages and the implicit question raised thereby of their relative seniority in the ruling genealogy. He neglected his wife and his three children, and Moutloatsi Setlogelo was effectively brought up and educated by Fenyang. The bitterness caused by this was reflected in family dissension at the funerals both of Israel Tlale himself, in 1958, and of his son Moutloatsi, in 1981. Shortly before his death, Israel Tlale bought the farm Gogothuse 631, part of the original Meloendrift 128, adjoining his old inherited property of Matlapaneng, in a transaction which left him heavily in debt to his two sons, Moutloatsi and Bathobatho Setlogelo, and to two others.[65]

As we have seen in Chapter 3, W.Z. Fenyang was a close friend of Sol Plaatje. *Ephraim Mabilo Mojanaga* (1884–1965) was a first cousin of Sol Plaatje, his father having married Sarah, a sister of Plaatje's father. The Mojanaga family had moved from the Berlin Mission station of Bethanie in the southern OFS to Pniel Mission on the Vaal river, a journey similar to that of Sol Plaatje's family recorded in Brian Willan's biography of Plaatje. They were all under pressure to reduce their stock. Nevertheless the Mojanaga family prospered sufficiently on livestock to move north to British Bechuanaland, where Ephraim Mabilo's father bought the farm Buccleugh in 1908, for £2,100. The farm lay on the Kabe tributary of the Molopo river, just south of the Molopo reserve.[66]

In 1913 Ephraim Mabilo married Lydia Morwaledi Goronyane, a daughter of Reverend Joel Goronyane. They settled in the Thaba Nchu district a few years later. On Goronyane's death in 1926, his two daughters jointly inherited one of his properties, the farm Vaalkop 66 (see Figure 1.3). Ephraim Mabilo farmed at Homeward, comprising half of Vaalkop 66, for the rest of his life. But he never owned the property, which was registered in his wife's name and, after she died in 1934, jointly in the names of their six children. In 1938 Ephraim Mabilo and his brother Philip Mojanaga inherited the farm Buccleugh, in the Mafeking district, from their father. Ephraim Mabilo could not work the farm efficiently from his home at Thaba Nchu. He therefore sought to exchange Buccleugh, within the terms of the Trust and Land Act 1936, for a suitable farm in the Thaba Nchu district. The Native Affairs Department refused to effect any exchange, on the grounds that all land close to Homeward which had been bought by the Trust in Thaba Nchu was required for the Gladstone settlement initiated in 1941. The Mojanaga brothers eventually sold Buccleugh, which was a 'black spot' surrounded by white-owned land, to the Department of Lands for £4,500 in 1942; and, following repeated appeals through Senator Rheinallt Jones for official permission to do so, they were able eventually to buy for cash a portion of the farm Dankbaar 206 from the estate of Charlie Morgan, who died in 1939. The latter's younger brother, Cecil Morgan, was an executor of Charlie Morgan's estate and also on very friendly terms with Ephraim Mojanaga.[67]

Mojanaga was a single-minded and hard-working farmer, who concentrated on rearing sheep for the wool market. He never got into debt. He also had a substantial interest in Thaba Nchu African Trading Stores, the largest African-owned general dealers in the district. The other proprietors were Dr Moroka, Bennett Herbert Keikelame (see below) and Paul Mosaka, an entrepreneur from Johannesburg who was headmaster of St. Paul's School in Thaba Nchu for some years in the 1930s. Mosaka was also one of the founders of the African Democratic Party in 1943, and a member—with Dr Moroka—of the Native Representative Council. Mojanaga had two sons and four daughters. His eldest son, Henry Rebolang, was manager of Thaba Nchu African Trading Stores until the partnership was dissolved in the 1950s. One of his daughters married Silas Motshumi, son of Nehemiah Mogorosi Motshumi, who worked closely with Rheinallt Jones on the resolution of the complex issues which arose out of the 1936 Trust and Land Act (see Chapter 4). Silas Motshumi was a member of the Tribal Authority, and rose to become Speaker of Bophuthatswana's Legislative Assembly. Ephraim Mabilo himself was also a member of the Tribal Authority, until the regent requested his removal in 1960.[68]

Ephraim Mabilo's other son, Eric Lebogang ('Boy') Mojanaga, who had been educated at Adams College in Natal, took over the management of Homeward on the old man's death in 1965; he suffered severe loss of livestock, however, in the 1969–70 drought, and thereafter worked as a clerk in the agriculture and health departments in Thaba Nchu. He leased Dankbaar for ten years to Alex Shuping, a successful businessman from Thaba Nchu, because he could not afford to run that farm as well as Homeward. In the 1980s, after the slum of Onverwacht/Botshabelo was established, which lay immediately to the west of Dankbaar (see Chapter 6), the livestock on the farm were repeatedly raided by inhabitants of the slum. These incidents came to a head early in 1989 with the murder of the herdsman employed by Ephraim Mabilo Mojanaga's elderly widow, and the violent theft of sheep and cash. Eric 'Boy' himself died in March 1989. His widow remained at Homeward, with most of their children and several grandchildren. In 1989 the three eldest daughters were, respectively, a social worker in Onverwacht/Botshabelo; a croupier at the Thaba Nchu Sun Hotel which was built in the 1980s to the north of Homeward farm (see below); and a librarian in Windhoek (Namibia). One son was looking for a job in Mafikeng, being unable to afford his fourth year of study at Fort Hare University. Another son was a barman at the recently-opened Naledi Sun hotel in Thaba Nchu. Of the two remaining daughters, one worked at the Thaba Nchu airport nearby, and the other was finishing Standard 8 at Albert Moroka High School in Thaba Nchu.[69]

*James Sebe Moroka* (1892–1985) was born to Maggie Ketshogile, the eldest daughter in Tshipinare's sixth house (see Figure 5.2), when she was 18 years old. His father was said to be a white man. His mother was later married to Stephen Mokitlane Nyokong, son of John Mokitlane Nyokong of Maseru 64 (see Figure 1.3), whom she divorced for adultery in 1908. She had two children by him, Richard and Jacobeth Nyokong; and two others by Hermanus Ntsieng, Gideon and Esther Ntsieng. [In 1933, as an illustration of the marital mobility of the sons and daughters of the elite, Esther Ntsieng was married to Bathoen II Seepapitso Gaseitsiwe, chief of the Ngwaketse tribe in Bechuanaland]. As one of Tshipinare's sixteen heirs, Maggie Ketshogile was granted in 1886 the three farms Middelerf 114, Bittervlei 115 and Walhoek 116 (see Figures 1.3 and 1.5), and also one-sixteenth of Egypte 107. She died in 1928.[70]

James Sebe Moroka had several reputations. As a medical doctor, he was trained in Edinburgh (Scotland) and later, for three years from 1933, in Vienna (Austria). He maintained a lucrative private practice in the eastern OFS for fifty-eight years, from 1918 to 1976, and he is remembered particularly for his diagnostic skills. As a politician at the national level, he was prominently involved in the All-African Convention, which was formed to oppose the Hertzog legislation of 1936. He was a member of the Native Representative Council in the 1940s, and with others proposed its adjournment in 1946, during the African miners' strike, in frustration with the government's failure to heed any of its recommendations. He was elected president of the African National Congress in December 1949, as a compromise candidate in the confrontation between Xuma and the Youth League over the 'Programme of Action' adopted at that time. He stood trial at the end of 1952 with Mandela and Sisulu and others for participation in the Defiance Campaign. They were convicted of 'statutory communism' and sentenced to nine months' imprisonment with hard labour, suspended for two years. During the trial, Dr Moroka made his 'great political error' of engaging separate defence counsel and entering a plea of mitigation that stressed his friendship with and assistance of

Afrikaners.[71] This soured his relationship with the national liberation movement, but he remained active in local politics thereafter, albeit subtly and seldom overtly.

Dr Moroka's career as a politician was based on his advanced education and his impeccable professional credentials. His success as a farmer was based on the income he derived from his medical practice. He developed his inherited property of Mafane 683, on the western edge of the mountain and the southern border of the Thaba Nchu reserve. He also bought a number of other farms in the district, including three subdivisions of the original Makgothi family estate of Good Hope 70, adjoining the Mojanaga farm of Homeward; and portions of Ngakantsispoort 76 and Meloendrift 128. In addition, he built himself a substantial mansion, known as the 'palace', opposite the Moroka Hospital in Thaba Nchu. He lived there with his first wife, Maggie Harvey; they had no children. After her death in 1967, he married Susan Motshumi, who lived at Malane farm and had borne him ten children over the years, most of whom were brought up in Thaba Nchu. He had also adopted his own eldest son, Kenosi, by another woman. At Dr Moroka's funeral in November 1985, the family acknowledged ten children, twenty-four grandchildren and five great-grandchildren.

The key to his life's work, and to his philosophy of change in South Africa, lay in his education first at Lovedale (eastern Cape), then at the Royal High School (Edinburgh) and at Edinburgh University. It is of some interest, therefore, in respect both of the biography of a national political figure and of understanding the emergence of the modern Barolong elite at Thaba Nchu, to trace the material basis of James Sebe Moroka's education. In his later years, Dr Moroka consistently attributed his trajectory of success to the help he had been given by a local white farmer, Pieter Frederik Ryk Steytler, who both lent him a substantial sum of money [variously £800 or £1,000] and looked after his farm during his absence in Scotland from 1911 to 1918. This relationship prompted Dr Moroka to assist many others, including whites, with their educational expenses. As he expressed it in 1981, 'I cannot forget that it was white money which enabled me to study medicine overseas. When I returned home many whites came to me for treatment'.[72]

From the records available in Bloemfontein, it appears that Steytler's assistance was an entirely businesslike transaction. P.F.R. Steytler is recorded as a burgher of the OFS republic in 1899, resident on the government farm Salisbury 79, in the south of the Thaba Nchu district. He did not, however, hold a lease on one of the subdivisions of the farm.[73] After the war, he was living at Victoria Nek, on or near the property of Ketimetse, widow of Chief Tshipinare in his sixth house, and grandmother of James Sebe Moroka. James Sebe grew up on her farm, while his mother was married elsewhere. Ketimetse had been granted the farm Victoria 127 (2,023 morgen) in 1886 as part of the Gregorowski dispositions. On her death in 1906, when it was valued at £4,048, the farm passed jointly, according to the terms of her will, to her younger son, Morokanyana Moroka, and her grandson, James Sebe Moroka.

Victoria 127 was already bonded for £200 to Steytler. James Sebe's mother, Maggie Ketshogile, required funds to pay off this bond and other small debts, to meet the costs of administration of her mother's estate and to maintain James Sebe himself. She accordingly arranged another mortgage for £450 on his undivided half of the property, again in favour of Steytler. A balance of £45.4s.8d was deposited in the Guardian's Fund, to be paid out in instalments as required for James Sebe's benefit. From the same date, October 1907, the whole farm Victoria 127 was leased for five years to Steytler, for a rent of £100 per annum. The arrangement was technically illegal, since African landowners were not allowed to lease their property to whites for more than six months at a time, but it was secured by the lawyers, in effect, through a repeated series of six-month leases over a period of about ten years. James Sebe's share of £50 per annum in rental income from Steytler was used to pay the interest due at 6 per cent on the £450 mortgage bond held by Steytler, and, from 1909, to meet the costs of his education at Lovedale. In 1911, at Lovedale, the opportunity arose for him to go to Scotland to pursue his education, having been selected for the purpose by a visiting missionary, Mr MacDonald. James Sebe was described at the time as a 'very fine intelligent boy'.[74]

The church assisted with these arrangements but provided no direct financial support for James Sebe's education. Money for his passage by steamer and for clothing appropriate for the journey was drawn from the Guardian's Fund deposit. Otherwise his mother and guardian, Maggie Ketshogile, assumed responsibility for meeting his expenses. His uncle, Morokanyana Moroka, also 'promised to contribute something'. Maggie Ketshogile borrowed £500 from the local attorney Faustmann in 1908, and £1,200 in 1909, on the security of her own three small farms east of the Thaba Nchu reserve. Morokanyana Moroka borrowed £700 in 1907 and £1,587 in 1910 from P.F.R. Steytler, on the security of his title to an undivided half-share of Victoria 127.[75] Whatever the precise combination of financial resources mustered by the family for the purpose, it is clear that James Sebe's education in Scotland was made possible by his own inheritance of title to landed property and by the capacity of his close relatives to borrow money on the strength of their titles to landed property. The relationship with Steytler was one of mutual convenience rather than charitable assistance.

W.Z. Fenyang's full-sister, Naomi, married George Modiko Keikelame of Brandkop 78, adjoining her mother's property of Rietfontein 119. *Bennett Herbert Keikelame* (1906–80) was their second son. His father was drowned at Dakpoort in 1916; and Naomi Keikelame took transfer of Brandkop 78 on behalf of her three minor sons. Two mortgage bonds were then taken out: the first for £600 in favour of Naomi's mother, Elizabeth Nkhabele Fenyang, to meet the liabilities and liquidation costs of the estate; the second for £2,971 in favour of Naomi herself, in respect of the half-share of the farm to which she was entitled through her marriage in community of property to George Modiko. Thereafter Naomi Keikelame maintained her minor sons and paid the interest due on the first bond, while her mother-in-law, Nerea Keikelame, retained exclusive usufructuary rights over Brandkop.[76]

This awkward family situation was resolved in 1930, when the youngest of Naomi's three sons, Hermanus Hamilton, attained his majority. A portion of 300 morgen was sold to Nerea for £1,800, of which £1,200 was paid in cash to her grandsons and £600 represented their purchase from her of the usufructuary rights over the remainder of the farm. This remainder was then divided equally between the three sons: Austin Michael (Brandkop 793), Bennett Herbert (Makgabana 792) and Hermanus Hamilton (Hermanus Rust 791). Austin Michael and Bennett Herbert each took out mortgage bonds for £1,000 in favour of the South African Mutual Assurance Society. Hermanus Hamilton died without issue in 1934 and his two brothers jointly inherited his portion of the farm. They took out bonds respectively for £1,500, in favour of Cecil Rayner Morgan, and for £1,193.13s.4d., in favour of their mother, in order to pay off the outstanding bonds. In 1938, when these bonds were called up, Bennett Herbert took over Austin Michael's half-share in Hermanus Rust 791 and sold his own portion of the farm, Makgabana 792, to the South African Native Trust. There were fifty-seven adults and sixty children then resident on Makgabana, which had been worked on a share-cropping basis.[77] Nereas Rust 790 was also sold to the SANT in 1938. In due course the Trust village of Balaclava was established on these two portions of the original farm.

In 1935 Bennett Herbert Keikelame married Maria Setlogelo, eldest daughter of Fanny Mmutsinyana and Ephraim Setlogelo. Fanny Mmutsinyana and her children were heavily in debt, and he rescued them from imminent legal proceedings by buying the undivided shares of Somerset 55 which were vested in Maria's younger siblings (see Chapters 3 and 7), so that their creditors could be paid off. Later, he launched Thaba Nchu African Trading Stores, in partnership with Ephraim Mojanaga, Dr Moroka and Paul Mosaka. He emerged as sole proprietor in the mid-1950s. In 1964 he acquired a portion of Rapulana 776, a subdivision of Rietfontein 119 which adjoined his mother's property of Dithotaneng 775, from the estate of Dr A.B. Xuma, erstwhile president of the African National Congress, for R25,300. All his landed property was heavily mortgaged at this time, for R27,000. Finally, in the last year of his life, Bennett Herbert Keikelame inherited half of his mother's landed property, Dithotaneng 821. The other half, Mashalana 773, went to her grandson, Paul Keikelame, son of Austin Michael, who in 1986 was living at his grandmother's house in Moroka location.[78]

Just before he died in 1980, in order to pay off the large bond of R27,000, B.H. Keikelame sold Hermanus Rust 791 to Samson Seape, a former teacher and successful farmer who already owned a block of freehold land, known as

Morago Farms, to the north-west of Thaba Nchu town. Bennett Herbert's affairs were so complex, however, that his estate had still not been wound up six years later, in 1986, when I interviewed Maria Keikelame at Thaba Nchu. The papers were held by the Master of the Bophuthatswana High Court. She was bequeathed the dwelling house in Moroka location, and his van and lorry and planters. She had leased his business to various tenant managers, none of her children being 'business-minded'. Bennett Herbert and Maria Keikelame had seven children. In the mid-1980s, three were local teachers, one of whom was killed in a road accident in 1988; one was a nurse at the Moroka Hospital; one a salesman at Ellerine's furniture store in Thaba Nchu. Another son, Ephraim Keikelame, was Minister of Economic Affairs in the Bophuthatswana government, based at Mmabatho. He had a degree in commerce from the University of the North (Turfloop). The youngest son, Hamilton Keikelame, was Regional Director of Works at Thaba Nchu.[79]

*Robert Frederick Setlogelo* (1888–1963) was the younger full-brother of Israel Tlale, and W.Z. Fenyang's other half-brother (see Figure 5.2). I described in Chapter 3 how he acquired two portions of his father's original estate, Moroto 68. In 1924, he bought Vrywoning ('Free Residence') 659 (338 morgen) from his brother, Israel Tlale, with capital to which he was entitled as part of the complex resolution of Israel Tlale's affairs after the death of his first wife.[80] In 1931, he bought the adjacent subdivision, Matlapaneng 455 (rest) (702 morgen), when its owners, the Greenwells, were sued by their creditor, Charlie Morgan. Meanwhile, in 1929, he had inherited the farm Dithotaneng 775, a portion of Rietfontein 119, as a result of the division of his mother's estate. He bought Matlapaneng on the strength of his title to Dithotaneng.

As a young man, Robert Frederick Setlogelo was provincial secretary of the African National Congress. In that capacity he investigated a 'condensed flurry of unbridled violence'—shootings and assaults of Africans by white farmers—that swept the OFS countryside between 1918 and 1922. He married twice, but both wives died childless. In 1931, at the age of 43, he followed the example twenty years earlier of Dr Moroka, who was several years younger than him, and went to Scotland for medical training. For six years, from 1931 to 1937, he attended the Extra Mural Medical School of the Royal Colleges of Edinburgh and Glasgow, which was substantially cheaper than registration through the University of Edinburgh. The expenses were met initially by borrowing £1,900 from his half-sister, Naomi Keikelame, by mortgaging Matlapaneng 455 and Dithotaneng 775 in her favour, and then in 1935 by selling Dithotaneng to her for £4,200. Allegedly, during Robert Frederick's absence in Scotland, W.Z. Fenyang and Dr Moroka 'sold' his remaining property, Vrywoning 659 and Matlapaneng 455, to a gullible white man who paid them in cash but could not obtain transfer of the farm because, under the terms of the 1936 Trust and Land Act, it lay within the Released Areas and therefore could not be legally acquired by a white person. He never got the money back. This

story still caused amusement in Thaba Nchu fifty years later. As glossed by
Solomon Ramolehe Ramagaga, in Sesotho for my benefit, in the light of
growing political divergence at the time between Fenyang and Moroka, *pho-
kojwe le phiri ha diutlwane, empa ha dija nku diakopana*: 'the jackal and the
hyena don't get on, but when they eat sheep they come together'.[81]

Dr Setlogelo returned home in 1938, established a medical practice in
Bloemfontein, and married a 'Coloured' woman, Dorothy Maasdorp. They
had ten children—six daughters and four sons—born between 1939 and 1957.
By the late 1950s, he had retired to live at Vrywoning. At this time, Matlapaneng 455 was leased to four African farmers: Moses Ramagaga, Moses Nehemiah Ramagaga (a member of the Tribal Authority), Ernest Modiakgotla
(secretary of the Tribal Authority) and Michael Malebo. There were seven
resident labour tenants. The farm was heavily over-stocked and 'badly denuded' as a result. In 1959, Dr Setlogelo proposed to subdivide Matlapaneng
and sell off two portions of 200 morgen each, in order to pay off a bond of
£4,500 which had remained outstanding since 1938; to settle other debts; to
send two of his daughters overseas to study medicine; and to obtain proper
treatment for his rapidly failing eye-sight. Officials attached conditions relating to conservation measures and proper cultivation of the farm, including
limits on the numbers of livestock allowed, and in the event Dr Setlogelo was
unable to find buyers. Instead, he took out another bond on his property for
£3,000 in favour of Phyllis Ennis Morgan, the wife of Cecil Rayner Morgan.[82]

Thus, at his death in March 1963, two large bonds of R9,000 and R6,000
were outstanding. The total liabilities of his estate were R17,816. Under his
will, his ten children were equal beneficiaries of his estate, but eight of them
were still minors, and six of them had not completed their education at private
boarding schools in Aliwal North and Cradock (Cape) and Ixopo (Natal).
Albert Mohale, his senior son-in-law, recalled that Dr Setlogelo found Serolong funeral customs inconvenient: they required the cutting of hair for the
mourning period, and played havoc with his daughters' expensive hairstyles.
Dr Setlogelo had also adopted Robert Maasdorp, the child of his wife's sister,
whose education was likewise a charge on his estate. In order to cover the debts
and costs of administration, the administrators of his estate, Dr Moroka and
Thaba Nchu attorney N.J. Klopper, negotiated a bond of R19,000 with the
South African Bantu (Native) Trust, which was repayable in half-yearly
instalments over twenty years, with interest at 4.5 per cent. The annual capital
redemption was R950 and the interest R855, both of which were drawn against
the rental income of R2,672 per annum that accrued from leasing Matlapaneng
455 to three African farmers and Vrywoning 659 to Walton Zacharia Fenyang
Setlogelo, the eldest son, who later worked for the Bophuthatswana
government.[83]

Dr Setlogelo's widow, Dorothy, died in 1966, and the responsibility for
bringing up the younger children rested primarily on his eldest daughter,

Catherine Keitumetse, who was by this time married to a senior civil servant in the Lesotho government, Albert Mohale. In this way, most of her younger sisters passed through Roma University in Lesotho, with or without degrees, and then worked for the Lesotho Bank and the Standard Bank in Maseru. They also passed through Cathy Mohale's house in Maseru, where they met a stream of British expatriates. In 1989, these daughters were variously distributed around the world: Elizabeth Nkhabele was married to a black South African electrical engineer in Winnipeg (Canada); Dorothy Lillian was married to John Hurst, who worked in real estate in Birmingham (England); Naomi Rebecca was married to David Morton, who worked for the United Nations World Food Programme in Addis Ababa (Ethiopia); and Constance Esther Kelopile was married to Michael Bevis, on contract with the International Red Cross in Burma. One son, James Sebe Moroka Setlogelo, was well-known as a mural artist in Maseru in the 1970s, under the name of James Dorothy. By 1989, he was living in Middlesbrough (England).

Catherine Keitumetse herself, with her husband, Albert Mohale, had found it necessary to withdraw from Lesotho after the military coup of January 1986 which displaced Prime Minister Leabua Jonathan from power. They found refuge on the family farm, Vrywoning. There Albert Mohale quarrelled with Clement Seape, Samson Seape's elder brother, over the payment of rent for Matlapaneng. It was difficult to resolve this matter through legal action which involved, of necessity, all ten beneficiaries of the estate, who were scattered around the world. Clement Seape had his own farm at Potsane, north-west of Thaba Nchu. He had worked in Lesotho for many years, in the Department of Agriculture, and was Permanent Secretary for Agriculture in Bophuthatswana until he resigned in 1983. His grandparents had been on Samuel's side in the Barolong civil war and had lost their land for that reason. Clement Seape and his brother Samson Seape were perhaps the prime examples in the district in the 1980s of progressive and successful African farmers who had not inherited landed property.[84]

In combination, the lives of the six men briefly profiled here approximately spanned the period from the destruction of the political independence of Moroka's chiefdom in the 1880s to the emergence of a substantially diminished territory as part of the Republic of Bophuthatswana in the 1970s. Their lives thus illustrate the transformation of the Barolong elite that took place over this period. Walton Zacharias Fenyang was a loyal and energetic public servant; Israel Tlale Setlogelo was an entrepreneur, of diverse talents, who lost his own land and strove to profit from the loss of other people's; Ephraim Mabilo Mojanaga was a single-minded and successful farmer; James Sebe Moroka was a doctor, farmer and nationalist politician; Bennett Herbert Keikelame was a business 'tycoon'; and Robert Frederick Setlogelo was a doctor and, in retirement, a country gentleman. Of these six men, five directly inherited land in the district, and all of them built their careers, and paved the way for the careers of their sons and daughters, to a greater or lesser extent on the basis of the financial liquidity they derived from bonding their landed property. One of the six 'married into' his wife's estate and also, in effect, exchanged his own landed property elsewhere for private land in Thaba Nchu. Their numerous descendants duly took their place amongst the 'cream of the Barolong' in the 1980s.

## EPILOGUE: THE MEANING OF NATIONAL DEVELOPMENT

South of Thaba Nchu mountain, north of the Mojanaga farm of Homeward, the Khabanyana stream used to meander across Groothoek farm, a natural amphitheatre. Passing between two rocky outcrops, it flowed westwards across Morokashoek, eventually to join the Modder river. The Voortrekkers encamped above the stream through the summer of 1836–7, on the lower slopes of the mountain. The original farm of Groothoek 125 belonged to Chief Tshipinare's daughter Majang, who sold it when she left Thaba Nchu with her husband, Michael Tshabadira, in 1887. The two adjoining farms, Morokashoek 58 and Khabanyana 57, were vested in Tshipinare's private estate in 1885 and sold off at the end of that year to pay the Barolong public debt (see Chapter 1). Most of the land was recovered from white owners in the first and second waves of purchase by the South African Native Trust (see Chapter 4). It was eventually planned to accommodate two Trust settlements: Groothoek and Morokashoek (see Figure 6.1).

The Khabanyana stream no longer meanders across that splendid natural amphitheatre. By the early 1980s, the Groothoek dam was built across the narrow passage between the two rocky outcrops which form the boundary of Groothoek 125 and Morokashoek 58. The water was stood back about 3 kilometres, and the Bophuthatswana government declared Groothoek and Morokashoek a National Park. Game was to be introduced. In September 1981 it was announced that a luxury hotel and casino would be built, for which purpose the Bophuthatswana National Development Corporation floated a loan of R15 million for construction by the Southern Suns Hotel group, owned by Sol Kerzner.[85] The people who lived in the area, therefore, had to be removed.

About sixty families from Groothoek and thirty families from Morokashoek were removed from their homes in late January 1982, and the two villages were razed to the ground. Reporting for the Bloemfontein *Friend* at the time, Gaye Davis described some of the livelihoods they had built up over the two decades since the settlements were established:

> Miriam Motlhatlhedi is proud of the five-roomed brick and mud home her husband Joseph built for her. It is one of the biggest in the village, and in her garden grow onions, cabbages and peach trees. Now she will break her house down and take the bricks to Gladstone, where Joseph will build another home for her. She expects remuneration from the Bophuthatswana Government: agricultural officers measured sites and evaluated

homes in the village last month. Her husband works on the construction site at the dam. Instead of walking to and from work, he will now have to travel from Gladstone and back by bus.[86]

Of the sixty families from Groothoek, fifty-four were moved to Yoxford, another Trust village in the south of the district; two went to Dipudungwaneng (Gladstone); two to Tweeefontein; one to Seroalo and one to Potsane, in the north of the district. Most of the thirty families from Morokashoek went to Dipudungwaneng (Gladstone). They said that the Bophuthatswana government moved their window frames, roofing and furniture but they had to move the bricks, livestock and other possessions themselves. There were promises of compensation: as reported above, officials had been to the villages to measure sites and value houses.

Seabata Mehlolo, interviewed at Yoxford in August 1983, had been living with his family in Groothoek for about five years before the move. They had previously been on a white-owned farm near Bethulie, but had left because of a disagreement with the owner. They brought five cattle with them from Groothoek to Yoxford, of which one had died. There was plenty of land for grazing and ploughing, however, because Basotho households resident in Yoxford had already been moved to Onverwacht/Botshabelo (see Chapter 6). Seabata Mehlolo's household was evidently a prosperous one, relative to most households in the Trust villages: the house contained soft furnishings, a television and radiogram and the yard was extremely neat. The reason for this was not the opportunity to engage in agriculture but the fact that nine adult children were in diverse employment elsewhere, able to contribute substantially to the welfare of their parents.[87]

Several years later, in July 1986, also at Yoxford, Selekisho Segoneco recalled his circumstances. He was born in Morolong location at Thaba Nchu in 1942 and had moved to Groothoek in 1964, 'when the cattle were removed from the locations'. At that time the family had 28 cattle; some had died, but they were able to build up a good livelihood at Groothoek; and he was employed at Kaplan's General Dealers in Thaba Nchu. The move from Groothoek in January 1982 severely disrupted their lives. Nevertheless, having been evicted with all the other residents of Groothoek in order to make way for the animals and the tourists, Selekisho Segoneco was able to find a job as a driver at the Thaba Nchu Sun hotel, which opened in October 1984. He had to leave Yoxford at 5 a.m. to get a bus into Thaba Nchu and then another bus out to the hotel. Each journey to work was thus about three times the distance from Yoxford to the hotel, which cost him heavily both in time and in bus fares. He found that his monthly wage of R229, after deductions, did not compensate for that.[88]

By the late 1980s, the Maria Moroka National Park was stocked with springbok, blesbok, zebra, red hartebeest and eland. Jaded urban visitors from Kimberley, Bloemfontein and Welkom could indulge themselves at the

Thaba Nchu Sun in response to the extravagant imagery evoked by the Southern Suns publicity department: 'Picture a fantasy of shape, colour and sound. Picture a Twenty-first century African village mushrooming in the heart of the Southern Bophuthatswana mountains; a magical whirligig of sun-drenched pleasure and ethnic mystery'.[89]

All this cost R25 million. Meanwhile, the people who were summarily expelled from Groothoek and Morokashoek had received no compensation. They were called to a meeting in June 1985, attended by three ministers from the Bophuthatswana cabinet, one of whom was Ephraim Keikelame. There was a 'blockage' in parliament, these important men explained. Nothing was done to shift it. The people felt aggrieved and powerless. That was their experience of 'development' in Bophuthatswana.

Early views of Thaba Nchu: 1. 1834, by Charles Bell
2. 1839, by James Backhouse

3

4

5

6

Rivals for the chieftainship, early 1880s: 3. Tshipinare, the incumbent
4. Samuel Lehulere, the challenger
Members of the Barolong progressive elite: 5. Reverend Joel Goronyane, 'Father of the Barolong'
6. Jeremiah Makgothi, farmer, teacher, interpreter

7

8

New capital: 7. the Newberry mill on the Leeuw river, built in 1893
8. the 'Big House' at Westminster, built in 1904

9

10

Milner settlers:   9. Ernest Langbridge
              10. Daniel McPherson and family, c. 1920

11                                                      12

13                                                      14

Law agents, Thaba Nchu:      11. John Henry Faustmann
                             12. Gideon Jacobus Van Riet
The Barolong establishment:  13. Walton Zacharias Fenyang, in the year of his death
                             (1957)
                             14. James Sebe Moroka, as a young man in Edinburgh

15

Onverwacht/Botshabelo: one patch of land. 15. from barren veld (the farm Toekoms 771, in 1975)...

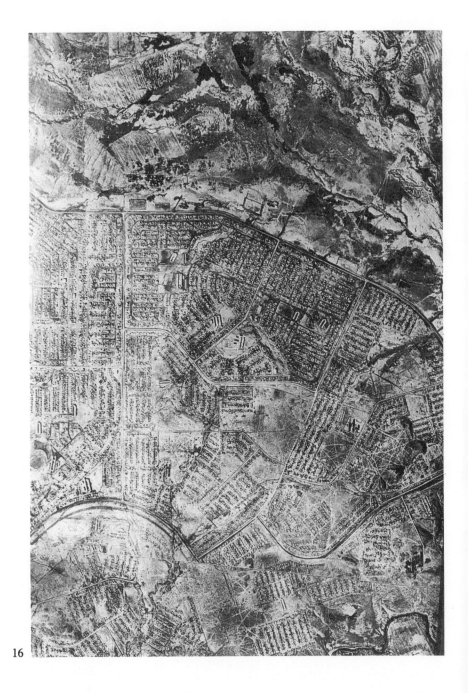

16

Onverwacht/Botshabelo: the same patch of land. 16. . . . to crowded slum (the D section, in 1987)

17

18

From railway slum to 'place of refuge': 17. the remains of Kromdraai, 1980
18. part of Botshabelo, 1983

19

20

Onverwacht/Botshabelo: a struggle to survive: 19. Mmaserialong Ntomane and family
20. Tozi Xaba and family

Onverwacht/Botshabelo: a struggle to survive: 21. Mmaboraki Mmeko and family

Onverwacht/Botshabelo: a struggle to survive: 22. Mmadiphapang Thakho and family

23

24

Ruins at Ngoananyana: 23. the African huts, 1980
24. Daniel McPherson's house, 1986

# 6

# RURAL SLUM: BOTSHABELO

Our burden is this. We are trapped. Our hands are tied. We have no right to seek work for ourselves wherever we want to go. We are supposed to stand around here maybe three months, five or six months or longer, waiting for work that never comes. When you go to Bloemfontein you spend your own money on the bus fare. You might get a job sometime, if you're lucky, but when you have to get fixed up at the pass office at Bloemfontein you are chased away. They say you've got no right to seek work for yourself: 'Get back to Onverwacht and wait there!' We are men with families, we have children going to school. We need money for everything. We ask how can we manage to raise our families and feed them and keep the children in school when our hands are fastened like this?

Work-seeker, Onverwacht/Botshabelo, July 1980

On a week-day morning, south of the main tarred road from Bloemfontein to Maseru, a thick pall of dust hangs in the air. Below it, a vast parade of *masenke*—corrugated iron shacks—stretches, it seems, as far as the eye can see. This is Botshabelo: 'place of refuge' for half a million people displaced from towns and farms in 'white' South Africa. In 1979 the site was bare veld. In 1986 it was the largest rural slum in the country. The morning pall of dust rises from the rutted dirt tracks around the settlement as an apparently endless trail of yellow Jakaranda buses rumbles off to Bloemfontein, 60 km distant, to disgorge tens of thousands of daily commuters.

Botshabelo is not unique. Elsewhere in South Africa, huge rural slums sprang up through the 1970s and 1980s. Examples on the highveld alone are the Winterveld, KwaNdebele and Qwaqwa (see Figure 6.1). The population of the Moretele-Odi area of Bophuthatswana, to the north-west of Pretoria, was estimated at between two million and two and a half million in 1985. Many of them were victims of forced removals from around Pretoria in the 1950s and 1960s, and lost their Section 10 rights under the pass laws as a result. During the 1970s, part of this area—the freehold farms known as the Winterveld—filled up with more than half a million people desperate to find somewhere to stay within daily reach, albeit expensive and time-consuming, of the industrial centres of Pretoria-Rosslyn and the Rand. An estimated 80 per cent of them were not Tswana and they were regularly harassed by the Bophuthatswana authorities.

To the north-east of Pretoria, in the heart of the central Transvaal, lies a series of sprawling slums which in the 1980s comprised the newest Bantustan, KwaNdebele. Ninety per cent of their inhabitants were recent immigrants.

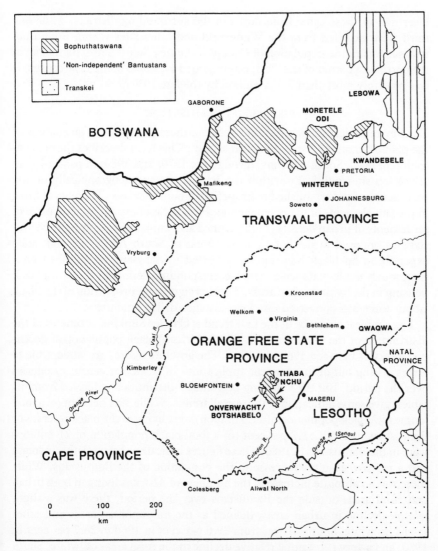

*Figure 6.1* The southern highveld, showing Bophuthatswana, early 1980s.

Over half of these came from farms in the surrounding districts, while one third were expelled from the Winterveld and other sites within Bophuthatswana. Again, the population of Qwaqwa, the tiny South Sotho Bantustan in the north-east corner of the OFS, was recorded as 24,000 in the 1970 census. It was probably more than half a million by the late 1980s.[1]

### DISPLACED URBANISATION

The key to understanding the emergence of these places lies in an analysis of the phenomenon of 'displaced urbanisation'. This term describes the concentration of black South Africans, through the 1970s and 1980s in particular, in relocation sites politically within the Bantustans and geographically on the peripheries of the established metropolitan labour markets. There were three important elements of the phenomenon. First, a rapid expansion took place of settlements of urban density, both planned and unplanned, within the Bantustans as opposed to the 'white' urban areas of South Africa. Second, state expenditure on black housing was diverted to the Bantustans, albeit on a grotesquely inadequate scale, with a corresponding deliberate freeze on black housing in the 'white' urban areas. Third, a significant proportion of the black labour force was converted into long-distance daily commuters.

The simplest evidence of the first trend is Charles Simkins' estimates of the distribution of the 'domestic' (i.e. South African) black population at decennial intervals between 1960 and 1980. The absolute figures are susceptible to errors arising out of inconsistent applications of particular census categories over the period. But the following percentage distributions, derived from his tables, give some indication of the overall trends. While 39.1 per cent (of a total 'domestic' black population of 11.5 million) were living in the black reserves or Bantustans in 1960, 52.7 per cent (of a total black population of 21 million) were in the Bantustans in 1980. These figures indicate a sharp relative increase and a massive absolute increase in the population of the Bantustans. While there was an absolute increase in the numbers of Africans living in both urban and rural areas outside the Bantustans over the period, there was a slight *relative* decline in urban areas, defined as the metropolitan areas and other towns in 'white' South Africa, from 29.6 per cent in 1960 to 26.7 per cent in 1980; and a very substantial relative decline in the rural areas of 'white' South Africa from 31.3 per cent in 1960 to 20.6 per cent in 1980. This decisive redistribution of the black population reflected a massive effort by the state to reverse the tide of black urbanisation that would otherwise have occurred in 'white' South Africa as a result of deepening poverty in the black reserves and rapidly rising black structural unemployment in 'white' agriculture.[2]

According to one estimate, 56 per cent of the population of the Bantustans were 'urbanised' by the mid-1980s.[3] Several million people had been relocated from white farms, from 'black spots', from small town locations and from the metropolitan areas.[4] In addition, some densely populated zones—such as

KwaMashu outside Durban and Mdantsane outside East London—were formally incorporated into Bantustans by the redrawing of boundaries on the map. Some of the concentration had taken place in 'proclaimed' (officially planned) towns in the Bantustans, whose population was 33,500 in 1960, 595,000 in 1970 and 1.5 million by 1981.[5] But most of the concentration had taken place in huge rural slums, which were 'urban' in respect of their population densities, but 'rural' in respect of their distance from established conurbations and of the absence of proper urban infrastructure or services. Most housing in the rural slums was built by the inhabitants themselves.

For many years the acute shortage of housing afforded an administrative barrier to black urbanisation in 'white' South Africa that was repeatedly exploited by both central and local government authorities. In many townships, for example, new building was frozen as a deliberate tactic to enforce 'voluntary' removal to new towns or closer settlements in the Bantustans. The 'orderly urbanisation' strategy which replaced the pass laws in 1986 merely made housing shortages a more explicit instrument of the policy of influx control.[6] Estimates and projections of housing shortage differ widely, of course, depending on diverse premises and methods of calculation relating to where people 'ought' to be living, what indices of over-crowding are used in practice and what rates of urbanisation, 'orderly' or otherwise, may be expected in the future. The official estimate of African housing shortage in 'white' urban areas at the end of 1985 was 221,572 units. An economist from the Council for Scientific and Industrial Research in Pretoria, however, estimated in 1986 that, taking account of the needs of compound and hostel migrants and private tenants, the housing backlog for Africans in 'white' areas was a much larger total of 538,000 units. By 1990 this figure had been revised upwards to two million units, required both to overcome the accumulated backlog and to meet the surge of movement to the metropolitan areas that followed the repeal of the pass laws in 1986.[7]

Associated with the trend of rapid 'urbanisation' in the Bantustans was an increase in the numbers of frontier commuters, defined as people who live in a Bantustan and commute daily or weekly to work in a 'white' area. Official figures recorded 615,000 commuters in 1978 and 773,000 in 1982; while the total number of migrants from the Bantustans officially recorded in 1982 was 1.395 million.[8] Thus there were still substantially more migrants than commuters but, taking into account unofficial estimates from different areas and booming bus transport in the early 1980s on certain key routes, it is evident that commuters represented an increasing proportion of the black labour force as a whole. A particularly stark indication of this development was recorded by Joseph Lelyveld in his excellent book, *Move Your Shadow*. The number of daily buses running between the desolate slums of KwaNdebele and the Pretoria region, operated by the major private bus company Putco but heavily subsidised by central government, was two in 1979, sixty-six in 1980, 105 in

*Figure 6.2* The Thabu Nchu district, Bophuthatswana, early 1980s, showing African freehold land at 'independence' (1977). The white-owned farms Onverwacht, Toekoms, Mariasrus, Mt Pleasant and Ngoanyana are also shown, to illustrate the story of Ngoananyana in Chapter 7.

1981, 148 in 1982, 220 in 1983 and 263 in 1984. Lelyveld commented: 'In a period in which South Africa is alleged to be changing and phasing out apartheid, the expansion of Putco into . . . the homeland provides as accurate a measure as can be found of the real thrust of change'.[9]

This 'real thrust of change' represented by the phenomenon of displaced urbanisation is the analytical focus of this chapter. Its empirical focus is the huge rural slum of Onverwacht/Botshabelo outside the Thaba Nchu district of Bophuthatswana (see Figure 6.2).[10] Any adequate explanation of the genesis of this place and of its significance in the contemporary political economy of apartheid must take account on the one hand of long-term and fundamentally important processes of structural change at the macro level of the national economy; and on the other hand of more immediate and more regionally specific pressures and conflicts which arose out of the politics of Separate Development in the eastern OFS. The next section identifies two such processes of change at the macro level: the squeeze out of black urban locations in 'white' South Africa and the squeeze off white-owned farms.

The following section explains how a slum of 'illegal squatters' which grew up in the heart of Thaba Nchu in the 1970s became a cauldron of inter-ethnic antagonism. Thereafter, I present some detailed case studies of the experience of individuals and their families through the 1970s and the 1980s. Such case studies, in my view, offer the best prospect of integrating the macro and the micro levels of analysis and thence of comprehending the sheer variety and complexity of the phenomena collectively embraced by the phrase 'forced relocation'. The final section of the chapter reviews, with reference both to the contradictions of state strategy and to various dimensions of popular struggle, what I take to be the two vital questions relating to the future of the inhabitants of the rural slums. To what extent and in what senses will they be economically integrated into the principal metropolitan labour markets? To what extent and in what senses will they be politically integrated into a unitary South Africa? As will be seen, the answers to these questions are vitally inter-connected. While political integration is a necessary condition of economic integration, however, it is not a sufficient condition. Herein lies, perhaps, the greatest challenge facing a 'new' South Africa.

In seeking to identify strategic lessons for the future, it is vital to be clear about the criteria of 'urbanisation' which are deployed in the argument. In the past the term was used to refer to the scale of the movement that took place into the 'prescribed' (urban) areas of 'white' South Africa, as a result of conflict between two opposing forces: the overwhelming pressure of poverty in the rural areas; and the remorseless effort of the state to push people back to the black reserves. The terms of the debate have shifted in response to the tidal wave of urbanisation displaced to the Bantustans. As a result, the term 'urbanised' may be used to refer to daily access to or effective integration into or functional dependence on the urban labour market.

Integration and dependence, however, are very much matters of degree. A criterion of functional dependence on the urban labour market may be sensibly applied to incorporate the 'urbanised' population of the Bantustans in an analysis of contemporary trends in the political economy of apartheid. But it should not be used to imply either, on the one hand, that recognisably rural households are not dependent on an urban wage for their livelihoods, through migrant household members. Nor, on the other hand, should it be used to imply that people who live in the slums no longer aspire, ultimately, to recover a past livelihood on the land. We should rather be profoundly impressed by the sheer tenacity with which, over decades of mounting historical odds against them, they have struggled to maintain a 'toehold on the land'.[11] As I demonstrate below through detailed case studies, households in the rural slums survive only through the distribution of their members between a wide range of economic activities undertaken in different parts of the country. Here as elsewhere in the southern African region, therefore, strategic planners for the future should hesitate before prescribing the end of migrant labour or presuming that the urgent need for urban employment precludes the simultaneous pursuit of other options.[12]

## THE SQUEEZE OUT OF 'WHITE' SOUTH AFRICA

As Simkins' figures indicate, there were two major elements of dislocation of the African population in the 1960s and the 1970s in particular. In the first place, people were pushed out of black urban areas in 'white' South Africa, through the repeated harassment of 'illegal squatters' and through rigid limitations, imposed by municipal authorities and backed by the central state, on the expansion of black townships. In the second place, and on an even larger scale, people were pushed off white-owned farms, through a diversity of structural pressures which I examine below. Here I elaborate a framework within which to understand these pressures and their outcomes in the eastern OFS.

The movement of Africans into towns was always controlled with particular harshness in the OFS. Until the Land Act was passed in 1913, the OFS was the only province which specifically prohibited Africans from acquiring freehold land in towns, despite the prevailing stereotype that they were only 'temporary sojourners' in 'white' urban areas. Again, at the turn of the century the OFS was unique in requiring women to carry passes as well as men: Bloemfontein passed its first municipal regulations for its black locations in 1893, which applied equally to men and women. According to Sol Plaatje, these measures of the old Republic were applied with much greater rigour under the Union:

> no native woman in the Province of the Orange 'Free' State can reside within a municipality (whether with or without her parents, or her husband) unless she can produce a permit showing that she is a servant in

the employ of a white person, this permit being signed by the Town Clerk.[13]

A determined campaign of passive resistance to passes was mounted by women throughout the OFS in 1913. The pressure on municipal and provincial authorities was sufficient, in the end, to force the suspension of passes for women for thirty years from the passage of the 1923 Urban Areas Act. Julie Wells concluded, from her examination of the records relating to Bloemfontein, Winburg and Jagersfontein, that the issue of passes for women was too 'dangerous and volatile' for legislators to force in 1923.[14] Thus women's freedom from passes remained in effect until 1956, when the Nationalist government insisted on their re-introduction. The immediate response—an angry mass demonstration by women in Pretoria—showed how dangerous and volatile the issue remained a generation later, although this time the women were not successful.

The pass laws were repeatedly amended after 1923, with a view to enforcing more and more rigorous control of the movement of black people into towns. The pressure intensified from 1948 under the Nationalist government. Pass law contraventions nationally soared to well over half a million per annum by the late 1960s.[15] But it is impossible to assess from the available official statistics how many people were forcibly relocated from the urban areas of South Africa. First, there was confusion and overlap between different pieces of discriminatory legislation. Second, the number of pass law contraventions did not coincide with the number of people affected in these different ways. Third, there was a wide variety of forms of harassment available to the state: arrest and conviction under the 72-hour rule; 'endorsement out' of people who for one reason or another failed to qualify to live in town under Section 10 of the Black (Urban Areas) Act as amended; eviction of families from municipal accommodation when they were late in paying the rent or when the male breadwinner died; official refusal to register dependents; and, quite simply, the indirect but deliberate pressure of acute shortage of housing. In addition to these ubiquitous forms of pressure, however, the original black townships attached to a number of white towns in the OFS were deproclaimed and razed to the ground in the 1970s, in the course of which many of their inhabitants were relocated to Qwaqwa and Thaba Nchu.

Mangaung township outside Bloemfontein was 'frozen' in 1968, mainly in order to enforce very tight control of the urban labour market in the region and to displace 'surplus labour' elsewhere.[16] The overall strategy of urban relocation for the OFS was spelled out in May 1979 in a sinister report of the development of a huge new township outside Thaba Nchu. According to the Bloemfontein *Friend*, a spokesman for the Southern Free State Administration Board:

> stressed that people would not be forced to leave their homes in Bloemfontein, the surrounding smallholdings and other Free State towns, but

would move of their own free will ... Mr Spies estimates that 30,000 people will be resettled from Bloemfontein, the smallholdings and country towns over a long term ... In Bloemfontein alone, where the housing backlog is currently 5,000—he expects more than 13,000 people to qualify for resettlement. These figures are made up of 2,000 families who are mainly boarders and 717 families who must be rehoused because of poor housing. At an average of five a family, this means 13,585 people. There are about 40,000 South Sothos on the surrounding smallholdings. Of these the Administration Board estimates 3,000 families or 15,000 people qualify for resettlement. There are another 372 South Sotho families or 1,860 people in the Southern Free State who are unemployed. Mr Spies did not foresee problems with job opportunities. Bloemfontein would be an important source, he said. The Free State goldfields would provide employment and the existence of a new city (Onverwacht) would create job opportunities. There was also the possibility of industrial development. He did not think transport for commuters between the new city and Bloemfontein would be a problem either.[17]

The transport problem would be solved by the building of a double electrified high-speed railway line from Bloemfontein to Onverwacht, Selosesha and Thaba Nchu, which was announced in June 1981.[18] The problem of employment and the possibilities of industrial development are discussed in the following sections of this chapter.

The criteria of 'qualification for resettlement' were not elaborated in this revelation of official strategy. It rapidly became clear, however, that the elderly and the unemployed were particularly well qualified for resettlement away from the urban areas. The repercussions on their lives were often wholly destructive. One story that achieved publicity in 1980 was merely the tip of an iceberg. Emily Modise, aged 70, was evicted by the East Rand Administration Board from a 'squatter' camp outside Springs in the southern Transvaal. She had a resident's permit to live in the area but had to stay in the camp because of a chronic shortage of housing in KwaThema, the Springs black township. She was dumped in Qwaqwa with a very young grandchild, with hardly any money and no place to go to. She built a shack in Namahadi Rakopane, a village outside Phuthaditjhaba, the capital of Qwaqwa, where she was joined in due course by two daughters and two other grandchildren. Soon after her arrival in Qwaqwa she made three separate journeys without success to collect her pension at Nigel (southern Transvaal), where officials told her she would be paid in Qwaqwa. Qwaqwa officials repeatedly referred her back to the Transvaal. Meanwhile she and her family were starving. Under pressure of adverse publicity, the Minister of Co-operation and Development [sic], Piet Koornhof, promised a departmental investigation.[19] But thousands and thousands of similar cases received no publicity, no pension and no justice.

Some townships were officially reclassified under the Group Areas Act. For example, the township of Luckhoff had a mixed African and 'Coloured' population. It was proclaimed a Coloured Group Area in June 1984, allegedly to facilitate its administration under the new tri-cameral constitution. As a result, ninety-four African families were removed to the K section of Botshabelo. The Deputy Minister of Co-operation and Development [sic], George Morrison, explained in Parliament that 'the continued existence of the black town at Luckhoff is not economically justified'. He did not know what criteria were applied in reaching this judgement.[20]

People removed from black townships were not, however, the largest category of forced relocation. The Surplus People Project estimated that 1.13 million people were moved off white-owned farms between 1960 and 1982.[21] Nationally, about 834,000 Africans were employed on white-owned farms in 1986, by contrast with 1.4 million in 1971.[22] These figures indicate a massive decline in black employment in white commercial agriculture, a decline which is attributable to an intensified drive by the central state to eliminate labour tenancy and also to the effects of rapid capital intensification from the late 1960s. In itself, of course, a dramatic reduction in the proportion of the labour force employed in agriculture is by no means peculiar, although it was somewhat belated in South Africa by comparison with other regions of advanced capitalist development. I would argue, however, in view of the barriers to urbanisation described above and the prevalence and intensity of poverty in the black reserves, that the extrusion of labour from white-owned farms within the political economy of apartheid was rendered a peculiarly painful experience for black farm workers and their families.

In respect of South Africa's highveld 'maize triangle', capital intensification implied mechanisation mainly of the harvesting and delivery of maize, through the widespread purchase of combine harvesters and the expansion of bulk storage facilities. The effects of this process of capital intensification on the structure and composition of the labour force were not simple, however, and required further investigation from the point of view both of farmers and of farm workers. Some pioneering work in this field was undertaken by Michael De Klerk in his study of sixty-one maize farms in six districts of the western Transvaal between 1968 and 1981. He found that, taking into account a substantial increase in the mean size of farming units over the period, there was a 70 per cent decline in the number of seasonal jobs and a 50 per cent decline in the number of permanent jobs for the major task of harvest and delivery of the maize crop. Further, there was a 60 per cent decline in the number of seasonal jobs for the important subsidiary task of weeding.

This decline of employment opportunities was not, however, directly reflected in removals from the 'white' farming areas to Bantustans, partly because much seasonal labour had in any case been drawn from the reserve areas of Bophuthatswana, and partly because a degree of structural unemployment was absorbed by the families of permanent farm workers, in the sense

that available permanent jobs were spread more thinly amongst fewer established farm families. As De Klerk expressed it, 'more mechanisation has gone
hand in hand with fewer permanent workers per family, and this in turn has
meant lower family incomes in spite of higher wage rates'.[23] One potential
social benefit, on the other hand, might be the release of younger family
members for schooling.

Thus, drawing his evidence from white farmers and not from black farm
workers, De Klerk was cautious about linking black structural unemployment
in white agriculture directly to the scale of forced relocation which took place
from 'white' rural areas to the Bantustans. The testimony of ex-farm workers
in rural slums such as Qwaqwa and Botshabelo, by contrast, is unequivocal in
this respect. Again and again, their experiences indicate that residence on
farms was generally tied to employment there. Many of these people were not
'forced' to move in the narrow sense of being directly evicted by the landowner
or of being transported and dumped by GG (South African government)
lorries. They invoked a wide variety of particular circumstances to explain
their decision to leave. But the implied distinction between 'forced' and
'voluntary' removal is misleading, here as elsewhere. For individual decisions
to leave were commonly taken under acute structural pressure. Farmers
resented the presence on their land, for example, of adult men who were not
employed on the farm. Typically, an elderly farm worker with adult sons still
resident on the farm but employed as migrants elsewhere was under strong
structural pressure to leave, although the actual decision may have been
triggered by any one of a number of particular incidents or by a combination of
circumstances that was perceived as unique. The point is that the particular
circumstances differed widely but they worked themselves out within a framework of law enforcement which allowed, indeed encouraged, farmers to evict
on the slightest whim. Alternatively, farm workers may have decided they
would no longer put up with arbitrary impositions by the farmer, even though
the only defence they had was the ultimate one of rendering themselves
homeless and jobless.

## Case study A: Ha Rantsatsa

North of the landmark of Mohono hill, halfway between Thaba Nchu town
and Tweespruit, the railway line cuts across the original farm Meloendrift 128,
which links the old Setlogelo estate of Moroto 68 and Somerset 55 to the rest of
the modern Thaba Nchu district (see Figure 6.2). In 1983, scattered on various
privately-owned subdivisions of Meloendrift 128, were half a dozen makeshift
settlements. The people who lived in them were transient refugees from
white-owned farms in adjacent districts of the eastern OFS: the human flotsam
and jetsam, so to speak, of a tidal wave of structural unemployment on the
farms which swept this part of the highveld in the decade of the 1970s. Their
presence in these makeshift settlements was briefly tolerated until, under

pressure from white farmers who complained repeatedly of stock theft, the magistrate of Thaba Nchu (Bophuthatswana) abruptly ordered the land-owners concerned to ensure their removal by the end of September 1983. A few weeks before this deadline, at the end of August 1983, I carried out a rapid survey of ten households which comprised half of one of these settlements, Ha Rantsatsa, which lay close to the railway line on a portion of Segopocho 508 (a subdivision of Meloendrift 128), owned by Molapo Ngakantsi. This survey thus represents a fleeting glimpse of the lives of these refugees in their tor-mented progress from the farms, whither they did not know. As it turned out, many of them—by no means all—fetched up in Botshabelo.

Household 1 had been evicted from the farm Naauwpoort 74 (Bophutha-tswana, see Figure 6.2) in February 1983, having quarrelled with the Masisi family who owned it over the terms of their employment. They had been paid R30 a month there, and they brought two cattle with them to Ha Rantsatsa. Three older sons were on mine contracts; four younger sons and two daughters remained with their parents. They had no idea where they would go.

Household 2 was expelled from a white farm near the Modderpoort pass (Ladybrand district) in April 1982, apparently because they had an adult son in mine employment. The elderly parents had seven adult children, variously dispersed. Of their five sons, the eldest was unemployed 'at home'. His younger brother, born in 1946, had been working on the mines since 1966; it was he who, after searching everywhere, found the family a temporary refuge at Ha Rantsatsa, and exhausted his own resources in building a hut and buying doors and windows. The third son was in Qwaqwa, where he had a disability pension and 'bits and pieces' of employment. The fourth son, then 27 years old, was working at President Steyn gold mine (Welkom, OFS); he was the main support of the household. The last son was in his third year in Johannes-burg, working for a construction firm. Of the two daughters, the younger was a domestic servant in Johannesburg. The elder had remained on the farm at Modderpoort, a widow whose husband had been killed in a mining accident. She worked in the owners' fields, and she had two grown-up sons, also on the mines, who were vulnerable to expulsion from the farm in the same way as her parents had been.

Household 3, related to Household 2, had come to Ha Rantsatsa in April 1983 from a farm near Marseilles (Ladybrand district), the junction of the main railway line with the short branch line to Maseru in Lesotho. The circumstances were unclear, except that the household head, who worked in Bloemfontein, wanted to find 'a place to live', implying that he felt insecure on the farm. They had not been evicted, however, and his mother, who had worked for the farmer for more than twenty years and remained on the farm, was visiting the household at Ha Rantsatsa in August 1983 to help out with the house. Three older sons were, in effect, 'lost' to the family: one of them had not been in touch for years; another was in Maseru with his own family, employed on the railway; a third was based in Qwaqwa but working somewhere on the Rand. One daughter was still working on the farm, but her two daughters— each of whom had small babies—had come to live with their mother's brother and his family at Ha Rantsatsa. There were usually six people in the household.

Household 4 had come originally from farms in the Marquard district but had stayed since May 1981 on a farm near Westminster, where they had paid R5 a month in rent for a place to stay, and had to help out with crops and livestock when required. They left in September 1982 to come to Ha Rantsatsa. The core of the family was two brothers, born in 1948 and 1956, the elder married with four children, the younger married with one child. The elder had been a self-employed builder in Bloemfontein for four years; the younger had worked at Hennenman (northern OFS) for three years but left there when the family left the Westminster farm, and 'scratched around' for alternative employment. In August 1983 he had been working for four months on the secondary road between Excelsior and Verkeerdevlei for R127 a month, but both he and his brother were at Ha Rantsatsa throughout the last week of August because of the imminent threat of removal. They did not know where they would go.

Households 5 and 6 occupied physically discrete huts but were one family and clearly, in most respects, managed their daily lives as one unit. The family consisted of a grandmother, her son and his wife and ten children. They had left the farm Phillipina, near Excelsior, where they had lived since 1970. Two of the older children were absent from Ha Rantsatsa: a daughter had a job in Excelsior and a son was at secondary school in Qwaqwa. Another daughter, then aged twenty, had a three-month-old son. Her younger sister was at a local school, on the neighbouring farm Leeuwfontein which belonged to Elisha Ramagaga's son-in-law, John Makgothi, a retired teacher. Some of the younger children were also in school. Only one member of the family—the household head—was employed: he worked with his neighbour of Household 4 on the secondary road from Excelsior to Verkeerdevlei.

Household 7 came from Fairview, a farm at the eastern end of the Mensvretersberg. The old man's story embraced his wife, ten surviving children, one daughter-in-law and two young grandchildren. Most of his children were still distributed between farms in the Excelsior district, but he had left Fairview together with his wife and son and son's family, after many years of service there, because of the owner's unreasonable demands on his daughter-in-law. She was a domestic servant in the farmhouse, and her employer wanted her to accompany them on a holiday trip to the sea but to leave her baby behind. With whom? Her husband was working for the farmer but he could not look after the child and carry out his farm duties. So they decided this was too much, they should rather leave. Her husband had recently taken a contract on an asbestos mine in the Transvaal.

Household 8 consisted of an elderly couple who had been expelled two months previously, together with six other families, from George Barnett's pig farm Bally Ho, near Tweespruit. He wanted to reduce his labour force. The couple had one son, working on a Transvaal coal mine. They had come to Ha Rantsatsa with two beasts, of which one had died.

Households 9 and 10, closely related to one another, had come to Ha Rantsatsa in December 1982 from neighbouring farms in the Ficksburg district. Together, the two households comprised an elderly widow, her son and his family and another grandchild. Six of the widow's ten children survived. The eldest son was still employed on the Ficksburg farm. The second son, who was unable to work because he had been ill for a long time, brought his wife and some of their seven surviving children to Ha Rantsatsa. A daughter was married on a farm. The next two sons were both based in Qwaqwa: one was a peripatetic labourer on the railways; the other had a construction job in Boksburg (Transvaal) but had built a homestead in Tseki, one of the new closer settlements in Qwaqwa. Another son had remained on the farms but his child accompanied his grandmother to Ha Rantsatsa. The family had brought eight cattle with them.

Such testimony points to one clear trend, at least, through the 1970s and 1980s: that of growing integration between the agricultural and the industrial labour markets. One element of this partial integration was the relative 'skilling' of a few men trained as drivers and mechanics who then discovered they could compete for employment in manufacturing industry for much better wages, providing a disincentive from some farmers' point of view to taking advantage of training programmes for their workers. Another element was the semi-permanent loss of the next generation to the towns. Sons grew up on farms, refused to work for the farmer, obtained urban jobs for themselves but strove to retain a place for their own families to live on the farm until, exposing their father as vulnerable to eviction in his old age because he had not produced farm labourers to succeed him, the sons 'voluntarily' removed the whole family to a new home base in a rural slum. Alternatively, the farmer evicted the whole family in his frustration at having to accommodate the dependants of able-bodied urban 'layabouts' on his land.

These vicissitudes of the extrusion of labour from farms suggest intense inter-generational conflicts within farm families over strategic options for survival under changing conditions. Changes in the level and composition of employment on farms induced other complex conflicts also: between men and women. John Sharp, investigating the experience of ex-farm workers and their families who were relocated from farms throughout the OFS to Qwaqwa, found that the position of permanent male workers as heads of households was undermined, particularly from the mid-1950s, as farmers increased pressure on residual labour tenants, cut down access both to grazing and to arable land, reduced payments in kind as cash wages went up, and started paying wages directly to women employed as domestic servants in the kitchen or as seasonal labourers on the land. Accordingly, men and women had different perspectives both on their experiences on the farms and on opportunities and constraints, respectively, which applied after their removal to Qwaqwa.[24]

Meanwhile white farmers found themselves under increasing pressure through the late 1970s and the 1980s. Many succumbed to insolvency. The economic viability of white farming enterprises was undermined by three critical factors. First, an extended drought gripped the region in the early 1980s. Second, prevailing interest rates outstripped inflation, so that farmers' debts became hopelessly over-extended. Third, they experienced declining terms of trade, in the sense that the rise in costs of inputs exceeded the rise in prices of outputs. As a result of these three factors, aggregate levels of agricultural debt and of state subsidies approximately trebled between 1980 and 1985. Land values continued to rise, nevertheless, and large industrial and financial corporations rapidly expanded their interests in commercial agriculture.[25]

Opportunities for investment in land also arose within the bureaucratic citadel itself. Jakaranda Motors, for example, the proprietor of that endless trail of commuter buses from Botshabelo to Bloemfontein, was founded by two erstwhile civil servants from Pretoria, Erasmus and Smit. With the advantage of official prescience, they obtained the monopoly licence for this transport route and reputedly invested the profits in large-scale land purchase in parts of the OFS.

### KROMDRAAI: THE RAILWAY SQUATTERS

The 1970 census recorded an ethnically mixed population in Thaba Nchu: 24,300 Tswana, 12,000 South Sotho and 3,600 Xhosa in a total population of 42,000, all politically subordinate to the Barolong Tribal (Regional) Authority.[26] In the early to middle 1970s, tens of thousands of people—mainly Basotho—left white farms, the smallholdings around Bloemfontein and small towns all over the OFS. They drifted into the Thaba Nchu locations— Morolong, Mokwena, Moroka, Ratlou, Ratau, Motlatla; to the Bultfonteins (see Chapter 5); to the Trust villages; and to some of the remaining privately-owned farms. A large concentration of 'illegal squatters' developed in a bend of the railway, east of Thaba Nchu station and west of Mokwena location, in an area which became known as Kromdraai (see Figure 6.2). Part of the original Thaba Nchu reserve, it had been demarcated as grazing land, but thousands of people moved there apparently because plots had been fraudulently sold to them or because they had been led to believe that stands would be allocated to them. According to a press report:

> It is the rejected who come to Kromdraai—those who can no longer work, those who cannot 'fix up their passes'—from the small dorps and farms all over the Free State. The authorities of Thaba Nchu (in Bophuthatswana)

do not want them and say they must go to their own place—Qwaqwa. But Qwaqwa is far away and over-crowded already.[27]

Initially, an attempt was made to deport the squatters to Qwaqwa. 'Big GG lorries left Thaba Nchu piled high with furniture, corrugated iron and chicken-wire, with bewildered faces peering down.'[28] In 1974 Chief Minister Mangope was reported to have made Bophuthatswana government vehicles available for this purpose.[29] A reader of the *Friend* commented on this in 1976:

When approaching Thaba Nchu by rail one is alarmed to notice the uncontrolled development of the squatter town now generally known as Kromdraai. For those who have the welfare of the Black people at heart, it was a great relief to see Government vehicles transporting these squatters to Witzieshoek [Qwaqwa]. Black leaders in Thaba Nchu were happy to see one of their major problems so easily solved ... It is only hoped that the (Sotho) politicians using these squatters for their own political gains will realise what hardships they have caused and are still causing to innocent people and that they will have the courage to accept responsibility for the problems they are creating.[30]

At the time, the new Chief Minister of Qwaqwa, Kenneth Mopeli, was seeking to articulate a wider political constituency than could be found in Qwaqwa itself, the South Sotho Bantustan. According to the 1970 census figures, less than 2 per cent of the 'South Sotho national unit' were resident in Qwaqwa; 90 per cent were in 'white' South Africa, two-thirds of these in the OFS, one-third in the Transvaal; and substantial numbers were in the Transkei and other Bantustans.[31] The Kwena chieftainship and the Qwaqwa bureaucracy together launched a campaign to persuade Basotho to 'come home'; and Mopeli himself took up the grievances of Sotho minorities in Transkei and Bophuthatswana. He said in 1976, shortly before the Transkei became 'independent', that the ultimate aim of Qwaqwa was to 'form a union with Lesotho which will include the South Sotho living in the Transkei and Eastern Free State'.[32] The Qwaqwa cabinet declared Transkei Independence Day, 26 October 1976, as a day of mourning for many thousands of South Sotho of the Herschel and Maluti districts who were not consulted about their future status and who felt directly threatened by the Matanzima regime.[33]

Mopeli also took a particular interest in the predicament of South Sotho immigrants into Thaba Nchu. Agents from Qwaqwa carried out a clandestine survey to induce Basotho in Thaba Nchu to sign up as citizens of Qwaqwa and thus to generate evidence in support of a campaign to establish Thaba Nchu as a South Sotho area rather than a Tswana area.[34] Initially, as we have seen above, the Bophuthatswana authorities attempted to deport the Kromdraai squatters to Qwaqwa. But mass immigration into Thaba Nchu continued. The immigrants, most of whom were Basotho, found difficulty in obtaining residential permits and they could not register as work-seekers at the tribal labour bureau in Thaba Nchu. Their children could not be taught in Sesotho since Setswana was the only official medium in primary schools within Thaba Nchu.

A public row over these issues took place in the correspondence columns of the *Friend*, between J.R. Ngake, Minister of Education for Qwaqwa, and S.O.O. Seate, one of the representatives of Thaba Nchu in the Bophutha-tswana Legislative Assembly. Ngake complained that South Sotho in Thaba Nchu were being discriminated against in respect of work permits, residence rights and language of instruction in the schools, while simultaneously they were subject to taxes and levies imposed by the Bophuthatswana authorities. In turn, Seate accused Ngake of interfering in the domestic affairs of Bophutha-tswana. Lazarus Sebolai wrote from Welkom to say that the Barolong at Thaba Nchu simply could not 'cater for people who are not our subjects'.[35] Sebolai was by no means a disinterested or casual correspondent of the paper. He was a successful 'tycoon' with a number of shops in Welkom whose profits were drawn from an overwhelmingly South Sotho local populace. He invested those profits in buying land in the Thaba Nchu district—for example, a portion of the Fenyang family farm of Rietfontein 119—and employed Se-sotho-speaking farm labourers in the 1980s. In another sense than the one he intended, therefore, his own prosperity was based on 'catering for people who are not our subjects'.

In 1978, the population of Kromdraai was estimated to be 38,000 people. They were living in poverty and squalor, in shacks roughly constructed from mud-bricks and corrugated sheeting.[36] They had been regularly harassed by the Bophuthatswana police as 'illegal foreigners' and this pressure was in-tensified shortly after 'independence' in December 1977. Several massive raids took place in 1978. On 24 April, for example, 301 people were arbitrarily arrested, their children intimidated, their livestock dispersed and impounded; some were shot, others were raped. Those charged and convicted for squatting were fined R40 or imprisoned for forty days in Bloemfontein gaol, by arrange-ment with the South African authorities. In May 1978, Mopeli appealed to Mangope to leave South Sotho in Thaba Nchu alone until they could be resettled.[37] Nevertheless, another big raid took place on 21 December 1978 which led to R60 fines or sixty days' imprisonment. The practice had become a lucrative one for the Bophuthatswana authorities. On several occasions, indeed, the South African police intervened to persuade the Bophuthatswana police to behave more moderately. Basotho tenants in the Thaba Nchu lo-cations also complained of exploitation and harassment by Barolong landlords.

During 1977 and 1978 negotiations took place between Bophuthatswana and Qwaqwa and the South African government over the provision of land for the relocation of Basotho from Thaba Nchu. An agreement was reached by which 25,000 hectares of land in the Bophuthatswana regions of the northern Cape would be excised in exchange for an additional 25,000 hectares in the OFS, of which 15,000 hectares would be for Bophuthatswana and 10,000 hectares would be for the resettlement of South Sotho from Thaba Nchu and elsewhere.[38] A number of white-owned farms was compulsorily purchased by the central state in the first half of 1979. Removal of the Kromdraai squatters to the area known as Onverwacht began in late May 1979—in winter—and was completed by December of the same year. Basotho were also removed from the Bultfonteins; from the old locations in Thaba Nchu; from freehold farms such as Meloendrift 128 in the east of the reserve (see previous section); and from Trust villages such as Paradys and Longridge in the north and Dipudung-waneng (Gladstone) in the south. Dr Mervyn Griffiths, then medical superin-tendent of the Moroka hospital in Thaba Nchu, remembered the exodus very clearly:

> We saw lorries go past the hospital daily, laden up with people with everything on they could salvage from their homes, together with pigs and fowls and things in little wire cages . . . Laden lorries would go past all day for months and months and months . . .[39]

Following this mass exodus of Basotho from Thaba Nchu, the slum of Kromdraai was razed to the ground and the site reverted to bare hillside, scrub and grazing. In March 1980, all that remained of the squatter slum was a scatter of rusting, upturned vehicles and, in the community's graveyard, a pathetic miscellany of medicine bottles and small household items left to accompany the dead. The tragedy of very high infant mortality remained crudely inscribed on many headstones.

The refugees from Kromdraai were concentrated in one section of Onver-wacht initially known as the 'Singles' (later redesignated the A section) because they had no letters, only numbers, painted on their toilet doors. The women brought with them their virulent terror of 'MaYB', the Bophuthatswana police, who became known by the YB numberplates of their vehicles, just as refugees across South Africa identified the agents of their forced relocation as 'GG', after the numberplates of the government trucks that carried out the task. Amongst a group of women from Kromdraai interviewed in Onverwacht in May and June 1980, Mmaboraki Mmeko recalled one of the big raids:

> That time the vans came—so many of them—from Bloemfontein, I heard people say they were coming to carry on the war they'd plunged us into. Hao! They were killing us, really! A van stopped and [one of the police-men] said, Get in with these stones, don't throw stones at my van, Come, get in, I'll give you all a ride. So we got in, silently, just like sheep going to the slaughter. Well, we got there [the police station] and he said, These people, they were swearing and shouting at me, just like this, they threw stones at my van, and insulted me. So I've brought them in. Let them be arrested! So we were taken in, though we had done nothing wrong. But we had to pay, of course, we had to pay. As soon as you opened your mouth, they just said, You, Mosotho, sixty rand, sixty rand. If you didn't have the money, you went to gaol. And they came to gaol too, those Barolong, with

a torch. They came for the young ones, to be 'married'. There was 'marriage' there, they said, and the better-looking ones were taken out, Out! Out! Out! Women off to be 'married'! As for the ones left behind, Go to sleep, you old woman, the torch shone over your eyes. What shame! We prayed night and day, Oh God, we just prayed, we were all there [indicating two companions in the shack], we call it the prayer of Troubles, we prayed to Jehovah, God of Mishack, Shadrack and Abednego, we said please God, feel our pain, just like those three men who went into the midst of the fire with the angel . . .

Another woman who was there broke in to Mmaboraki's account:

You know when you speak about MaYB my heart feels such pain . . . it's even better to die if you come across those MaYB, because they held us in such contempt [*ka mokha oo ba neng ba re nyonya ka teng*]. Some women, you know, their husbands divorced them on account of those MaYB, women who'd got children with them, their husbands threw them out, that's what life in Kromdraai was like. These women were just given children on the side, against their will, while their husbands were off at work, MaYB just went into the gaol . . . I don't know what I can say, when I remember MaYB I feel very shaken and upset.[40]

## Case study B: 'MaYB' versus one widow

Hanyane Rebecca Mofihli was summoned over from a neighbouring shack to tell the story of her experience on 24 April 1978:

It was in the morning, about the time the kids go to school. I saw them coming back so I said, what's the matter? They said the police are many there at the school. I said, well, if the police are many, leave off going to school. They went into the hut and took off their school-clothes. After a little while my daughter went to the doorway and said, Mother, I see them coming. I said, Oh, are they coming? She said yes. I told them to sit down. Then the policemen came—there were two of them—and asked my son, who was there with a friend, to stand up in front of me. My boy stood up. One policeman said to him, Come here, you teacher. My boy said, No, I'm not a teacher, sir. When he asked him a second time he just grabbed him and went off with him. Over there on the path he came back saying, His friend, why am I leaving him behind? He took him as well. When they were a little distance away, [the policemen] beat them with their guns, they beat them about four times about the head with their guns. I cried out, Hao! Since you are holding them, why are you beating them? That's when this young one who had grabbed the boys came back to catch me and he pushed me towards the boys. Then he hit me behind here, I didn't know what with, whether his fist or what, he hit me once, twice, three times. The fourth time, he shot me. I fell over and fainted on the spot. I woke up in hospital. It felt like I died just as I fell.[41]

The bullet entered below her left scapula and emerged in her left armpit. She was vomiting blood and she underwent immediate surgery in the Moroka hospital at Thaba Nchu, where she remained for two months from April to June 1978. It was four and a half months before she felt any better. More than two years after the shooting, at the time she told her story to me in mid-1980, she still suffered acute pains and she could not lift any weight or even fetch water for herself. Any sudden exertion left her chronically short of breath.

The policeman who had shot her was charged, and a trial was held at Thaba Nchu Regional Court on 4 December 1978. Four times the case came before the court, and there was no judgement until August 1979. The policeman's mother found lawyers for his defence who got him out on bail, and he left Thaba Nchu for Mafikeng. Eventually they gave him a suspended sentence of one year and eight months. When the case was over the police said Hanyane Mofihli had been the cause of his arrest, so she should pay for the lawyers. She said she had no money. They said she could borrow it from the men at Onverwacht. She said there was no one who could lend her money. They did not press the policeman for the lawyers' fees. How could they when they were helping him? On his side they were all in a huddle, advising him what to say. She was on her own.

In the latter part of 1979, after removal to Onverwacht—it was hopeless to attempt anything from Kromdraai where none of the people had any legal status—Hanyane Mofihli set about tackling the bureaucracy with a view to obtaining a disability pension. In response to a request from the District Pension Officer in Bloemfontein, Dr Mervyn Griffiths, who had treated her at the Moroka hospital, certified in September 1979 that her arm movements were limited, her shoulder was stiff and her left arm was shorter than her right. The District Surgeon then reported that she was not 'suitable for open labour market' [What open labour market, it might be asked, since in the first place she was a woman and in the second place she had no *soekwerk* stamp?]; she was not 'suitable for light work'; and she was 100 per cent permanently disabled. Nine months later, however, no progress had been made with the application. She had repeatedly tried to return the forms to be forwarded to Pretoria; but this meant standing in the interminable queue at the Onverwacht office. 'The police there just cut us off and eliminate us—you know when you go there you just stand in a line, and they take you ten at a time'. And then she had not gone at all for three months, because her feet were swollen and she was exhausted with the strain and uncertainty and the resurgence of pain from the wound. In addition, the police sergeant at Onverwacht was the uncle of the Bophutha-tswana policeman who had shot her. He knew all the details of the case, and obstructed her from bringing her application for a disability pension forward through the Onverwacht office.[42]

Hanyane was born near Mafeteng in Lesotho in 1930, but she grew up on farms east of Thaba Phatshwa where her parents had moved before the great drought of the early 1930s. She had two children with a man who then deserted her. She returned to her parents' place in 1957 where her third baby died at two months old. Later she married a man who worked on construction sites south of Bloemfontein. They lived in Thaba Nchu for years, renting a place to stay in one location or another. Her husband died in 1970 at the Moroka hospital. Hanyane herself had been a domestic servant in Bloemfontein, Brandfort and other towns in the OFS. From Kromdraai, unable to obtain a *soekwerk* stamp, she had worked again in Bloemfontein illegally for two years until the end of 1977, leaving the younger children in the care of her eldest son.

She had seven surviving children. In 1980 her eldest son was working on a building site in Bloemfontein, for about R25 a week, getting up at 4 a.m. to commute and arriving back in Onverwacht after dark. His wife and two young children stayed with her in the household. Her eldest daughter had two children of her own and she was waiting for a stand of her own at Onverwacht. The father of these children, on the farms near Dewetsdorp, had not visited or sent any money for two years. The next son had just started his fourth mine contract at Rustenburg, and sent perhaps R50 a month, the household's main source of income. Hanyane's second daughter, born in 1960, left school in Kromdraai at Standard 4 in 1977, because there was no money to keep her in school. Hanyane was waiting to get her registered for a reference book, so that she could try and find a job. Her younger sister, born in 1962, had a child born in February 1980, but felt she was too young to get married and wanted to go back to school. Hanyane's two youngest children were at school locally. Thus thirteen people were living in the shack in June 1980: Hanyane herself, six of her seven children, her eldest son's wife and five grandchildren. There were three small compartments: a living room with a stove and two beds; a curtained-off sitting-room with a furniture suite and a radiogram belonging to her second son, bought with his mine wages; and a separate space for her eldest son and his wife.

Nine years later, in August 1989, when I sought out Hanyane Rebecca Mofihli again, she was living in the E section with her daughters, the eldest of whom was earning R70 a month as a sewing instructor at a firm in the industrial area of Botshabelo. Hanyane had eventually succeeded in obtaining a disability pension, in 1986. The policeman who had shot her, she told me, had himself been shot and killed in Mmabatho, the capital of Bophuthatswana, two or three years after moving up there.

The flood of immigrants into Thaba Nchu in the 1970s, as into Qwaqwa, reflected the acute insecurity people experienced on white farms and in black townships throughout the OFS and southern Transvaal. Conflicts developed within Thaba Nchu along ethnic lines because of official insistence that all black South Africans should be identified as belonging to one or other exclusive 'ethno-national unit'. As shown in Chapter 5, Thaba Nchu was defined as the 'land of the Barolong', and here as elsewhere—most viciously in the Winterveld, north-west of Pretoria—the Bophuthatswana authorities pursued a policy of strident Tswana nationalism in respect of access to very scarce resources. In Thaba Nchu, after all, Sotho immigrants in the 1970s rapidly outnumbered established Tswana residents. There is no doubt that the Mangope regime perceived this as a major threat to its political grip on this isolated territorial enclave, distant as it was from the other territorial fragments that comprised Bophuthatswana. There had been much intermarriage over the years between Barolong and Basotho in Thaba Nchu. But the identity of persons of 'mixed' parentage had not been politically important, and it is this fact that lies behind press depiction of Thaba Nchu as a notoriously 'peaceful place' until the 1970s.[43]

That reputation is belied by the successive eruptions of factional conflict recorded in Chapters 1 and 4 of this book. In retrospect, however, it is clear that the events of the 1950s and 1960s, recorded in Chapter 5, induced a significant shift in the patterns of political cleavage that prevailed in the district. Factional conflict within the community of the Seleka Barolong was transformed by the politics of Separate Development into inter-ethnic antagonism between Barolong and Basotho. This antagonism was sharply intensified by the events of the middle and late 1970s. Thaba Nchu, the 'place of the Barolong', became an inferno of communal contempt.

Accordingly, the Kromdraai refugees in the 'Singles' section of Onverwacht in 1980 expressed profound relief that they were no longer subject to arbitrary arrest and intimidation by 'MaYB'. In the Qwaqwa election of March 1980 they voted solidly, they said, for the Dikwankwetla party because they believed that Chief Minister Mopeli had persuaded the South African government to provide a refuge for the Basotho who were being harassed in Thaba Nchu. Mopeli thus gained considerable political credit at the time for leading his subjects 'out of the land of Egypt into the land of Canaan', as some of them expressed it. But he was unable to provide land or jobs for them. As the erstwhile Kromdraai squatters were rapidly outnumbered by other refugees in Onverwacht who had no cause to be grateful to the Chief Minister of Qwaqwa, this political credit swiftly evaporated. On 14 September 1980, two men were arrested by Bophuthatswana security police while Mopeli was addressing a crowd of 20,000 at Onverwacht, after rumours of a possible assassination attempt against him.[44]

### 'SEVENTH HELL': STRUGGLES OVER DAILY LIFE

A year after the settlement's foundation, in June 1980, church workers estimated there were 100,000 people living there, and newcomers were arriving steadily. People qualified for residential stands in Onverwacht by producing a Qwaqwa citizenship card, a valid reference book and a marriage certificate, and by paying R1 for the allocation. Qwaqwa officials were not insisting on

Sotho identity as a criterion of Qwaqwa citizenship, with the result that there
was a significant minority in Onverwacht who were identified as members of
the Xhosa ethnic group but as citizens of Qwaqwa. The stands were 30 metres
by 15 metres, each consisting of a patch of bare ground with a tin prefabricated
toilet whose number—painted on the toilet door—was the new address. People
were provided temporarily with tents and told to build their own shacks. The
price of secondhand corrugated sheeting immediately rocketed in response to
the heavy demand, so that many families had the greatest difficulty in providing themselves with alternative accommodation. The tents, meanwhile, were
bitterly cold, far too small and a dangerous fire hazard. Possessions could not
be protected from theft or damage. Some of the sites had large boulders on
them, others were subject to flooding in the rains. The bucket toilet removal
system was thoroughly inadequate, and there was an outbreak of typhoid early
in 1980, denied by officials in Bloemfontein and Pretoria. Despite the provision of piping and tap outlets there was a severe shortage of water in most
sections of Onverwacht throughout 1980 and 1981. By 9 July 1980 there were
258 'adult' graves and 269 'children's' graves in the cemetery: a stark index of
the vulnerability of babies in this desperate environment. Despite all the
difficulties, many people showed remarkable ingenuity in building, improvis-
ing, furnishing and decorating their tin shacks, which were intolerably hot in
summer and very cold in winter.

Facilities were grossly inadequate for such a large concentration of people. A
visitor at the end of 1981 observed one clinic, one police station and one
supermarket, no post office and no electricity. There were nineteen schools,
with nearly 20,000 pupils operating a double-shift system which gave rise to
acute anxieties for parents as young children returned home in the dark. It was
proving impossible to find qualified teachers to staff the two secondary
schools.[45] Some building of brick houses took place in 1981, but these were
available at a price of R3,000 or R4,000 which, even spread over twenty years,
very few people at Onverwacht could afford.

Onverwacht was then administered by the Black Affairs Commissioner,
Bloemfontein, on behalf of the South African Development Trust which
owned the land. Representatives of Dikwankwetla, the Qwaqwa ruling party,
had an informal advisory function in the slum and they purported to 'represent' the South Sotho political constituency in its dealings with the South
African authorities. Unemployment was certainly very high, although it was
impossible to quantify since the total population could only be guessed at and
so many people experienced difficulty in registering as workseekers. Particular
focal points of frustration and anger were the forced auctions of livestock
which took place; and the inadequate facilities and gross overcrowding of the
schools. Six hundred students stormed the police station at Onverwacht on
10 July 1980.[46] People also complained bitterly about the restrictions placed
on informal sector activities. Petty traders without licences were constantly

harassed, yet this was one of the very few activities open to people who had to find a *local* source of income in order to look after a young family at Onverwacht.

The boundary between the slum of Onverwacht and the (new) Thaba Nchu district was subject to continuing dispute, as was the boundary between Onverwacht and white farming areas to the south. Examples of both sorts of dispute recurred in press reports. In March 1981 Napoleon Khomo, national organiser of Dikwankwetla, warned of a 'bloody confrontation' if the Bophuthatswana police did not stop impounding the livestock of Onverwacht people and auctioning them off without informing the owners.[47] The Kromdraai women in the 'Singles' section of Onverwacht still complained of harassment by 'MaYB', who lurked in their vehicles on the Bophuthatswana side of the border and demanded instant fines of R5 or R10 from Onverwacht women collecting firewood who allegedly trespassed into Bophuthatswana. At about the same time, Dewetsdorp farmers vigorously complained of escalating stock theft in the area, attributed to the prevalence of unemployment in the slum and the large number of 'hungry Onverwacht dogs'.[48] Onverwacht inhabitants had nowhere to graze the few animals they had been able to bring with them, partly because, despite compulsory purchase of other lands than those on which the settlement itself was concentrated, several farms which had been bought by the Trust—namely Labora (a subdivision of Travalgar 2), Kromdraai 120 and Vaalkraal 30—had been leased to white farmers.[49]

Again and again, Onverwacht residents complained of the ruthless and arbitrary bureaucratic obstruction they received at both ends of their desperate search for employment. One end was the Onverwacht office, at that time an ex-farmhouse—ironically, that of Spes Bona—that also served as a labour bureau. The other end of their travail was the Bloemfontein offices of the Southern Free State Administration Board and the Black Affairs Commissioner. People pointed out that, in the first place, it was difficult to get a *soekwerk* (workseeker's) stamp at all. This was dependent on having Qwaqwa citizenship and a valid reference book and (sometimes) on being registered as occupier of a stand as opposed to sharing someone else's stand. It was often necessary in practice to bribe the black office staff for access to the senior whites who controlled the use of such stamps. In the second place, the *soekwerk* stamp did not allow people to seek work but merely to compete with many others for the occasional unskilled labouring jobs for which requisitions came to Onverwacht. In the third place, even if individuals were lucky enough to find employment in this way, there was no guarantee that they would be paid even the very low wages they were promised; there was no effective means of redress if they were not. Many stories circulated of the utterly unscrupulous behaviour of employers. These stories help to explain why people resisted, when they possibly could, the most low-paid and insecure prospects of employment, especially seasonal labour on the farms. They could not afford to be absent from Onverwacht for two weeks and discover that they were only paid R5 for a week's work instead of, say, the R20 promised.

### Case study C: The bureaucratic nightmare

Tozi Xaba was born to Xhosa parents in 1952 in the Edenburg district. She went to Kromdraai on her own in 1974, leaving her mother and family on the smallholding near Ferreira station, outside Bloemfontein, where they had lived for many years. As Tozi put it, 'the whites there didn't like it when I stood up for myself, they resented my behaving like a white madam'. She rented a room at Kromdraai from a Basotho family already established there, and once tried to arrange (by night) for her elderly mother to move to Kromdraai with her young grandchildren and her belongings. But they were caught by Bophuthatswana police, who chased them away from Thaba Nchu. Tozi stayed in Kromdraai herself, however, giving birth to her second surviving child (three had died) in March 1978. She was joined by her elder sister, who daily commuted to Bloemfontein as a domestic servant in the city, and the latter's boy friend, who was unemployed at the time. In 1979 Tozi worked as a domestic servant in Kempton Park, Johannesburg, for six months. When she returned in December, having been given a 'back to' stamp (return to place of origin) in her reference book, the move from Kromdraai to Onverwacht had taken place. In May 1980 the family occupied two tents on a stand in the 'Singles' section.[50]

Tozi's elder sister was the only member of the family in regular employment. She had to leave her three children in order to stay in Bloemfontein, visiting home once a month, because she could not afford the daily bus fare from Onverwacht, which took R12 out of a month's wages of about R30. Her boy friend had been in and out of various jobs in the middle and late 1970s: a Bloemfontein construction site; the bakery at Thaba Nchu; a mine contract at Carletonville (Transvaal); a garage at Pietersburg (northern Transvaal); and, illegally, the military base outside Bloemfontein. As soon as the family moved to Onverwacht and he tried to regularise his reference book, he was repeatedly refused a *soekwerk* stamp because he allegedly owed two years of tax. How was he supposed to pay the outstanding tax if he could not get a job? No one explained. Tozi herself could not get a *soekwerk* stamp because she did not have her own stand, and the Onverwacht office refused to register a stand in her name because she was an unmarried mother. She could not apply for a stand as a nominal dependent of her mother because the latter was already registered as a dependent of her elder daughter in whose name their present stand was registered. She was frustrated and outraged by the absurdity and injustice of such bureaucratic obstruction, and she used the phrase *diheleng tsa bosupa* ('Seventh Hell') to describe her experience of Onverwacht. The five children for whom, in her sister's absence, she was largely responsible, were all visibly undernourished.

Tozi's elderly mother, who was born in Bloemfontein in 1910, had spent much of her adult life on the Ferreira smallholding, working on and off as a domestic servant. She moved to Onverwacht in July 1979 with the rest of the family. On her arrival she applied for a pension at the Onverwacht office but was told that she was 'too young'. So she returned to the Ferreira smallholding 'where she had grown up', and enlisted the help of her daughter's employer in Bloemfontein in making a pension application there. By May 1980 they had received some papers that had to be completed at the Black Affairs Commissioner's office in Bloemfontein and then returned to Pretoria. This involved a further indefinite period of uncertainty and delay. Meanwhile the old woman returned to the Ferreira smallholding to await the approval of her application and had to beg the owners for permission to stay with a black family employed by them. She was still waiting there in July. If her pension were to come through and she could then return to her family at Onverwacht, she would still have to travel from Onverwacht to Ferreira to receive it every two months, since an attempt to transfer payment to Onverwacht would not be worth the further trouble and delay that they knew from experience would arise. A small sum as it was—R55 every two months at that time—her pension was a vital source of income for this family.

The circumstances of this household illustrate extreme poverty, frustration and insecurity. Whatever problem they tried to solve—employment, housing, pension—they encountered an obstructive bureaucratic maze. Even those in relatively stable employment had to pass through routinely obstructive hoops of this kind. The following extended case study illustrates this.

### Case study D: Working a passage

In late April and early May 1980 Motlatsi Ntomane was at home in Onverwacht, between annual contracts of employment as a *sakdraer* (unskilled labourer) in Klerksdorp, western Transvaal. He saw his family twice a year: on Christmas leave and when he returned to his 'place of origin' to renew his contract. His wife, his mother and the children moved to Onverwacht in September 1979 from Morolong location in Thaba Nchu, and they occupied a two-room L-shaped shack in the dusty B section. Motlatsi was born in 1936 at Hennenman, a small town between Virginia and Kroonstad in the OFS, where his father worked for twenty-five years in the Anglo Alpha cement factory, and they stayed in the company location. Motlatsi went to work in the cement factory in 1955. He married in due course—his wife was also from that area—and they had their own place in the company location. On his father's retirement with a lump-sum pension in 1964, his parents were no longer entitled to company accommodation, and they moved to Morolong location, Thaba Nchu, where they built a house for themselves.

Some time after 1964, Motlatsi lost his job as a result of a dispute with his
employer, and came with his family to Thaba Nchu, where he picked up
occasional bits of work for the municipality and in the town. He was often out
of a job and it was a real struggle to make ends meet. His wife worked for three
years 'in the kitchen of the commissioner' and she begged this official to
arrange a job for her husband. This contact helped for a while. However,
Motlatsi was refused permission to build in Thaba Nchu on a site of his own.
The old arrangement no longer applied, he was told, and Basotho were not
allowed to build in Thaba Nchu any more. So the family stayed on Motlatsi's
parents' stand. The authorities also refused to stamp Motlatsi's reference book
to show that he belonged to Thaba Nchu. They said, 'Go to your own place in
Qwaqwa'. Motlatsi went to Qwaqwa in desperation, in the end, and they gave
him a *soekwerk* stamp in Qwaqwa on 13 May 1974. Soon afterward he was
employed by a firm in Klerksdorp that hired migrants on contract from
Qwaqwa. Meanwhile, his wife and the children were still in Thaba Nchu.
Motlatsi's father died in 1977 and with many others the family was under
pressure from the Bophuthatswana authorities to leave Thaba Nchu. They did
so in September 1979. By Easter of 1980 Motlatsi had completed six annual
contracts for the same employer at Klerksdorp, on average earnings in that
year of R26 a week. He had to sign up for every new contract in Qwaqwa,
involving an expensive and time-consuming journey from Klerksdorp to
Thaba Nchu and Onverwacht to Qwaqwa to Klerksdorp.

The extremely cumbersome bureaucratic process involved in administering
the pass laws may be illustrated through Motlatsi's 'call-in-card' (in fact a long
form), issued by the Western Transvaal Administration Board under the
Bantu Labour Act of 1964. It consisted of three sections. Part A was completed
by the employer, who set out the period, nature and conditions of employment, with evidence of 'approved accommodation'. Such accommodation in
this case was an Administration Board hostel, costing Motlatsi R4.50 a month
for a room shared with two other men, without any form of heating supplied.
The employer then certified: 'Please note that the holder of this card
_____ was employed by me during the period _____ as
_____. He desires to return to my service and I shall be pleased to
re-engage him provided he reports to me within one month of the date hereof'.
Part B of the form was completed by the Labour Officer of the Administration
Board as follows: 'I certify from my own records that the above-named Black
was lawfully employed as indicated above. Suitable and approved accommodation is available. There is no objection to the attestation of a contract of
employment provided this is done within one month of the date hereof'. Part
C was completed by the 'attesting officer or by tribal labour officer of
labour bureau of area of domicile of worker' to the effect that the contract was
attested on _____ (date), and the worker's reference book was endorsed

accordingly. Motlatsi had not yet tried to transfer the office of attestation from Qwaqwa to Onverwacht. The latter office was so notoriously obstructive that he would not bother.

In May 1980, before he set off again for Qwaqwa to renew his contract, Motlatsi was waiting to receive money for the journey from his eldest daughter, Serialong, who had been working in a Qwaqwa government office since January 1977. She had passed her Matriculation at Mariasdal, a Catholic secondary school in the Excelsior district on the north-eastern border of Thaba Nchu (Bophuthatswana), which she attended between 1972 and 1976. Her salary in Qwaqwa was R152 a month in 1980, of which she sent perhaps R40 a month to her family in Onverwacht. She paid R2.50 a month to rent one room and communal facilities—kitchen, toilet, backyard—in one of the municipal boxes in Phuthaditjhaba. She shared her room, barely 5 by 3 metres, with her younger sister, who was then at school in Qwaqwa, having previously been to school in Thaba Nchu where the official medium was Setswana; and with her close school friend for whom she had just been able to get a job as typist to the secretary of the Qwaqwa Minister of Justice. Serialong had a Qwaqwa citizenship card, and the family stand at Onverwacht was actually registered in her name, since her father was absent at work at the time of the move and her mother's reference book was lost. She had had to go down to Onverwacht from Qwaqwa for the purpose. Serialong had a child in 1978 who in 1980 was living with her mother in the household at Onverwacht, which also contained a distantly related boy attending primary school in the slum.[51]

These two detailed case studies are selected because they encapsulate a variety of common experiences related to me by inhabitants of Onverwacht over a period of several months in 1980. They are not, of course, statistically representative in any sense. It may be helpful, therefore, to complement this kind of evidence with some quantitative evidence relating to the distribution of employment and earning capacity at different points in time. For this purpose I refer to two surveys, undertaken in 1981 and 1984, whose results are not precisely comparable but from which may be drawn crude profiles of the 'average' household in Onverwacht/Botshabelo in these years.

In 1981, less than two years after the slum was established, the Surplus People Project (SPP) carried out a survey of ninety-three households in Onverwacht/Botshabelo, as part of its comprehensive investigation of forced relocation throughout South Africa. The ninety-three households contained 361 persons classified as 'permanently resident', seventy-four as 'commuters' and seventy-four as 'migrants'. The mean household size (including commuters and migrants) was 5.47 persons. Migrants and commuters made up 95 per cent of all persons in employment at the time of the interviews. Women comprised 25 per cent, of whom three-quarters were domestic servants, with rates of pay and conditions of social isolation and economic exploitation amongst the worst in South Africa. Just over 50 per cent of male migrants were concentrated in the mining industry; and half of all male employees in the sample (migrants and commuters) were unskilled labourers.[52]

Three years later, in September–October 1984, by which time the population of Botshabelo had greatly increased, the Bureau of Market Research (BMR) in Pretoria carried out a survey of the income and expenditure patterns of 496 households. Classified by ethnic group, the household heads were 80 per cent 'Sotho' and 15 per cent 'Xhosa'. The 496 households contained 318 'commuting and non-commuting earners in households working outside Botshabelo'; and 382 'family members, temporarily absent'. These categories correspond approximately with the respective categories 'commuter' and 'migrant' used by SPP. Thus the mean household size (including commuters and migrants) was 6.81, an increase which probably reflects the gross over-crowding on stands that people routinely complained about in the early 1980s. Of the 382 migrants, 175 (46 per cent) were employed on mines, predominantly the OFS gold mines in the region of Welkom and Virginia; 101 (26 per cent) in 'community, social and personal services', within which group it may be readily inferred that women domestic servants formed the largest number; and forty-two (11 per cent) in construction. Of 318 commuters, an overwhelming 92 per cent were employed in Bloemfontein. Of 918 men (including commuters and migrants) aged between 15 and 64 in the sample, 112 men were classified as 'unemployed', i.e. the male unemployment rate was 12.2 per cent.[53]

Such sample surveys provide some plausible bases for statistical generalisation, but are subject to the disadvantage that the presentation of aggregate results in the manner cited above is typically insensitive to variation between households. For this reason, I would argue strongly that sample surveys should be complemented by detailed household studies through time, from which may be drawn a valuable understanding of significant trajectories of household development or decline. One study of this kind follows below. It shows how individual household members move between various sectors of employment in the course of their working lives; how they are distributed between different sectors at any one point in time; how rapid turnover takes place in household membership over time; and, finally, how the exigencies of individual experience at the micro level reflect changing structural pressures at the macro level. Investigation of the routine struggles for survival in which household members are engaged thus demonstrates, firstly, that all sectors of the economy are fundamentally inter-connected; and, secondly, that the labour force as a whole is significantly differentiated—between 'insiders' and 'outsiders', between men and women, between migrants and commuters and the unemployed, between the skilled and the unskilled.

## Case study E: One household through time

Mmaboraki Mmeko was the dominant figure in a household of refugees from Kromdraai who were settled in the 'Singles' (later the A section) of Onverwacht. She was born in 1927 on a farm in the Zastron district, but the family moved repeatedly and she married her husband, born in 1922, at Dewetsdorp. She bore fourteen children, of whom seven died very young and seven survived: three boys and four girls. She was severely affected by high blood pressure. In a varied working life her husband moved from farm work to mine work—three shaft-sinking contracts at Virginia, presumably at the time the OFS gold mines were being opened up after World War II—and back to farm work. Their last place was on a farm in the Wesselsbron district. The family spent about five years at Kromdraai but the move was a protracted one, with Mmaboraki herself travelling frequently between Wesselsbron and Thaba Nchu. Initially her eldest daughter B3 (see Figure 6.3 for numbered letter references) was living at Kromdraai on her own, while Mmaboraki's husband A1 was still working on the Wesselsbron farm. He finally left the farm in 1977 when a new owner expelled many of the old workers and their families. Mmaboraki and her husband were arrested at Kromdraai during one of the raids by Bophuthatswana police in 1978, but were released after persuading the authorities that they did not intend to stay. Her husband found a cooking job later in 1978 but it did not suit him and he got another job at Welkom in February 1979, with a firm involved in dam construction. The family moved from Kromdraai to Onverwacht late in 1979.

In mid-1980 the eldest son B1, born in 1950 in the district of Virginia, was a driver at Crown Mines, Johannesburg. He had been married but his Xhosa wife had deserted him and taken their two young children to the Transkei. Mmaboraki's next son B2 worked at Western Holdings gold mine as a surface worker in the reduction plant, earning R194 per month. He had not joined on contract but directly, he said, from the farm in Wesselsbron district. He would prefer to stay at home and 'make a business', if he got the chance. The eldest daughter B3 was a professional Moposetola—an adherent of an Independent (Zionist) church—in Pretoria. The next daughters B4 and B5 were both at school in Virginia, staying with their father's sister in the township. Their younger brother B6 was at school in Onverwacht, as was the youngest child B7.

Mmaboraki's younger brother A3, born in 1942, began his working life as a farm labourer, moving with his family from the Dewetsdorp district to farms in the Brandfort and Wesselsbron districts. At the beginning of 1974 he took a mine contract at Welkom, paying R14 a month to rent a place for his family to stay on a white-owned farm outside the town. In addition, his wife A4 had to work for the farmer without payment in the weeding and reaping seasons. At the end of 1975, through knowing some of the workers there, he was able to get a job with Boart Drilling for R120 a month, compared with his earnings at the

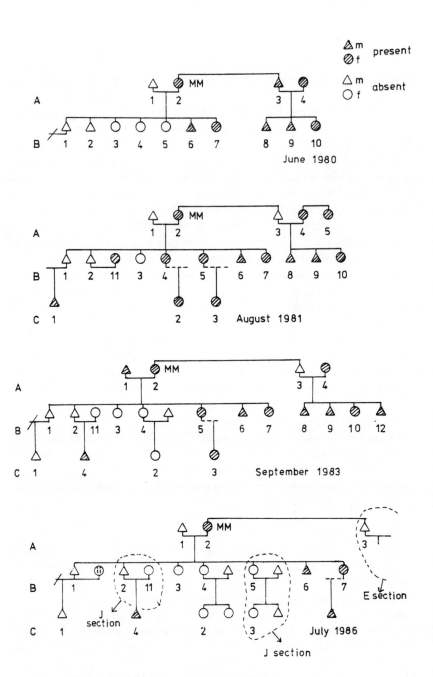

*Figure 6.3* Mmaboraki Mmeko: household turnover.

mine of R70 a month at that time; and he was able to fix his pass accordingly. His family remained on the farm, his children unable to go to school, until December 1979, when they were evicted by a new owner who did not want to farm his land as a labour reserve. His wife and children were arrested and fined R90. He was eventually able to arrange for them to go and stay in Onverwacht, where his brother-in-law was already established with his family. Their stand was intolerably crowded as a result, and A3 was anxious to register at Onverwacht so that he could be allocated a stand of their own. His wife could not do this in his absence because the office would insist on seeing her husband's reference book, and he could not risk remaining in his job at Welkom without this. So in February 1980 he gave up his job and came 'home' where he was only able to find occasional piece work. They registered for a stand in June 1980 but were told, along with everyone else resident at Onverwacht already, that they were unlikely to be given a stand until August 1981, since the priority was to remove people from oppression by the Barolong in Bophuthatswana. It was then extremely difficult for A3 to find another job.

By August 1981, B1 had recovered one of his sons from his wife's family in the Transkei, and this boy C1 was now living in the household. B2 had got married, while on leave, to a girl B11 from the D section of Onverwacht who had just moved in with the family. B4 and B5 had both returned from Virginia to Onverwacht where, within several weeks of one another in June 1981, they both gave birth to baby daughters by men who were working respectively at Virginia and Welkom and whose prospects were relatively good, although it was unclear at the time whether marriages would take place. A3 was away on a one-year contract on one of the new gold mines in the OFS. His wife's sister A5 had been staying in the household for eight months. Thus there were fourteen *de facto* residents by August 1981, by contrast with eight in June 1980.

In early September 1983 Mmaboraki's husband A1 was on weekend leave from his job at Welkom. B1's son C1 was in the Pokolo sanatorium at Thaba Nchu for long-term disabilities arising out of a bad fall as a baby. B2's wife had had a baby C4 in September 1981. B4 was living at Virginia at her husband's place with her child C2. B5 was still resident in the household while the family of her child's father were near neighbours in the A section. A3 was still working at the new mine near Theunissen, and his family still had no stand of their own. The walls of a cement-block house were half-finished. The household was relatively well off at this time, having at least three male members in regular paid employment.

By July 1986 the household had significantly contracted. A3's family was now established on their own stand in the E section of Botshabelo. It had taken more than three years to achieve that. Having seen his family expelled from a rented site on a white farm at the end of 1979, A3 had been forced to give up his job as well in order to wait for the opportunity to register at Onverwacht and then to be allocated a stand of their own at some indeterminate point in the future. A3 could begin again from scratch, meanwhile, to compete in the labour market from a distance that enforced the migrant as opposed to the commuter mode.

By 1986, also, two of Mmaboraki's children, B2 and B5, had their own stands in the J section of Botshabelo. In the three years since 1983, Botshabelo had expanded steadily north-westwards and south-westwards (see Figure 6.4). B2's wife B11 lived on her own, in the absence of her husband at work in Welkom, while her child C4 spent most of his time at his grandmother's. B5's husband was similarly absent at Welkom, and both B4 and B5 had had another child. B6 had completed his matriculation and was anxious to find some way of further pursuing his studies. B7 had a child in 1985 and also spent two months in hospital as a result of severe burns from a flaring primus stove. It was now possible for individuals to buy stands at Onverwacht. Significantly, B5 distinguished between those who had bought stands—a once-only payment of between R60 and R80 depending on size and situation; they then built for themselves as they could afford to—and those like herself who had bought a four-roomed house as well as a stand and were locked into a heavy long-term financial commitment: R52 per month in 1984, R58 in 1985 and R75 in 1986. The former, she reflected, was the sensible thing to have done, given pervasive insecurity of employment.

She might have added that investment on this scale was also vulnerable to the pervasive insecurity of marriage. In August 1989, B5 was back in her mother's household with her two children, having split up with their father. By this time, however, her brother B6 was helping to support the household through a job as clerk in the local health clinic which he had held since August 1986.[54]

Some of these working lives suggest a degree of mobility between farms, and between farms and industrial employment, that is not altogether consistent with the assumption that farm workers, being formally precluded from access to the urban areas, were tied either to particular farms or to farm work in general. Such mobility reflects the well developed intelligence networks by which farm workers and their families knew very well which farmers treated their employees well and which badly, and it explains the otherwise paradoxical but common observation through the decades that labour shortages have co-existed with labour abundances. But the constraints were severe nevertheless. People brought up on farms experienced the enduring structural disadvantages in the labour market of very little education, relative illiteracy and the non-transferability of limited skills. And when they attempted to establish a foothold in urban employment, they and their families were exposed either to official harassment or to the arbitrary whims of landowners with a monopoly of state power on their side. It should be remembered that evictions from farms or from towns under the pass laws did not simply remove people to Bantustans.

They also destroyed years of patient accumulation of family livelihoods. A crucial condition of resilience in such circumstances was finding a secure place to stay, albeit at the cost of physical distance from opportunities of employment that imposed severe strains on marital and other social relationships.

## WHAT SORT OF 'INTEGRATION'?

The population of Onverwacht/Botshabelo massively expanded from a figure of 64,000 at the end of 1979 to an unofficial estimate of 500,000 in 1986.[55] It was gazetted as a township in November 1982, and responsibility for the provision of services was transferred from the Southern OFS Administration Board to the Department of Development Aid on 1 April 1984.[56] According to a large-scale official *Meesterplan* dated September 1985, twenty-four residential sections were planned, spanning the entire alphabet except for 'I' (Industrial Area) and 'O'. This Master Plan shows facilities which include a sports stadium, two burial grounds, picnic sites and ground for 'youth camps'. A rocky hillside on the eastern side is marked 'nature reserve', bounded by residential sections to the west and south, the new graveyard to the north and the Country Bird chicken factory to the east (see Figure 6.4). A day hospital was opened in November 1986. At the same time there were said to be eighty educational institutions in Botshabelo, including thirty-one primary schools and forty-two kindergartens.[57] The schools were administered by the OFS regional office of the Department of Education and Training.

From its inception, officials envisaged that Onverwacht/Botshabelo would eventually be politically integrated with Qwaqwa. Its establishment within commuting distance of Bloemfontein, however, and at a great distance from Qwaqwa itself, contradicted the ethno-national logic of the Bantustan strategy, since it was equally obvious that these two over-crowded rural slums would never be territorially integrated. Such contradictions, reflecting some of the injustices, the failures and the absurdities of the original strategy, were acknowledged in President Botha's formulation of an alternative strategy of regional development in 1982.[58] Nine Development Regions were then identified. They were supposed to transcend the political and economic boundaries of grand apartheid under which South Africa was divided into ten Bantustans on the one hand and 'white' urban and rural areas on the other. Onverwacht/Botshabelo was the core of Development Region C which embraced both the provincial capital of Bloemfontein, with its own black townships in 'white' South Africa, and also the Thaba Nchu district of the 'independent' republic of Bophuthatswana. The burgeoning slum was explicitly adopted as a prime site of experiment for pragmatic modernisers within the state who were committed to technocratic reform of apartheid 'from above'.[59] Accordingly, one of the critics of 'regional development' analysed Onverwacht/Botshabelo as a test case for the strategy of 'orderly urbanisation'.[60]

One important implication of the rapid expansion of the rural slums was that

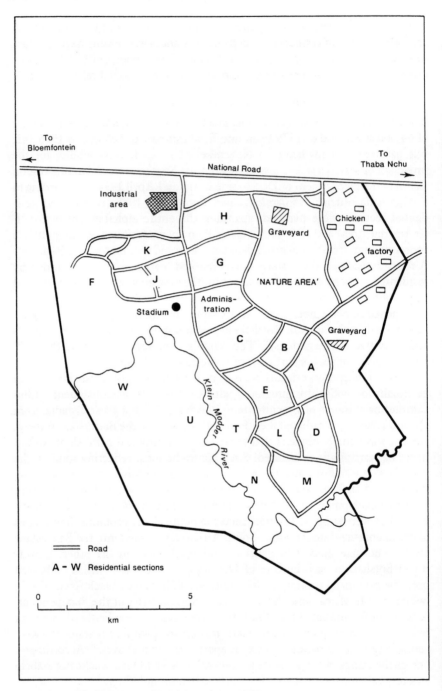

*Figure 6.4*  Botshabelo: residential sections, 1987.

the black labour force was no longer simply divided, as in the Riekert philosophy of 1979, into relatively privileged urban 'insiders' with Section 10 (1)(a)(b)(c) rights to live and work in 'white' South Africa on the one hand, and disadvantaged 'outsiders' from the Bantustans and from foreign labour reserves who had no such rights and had to seek work in the 'white' areas as temporary migrants on the other hand. Rather, frontier commuters were to some degree integrated into the metropolitan labour markets, in terms of their access to and dependence on wage incomes in the major industrial regions. But housing was not available for them in those industrial centres, and they and their families had to find a place to live in the fragments of this or that Bantustan not wholly beyond the reach of the Putco and the Jakaranda buses.

Consistently with the shift of strategic emphasis identified above, the predicament of work-seekers from Onverwacht was eased somewhat by an act of administrative discretion. From 1982 commuters from Onverwacht to Bloemfontein, and aspirant job-seekers based in Onverwacht, were given Section 10 (1)(d) rights to compete in the labour market on equal terms with urban 'insiders' who had Section 10 (1)(a)(b)(c) rights. Even this formal distinction fell away—with important qualifications relating to 'aliens' which are noted below—when the pass laws were repealed in June 1986. But this did not imply that it was easier to find either employment or accommodation in the metropolitan areas. Rather, the acute shortage of jobs and housing became the prime index of the practical severity of the new system of influx control which replaced the pass laws and was dignified by the official euphemism of 'orderly urbanisation'. At the end of 1984 the labour force domiciled in Botshabelo included some 23,000 commuters to Bloemfontein and 30,000 migrants to the OFS goldfields.[61] The implication of those figures is that the absolute numbers of jobs held outside the slum by residents of Botshabelo had increased. But it must also be true that the number of commuters and migrants *relative* to the total population of the slum had declined. Unemployment within Botshabelo, in other words, escalated much faster than employment of residents of the slum within the economic region of which Botshabelo was a part.

Corresponding to the state's refusal to accommodate blacks residentially within 'white' South Africa was a strategy of industrial decentralisation intended to disperse productive activities away from the established metropolitan areas.[62] Thus, in the eastern OFS, Bloemfontein was identified in 1982 as an Industrial Development Point (IDP) along with Botshabelo outside Thaba Nchu and Selosesha inside Thaba Nchu. In 1986, rising on the veld beside the Bloemfontein-Thaba Nchu main road, and one third of the way along it, was a site called Bloemdustria which was intended to develop in relative proximity both to Bloemfontein and to the vast pool of potential labour concentrated at Botshabelo.

The Botshabelo IDP was administered by the South African Development Trust Corporation (STK), which was itself established in March 1984 to take over the residual functions of the Corporation for Economic Development and the Mining Corporation in 'developing areas' outside the Bantustans. At the time the STK assumed this responsibility, five factories had been completed at Botshabelo, of which three were occupied, employing 296 people. Nearly two years later, in early 1986, according to official sources, there were fifty-four factories employing approximately 7,000 people. The total cost of these projects was assessed at R11,200 per job created, of which the public sector contribution was R3,700. The STK had also substantially invested in the Country Bird chicken factory, near the edge of Bophuthatswana, which in 1985 employed 500 workers and slaughtered 180,000 birds per week.[63]

Such figures appear to reflect a relatively successful investment programme. The question arises, however: successful for whom? The strategy of industrial decentralisation depended on generous wage and transport subsidies and tax incentives from the central state. In March 1987 William Cobbett investigated how these state subsidies worked at Botshabelo. He found a range of corrupt practices and published some detailed examples of these. Firstly, businessmen colluded with contractors to submit artificially high estimates of refitting costs which qualified for a relocation allowance from the state, and then shared between them the difference between the state grant and the actual cost. Secondly, businessmen claimed a 70 per cent state subsidy of the interest on capital loans arranged to pay for new equipment, but then installed inferior or secondhand equipment at a much lower cost and passed the balance of cheap capital back to the holding company. Thirdly, employers took advantage of the 95 per cent wage subsidies available from the state up to a maximum of R100 per employee per month for seven years. Either they claimed a larger wage subsidy than they were entitled to by declaring a false number of employees, or they actually paid their employees at rates lower than those they declared to the state.

The only possible explanation of this state of affairs, Cobbett concluded, was that the state agencies which administered the subsidies, notably the STK and the Board for Decentralisation of Industries, were so desperately committed to the 'success' of the programme that they either failed to apply elementary accounting checks or deliberately overlooked corruption on a grand scale, or both. The reason for state officials' inefficiency or corruption in this respect was not simply the need to make credible the state's extravagant claims of the progress of 'economic development' in the rural slums. There was the longer-term political objective of subverting the possible effects of sanctions on South Africa's export capacity. Thus, Taiwanese and Israeli firms had actively colluded with the South African state to manufacture at Botshabelo and other IDPs products whose origin was then concealed for purposes of export to the US and to countries of the European Community.

At the same time as they were exploiting the subsidies available from the state, these companies were exploiting their workers in an appalling manner.

Ninety-three per cent of the employees of the companies Cobbett surveyed were women. Most were paid between R40 and R80 a month. There were very few facilities at work and negligible fringe benefits. The work was of an exceedingly routine and boring kind. Wages were subject to arbitrary deductions by management. The managers themselves were unanimously hostile to any form of union organisation. Despite these conditions, groups of men and women clustered outside the high security fences that surrounded the industrial area in the hope that some casual vacancy would arise.[64]

It was this labour force that was described by the technocrats of state reformism, in their blandly enthusiastic advocacy of regional co-operation and regional development, as 'highly motivated and responsible'.[65] 'Highly motivated' in effect meant extremely poor and desperate for any kind of employment; 'responsible' in effect meant unorganised. Regional co-operation was recognised, however, as a 'delicate bloom'. This was also a coded phrase and acknowledged the fact that conflict between different agencies pervaded the implementation of regional development. In the mid-1980s Bloemfontein IDP and Bloemdustria were administered by the Bloemfontein City Council. Botshabelo was on land owned by the South African Development Trust (SADT), and was administered by the Department of Development Aid, the rump of the old Department of Co-operation and Development. For its part, Selosesha IDP fell under the Bophuthatswana National Development Corporation (BNDC), whose headquarters were in Mmabatho, Bophuthatswana.

Such bureaucratic proliferation greatly compounded the difficulties of planning and implementing regional development initiatives. For these initiatives had an important constitutional corollary. Elaborate and ingenious proposals emerged in the early 1980s for a third tier of government, known as the Regional Services Councils (RSCs). The RSCs would administer the distribution of local services in the Development Regions and all communities would be represented on them in proportion to their consumption of services provided. Since white municipalities had a much greater capacity to consume services than black townships, it may be inferred that the RSCs were intended to manage the putative incorporation of the rural slums into a loosely federal political framework without making any concession to the demand of black South Africans for a unitary democratic state. This 'solution' was sponsored by reformists within the state who acknowledged, apparently, that the Bantustans would eventually be re-incorporated but who were anxious to retain the substance of white power. The implementation of RSCs was substantially delayed, however, for the obvious reason that, in the wake of the demise of the black local authorities, they were fatally deficient in political credibility.[66] They also conflicted with, and were opposed by, the established administrative authorities of the Bantustans.

This last form of conflict was thrown into sharp relief by the apparent refusal of the Bophuthatswana authorities to allow dual citizenship. With the repeal of the pass laws in mid-1986, and President Botha's vague promises to restore South African citizenship to citizens of the 'independent' Bantustans (Transkei, Bophuthatswana, Venda, Ciskei—the TBVC states), there remained much confusion about what would happen in practice. It emerged that South African citizenship would be restored only by a complex formula of administrative concession to TBVC citizens who were 'permanent residents' of 'white' South Africa in July 1986—an estimated 1.75 million out of a total of approximately nine million TBVC citizens.[67] Otherwise, TBVC citizens would remain aliens and were therefore formally precluded from a right of access to jobs and housing in 'South Africa' (in the reduced sense used by Pretoria to exclude the TBVC states). Thus the political boundaries between the 'independent' Bantustans and 'South Africa' remained extremely important formal barriers to the freedom of movement of many millions of people who considered themselves to be South African.

The political boundary between Thaba Nchu and 'South Africa' appeared to be reinforced when, on 12 July 1986, senior representatives of Mangope's government held a public meeting in Thaba Nchu. They threatened the people that, if they applied for the new (allegedly uniform) South African identity documents which were replacing the hated *dompas*, but which remained a condition of employment in 'South Africa', they would forfeit all rights in Bophuthatswana, including citizenship and residence. If this was a serious threat, several hundred thousand commuters from Moretele-Odi to the Pretoria region and from Thaba Nchu to Bloemfontein faced the appalling dilemma of whether to give up a job in 'white' South Africa or a place to live in Bophuthatswana. The people were confused and angry. 'Negotiations' subsequently took place, allegedly, to resolve this problem.[68]

School students in Botshabelo, as elsewhere in South Africa, were in the forefront of resistance to the machinations of the state. Local unrest came to a climax in June 1986 with the imposition of a general State of Emergency throughout the country. Students demanded qualified teachers and the right to elect Students' Representative Councils. A series of confrontations with the police took place; some students were arrested; a Crisis Committee was elected which persuaded students to write their exams, but its members were repeatedly harassed. Sheaves of threatening leaflets were distributed by the police, warning parents against intimidation by 'radicals and rascals'. It identified as radicals 'those people who are going to ignore banning restrictions on meetings and gatherings between 4 and 30 June 1986'. Further notices were flung out of armoured trucks (known as 'hippoes') on 12 July 1986, immediately prior to the re-opening of schools on 14 July. Parents were instructed by the OFS Regional Director of the Department of Education and Training to make sure their children attended school on time and to enforce the rules that schools were out of bounds out of school hours and that children could not loiter in the vicinity of schools. Students had to go through an elaborate procedure for registration in January 1987, by which parents committed themselves to supervise their children and pay for any damage, etc. These instructions were issued for the purpose of 'legalising, normalising and regularising admissions'.[69]

On 9 July 1986, within the first month of the general State of Emergency, it was confirmed that Botshabelo would indeed become part of Qwaqwa, although the timing was left open. Rumours flared in February and again in May 1987 that incorporation was imminent. Students demonstrated against incorporation and organised a school boycott. A teacher who tried to prevent the demonstration was stabbed. A large number of unemployed men had been hastily recruited for training as *kitskonstabels* (special constables).[70] Survey evidence suggested that a large majority of the inhabitants of the slum did not want to join Qwaqwa.[71]

In the face of pervasive tension over the issue, the announcement of the political and administrative incorporation of Botshabelo into Qwaqwa came on 2 December 1987. *Kitskonstabels* were guarding schools and churches to prevent the organisation of any protest meetings or demonstrations. A local teacher, backed by the National Committee Against Removals, mounted an immediate challenge to the validity of the proclamation, on the grounds that the State President had exceeded his power under the National States Constitution Act of 1971 to 'amend or modify' the area for which a particular legislative assembly was established, and that Botshabelo had not passed through any of the stages of the gradual evolutionary process envisaged by the Act. The South African government rapidly tabled a new bill, the Alteration of Boundaries of Self-Governing Territories Bill, which appeared to extend the State President's powers to incorporate land into the Bantustans; to exclude legislation passed by legislative assemblies of the 'non-independent' Bantustans from being tested in a court of law; and thence to over-ride the legal objections to Botshabelo's incorporation.[72] Despite such blatant retrospective intervention by the state, the Bloemfontein Supreme Court ruled in late August 1988 that the incorporation of Botshabelo had been incorrect, and Botshabelo residents 'threw feasts' to celebrate this probably transient success. The state immediately gave notice of appeal against the judgement.[73]

Irrespective of its formal invalidity, the partial incorporation of Botshabelo into Qwaqwa caused a great deal of practical confusion. The land still belonged to the South African Development Trust. The police remained under the control of the central state. The judicial system, however, was 'secretly handed over' to the Qwaqwa government. Responsibility for schools in Botshabelo was also transferred to Qwaqwa. Serious shortages of staff and resources quickly developed. Teachers lost medical and pension benefits. They were forced to join the Dikwanketla party. Schools were grossly over-crowded and students were repeatedly harassed. More than 50,000 residents of the slum marched in protest on 1 October 1989 to present a petition against incorporation. In March

1990, the Appellate Division of the Supreme Court rejected the state's appeal against the earlier judgement, with the implication that Botshabelo once again fell under the administration of the central state.[74]

It is a story of confusion and contradiction at both economic and political levels. The logic of political incorporation could only be to push Qwaqwa into 'independence' alongside the TBVC states. This represented a setback for the reformist technocrats since their strategy was based in part on the erosion of the political boundaries of the Bantustans. Regional development, the new reformism, was supposed to transcend the boundaries of Bantustans. But the attempt to incorporate Botshabelo into Qwaqwa and President Mangope's aggressive insistence on the exclusive integrity of citizenship of Bophuthatswana represented a 'hardening', not a 'softening', of the boundaries.

Thus in the late 1980s there lay a cloud of uncertainty over the future of the rural slum and the life chances of its disparate half million inhabitants. On the one hand, the partial erosion of legal barriers to freedom of movement within 'white' South Africa eased the predicament of those who, like Tozi Xaba and her family in 1980, experienced impervious bureaucratic obstruction whichever way they turned. On the other hand, in August 1988 the state introduced a series of bills on squatting, group areas and slums whose overall effect would be to make homelessness a criminal offence and to exacerbate the difficulties of finding a job and a place to stay in both urban and rural areas of 'white' South Africa.[75]

Through the 1980s, in any case, the problems of poverty and unemployment and personal frustration intensified in proportion to the physical concentration of displaced and dispossessed people within the slum. Many of these people had spent their working lives on South African farms and struggled to build new livelihoods with decisive disadvantages in the wider labour market. Women in Botshabelo, in particular, experienced acute structural disadvantage. They had three options only: domestic service under conditions of extreme exploitation by white employers beyond the reach of daily commuting; residual employment at very low wages in a local industry established precisely to take advantage of an unlimited supply of cheap labour on the doorstep; or various forms of informal enterprise within the slum characterised by low returns, strong competition and official harassment. Given deepening structural unemployment across the country as a whole, the economic 'integration' of the inhabitants of Botshabelo within the regional labour market was highly tenuous, partial and differentiated.

Their political integration was similarly tenuous in the late 1980s. On the one hand, consistently with the strategic initiatives of 'regional development', Botshabelo was formally incorporated within the Bloemfontein Regional Services Council (RSC) which was gazetted on 3 January 1986. A special guarantee of central state support had to be made, following howls of protest from the white Bloemfontein municipality which anticipated, no doubt correctly, that

Botshabelo would entirely exhaust the financial resources of the RSC.[76] On the other hand, the central state was simultaneously driving Botshabelo into the political embrace of Qwaqwa, which implicitly if not explicitly increased the pressure on Qwaqwa to take 'independence' and thence threatened the conversion of Botshabelo's inhabitants into aliens without rights in 'South Africa'. Accordingly, the Kromdraai refugees in Botshabelo no longer struck the Qwaqwa ruling party salute ('Sekwankwetla!') to celebrate their deliverance from 'Egypt' into 'Canaan'.

Early in 1990, the log-jam began to break, and the incorporation of Botshabelo into Qwaqwa lost its political momentum. The immediate reason for this was the judicial decision of March 1990, at the highest level, that incorporation was legally invalid. The wider political context was the forced retirement of President Botha in late 1989 and the unbanning of the African National Congress by his successor, President De Klerk, in February 1990. This opened up the probability of political re-integration of the Bantustans into a unitary South African state. By the end of the year, the outcome still hung in the balance. Three of the four 'independent' Bantustans had military rulers committed in principle to negotiations over re-integration. By contrast, in striking isolation, President Mangope remained committed to the 'independence' of Bophuthatswana. Chief Minister Mopeli of Qwaqwa, for his part, maintained a studied ambiguity on the matter.[77] At last, the people of Botshabelo had cause to celebrate their resistance to his embrace.

# TWO FARMS: ONE HUNDRED YEARS

> At the homestead patches of hard earth floor are sagging under the fast growing reeds, where once our little feet moved swiftly. How sad.
>
> Ellen Kuzwayo, who grew up at Thaba Phatshwa
> *Call Me Woman* (1985), p. 57

> For a child it was a wonderful, a marvellous place in which to grow up . . . You were privileged . . . You could live the cycle of history, you were like a feudal lord . . .
>
> John Nieuwenhuysen, who grew up at Ngoananyana
> Interview, London, December 1983

> We worked the potatoes. It was very hard. We got up in the dark, as soon as the call reached the village, and went off to work . . . It was tough. We had no blankets, we had nothing . . . That's how it was all the time we were growing up.
>
> Mmadiphapang Thakho, who grew up at Ngoananyana
> Interview, Thaba Nchu, July 1986

I climbed Thaba Phatshwa (2,049 m) on the first day of July 1986. It was mid-winter. Three weeks before, a State of Emergency had been imposed throughout South Africa. Hippoes, casspirs, etc.—the metal juggernauts of repression—were chasing children in Botshabelo (see Chapter 6), in Soweto, in Guguletu. Alone on the summit of Thaba Phatshwa, it was intensely quiet but for the rustle of a light wind. I could see for miles in every direction, although not as far as the Maluti range in Lesotho, which was shrouded in a dusty haze. Gazing 180 degrees across the barren countryside from east to west, I felt giddy because I could see the earth is round.

On the northern horizon lay the distant hills of Moroto and Lokoala (the Mensvretersberg), the distinctive landmarks of the old Setlogelo family estate. Near at hand and to the south was the lumpy Mokopu (Pumpkin), which overlooks Naauwpoort farm. Immediately below the plateau of Thaba Phatshwa, on its eastern side and bounded now by the Armenia dam, were the arable and pasture lands of Thaba Patchoa farm.[1] The names of its modern subdivisions evoke poignantly the history of the Makgothi family who no longer own it: Tshiamelo, Place of Goodness, at the south end; Sweet Home at the north end; and Segogoane's Valley between (Figure 7.2).

About 20 km to the north-west was Thaba Nchu itself (2,138 m), the mountain that gave the district its name. It seemed blue, not black, in the thin winter sunlight. To the west, there were two roughly conical bumps on the undulating landscape. The larger is Ngoana, Child; the smaller is

Ngoananyana, Small Child, which overlooks Ngoanyana 98.[2] In the fore-ground was laid out a rectangular grid of ploughed fields and open stubble, dotted with small dams and clusters of trees marking the homesteads. This was the arable heartland of the Milner settlers. Some of the farm names—Fort Kelly, Sheen's Post—betray the sites of Lord Kitchener's blockhouses, dubbed 'blockheads' by Christiaan De Wet. A line of small fortifications built at the end of 1901, and connected with barbed wire, the blockhouses were part of an elaborate network of defensive and offensive cordons designed to pin down the Boer guerillas in the later stages of the South African war.[3]

Bending my imagination to the task, I could rotate parts of this giddy panorama on a temporal axis, stretching back one hundred years and more. This chapter is about people who lived and worked on two of the farms which were spread below me: Thaba Patchoa 106, immediately to the east, and Ngoanyana 98, a little further to the west. By reconstructing the disparate human lives that have been rooted in their soil, it is possible to grasp, almost as a whole, the diverse trajectories of social and economic change in the district. Through the experience of some of those people—black, white and 'Coloured'—these two particular stories connect most of the large themes which are analysed separately in the previous chapters of this book.

The stories are different but complementary. From the late nineteenth century, Thaba Patchoa 106 was owned by the Masisi and Makgothi families, prominent members of the Barolong progressive elite. Parts of the original farm were sold in the 1930s and early 1940s to the South African Native Trust, after two Makgothi heirs had fallen into irretrievable debt. Three subdivisions of it survived, however, as 'black spots' into the 1970s. By a curious shift of circumstance, Thaba Patchoa 106 was eventually re-integrated, as a desolate Coloured reserve. For its part, Ngoanyana 98 was granted to Michael Tshaba-dira, one of Chief Tshipinare's close collateral kinsmen (see Figure 1.2), but passed rapidly into the hands of a land speculator who had made his fortune at Kimberley. In the first half of the twentieth century, the eponymous fragment of the original farm was the home base of an outstandingly successful agricul-tural enterprise, founded by a Milner settler. After the old man's death in 1951, his enterprise fell into decline and one of his grandsons went bankrupt in 1979. Ngoanyana 98 had to be sold, and eighteen black families were evicted from the farm at gunpoint in October of that year.

## THABA PHATSHWA: AFRICAN FARM

In May 1836 the French missionaries, Arbousset and Daumas, stopped for two days at Thaba Phatshwa. They were on the last stage of their journey of exploration of the country north and west of the Mohokare (Caledon) river which had been ravaged by the *difaqane*. They found Thaba Phatshwa occu-pied by a Mosotho chief, Mpolu, whose people had sought refuge there from attacks by Moselekatse. It was, Arbousset recorded:

one of the most beautiful mountains of the country, and one of the best peopled. It presents an imposing aspect . . . It rises in a plain, by regular steps, composed of very hard rocks . . . These immense banks or shelves of stone form terraces all round the mountain . . .[4]

He conjured for his readers a scene of pastoral serenity which contrasted starkly with the waste and desolation of the many 'deserted villages' he inscribed on the map of the earlier stages of their journey.

When, from these various points, one sees a thousand little columns of smoke rise, expand and finally lose themselves in the air, when one hears the noise of the shepherds mingling with the bleating of their goats and the lowing of their oxen, one finds in all this an air of life—an indescribable feeling of wildness, which produces a sensation of pleasure, particularly in those who have still to endure for some time longer the tedious silence of solitude.[5]

In the early 1880s Thaba Phatshwa was a densely populated community of peasant cultivators on the south-eastern periphery of the Barolong political domain. Many of them were 'loyal' Basotho who fled from Basutoland at the time of the Gun War in 1881 or afterwards from the relentless hostility of Chief Masupha towards 'loyals' who had sided with the Cape government. In due course, many of these itinerant refugees either moved on to Nomansland, in the north-eastern Cape, or returned to Basutoland. Tshipinare's magistrate, John Cameron, recorded in his census of 1884 that Thaba Phatshwa had twelve settlements with 315 huts, inhabited by 515 Barolong adults and 140 Basotho—the largest Basotho minority recorded anywhere in the district.[6]

The farms surveyed by Bourdillon in this south-eastern corner of the Moroka territory were claimed, after the annexation, by two members of the Barolong political establishment. Joseph Thoto Masisi, who had been a senior councillor both of Moroka and Tshipinare, claimed Naauwpoort 74, England 28, Commissiehoek 32 and Mokopu 38. Stephanus Koko Moroka, a son of Chief Moroka in his fourth house, claimed Thaba Patchoa 106, Patchoana 27 and Leeuwdraai 39 (see Figure 1.3). He had been subchief at Thaba Phatshwa since 1870. Following Judge Gregorowski's recommendations of June 1885, Masisi was granted two farms: Naauwpoort 74, in the south-eastern corner, and Langbewoond 73, on the north-western border; while Stephanus Koko was granted only Thaba Patchoa 106. Their additional claims had been rejected by the Prinsloo commission in August 1884, a month after the annexation, and Gregorowski did not alter that decision. Thus a large block of land in the south-eastern corner, including a narrow corridor between Thaba Patchoa 106 and Naauwpoort 74, emerged in 1885 as government farms which were to be leased to white settlers.[7]

People resident on government farms were supposed to move to the two reserves of Thaba Nchu and Seliba by 20 August 1885. None went to the reserves, but many left Thaba Phatshwa and went to the Transvaal or

Kroonstad and Winburg and other parts of the OFS, or to Basutoland. About 125 families who remained in the Thaba Phatshwa area felt acutely insecure. Senior Barolong sent a deputation to President Brand, complaining that the land settlement 'would entail misery and ruin upon a large portion of the people'. They were particularly angry about exclusion from the block of government farms in the south-east, some of the best land in the district. By contrast, the locations were bleak and barren and 'mostly occupied by Samuel's followers'. Brand was sufficiently sympathetic to suggest to the Volksraad in the following session that the government farms in the south-eastern corner be turned into a location; but this was strongly rejected by the Volksraad on the grounds that the farms were too near the Basutoland border and must therefore be settled by whites. Accordingly, in July 1886 these farms were advertised for hire for a period of ten years to burghers of the OFS. John Daniel reported at the end of the year that the Thaba Phatshwa circuit had been 'almost depopulated by the hiring out of three-quarters of the land and the consequent eviction of the people'.[8]

Joseph Thoto Masisi had two children, by different wives (see Figure 7.1). In 1885 his son Moses Masisi married Julia Motshumi, the daughter of an African minister in the Methodist church. He acquired Klipfontein 110 from the heirs in Tshipinare's estate: nine-sixteenths of the farm in 1888 and the remaining portions between 1899 and 1904. In 1886 Joseph Thoto Masisi's daughter Magdalena Segogoane was married to Jeremiah Makgothi, third son of Stephanus Makoloi Makgothi, owner of Good Hope 70. The Masisi and the Makgothi families were close, having the reputation of 'marrying one another' in successive generations. Moses Masisi and his brother-in-law, Jeremiah Makgothi, had been at school together at Lovedale in the eastern Cape. Masisi thereafter concentrated on farming. Makgothi graduated in 1883 with a teaching certificate, and became headmaster of the first boarding school in Thaba Nchu for African boys. He was an invaluable assistant to Canon William Crisp, the Anglican missionary at Thaba Nchu through the early 1880s, in translating the Bible into the Serolong dialect of Setswana. Jeremiah Makgothi also taught about twenty white children for five years, before a government school was built. At the end of the South African war, he sought employment in the local Land Settlement office, and later became an interpreter in the magistrate's court.[9] He must have spent most of his working life in Thaba Nchu town rather than on his farm.

Stephanus Koko Moroka died shortly after obtaining title to Thaba Patchoa 106 in 1886. Reputedly, he liked brandy very much, and circumstantial evidence suggests that he became heavily indebted to local traders. A family dispute followed his death, concerning livestock in his estate which were claimed by his mother, Mmabathobatho.[10] At any rate, his wife Magaisang assumed liability for his debts and for the costs of redeeming the farm title. In 1889 she took out a mortgage bond for £850, half the value of the farm, in favour of James Robertson, the miller of Jammerberg Drift, whose speculative activities in the district were described in Chapter 2; and in 1890 she sold Thaba Patchoa 106 in two undivided halves to Robertson and to William Edward Higgs, trader of Ladybrand. Higgs sold his half to Robertson, and Robertson sold the whole farm to Joseph Thoto Masisi in September 1891. The staggeringly high price of £10,000 which is recorded in the relevant transfer deed appears to reflect a complex transaction by which Robertson provided capital for Masisi's farming operations. At the same time, Masisi sold his other property, Langbewoond 73, to Robertson for £3,000; and took out a mortgage bond in favour of Robertson for £6,000, representing the balance of the purchase price of Thaba Patchoa 106, which capital sum was to be repaid in four equal annual instalments by 1895. Immediately before the first repayment of capital of £1,500 fell due at the end of July 1892, Masisi took out a bond for £2,500 on Naauwpoort 74 in favour of the Provident Assurance and Trust Company of Port Elizabeth.[11] By these means, Masisi both consolidated his landed property—Thaba Patchoa 106 and Naauwpoort 74 were nearly contiguous—and imposed a heavy financial burden on his legal titles.

Joseph Thoto Masisi died in 1903, aged over 80. His joint estate, comprising the two farms, several plots in Thaba Nchu and also significant movable property, was valued at nearly £30,000. His liabilities, for the most part comprising the capital and interest payments due on a series of mortgage bonds, exceeded £15,000. His property was inherited equally by his two children and a division of the estate was agreed: Naauwpoort 74 was registered in the name of his son, Moses Masisi, and Thaba Patchoa 106 in the name of his son-in-law, Jeremiah Makgothi. One bond of £2,500 was ceded to Adam White Guthrie, cartage contractor of Port Elizabeth, in 1904 and cancelled in 1905 when the elder Masisi's estate was wound up. Jeremiah Makgothi took out new bonds in favour of Guthrie for £2,500 in October 1905 at 6 per cent interest and £3,500 in June 1906 at 6.5 per cent, on the security of his title to Thaba Patchoa 106 and an undivided half-share of certain plots in Thaba Nchu.[12]

Throughout the period of his formal ownership of Thaba Patchoa 106, then, from 1905 until his death in 1922, Makgothi had to meet interest payments on bonds totalling £6,000. He was politically active for much of this period, as was Moses Masisi, particularly in the Becoana Mutual Improvement Association in the years before Union, and in the South African Native Convention which preceded the founding of the African National Congress in 1912. Again with Moses Masisi, he was also a member of the Thaba Nchu syndicate that helped to finance Sol Plaatje's newspapers.[13] In order to assist him to meet these obligations, he leased 1,000 morgen portions of Thaba Patchoa 106 for six months at a time to his friend Edward Worringham, local Justice of the Peace and settler on the farms Scotland and Ireland (subdivisions of the original England 28), to the south of Naauwpoort 74. In 1908, the rent for 1,000 morgen was £10.8s.4d. per month. The inference may be drawn that Makgothi was able to meet between one-third and two-thirds of his annual interest payments through leasing portions of his land in this way. The arrangement required the approval of his mother-in-law, Isabella Moseetsi Masisi, who retained usufructuary rights in the farm until her death in 1916. According to his youngest daughter, Blanche Tsimatsima, Jeremiah Makgothi was known as the black Scotchman because of his friendship with Worringham.[14]

One of Jeremiah Makgothi's grand-daughters, Ellen Kuzwayo, born Merafe in 1914, remembered her childhood at Thaba Patchoa with deep affection and nostalgia. 'It was a beautifully cultivated farm, with plenty of rich grazing pasture . . . abundant corn and maize in winter and equally abundant wheat in summer'.[15] There were large numbers of farm animals: cattle, sheep, goats, pigs, horses, rabbits, turkeys, ducks, chickens. There was a vegetable garden and an irrigated orchard with various fruit trees about twenty-five yards from the homestead. There was also a nearby village, Mocweding, where lived the other residents of the farm, who raised their own livestock and cultivated their own lands on the farm. Makgothi kept a notebook in which he recorded in meticulous detail the assets owned and the crops reaped by each of these families. The most obvious purpose of this would have been to facilitate equitable division of the crops. According to Blanche Tsimatsima, however, the relationship was not based on share-cropping. People were paid in cash for their seasonal or intermittent labour services. In addition, there was a strong tradition of *matsema*, work-parties, which were most popular for the labour-intensive tasks of ploughing, weeding and threshing. Every family made an effort to be represented, including the Makgothis themselves. The men and women would bring their own equipment; the organisers would provide beer, meat and maize or sorghum porridge; and the women would supplement these with other provisions. The work-parties reached a climax with vigorous singing and dancing.[16]

In summary, it would appear that part of the farm was leased to Worringham; Jeremiah Makgothi farmed other parts directly, using his own livestock and machinery and some family labour but often hiring labour in addition; and the village residents had their own livestock and arable lands. Reciprocal work-parties were common. Ellen Kuzwayo's reminiscences convey an impression of strongly co-operative social and economic arrangements. Despite this, the fact of land ownership sharply distinguished the Makgothi family within the community. Jeremiah Makgothi was a gentle, mild-mannered man. For her part, Magdalena Segogoane would stand no nonsense: not from her grandchildren, not from white madams, not from neighbouring farmers. She insisted that Jeremiah Makgothi's Cape carriage should take up as much of the road as any cart or carriage travelling in the opposite direction. On one occasion in Thaba Nchu, an Afrikaner woman approached her with a request, 'I am looking for a maid to work in my kitchen'. Magdalena Segogoane

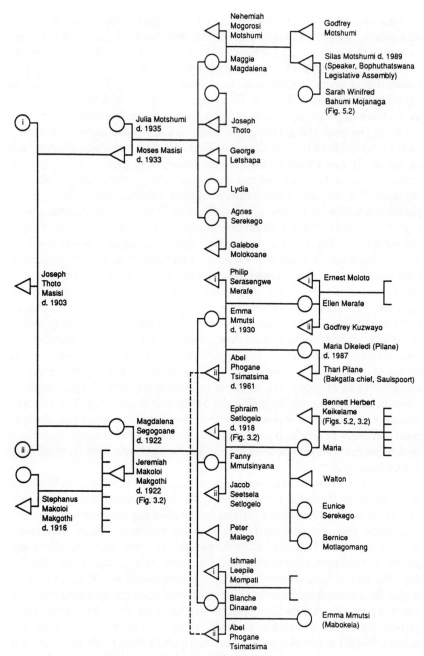

*Figure 7.1*  Partial Makgothi/Masisi genealogy.

retorted without hesitation: 'I am also looking for that type of person—can you help?' On such journeys to town, Ellen Merafe and her young Setlogelo cousins would have to wear full knee-length dresses with high yokes, starched bonnets with two or three frills and white coats. 'Our whole costume', Ellen recalled, 'made us look painfully different from the neighbourhood children ... we stuck out like sore thumbs'.[17]

Jeremiah Makgothi and his wife Magdalena Segogoane died within two months of one another, in April and July 1922. Their landed property comprised Thaba Patchoa 106 (4,237 morgen), valued at £21,185; Pilgrim's Rest 547 (476 morgen), Jeremiah's one-eighth portion of Good Hope 70, inherited from his father and worth £1,904.18s.8d.; an undivided one-eighth share of a 16-morgen plot in Thaba Nchu, likewise inherited from Stephanus Makoloi Makgothi, worth £50; shares in certain plots in Thaba Nchu which Magdalena Segogoane had inherited from her father, Joseph Thoto Masisi, worth £500; and a farm identified as Gamabot (949 morgen) in the district of Vryburg (northern Cape), worth £1,168. Movable assets of the estate were valued at £1,226, and consisted mostly of livestock and farm implements. The inventory included sixty-five cows, seventy-five oxen, twenty-four calves, twenty tollies [young oxen], twenty-nine calves and tollies, twenty-nine heifers, eleven mares, three fillies, six geldings, one colt, 179 ewes, 240 hamels [castrated rams]; five ploughs, three planters, five cultivators, two Cape carts, two wagons. The Makgothis were indeed a family of substance. But the liabilities of the estate were approximately £11,000. Jeremiah Makgothi's debts had been consolidated in 1918 and re-allocated in the form of a bond for £5,500 in favour of Miss H. Robertson—almost certainly Helen Robertson, unmarried sister of James Robertson—and two smaller bonds.[18] Capital repayments and interest were outstanding in respect of all these bonds.

Jeremiah and Magdalena Segogoane's joint will, drawn up in 1918, envisaged the necessity of selling part of Thaba Patchoa 106 in order to meet the outstanding liabilities. Complex arrangements had therefore to be made in order to facilitate payment of debts and to ensure a fair division of the estate between their four children: Emma Mmutsi, Fanny Mmutsinyana, Peter Malego and Blanche Dinaane. In the event, the amount of land they had envisaged for sale was not by any means sufficient to pay off the creditors of the estate, so major adjustments had to be devised by the executors. The original farm was divided into six portions: Tshiamelo 664 (607 morgen) went to Emma Mmutsi; Segogoane's Valley 665 (608 morgen) to Blanche Dinaane; Thaba Patchoa 106 (rest) (615 morgen) to Fanny Mmutsinyana; Dassieshoek 666 (896 morgen) and Sweet Home 667 (600 morgen) to the estate; and Thaba Patchoa Berg 668 (909 morgen) to Peter Malego. Since much of Thaba Patchoa Berg 668 comprised the mountain itself, that farm was exchanged for Sweet Home 667 on a valuation basis by which it could be established what contribution Peter Malego thereby made towards realising the necessary cash. Then

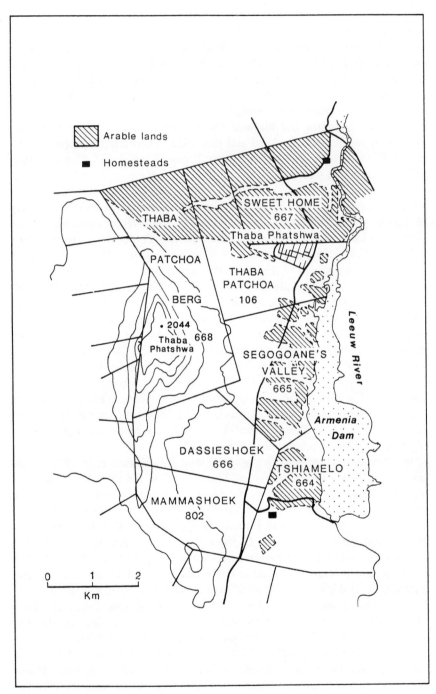

*Figure 7.2* Thaba Patchoa farm.

Dassieshoek 666 was sold by public auction to Moses Masisi for £3,408.9s.; and Thaba Patchoa Berg 668 to Gert Petrus Stofberg for £2,750.9s.6d. Each holding that remained in the hands of the four Makgothi heirs was diminished by roughly one third of the size envisaged by their parents in their will.[19]

At the same time the rest of the fixed property was sold by pre-arrangement to the heirs, according to the terms of the will, so that Fanny Mmutsinyana bought Pilgrim's Rest 547; Emma Mmutsi the several Masisi plots in Thaba Nchu; Blanche Dinaane the one-eighth share of the Makgothi plot in Thaba Nchu; and Peter Malego the farm in Vryburg district. These sales realised additional cash for the estate but, in order to meet the cost of purchase and to cover the remaining balance of liabilities, each of the four heirs took out mortgage bonds in 1924 at the time transfer took effect; Emma Mmutsi for £1,300; Fanny Mmutsinyana for £1,500; Peter Malego for £1,500; and Blanche Dinaane for £1,200.[20]

Emma Mmutsi and Philip Serasengwe Merafe were divorced while Ellen, born in 1914, was still an infant. Emma Mmutsi married Abel Phogane Tsimatsima in 1921. His father, not a landowner, was foreman at Rietfontein 119 for Elizabeth Nkhabele Fenyang, and owned many livestock. Abel Phogane apparently sold life assurance before his marriage, and then he started farming at Thaba Patchoa. Ellen Merafe remembered that her step-father integrated swiftly and easily into the Makgothi family. He was 'alert, sensitive and calm', and strongly encouraged Ellen to read and take an interest in current affairs. Ellen's half-sister, Maria Dikeledi, was born in 1922, and gave Ellen a sense of belonging and companionship which she had not always felt in the company of her Setlogelo cousins, being singled out sometimes as a 'Merafe child'. Her uncle Peter Malego, however, 'oozed with love' for both Ellen and her Setlogelo cousins.[21]

In the mid-1920s, Fanny Mmutsinyana was a widow with four young children, her husband and cousin Ephraim Setlogelo having died in 1918 at the age of 30. In 1926, on the death of Hessie Sealimo Setlogelo, as recounted in Chapter 3 with reference to Setlogelo family affairs, Fanny Mmutsinyana and her children jointly inherited from the estate of her late husband a portion of Somerset 55. Fanny Mmutsinyana later married Ephraim's cousin, Jacob Seetsela Setlogelo, owner of the farm Jordan 702, a portion of Moroto 68. His first wife died in 1930, leaving him with six children. Emma Mmutsi also died in 1930, and her husband Abel Phogane Tsimatsima became owner of Tshiamelo 664. In 1932 he married her youngest sister, Blanche Dinaane, who owned Segogoane's Valley 665, so that the two adjacent subdivisions of the original farm were effectively managed as one unit through the following decades. Blanche Dinaane had already been widowed herself, with two young children, by the death in December 1931 of her husband, Ishmael Leepile Mompati, a popular Bloemfontein composer and conductor.[22] These marital exigencies explain the complexity of the genealogical connections represented in Figure 7.1.

Blanche Dinaane had a distinguished nursing career. The youngest of Jeremiah Makgothi's children, she was born in 1900 and went to local primary schools at Naauwpoort and Thaba Patshwa. She trained as a teacher at Healdtown Missionary Institution at Fort Beaufort and then as a nurse at the Victoria hospital, Lovedale, from 1923 to 1925. She worked at the Moroka hospital in Thaba Nchu for many years, and did midwifery training in Johannesburg during the Second World War. This was followed by a decade of community service before her retirement in 1959. In 1985 she was presented with a 'Certificate of Merit to Service and Dedication' by the Thaba Nchu District Nurses Discussion Group. In 1986, frail but canny, she distinguished clearly between the family and other matters that she would talk about and those that she would not. 'I never wanted anybody to know what is in my wardrobe, how many dresses I have . . .'.[23] She had three daughters: two by her first husband and one, who was named Emma Mmutsi after Blanche's eldest sister, by her second husband.

Both Fanny Mmutsinyana and Peter Malego became heavily indebted through the 1920s. Fanny Mmutsinyana owned Pilrim's Rest 547, Thaba Patchoa 106 (rest) and an undivided share of Somerset 55. The first of these three properties was sold in 1930, to Cecil Rayner Morgan, a local land speculator and stock farmer. The second and third were sold in execution in 1932, in the depths of the depression, after legal proceedings brought by the bond-holders, the South African Association of Cape Town, a large finance and insurance company. As recorded in Chapter 3, Fanny Mmutsinyana may have been driven into bankruptcy by Israel Tlale Setlogelo, who had an unscrupulous lawyer behind him. Whether or not he was responsible, she lost all her own land. A small tract of Somerset 55 was only preserved for the family, albeit vicariously, by the intervention of Bennett Herbert Keikelame, who married Fanny Mmutsinyana's eldest daughter Maria in 1935, and whose career was briefly outlined in Chapter 5. In 1939, in order to forestall further legal action by bond-holders, he bought the undivided shares of Maria's three siblings in the farm. Thereafter Fanny Mmutsinyana stayed quietly at Somerset, occasionally helping with feeding schemes at St Paul's school in Thaba Nchu. She suffered from high blood pressure, and collapsed and died in 1953.[24]

Peter Malego trained in commercial studies at Bensonvale in the Herschel district. He then returned to help his father on Thaba Patchoa. He was very 'free-giving', according to Blanche Tsimatsima, and very extravagant. He was remembered, among other things, as the second black person in the district to buy a motor car. By 1929 there were four mortgage bonds registered against his property; respectively of £1,500, £1,000, £600 and £1,500. He sold Sweet Home 667 to Moses Masisi for £6,360, and acquired Dassieshoek 666 in return for £4,036.6s. He took out two fresh bonds, respectively of £2,018.3s. and £1,481.17s., which presumably, together with the balance in his favour derived from the exchange of Sweet Home 667 for Dassieshoek 666, covered his capital repayments and interest then due. He could not extricate himself, however, from a spiral of escalating debt. Moses Masisi, his maternal uncle, took legal action against him and in 1931 bought an undivided 2475/5606 share of Dassieshoek 666 for £1,782. A division of the property took place, so that Peter Malego became owner of Dassieshoek 666 (rest) (500 morgen) and Moses Masisi the owner of Mammashoek 802 (396 morgen). Once again, however, Peter Malego was unable to meet his obligations and Masisi bought the remaining portion of Dassieshoek 666 in 1932 for £1,900. After he lost his land, Peter Malego became the first boarding master at the Moroka Missionary Institution in Thaba Nchu. He later joined the church himself, and was sent to Francistown, Bechuanaland, where he lived for about ten years before his death in the 1960s.[25]

At his death in 1933, Moses Masisi was the owner of three registered portions of Thaba Patchoa 106: Sweet Home 667, Dassieshoek 666 (rest) and Mammashoek 802. His total estate was valued at £75,728.4s. He owed £5,000 to the local attorney John Henry Faustmann, but he was also recorded as the mortgagee in no fewer than twenty-one bonds, for amounts ranging from £85 to £1,000, a pattern quite contrary to the prevailing indebtedness of Barolong landowners. This reflects his exceptional shrewdness and ability both as a farmer and as an investor. Sweet Home 667 was inherited by George Letshapa Masisi, Moses Masisi's younger son, together with Klipfontein 110 (rest). Dassieshoek 666 (rest) and Mammashoek 802, which were taken over by Moses Masisi's widow Julia, were auctioned in 1936 after her death to George Letshapa Masisi for £4,484.16s. He took out mortgage bonds in favour of two members of the Dyke family, respectively for £2,450 and £2,350, with interest at 6 per cent per annum. In 1942, Masisi sold both properties to the South African Native Trust (SANT), for £4,500.[26]

Although not the eldest in age, Ellen Merafe was genealogically the senior child in the next generation of the Makgothi family (see Figure 7.1). She first went to school on Thaba Patchoa farm, in a church building about three minutes' walk from the homestead at Tshiamelo. She and her Setlogelo cousins used to exchange their bread and jam sandwiches for the tasty sour porridge which the village children brought to school. She moved first to St Paul's Higher Primary School in Thaba Nchu in 1927 and then, early in 1930, she went on to boarding school at St Francis' College at Mariannhill in Natal. The nuns there were rigid, cold and domineering. Through Elizabeth Makgothi, her mother's cousin who also lived at Thaba Patchoa, and who went to Mariannhill a year ahead of her, Ellen met and admired a group of senior students whose warmth, ideals and discipline inspired her. Then tragedy struck. She came home for the first school holidays in June 1930 and heard by telegram that her mother Emma Mmutsi had died in East London. Ellen moved on to Adams College, Amanzimtoti, in 1932 for her teacher training courses, and graduated at the end of 1935 with a higher primary teaching certificate. She then spent a year at Lovedale—a strong family tradition—before taking her first teaching job at Inanda seminary, Natal.

After six months her health broke down through sheer exhaustion, and she returned home to take a new post at St Paul's school in Thaba Nchu under Paul Mosaka, who later, in 1943, founded the African Democratic Party. She became secretary of the Thaba Nchu branch of the National Council of African Women. In mid-1938, suddenly and without explanation, Blanche Tsimatsima turned against her and evicted her from the Makgothi homestead in Thaba Nchu, telling her to go and find her father and his people in Johannesburg. Her whole childhood tumbled away. Beyond lay a brief period with her father, Philip Merafe, a civic leader and businessman in Pimville (Soweto), formerly one of the first trained black printers; then two years' teaching at Heilbron (OFS), where she lived with her mother's cousin, Elizabeth Makgothi, and her husband, Solomon Tlhapane. She had been bridesmaid at their wedding in December 1937, 'daintily dressed', according to the social correspondent of the *Free State Advocate*, 'in ankle length georgette',[27] and she was close to them both. During this period her half-sister, Maria Dikeledi, was married to Thari Pilane of Moruleng (Saulspoort) in the western Transvaal, who was heir to the South African branch of the Kgatla chieftainship. The senior branch of the Kgatla chieftainship is in Mochudi, Botswana, whither Maria Dikeledi Pilane moved after her husband's death and where she herself died in 1987.

In 1940 Ellen Merafe moved to Phokeng, near Rustenburg (western Transvaal), where she could visit her sister regularly. Shortly afterwards, she met her first husband, Ernest Moloto, who was headmaster of a large primary school in Moruleng. Marriage was a rude shock. She had two sons, and after a subsequent miscarriage she escaped from Moruleng early in 1947, leaving her two sons behind.

She got a teaching job in Orlando East and went through a divorce from her husband. She later married Godfrey Kuzwayo and lived in Kliptown, becoming involved in a youth work programme run by the Non-European Affairs Department. She resigned from teaching in 1952, trained as a social worker and developed a new career of community service, initially as General Secretary of the Transvaal Young Women's Christian Association, and latterly as architect of and adviser to women's self-help groups in Soweto. She was known through the 1970s as 'Mother of Soweto'. She was a member of the Soweto Committee of Ten for six years and she was detained without trial for six months in 1977–8. In 1983 she made a film with Betty Wolpert called 'Tshiamelo: Place of Goodness', about her grandfather's farm, the 1913 Land Act and the experience of compulsory expropriation by the state. The making of that film was the occasion, also, of her reconciliation with her aunt Blanche after forty-five years. In 1985 she published her autobiography, *Call Me Woman*.[28]

Of Fanny Mmutsinyana's four children, Ellen's Setlogelo cousins, the eldest and the youngest were still, in 1986, living in Thaba Nchu. Maria was the widow of the 'tycoon' Bennett Herbert Keikelame, who owned a large business jointly with Dr James Moroka, Ephraim Mojanaga and Paul Mosaka—Thaba Nchu African Trading Stores (see Chapter 5). Born in 1912, she was at Lovedale for nine years from 1921 and had a brief teaching career before she married in 1935. She had seven children. As indicated in Chapter 5, one of her sons, Ephraim Keikelame, was Minister of Economic Affairs in the Bophutha-tswana government in the late 1980s. Maria's youngest sister, Bernice Motla-gomang, born in 1919, was living on the edge of Moroka location, Thaba Nchu, in much poorer circumstances. Fanny Mmutsinyana's son Walton was a court interpreter who was transferred to Vanderbijlpark (southern Trans-vaal), where he died in 1953. Her other daughter, Eunice Serekego, married in Krugersdorp (western Transvaal) and died there in the 1970s.

Thus were Jeremiah Makgothi's children and grandchildren dispersed. But the story of Thaba Patchoa 106 is not yet complete. The farm was included in the Released Areas scheduled under the 1936 Trust and Land Act (see Figure 4.1). As we have seen, however, in Chapter 4, the two adjoining farms Aberfoyle 157 and Strathearn 396, among others, were excised from the Released Areas in response to pressure from the Vigilance Committee of white farmers in the district. The Minister of Native Affairs was initially 'hesitant about approving' this excision on the grounds that this separated Thaba Patchoa from the rest of Released Area No. 3.[29] Nevertheless the excision was formally gazetted in 1938 and the SANT acquired two portions of the original farm Thaba Patchoa in the same year: Thaba Patchoa 106 (rest) (615 morgen) from F.H. Swanepoel and Thaba Patchoa Berg 668 (909 morgen) from G.P. Stofberg. Subsequently, in 1942, the SANT also bought Dassieshoek 666 (rest) and Mammashoek 802 (together 897 morgen) from George Letshapa Masisi (see Figure 5.1).

From the early 1940s, then, three fragments of the original farm survived in black ownership: Tshiamelo 664, owned by Abel Phogane Tsimatsima; Sego-goane's Valley 665, owned by his wife, Blanche Tsimatsima; and Sweet Home 667, owned by her cousin, George Letshapa Masisi. Two of the three surviving Makgothi heirs—Fanny Mmutsinyana and Peter Malego—had entirely lost any material interest in Thaba Patchoa. The SANT owned the rest of the farm.

## FROM 'BLACK SPOTS' TO COLOURED RESERVE

At this point, the history of a quite different community, and of a quite different struggle for land, intersects with that of the Makgothis on Thaba Patchoa: that of the 'Coloured' people who were descended from Carolus

Baatje's Newlanders. The Newlanders, who spoke Afrikaans and are often described in contemporary sources as 'Bastards', settled in the early 1830s at Platberg, near what became the village of Ladybrand, with the Methodist missionary Thomas Sephton. Their settlement was constantly vulnerable to attack as a result of conflicts over land between the Basotho of Moshoeshoe, the Batlokwa, the Bataung, the Boers and other immigrant communities. The Newlanders were briefly displaced from Platberg in 1851. Later, before the outbreak of the second Sotho-Boer war in 1865, they moved to Rietspruit, 80 km to the north-west, on the site of the later village of Brandfort. There they were treacherously attacked in late June 1865 by a Basotho force several thousand strong under Chiefs Masupha and Lerotholi, who killed almost all the men and male children with assegais. The Basotho took all the women and girls and livestock and wagons with them. On the next day, however, a commando intercepted them at Verkeerdevlei, and recovered the captives and the booty.[30] The surviving Newlanders were sent to Bloemfontein, whence they were dispersed in the Moroka territory and parts of the Free State.

At least twice thereafter, in 1870 and 1890, the Newlanders petitioned the Volksraad for a grant of land to redeem a pledge apparently made to them by President Brand for their support in the conflict with the Basotho. John Weymers, a zealous guardian of the history of the Newlanders, kept in his trunk at Thaba Phatshwa an anonymous and undated manuscript which records a promise of a large area of land: fourteen farms around the Mensvretersberg. The chronology is confused, however, since the manuscript also refers to 'British settlers' on that land.[31] These farms were clearly within the territory of Chief Moroka's Barolong. Equally clearly, President Brand was in no position to make promises about any part of that territory before he annexed it in 1884. He died in 1888. Many farms between the Mensvretersberg and Excelsior emerged from the Gregorowski enquiry in 1885 as OFS government land which was leased from 1886 to whites who were burghers of the OFS, not 'British'. However, that same block of land was settled after the South African war by men of 'British' stock, mainly from the Cape Colony (see Chapter 2). At any rate, the surviving Newlanders were granted half of the farm Bofulo (1,800 morgen) in the Seliba reserve, in 1897, as a result of a commission of enquiry appointed in response to a petition from Carolus Baatje's descendants.[32] Some of them, as individuals, had previously obtained small land grants from Tshipinare. Gregorowski confirmed, for example, the grants to Stephanus Mey of Israelspoort 14 and to Stoffel Weymers of Bastard's Post 147, which was taken over by Weymers' neighbour Stephanus Makoloi Makgothi of Good Hope 70.

There was constant friction between the Barolong and the 'Coloured' community of Bofulo. In 1906, for example, Thomas Malebo complained that, 'ploughing on a fair scale', he was 'having trouble with the Bastards' in respect of the demarcation of their respective lands. The magistrate tartly responded by marking out three fields that were 'quite sufficient for a boy of his class'.[33] In 1912, it became necessary to establish a definite line of division of Bofulo. The Barolong and the 'Coloured' people both felt aggrieved. The area was denuded and there was insufficient pasture and arable land for their needs. Living in close proximity, they maintained separate lifestyles and they did not mix with one another.

In 1939, the 'Coloured' community at Carolusrus in Bofulo consisted of 500 people, including eighty taxpayers. They owned between them 113 cattle, forty-two horses, fifty-two donkeys and fourteen goats. In the context of the reclamation proposals of that year (see Chapter 5), the community was considered a 'stumbling block' to the development of the Seliba reserve. Thus the isolation of Thaba Patchoa 106 from the rest of the Released Areas at the end of the 1930s provided the opportunity for what must have impressed Assistant Native Commissioner Booysen as a masterly bureaucratic solution to the long-standing mutual irritation between the Barolong and the 'Coloured' people. Negotiations were therefore initiated for the Carolusrus community to move 'lock, stock and barrel' to Thaba Phatshwa to occupy the 1,525 morgen of ground there that now belonged to the SANT. At the same time, it was proposed that about ten 'Coloured' households, resident on three portions of the farm Brakfontein 140 which still belonged to the Terblans family, should also be removed to Thaba Phatshwa with their livestock. An exchange of land would take place, by which the SANT would acquire the three portions of Brakfontein and the Terblans family would be given an equivalent portion of Thaba Patchoa 106 (rest). This would leave only 1,112 morgen available for the Carolusrus community.[34] It is curious that none of the parties involved in these negotiations apparently drew attention to the fact that roughly two-thirds of the farm Thaba Patchoa Berg 668 consisted of the mountain itself and therefore could not be used for arable purposes.

At a series of meetings in April and May 1940, at least half of the Carolusrus community rejected the proposed removal, unless the full 1,525 morgen at Thaba Patchoa were made available to them. The NAD was forced to make this concession, with the implication that the exchange of portions of Brakfontein 140 for part of Thaba Patchoa 106 (rest) could not take place. The NAD also had to re-assess the levels of compensation payable for site improvements at Carolusrus. The removal took place late in 1940, when fifty-four heads of households were recorded.[35]

In 1942, as indicated above, the SANT acquired Dassieshoek 666 (rest) and Mammashoek 802 (together 897 morgen) from George Letshapa Masisi, and made these lands also available to the new Coloured village. However, strong feelings quickly developed amongst the descendants of the Newlanders against their administration as 'Natives' under the SANT. The community at Thaba Phatshwa was divided into two camps. One faction, led by village board member J. Van Wyk, a people's nominee, was 'adamant that the land they occupy is not Trust land because it was given to them in exchange for land given to them by the old Volksraad government'.[36] This faction even refused to occupy Dassieshoek and Mammashoek because these farms were Trust land. The source of their strength of feeling was not merely pride and sentiment. They specifically resented the Trust's regular attempts to brand and cull livestock, whose impact elsewhere in the district is analysed in Chapter 5.

Officials agreed that the position was anomalous. The Native Affairs Department therefore approached Social Welfare with a view to the latter department taking over control and administration of the Coloured settlement. Thaba Patchoa would have to be excised from the Released Areas and bought by another department from the Trust, and compensating land would have to be bought by the Trust elsewhere. An agreement was reached by which Social Welfare would buy the four farms from the Trust through the Department of Lands; but the matter was held in abeyance while the second wave of Trust purchases in the Thaba Nchu district was negotiated and implemented. In 1951 a price of £20,460 was agreed for Thaba Patchoa 106 (rest), Thaba Patchoa Berg 668, Mammashoek 802 and Dassieshoek 666; but the land transfer could not be effected until 1953 when provision was made for it in the relevant budget. Administrative responsibility was transferred to the Department of Coloured Affairs in 1954. Some members of the community then urged action towards expropriation of the two surviving 'black spots': Sweet Home 667, owned by George Letshapa Masisi, immediately adjoining the Coloured village; and Tshiamelo 664 and Segogoane's Valley 665, owned respectively by Abel Phogane and Blanche Tsimatsima.[37]

George Letshapa Masisi's widow, Lydia Masisi, recalled that the government had been writing letters since the 1950s about purchase of Sweet Home 667. In 1956 Masisi was described by Native Commissioner Welman as *'n gebore verkwister*, 'a born wastrel', and his estate was under legal curatorship at that time. But the Masisis resisted a series of official overtures to purchase their property, and the matter was never resolved. Meanwhile they allowed 'squatters' to live on the farm, who worked the land on half-shares and who were limited to two cattle each. George Letshapa died in 1971, and Lydia Masisi leased the land to a white farmer from across the Leeuw river. Sweet Home was finally expropriated in 1977, under the terms of Section 13 (2) of the Trust and Land Act 1936, because it was 'situated outside a scheduled Bantu area and a released area'. The compensation paid was R72,000. All of the 'squatters', about 300 people, had to move to Onverwacht. One old man remained, whose marriage to a Mosotho woman confounded the state's racial conveyor belts. This couple was not accepted at Onverwacht, because he was 'Coloured'. Nor were they allowed to live in Thaba Phatshwa village, immediately adjoining Sweet Home, because she was black. In this manner they were reprieved from having to leave Sweet Home. The old man died there in due course.[38]

The other 'black spot' consisted of Segogoane's Valley 665, owned still by

Blanche Tsimatsima, in retirement at Thaba Nchu; and Tshiamelo 664 which, after the death of Abel Phogane Tsimatsima in 1961, was inherited in equal undivided shares by his adopted daughter Ellen Kuzwayo of Soweto, his daughter by her mother, Maria Dikeledi Pilane of Mochudi (Botswana), and his daughter by Blanche Dinaane, Emma Mmutsi Mabokela of Mafikeng (Bophuthatswana). What seems to have happened is that, being informally advised in the early 1970s by a white neighbour on the opposite side of the Leeuw river that expropriation was imminent, Blanche Tsimatsima arranged to sell both farms to Nicolaas Mattheus Hendrikz of Armenia farm, on the other side of the dam, to secure a good price in advance of final intervention by the state. The price for both farms was R79,960 in 1974. Hendrikz died in 1978 and the government bought the farms for R93,000 from his estate.[39] The whole of the original farm of Thaba Patchoa 106 was then re-integrated, as a Coloured reserve.

John Weymers estimated that there were 115 families at Thaba Phatshwa in the early 1970s. Fifteen Afrikaans-speaking families moved to the village in 1974, refugees from the imminent political 'independence' of the Transkei, so that there were about 130 households in the mid-1980s. Initially, under the SANT, four morgen of arable land had been allocated to each man when he got married. In 1958, however, the Department of Coloured Affairs declared that the land must be contoured and people would farm on a rental basis in future. In 1986 about eleven arable lands of 28 morgen each were leased out to individual farmers. Cattle and sheep grazed on communal land. Otherwise, agricultural activities were supervised directly by an official from Coloured Affairs in Bloemfontein; and some men gained a partial livelihood as artisans on neighbouring white farms. People paid a rental of R36 per annum for their stands, but they owned their own houses.[40] Thaba Phatshwa village in the late 1980s was a small community of refugees from the past and the present. The older descendants of the Newlanders retained an obvious pride in their distinctive history. Caught in the middle of the South African racial sandwich, however, they were socially isolated and economically depressed.

Meanwhile a 'Coloured' foreman, Roelf Van Wyk, occupied the old homestead of Tshiamelo, at the south end of the original farm, with his Mosotho wife and eight children. They had refurbished the place that Ellen Kuzwayo remembered with such warmth and affection. Roelf Van Wyk grew up near Wepener and then worked on the farm Armenia, across the dam. His employer there, Hendrikz, was 'very rough'. The family moved to Tshiamelo in 1970 and farmed the land on a share-cropping basis with the three absentee owners. This arrangement had worked well, he said. When Blanche Tsimatsima sold up in 1974 on behalf of herself and the co-owners of Tshiamelo, Van Wyk found himself once more under Hendrikz, until the latter's death in 1978, when the state intervened to eliminate the last 'black spot'. In 1986 he was employed directly by the Department of Coloured Affairs and paid R120 a

month to supervise agricultural operations on Sweet Home and parts of
Segogoane's Valley. He also had his own tractor and cultivated some land on
his own behalf. One of his older daughters, who spoke English, Afrikaans and
Sesotho, was shortly getting married and going to train as a nurse at Nelspruit
in the eastern Transvaal, a professional opportunity of which he was very
proud.[41]

### NGOANANYANA: POTATO KINGDOM

Title to the original large farm of Ngoanyana 98 (4,945 morgen) was granted to
Michael Tshabadira Moroka, who also held the two neighbouring farms
Ngoana 104 and Springhaannek 105 and, in the name of his wife Majang,
Groothoek 125 (see Figures 1.3 and 1.5). On the day of Tshipinare's murder,
10 July 1884, Michael Tshabadira had arrived much too late to be of assistance
to his chief, which might reflect the distance of his lands from the capital but
might also reflect his thoroughly equivocal position in the ruling genealogy. He
was Tshipinare's son-in-law, having married Majang, one of the chief's daughters in his third house (see Figure 1.2). His father Tshabadira, who died in
1874, had been half-brother both to Tshipinare (same mother) and to Samuel
Lehulere (same father), who claimed the chieftainship after Moroka's death on
the grounds that he was the only surviving male descendant in the first house of
the old chief. Majang had previously been married to Motlhware, Moroka's
grandson and heir apparent in the senior house, but he predeceased the chief
without issue in 1879, and Moroka arranged that Majang should be taken over
in the levirate by her cousin, Michael Tshabadira (see Chapter 1). His son by
Majang, Percy Tshabadira, succeeded to Samuel Lehulere's exiled chieftainship in the Tati district of Bechuanaland in 1932, and made an unsuccessful bid
for the Thaba Nchu chieftainship in the late 1930s, as described in Chapter 4.
Thus Michael Tshabadira's various complex ties of kinship and affinity made
his position more delicately poised in the succession dispute than that of any
other senior member of the family. The fact that he was granted title to three
farms by Tshipinare is, however, *prima facie* evidence that any private sympathy he may have felt for Samuel's cause had not been publicly declared.

   In November 1887, nevertheless, Michael Tshabadira sold all of his lands to
James Robertson, miller and speculator, and departed with some of his followers to British Bechuanaland. In turn, Robertson sold them to Charles Newberry. Through the 1890s, Ngoanyana 98 was part of the Newberry estates in
the Thaba Nchu district, which were representative of the large holdings of
absentee landlords with no interest whatever in applying the anti-squatting
regulations. The dominant contractual relationship was undoubtedly share-
cropping, and there were also considerable opportunities for transport-
riding.[42] The predominance of share-cropping did not, however, imply an
absence of investment in capital-intensive operations on the part of Newberry
himself. Roderick Finlay recalled that he and his brothers were taken to the

concentration camp at Thaba Nchu in 1901 in wagons drawn by Newberry's steam tractor.[43] Although share-cropping continued after the South African war, the relative security of tenure that applied in the 1890s was decisively subverted by new conditions. In the first place, both black and white inhabitants of the district were removed to concentration camps in the guerilla phase of the war, and much livestock was stolen or dispersed. This caused such chaos that it was extremely difficult afterwards to assert residential rights successfully. In the second place, most of Newberry's land in the district was sold to the new colonial government in October 1901 (see Chapter 2).[44] Land Settlement was to prove a very different regime for black share-cropping peasants.

The three large farms of Ngoanyana 98, Ngoana 104 and Springhaannek 105, together comprising some 13,600 morgen, were divided into twenty-two farms of roughly 500 morgen each, although some were larger than this (see Figure 7.3). Ngoanyana 98 (rest, now 473 morgen) and its immediate neighbour Knowsley 287 were allocated to two friends, Daniel McPherson and Jimmy Nelson, late of the Irish Fusiliers. Settlers were expected to bring about £500 of their own capital to the enterprise, but McPherson and Nelson were two of half a dozen ex-soldiers without capital who were settled on farms in this block before the conclusion of hostilities and for whom special arrangements were made by the Land Settlement Board. They were advanced what was judged to be the minimum working capital of £350 for a span of oxen, other livestock, a wagon, plough and house materials. By November 1902 McPherson and Nelson had 40 acres of forage and 30 acres of maize put in by themselves, and 80 acres of maize and sorghum worked on shares; also '100 bags potatoes, planted and looking well'.[45]

Daniel McPherson obtained title to Ngoanyana 98 in 1914. He came to prosperity in the period between the First and Second World Wars, a period remembered by the settler families as one of strong rivalry between two 'Potato Kings' in the area south of Tweespruit. McPherson was one. The other was Jacob Boris Lurie, a Lithuanian immigrant who arrived in South Africa in 1892 with £2.10s. He worked as a butcher during the South African war and served Tempe refugee camp outside Bloemfontein. He speculated in produce and then grew potatoes on half-shares with the settler who had been placed on Kent 286. In 1907 he rented Fortuinspruit 233 from its owner, and later bought that farm and others nearby—Lovedale 89 and Prospect 649—making a total of 4,000 morgen.[46] As shown in Chapter 3, Lurie's farming operations in the late 1920s were singled out as a prime example of progressive agriculture. His dependence on seasonal and largely female wage labour from Basutoland was also subject to disparaging comment from Dr Moroka in his oral evidence submitted to the Native Economic Commission in February 1931.

There are no comparable figures on McPherson's operations based at Ngoananyana in the 1920s and the 1930s, but he was probably farming on a similar scale. An almost exclusive concentration on potatoes over more than twenty

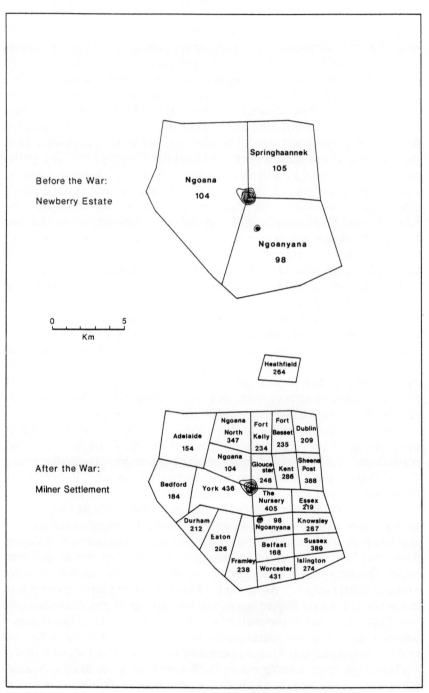

Before the War:

Newberry Estate

Springhaannek
105

Ngoana
104

Ngoanyana
98

0       5
Km

After the War:

Milner Settlement

Heathfield
264

Adelaide
154

Ngoana
North
347

Fort
Kelly
234

Fort
Basset
235

Dublin
209

Ngoana
104

Glouce-
ster
248

Kent
286

Sheena
Post
388

Bedford
184

York 436

The
Nursery
405

Essex
219

Durham
212

98
Ngoanyana

Knowsley
287

Eaton
226

Belfast
168

Sussex
389

Framley
238

Worcester
431

Islington
274

*Figure 7.3*    Ngoanyana farm: before and after the South African war.

years enabled him to buy up the following farms: Belfast 168 in 1916, Worcester 431 in 1919, Schuinsekop 126 in 1921, Kent 286 in 1923, Merrydale 638 in 1927, Cranborne 190 in 1931, Sussex 389 in 1935 and various subdivisions of Maseru 64 in the late 1930s (see Figure 7.4). He was buying land in the 1930s when many others were being forced to sell up. When he died in 1951 his property in land comprised roughly 5,600 morgen, more than ten times the size of his original allocation, and his estate was valued at over £100,000.[47] More significantly, he had no debts. This must be an unrivalled record of accumulation for a Milner settler in the Thaba Nchu district. He was, as his grandson John Nieuwenhuysen remarked, a 'most careful and excellent businessman'. Potatoes were his working life. But he also developed an interest in water-boring machines and indulged a passion for racehorses.[48]

Like Lurie, McPherson also employed hundreds of seasonal labourers in the height of the potato season. One of them, Mmadiphapang Thakho, who was born and brought up at Ngoananyana, recalled her experience as an adolescent in the late 1930s:

> We worked the potatoes. It was very hard. We got up in the dark, as soon as the call reached the village, and went off to work. And the papa [maize porridge] we took with us, there was nothing inside it, we ate it just as it was. Apart from that we used to steal his potatoes and cook them and hide the billycans where we were working so he wouldn't see them, [otherwise] he'd have a look inside to see if there were potatoes there. We worked the potatoes on all his farms—the lands to the south, Dawn, Kent Farm, Merrydale, all of them. It was tough. We had no blankets, we had nothing. We wore sacks. In the evening when we went to sleep your mother would take the sacks and sew them together, sew them together, to make a single cover. You got in a line and she'd cover you up with the sacking to go to sleep. That's how it was all the time we were growing up. And as you grew up you got a bit more money, up to R3 a month, £1.10s! They gave us rations of four tins of maize flour in the evenings.[49]

During the Second World War and afterwards, Daniel McPherson's eldest daughter, Iris, was effectively in charge of farming operations based at Ngoananyana. Potatoes had been killed off by eel-worm, and she introduced a mixed regime of maize, some wheat, cattle and dairy farming. She was at this time married to her second husband, by whom she had a son, John Nieuwenhuysen (b. 1937). They divorced in 1948. Her first husband, by whom she had her elder son Keith Ranger (b. 1934), had been drowned in the Lovedale dam. Iris's half-sister Marge was married to Eric Heath, a well-known attorney in Thaba Nchu and Bloemfontein. He played a prominent part in the late 1930s and mid-1940s in representing the views of local white farmers to the Native Affairs Commission, which was responsible for making detailed recommendations for the implementation of the Trust and Land Act 1936 (see Chapter 4). Daniel McPherson had two other daughters: Una, who married a

Bloemfontein vet, Johann Louw, in the 1940s; and Patricia, who remained unmarried. He had one son, Daniel (see Figure 7.5). Young Dan McPherson, as one of the South African Airforce 24 Squadron's 'great observers . . . led 65 raids and 108 sorties . . .' in the Middle East theatre of the Second World War.[50] 'He would really have liked to be a doctor', John Nieuwenhuysen recalled of his Uncle Dan, 'but you see there was this Irishness in my grandfather, he wanted continuity on the land'.[51] The old man's 'Irishness' embraced the qualities which made him a successful farmer. But it also left a residue of family bitterness for two decades after his death, for he inscribed in his will, under the influence (it is said) of Eric Heath, a provision which entailed the landed property inherited by his only son. The significance of this is outlined below.

There were perhaps seventy to 100 permanent employees in this period, including a number of 'Coloured' overseers who were paid more than the Africans and lived in separate and better houses. There were very many more seasonal labourers, mainly migrants from Basutoland. John Nieuwenhuysen recalled the big harvests when he was a boy, when they used to take the maize off the cob by hand. On pay-day at Ngoananyana, people would line up right down the drive and receive their wages in cupped hands through the barred office window—£1 or £2 for a few weeks' work, based on the quantity reaped. The great sandstone storage sheds down the hill were used as dormitories for the migrant workers.[52]

Nieuwenhuysen remembered his childhood at Ngoananyana as an exciting experience, 'rather like what I imagine the life of the landed aristocracy in Czarist Russia was'. The McPhersons were a close-knit and ebullient extended family. There were varied and intense relationships, a steady stream of visitors and large house parties, especially at Christmas. These house parties were also remembered years later, at Onverwacht, by the women who made the enormous salads that were served: some people's lavish hospitality was other people's unpaid overtime. As he grew up, however, John Nieuwenhuysen came to despair of the massive inequalities of lifestyle and opportunity both in the Tweespruit district and in the wider society. He left South Africa in the early 1960s to teach economics in Australia.[53] 'The last I saw of one of my closest playmates, with whom I used to steal neighbours' fruit, was when he was employed as the driver of the Tweespruit night (shit) cart'. In 1986 Nieuwenhuysen achieved some public prominence in Australia as the author of a sweeping review of the State of Victoria's labyrinthine liquor licensing laws.[54]

Mmadiphapang Thakho also grew up on Ngoananyana. She married one of the farm labourers, who graduated to tractor driving. She bore nine children, of whom eight survived. The eldest was born in the late 1940s, and she recalled the overwhelming frustration of blocked aspirations for progress at school:

While we were at Ngoananyana I often said to my husband, Let's leave here, we can't bring up our children properly here. They can't grow up properly here because they can't get schooling while we're just sitting here, there's no way they can get schooling, when we get to a point where we can educate them we'll be tired! Let's leave. He refused to leave. Well, my eldest boy—he's grown up now—said to me, 'Mother, speak to father, you should get out of here, I can't get schooling, I haven't got a bicycle to get to school, I haven't got any uniform, I haven't got anything and he gets so little money just to get a little maize flour for us to eat. I can't see how I can carry on with studying.' That really upset me and made me feel ill with worry, that my child really wanted to go to school but couldn't manage it. He had passed Six, he was supposed to enter Seven but I didn't know where I could get him to school. I looked for a place at Thaba Nchu, they said I would have to contribute forty [?fourteen] rand for the build-ing fund. I hadn't got fourteen rand. So my child couldn't go to school.[55]

In the late 1950s and 1960s more and more people moved in to live on the farm in response to the increasing severity of influx control elsewhere. Iris Nieuwen-huysen had to engage in 'fearful administrative procedures' with the Bantu Administration and Development (BAD) officials who attempted to enforce formal registration of every resident. Acute official anxiety in this period about *beswarting* ('blackening') of the *platteland* is reflected in the 1959 Du Toit Commission's publication of a map showing the extent of unsupervised occu-pation by Africans of white-owned farms in three districts of the OFS to the south-west of Thaba Nchu.[56] Although it was possible for farm owners, if they chose, to resist state pressure to reduce 'squatting', 'it was the easiest thing in the world to get people off the farm'; and rapid over-crowding made it very difficult to improve living conditions for Africans. Keith Ranger, who took over the management of Ngoananyana from his mother, never attempted to control the number of residents. 'When the BAD officials came, there'd be people drifting off into the veld or up the mountain or round the corner into the woods, you see, they'd be living like fugitives to a certain extent'.[57] Many of them depended on wage remittances from the mines or the towns.

## THE RUININGS: WHITE AND BLACK

By this time, the estate had been divided. Daniel McPherson died in 1951. His estate passed to his children in equal undivided shares, but there were re-strictive conditions imposed on the shares of Dan, Una and Patricia (see Figure 7.5). The portions of the estate inherited by Una and Patricia were to be administered in trust on their behalf by Eric Heath. Dan's portion—the northern block of Dawn, etc.—was entailed by the condition that 'in the event of his dying without lawful descendants then such fixed property shall revert to the estate . . .', apparently because, as Dan himself expressed it with bitter understatement years later, 'my marriage had not met with universal ap-proval'.[58] The old man feared that his daughter-in-law, an English woman,

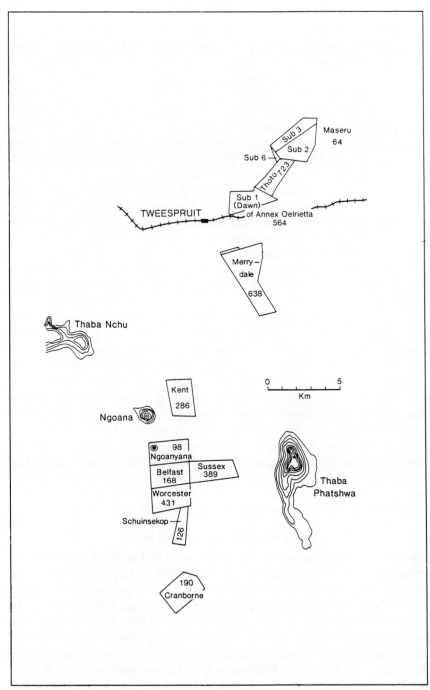

*Figure 7.4* Daniel McPherson's estate, 1951.

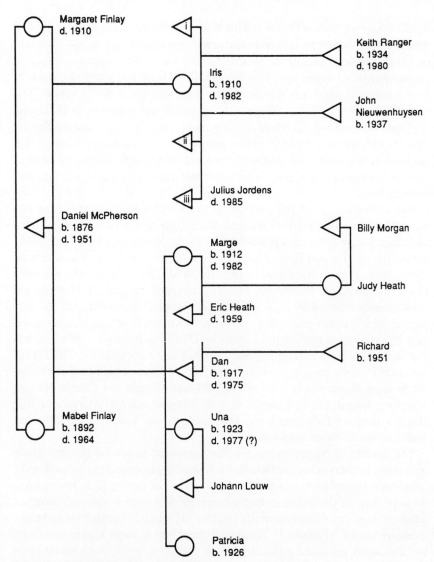

*Figure 7.5* Partial McPherson genealogy.

would otherwise induce Dan to sell his land and give up farming. The practical effect of this attempt to 'rule from the grave' was to impose a heavy constraint on Dan's farming operations, because he could not raise a mortgage bond on property entailed in this way. Dan felt that Eric Heath had usurped the role of paterfamilias through his effective control of four-fifths of the estate. The question of Eric Heath's allegedly misdirected influence over old Daniel McPherson remained, therefore, an extremely sensitive one within the family. Eric Heath's death in April 1959 was followed by the startling revelation that his trust account was in deficit to the amount of R30,000. Suspicion came to rest on his partner, however, who was some years later convicted for trust account fraud.

The ultimate irony of this part of the story is that the property of the two older McPherson daughters, Iris and Marge, on whose titles no conditions were imposed, was eventually lost to the family. Marge sold Merrydale in the 1960s. Iris and her son Keith Ranger, who inherited the block of land around Ngoananyana, went bankrupt in the late 1970s. By contrast, the northern block of Dawn and portions of Maseru, inherited by Dan McPherson and subsequently relieved by legal action of its onerous entailment, was the only part of the old man's estate that remained substantially intact. Heavily mortgaged, it was farmed through the 1980s by Dan's son Richard. Una's land was still farmed by her husband Johann, after her death in the late 1970s. Part of her sister Paddy's ground was bought by Billy Morgan, a grandson of Frederick William Morgan, a brother of Cecil Rayner Morgan and Charlie Morgan who were introduced in Chapter 4. Billy Morgan married Marge and Eric Heath's daughter Judy, and it was Judy Morgan who kept up the McPherson tradition of Christmas hospitality.

The decline of Ngoananyana may be attributed to several factors. Along with other farmers in the district, Keith Ranger over-committed himself to the 'wheat revolution' launched by Sam Bairstow of the nearby farm Jevington: a decisive shift in the 1950s to mono-cropping of winter wheat on a summer fallow system, involving caterpillar tractors to plough in the stubble and more intensive use of fertilizers.[59] This experiment was initially highly successful but ultimately produced a fragility of soil condition which made mono-cropping of wheat very vulnerable to drought. Other factors were more personal. Keith Ranger was slow to shift to sunflowers. He was not temperamentally suited to farming. And he was, in common with many others in the district, a heavy drinker. The farm never really paid its way. In the end they depended on his wife Ann Ranger's salary as a teacher in Tweespruit.

Keith Ranger and his wife and children left the farm at the beginning of 1979. His mother Iris remained, married now to her third husband, a retired Dutch sea-captain named Jordens. The bankruptcy put the farm workers and their families in a desperate situation. They were not paid for eight months, from January 1979 until their eviction in early October. They were harassed by the Tweespruit municipal police. Mmadiphapang takes up the story:

Then this white man—what was his name? who was that Baas?—Baas Fanthonnoro [Van Tonder], he came and ordered us off. We didn't go, we refused. He shut the water off. He said we shouldn't use it, we should pay for his water. We refused. We got up at night and took the water anyway when he wasn't around. Another time he came and waved a gun at us, and fired it tuu! tuu! a few times. We scattered. Then we went to tell Mrs Jordens. 'Hela! This Baas is provoking us, he is shooting at us with a gun and ordering us off the farm'. She said tell him to come here. But he didn't turn up again. The next thing was the police came and took us all, they came and rounded us all up. Some got away, others went to gaol. Kids were just left in the huts with nobody to look after them. Someone from central government came and asked us what was the problem? We told them. We were just staying there but we had nothing, there was nothing we could do. So they phoned up Qwaqwa to come and get us. The commissioner just told us get your stuff together, tomorrow I'm going to fetch you, you are going to Onverwacht because you're in a real mess here. Yes, we said, we were. That's how we came to Onverwacht.[60]

Mmadiphapang told me her story in June and July 1980. Because there were very many Van Tonders in the (old) Thaba Nchu district, especially in the area north of Dewetsdorp, and because this was one small thread amongst very many other threads of my enquiry, six years elapsed before I could confidently identify the 'Baas Van Tonder' who had evicted Mmadiphapang and the others. Who was he?

Johannes Hendrik Van Tonder was a victim of forced relocation. He owned one of the twelve farms, outside the western boundary of the (new) Thaba Nchu district (see Figure 6.2), identified in a press report of September 1978 as due to be compulsorily expropriated by the central government to create a vast new black township, as described in Chapter 6. The farm Onverwacht 704 was owned by Ignatius (Naas) Du Plessis, who had bought it only the previous year. He was the butcher in Thaba Nchu until 1985, when he sold the business to his son. He had lived there for forty years and he was known as Tsotsi to local Africans. The adjoining farm Toekoms 771 belonged to Coen Van Tonder, and Mariasrus 809 to Johannes Hendrik Van Tonder (apparently no relation). The owners were outraged to discover the imminent loss of their land. There were protracted negotiations with government officials, involving no less than three valuations and argument over how much of the compensation would be payable immediately in cash. Du Plessis and Coen Van Tonder were given seven days' notice in May 1979 to leave their farms. 'On Tuesday this week, government trucks rolled on to the farm of Mr Naas Du Plessis and workers began building a township to house 3,000 people . . .'. Eventually the question of compensation was settled out of court and those who were removed at a week's notice received 100 per cent of the farm valuations in cash, by contrast with the standard arrangement of 40 per cent in cash and 60 per cent in government securities. Naas Du Plessis was reported as not unhappy since he made a profit of R15 per morgen.[61]

Johannes Hendrik Van Tonder bought Mount Pleasant 54, north of Twee-spruit (see Figure 6.2), with cash from the compensation for Mariasrus 809 and a loan from the Land Bank. He then tried to buy Ngoanyana 98 for his son but could not raise a bond on the property. Pending his failure to do so, however, he evicted the eighteen families from Ngoananyana in the manner described by Mmadiphapang above. He had a row with Iris Jordens over his treatment of the people on the farm. A man of formidable size and weight, he personally supervised the eviction from Ngoananyana. He then pointed out to the re-fugees, when they were dumped in the D section of the new slum, where his farmhouse had been on Mariasrus 809 (Figure 6.2). One portion of the D section lies on a corner of his old property. Mmadiphapang and her neighbours commented bitterly on the irony of this.

There is another small irony in the tail of this story. J.H. Van Tonder failed to negotiate a bond for the purchase of Ngoanyana 98. The farm was bought, instead, by Naas Du Plessis with a bond of R110,000 in favour of the Bloem-fontein Board of Trustees, whose chairman (an ex-mayor of Bloemfontein) he knew.[62] The transfer was registered in June 1980. Keith Ranger died in the same month. And Mmadiphapang Thakho was describing, as she cleaned sheep's intestines in the yard at Onverwacht, her family's desperate circumstances:

> I'm running about even at night, I lie awake the whole night worrying about how we can survive, what I can do, what I can sell in order to look after these mites deserted by their menfolk. They depend on me, if I don't get up even at night, they don't eat, they just stay as they are. So I get up and go to this white man and beg him, 'Hao! Baas, if you would only give me meat on credit, I'll pay you when I've finished selling it'. Well, he hands it over, so that I can sell it and pay him off, and struggle to find maize meal for my children. He writes me down in his book, that I'll pay him another time when I've sold the meat, and with what's left I buy maize meal. That's the truth, there's no-one who can say I'm lying...[63]

The white man concerned was the butcher in Thaba Nchu, Naas Du Plessis. His manners were rough, she said, but he helped her by extending credit in this way. Having been brutally evicted from the farm where she had grown up and spent her working life, Mmadiphapang Thakho could get a dead sheep on credit from Naas Du Plessis with which to struggle for a very marginal livelihood in the informal sector of a huge rural slum. He borrowed R150,000 in 1985 from the Standard Bank of Bophuthatswana on the security of his title to Ngoanyana 98.[64] The contrast provides a starkly appropriate index of their respective opportunities to improve their lives.

I visited Ngoananyana in July 1980 and found that many of the African huts were already in ruins. The resident black community then consisted of remnants of the 'old' families and the families of seven farm labourers recently moved in by Naas Du Plessis. The former felt acutely insecure: someone remarked bitterly, 'We live by the gaol'. There had been another raid by the Tweespruit municipal police in February 1980; and people were in constant fear of being hauled off to gaol, or fined from R30 to R50, for being illegally resident on the farm. It was of course impossible to find that sort of money. On the morning of 9 July 1980, an ultimatum was given to three unemployed youths, that they must be off the farm by nightfall. Where were they to go to? Their parents lived and worked in a 'white' area, and the boys could not go and live with them. So they stayed on the farm with their grandmother, who had been born there, had grown up there, married there, lived there all her life. She asked rhetorically, with simple dignity, why should she move? She and her grandsons had nowhere else to go. On the same day, a vehicle from Onverwacht had also been at the farm, to register those who wished to go there. Opinion was divided: some wished to go, on account of the continuing insecurity at Ngoananyana; others wished to stay.

The African huts were the first ruins at Ngoananyana in recent times, but not the last. Naas Du Plessis allegedly ruined good farmland there by overloading it with stock reared for the slaughter-house. He was a butcher by profession, after all, not a farmer. Old Daniel McPherson must have turned in his grave. He lies in a small eucalyptus grove less than a stone's throw from the lovely sandstone mansion which he built in 1926 and which was destroyed by fire on 13 March 1982. His eldest daughter, Iris Jordens, sustained third degree burns in the fire and died of a heart attack on the following day.

## Case study F: Life in the D section

The eighteen evicted families were dumped at Onverwacht in early October 1979. Having no cash resources, they had no food for three days, Mmadiphapang reported, until a Catholic priest at Thaba Nchu was able to arrange an emergency supply of maize meal.[65] After nine months of surviving without wages on the farm, they had to pick up the wreckage of their lives in an unfamiliar wasteland that was both congested and chaotic.

Mmadiphapang's household consisted of her husband (X1), herself (X2), her husband's unmarried brother (X3) and various children and grandchildren (see Figure 7.6). She had eight surviving children. In June 1980 two older sons Y1 and Y3 were living with their families elsewhere in the OFS, with jobs at Virginia and Welkom. Her husband X1, who had been a tractor-driver on the farm, had been unable to find any employment. Mmadiphapang's eldest daughter Y2 was a domestic servant in Johannesburg, able to visit home only once a year, and her two children Z1 and Z2 were resident in Mmadiphapang's household at Onverwacht. Another daughter Y4 had been made pregnant at

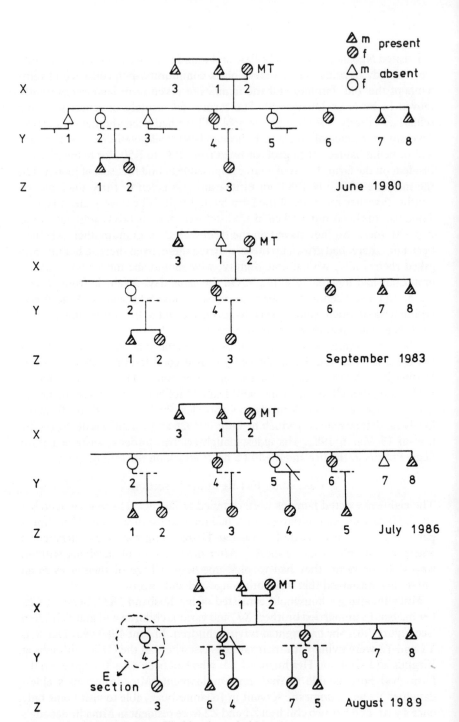

*Figure 7.6* Mmadiphapang Thakho: household turnover.

Ngoananyana by a youth who then deserted her, and her child Z3 was born in May 1978. In June and July 1980 this child had a severe chest infection. Mmadiphapang's youngest daughter Y6, aged 17, and two younger sons Y7 and Y8, aged 14 and 12, were also living in the household. Another daughter Y5 was married on a farm near Ngoananyana. Thus Mmadiphapang, with her husband, was immediately responsible for four of her own children and three of her grandchildren. Remittances of about R10 per month were the household's only regular source of cash income at the time. Mmadiphapang was desperate. Hence the sheep's guts.

In September 1983 Mmadiphapangi was still hawking meat, the shack had been extended to three sections in an L-shape, and foundations had been dug for a proper house, but the family could not afford to build. Mmadiphapang's husband X1 had managed to find a job at the Saaiplaas gold mine in April 1983. By July 1986 he was permanently at home, physically infirm with arthritis; Mmadiphapang's second daughter Y4 was employed at the Botshabelo chicken farm at a wage of R40 a fortnight; her younger sister Y5 had returned to her parents' household with her child Z4, following desertion by her husband, and was working as a domestic servant in Bloemfontein; the youngest daughter Y6 had borne a child in March 1984; Y7 had taken up his first mine contract at Virginia, with his eldest brother probably exerting some influence on his behalf; and the youngest son Y8 was still at school—although continuing administrative chaos and the takeover of schools by the police and army in July 1986 brought this status into question. The household had built and furnished a four-roomed cement-block house in the front of their stand. The corrugated sheeting shack was a storeroom and shebeen, with a high turnover in both bottled beer and Sesotho beer. This was the most lucrative activity in the informal sector. It was also illegal, and Mmadiphapang had been harassed from time to time. After years of struggle to establish a precarious livelihood, however, things were looking up.

By August 1989 the three younger daughters of the household, Y4, Y5 and Y6, were all employed at the local chicken farm. Wages there were now R57 a fortnight, a nominal increase but a real decline in view of the high rate of inflation prevalent in South Africa in the late 1980s. Y4 now had her own stand in the E section of the slum, but her child Z3 mostly stayed at her mother's household in the D section. Y5 and Y6 had each borne another child, Z6 and Z7, who were similarly attached to the household. The eldest daughter Y2 was still a domestic servant in Johannesburg, but neither of her two children was living in Botshabelo: Z1 was at school in Virginia, and staying in the house of his uncle Y1; Z2 was at a 'special school' in Bloemfontein, lodging with some relatives of Mmadiphapang. The two older married sons, Y1 and Y3, remained respectively at Virginia and Welkom, employed in mine or mine-related jobs. Y7 was also at Virginia, on a mine contract, but contributed nothing to the maintenance of his mother's large household. The youngest son

Y8 was unemployed, and he nursed an ambition to attend the University of the Witwatersrand to study law. Against the odds, he had achieved a matriculation exemption certificate, but it was quite improbable that his grades were good enough to gain him a place.

Mmadiphapang's family exhibits striking evidence of the differentiation of the labour force by gender and of the extent to which 'family life' in the rural slums is articulated by women. The five grandchildren resident with Mmadiphapang in July 1986 and August 1989, respectively, were all daughters' children, while her two married sons had established families elsewhere. The eldest daughter Y2, who had never been formally married, was a domestic servant in various suburbs of Johannesburg throughout the 1980s. Her youngest sister Y5 became a domestic servant in Bloemfontein on the failure of her marriage, and both relied on Mmadiphapang to look after their children in a distant rural slum. Y4 was also deserted by the father of her child, but she remained at home in the slum where the only possibility of employment was on the local chicken farm where wages were appallingly low. Mmadiphapang herself, on whose broad shoulders rested the immediate responsibility for feeding and clothing this large household, entered the informal sector with vigour and desperation but initially with very low returns from long hours invested. She graduated, in due course, to the most lucrative part of that sector: the concentrated weekend booze. But it was a risky business, and often violent and sordid as well.

Both original farms Thaba Patchoa 106 and Ngoanyana 98 were inside the (old) Thaba Nchu district but outside the (new) Thaba Nchu district. Their stories therefore counter-balance and complement, to a degree, the emphasis in Chapters 4 and 5 on the re-emergence of an African political community in a territory just over one-third the size of Chief Moroka's. On one farm, Thaba Patchoa 106, black landownership survived long enough to escape inclusion in Milner's scheme of Land Settlement and also the material benefits of deliberate state capitalisation of white agriculture. Some fragments of it fell prey to the more conventional predatory forces of finance capital: the 'cute lawyers' to whom Macmillan referred in the late 1920s (see Chapter 3). Other fragments emerged as 'black spots' susceptible, eventually, to expropriation by the apartheid state. The other farm, Ngoanyana 98, was 'captured' early by diamond capital from Kimberley, and developed by Milner settlers after the South African war. In the 1920s and 1930s, Ngoanyana 98 (rest) was a prime example of rapid capital accumulation based on a differentiated labour force of permanent wage labourers and seasonal migrants from Basutoland. In the 1960s and 1970s, it became a dumping ground for a black population that was 'surplus' in two senses. First, it was very difficult for black families to find anywhere else to live, and many drifted onto farms although they were primarily dependent on urban wage incomes. Second, a squeeze on black employment in white agriculture inflated the number of 'squatters' vulnerable to eviction either by landowners or by state agencies. White and black children who grew up together—or, as John Nieuwenhuysen expressed it, stole neighbours' fruit together—inevitably embarked on starkly different adult lives. Yet, as the story of Ngoananyana shows, their fortunes and misfortunes were inextricably intertwined.

# CONCLUSION: WHOSE LAND?

Thaba Nchu . . . is our land, and is the land of our forefathers . . . The wish of my people at Thaba Nchu is that they prefer no other country besides their country.

> Joel David Goronyane, October 1913
> UG 22-1914, pp. 24–5

We therefore claim from the OFS government the whole of the Barolong territory, with not a bit cut off.

> Kali John Matsheka, February 1933
> UWL, AD843, B62.11

The land shall be shared among those who work it.

> The Freedom Charter, June 1955

Thaba Nchu was contested ground for more than one hundred and fifty years. Chief Moroka's Barolong occupied it from 1833. Chief Moshoeshoe's Basotho claimed political sovereignty over it. The Wesleyan missionaries purported to have bought it. For barely three decades, from the establishment of the OFS republic in 1854, Thaba Nchu sustained a precarious independence. In the early 1880s, the territorial integrity of the Barolong chiefdom was undermined by the constant threat of civil war; by the envious intrigues of OFS burghers on its borders; by deep economic recession, spreading outwards from Kimberley; and by Chief Tshipinare's incipient privatisation of titles to land. The territory was annexed by the OFS in July 1884 and broken up by Gregorowski's dispositions into the several categories of land shown in Figure 1.3. Two-thirds of the land was granted to individual Africans.

Slightly more than 60 per cent of the land granted to Africans was very rapidly lost to whites in the late 1880s and early 1990s, in a manner reminiscent of the alienation of farms in East Griqualand in the same period.[1] Several reasons for this were suggested in Chapter 1. The most important factor was the rush of speculative capital associated with South Africa's mineral booms. James Robertson, miller and grain merchant, bought up many large farms and quickly sold them to Charles Newberry, who had made a fortune at Kimberley. In the 1890s Newberry alone owned more than 60,000 morgen of land in the Thaba Nchu district, most of which had belonged to three senior members of Chief Tshipinare's family, all of whom had left for British Bechuanaland. The Newberry estates were typical of the holdings of absentee white landlords of the period, on whose land black share-croppers with their own livestock and capital equipment not only survived but prospered.

The OFS republic, in its turn, was annexed to the British Empire in 1900 as the ORC. The Thaba Nchu district became the prime site of concentration, in the new colony, of Lord Milner's Land Settlement scheme. In aggregate, the scheme occupied one third of all land in the district. Half of this was inherited from the late government of the OFS. The other half was bought by the ORC government, mainly from Newberry, for the purpose of Land Settlement. These lands were subdivided into small farms of variable size, depending on the predominance of arable or pastoral use, and settled by ex-soldiers and others of 'British stock'. The whole experiment was under-written by a substantial imperial loan.

The first decade of the twentieth century was a critical period for the Milner settlers and, indeed, for other white landowners in the district who sought to recover from the devastation of the South African war. On the one hand, the settlers depended on a sympathetic state to defend and consolidate their fragile enterprises. On the other hand, under-capitalised themselves, they depended on share-cropping arrangements with black tenants who retained their own resources of livestock and equipment. This relationship was one of tenuous equality, in which the necessity of collaboration contradicted the formal rigidities of black–white relations in political and social life.[2] It came under pressure, however, from the momentum of state capitalisation of white agriculture which culminated in the Land Act of 1913 and which greatly weakened the bargaining power of black sharecroppers, as Keegan has shown.[3]

From 1913, the settlers were granted title to their farms on the strength of mortgage bonds in favour of the Union government for the balance of the purchase price. Some of the settlers made good in due course: Daniel McPherson's career, outlined in Chapter 7, is the outstanding example. Along with many other white farmers in the district, many fell heavily into debt, but were able to exert political pressure on Pretoria to relieve them of intolerable burdens of repayment in the great depression of the early 1930s (Chapter 3).

The ripples of British imperialism thus decisively affected the history of this part of the OFS. The new colonial regime formally dispossessed a stratum of impoverished Afrikaner *bywoners* who had rented portions of government farms before the war. Wealthy absentee landlords such as Newberry were also largely displaced. Both Afrikaner *bywoners* and speculative landlords gave way to an intensive programme for the establishment of small, under-capitalised white farmers of British origin. This experiment was carefully nurtured by the imperial authorities in a hostile political environment, until such time—after Union in 1910—that the central South African state rationalised its own protectionist policies on behalf of white farmers as a whole.

No such protection was available for black landowners, who also fell heavily into debt. The black landowners who retained their titles in 1913, when the Beaumont Commission identified their lands as 'additional' areas to be acquired for African occupation (see Figure 3.1), mainly comprised the educated Barolong elite of the period: members of the Goronyane, Masisi, Makgothi,

Nyokong, Setlogelo and Moroka families. Some of their complex consanguin-
eal and affinal connections are shown in the genealogies which accompany
case studies of family history (Figures 1.2, 3.2, 5.2 and 7.1). From their ranks
were drawn the local leaders of African opinion: men such as Reverend Joel
Goronyane, Moses Masisi, Jeremiah Makgothi, John Mokitlane Nyokong and
Walton Zacharias Fenyang. Some of them also played an active part on the
wider stage of nationalist politics.

They were subject, however, to remorseless pressure of three kinds. Firstly,
as their debts accumulated, they were acutely vulnerable to the threat of
dispossession. Many black landowners staved off legal proceedings only by
encumbering their property with further mortgage bonds or by consolidating
their debts and bonding their land all over again, for larger sums of money.
The inevitable outcome, in the 1920s and 1930s, was partial or complete loss of
their land. Secondly, while the aggregate area of land owned by Africans was
steadily shrinking in this period, the number of titles to land—whether to
registered subdivisions or to undivided shares—constantly proliferated in
successive generations, since under Roman-Dutch inheritance law every sibling was entitled to an equal share of the parental estate. The result was that the
viability of individual holdings was repeatedly undermined.

Thirdly, as indicated by Van Riet's evidence in 1931 on John Mokitlane
Nyokong's estate (Chapter 3), black landowners could not extract an economic
rent from their tenantry. They were unable to impose on their own relatives or
on the families of old retainers a regime of steadily declining independence that
was implied in the conversion from share-cropper to labour tenant and eventually to wage labourer. For this reason, they were compelled to lease substantial
portions of their land to whites in order to meet the regular interest payments
on their mortgage bonds. Inevitably, they incurred a degree of odium from
Africans thereby deprived of access to land.

The policy of land segregation, then, placed black landowners in a very
particular dilemma. The value of their land depended on its potential sale to
whites, since very few Africans could afford to buy land; and their capacity to
service their mortgage bonds depended on leasing their land to whites. As
community leaders, however, they were compelled to argue, within the terms
of the segregation policy, for the extension of the 'Released Areas' scheduled
under the 1936 Trust and Land Act. There were thus multiple ironies in the
implementation of land segregation in the Thaba Nchu district. First, black
landowners' private interest in a deracialised land market contradicted their
public obligation to secure more land for the Barolong community. Second, as
Rheinallt Jones discovered (Chapter 4), the way to maximise the land made
available for 'communal' African occupation was to defend private landowners, so far as possible, from the threat of dispossession by their creditors
and thence takeover by the South African Native Trust. Third, nevertheless,
the establishment of the Trust as the state agency responsible for purchasing

land for African occupation was the single most important factor subverting African landownership in the late 1930s.

Further, African landowners had no ready access to the range of services and institutional supports provided for white farmers by the central state. They had neither weapons of political repression nor the ideological whiphand of racial superiority to exact more labour from their tenants. From the late 1930s, state-sponsored credit was nominally available to African landowners, through the SANT, on similar terms to the Land Bank credit available to white landowners, i.e. fixed-term loans with half-yearly repayments of capital and interest at 4 per cent per annum, substantially lower than the 6 or 7 or 8 per cent interest that then prevailed in the private mortgage market. The SANT rarely exercised this discretionary function in practice, however. It excluded most applicants by reference to their alleged idleness and unreliability.

Thus few African landowners made a living from farming. Yet the gradual dispossession of African landowners in the Thaba Nchu district did not imply, as it often did for the sons and daughters of white landowners, inevitable descent into the urban working class. Outcomes for particular families depended on the balance between consumption and investment of the financial liquidity they derived from bonding their landed property. Much was wasted on liquor and motorcars and other extravagance. But much was invested in education. It was their differential educational opportunities, above all, that converted the descendants of the old landowning elite into the modern bureaucratic, professional and commercial elite. The careers of some of the individuals concerned readily illustrate this conversion: for example, those of Dr James Sebe Moroka, Dr Robert Setlogelo, Bennett Herbert Keikelame, Blanche Tsimatsima and Ellen Kuzwayo (Chapters 5 and 7).

Thus the fact of black landownership was of decisive importance in the process of class differentiation in the district, not because it was a condition of successful farming—it was not—but because it was the material springboard for a decent education and thence for socio-economic mobility within the district and outside it. In her autobiography, *Call Me Woman*, and her film, *Tshiamelo*, Ellen Kuzwayo rightly condemned the grotesque injustice of the 1913 Land Act and the subsequent expropriation of 'black spots'. 'Through iniquitous and inhuman legislation', she wrote, 'my family was rendered homeless and wanderers in the land of our birth'.[4] But the terms of her generalised indictment precisely miss the point. Her family was privileged, relative to other Africans, by the original land grants of 1886. Her own farm, Tshiamelo, was not technically expropriated by the state. More importantly, she and her co-owners, her half-sister and her step-sister, were dispersed respectively to Soweto, Mochudi (Botswana) and Mafikeng (northern Cape), all far away from Thaba Phatshwa, long before the threat of expropriation arose at all. The reason for that was the marital and occupational mobility they derived from an education superior to that obtainable by most Africans. It was funded essentially by the bonding of the Makgothi family farm in the 1920s and early 1930s (Chapter 7). The eventual loss of most of the farm was the other side of the same coin.

The majority of the African population of the district had long since been dispossessed of direct access to land. The Gregorowski dispositions of 1885 represented a conversion of administrative rights over land into virtually freehold rights for leading members of Chief Tshipinare's family and political faction. These titles were qualified by the servitudes which protected *bona fide* residents in 1884 from eviction. Nevertheless the private land grants worked to the disadvantage generally of those who had previously held land on a usufructuary basis, and specifically of supporters of Samuel Lehulere's political faction, whose leaders went into exile and whose ordinary followers either also left the district or were squeezed into the two African reserves. In addition, expropriation of many farms by the OFS government deprived the Barolong of direct access to much of the most fertile land in the district, particularly in the south-east. This was a focus of particular resentment well into the twentieth century.

As a result of the rapid alienation of much African-owned land to whites, many of the people who remained in the district became share-croppers who, after a brief period of relative prosperity, fell victim to systematic efforts by the central state to capitalise white farmers. Some were evicted from the land and drifted to the squalid townships of the OFS and southern Transvaal. Others left for Basutoland, already over-crowded, or the Bechuanaland Protectorate, where they suffered further extremities of deprivation (Chapter 3). Others again were pushed on to the surviving black-owned farms in the district, or into the two reserves, despite a rigorous official effort to control admissions. As the story of Nehemiah Gabashane suggests (Chapter 5), some erstwhile share-croppers retained a strong sense of 'shadow' rights to the land long after their eviction.

The 1913 Land Act did not put a stop to share-cropping in the district. On white-owned land it gave an impetus to the conversion, protracted as it was, of share-croppers into labour tenants. On black-owned land share-cropping continued as before, so that by the early 1930s, in the depths of the depression, most surviving black landowners derived an income partly from leasing portions of their land to whites, partly from their own employment in Bloemfontein or in the local state, and partly from such exactions as they could impose on an over-crowded tenantry. By the late 1930s, when the first wave of Trust purchases took place of both white-owned and black-owned land, all residents of that land became subject to settlement under the 'communal' regime imposed by the Trust. As we have seen in Chapter 4, this first wave of land purchase for African occupation opened up political 'space' for the Barolong Progressive Association (BPA). The BPA's populist rhetoric appealed to two constituencies of the dispossessed: landless Africans who sought to occupy newly-acquired Trust land on their own terms; and the heirs of the losing faction in the civil war of nearly sixty years before. In this way, the BPA's campaign subverted the authority both of the established chief and of the Native Affairs Department. The movement was therefore quickly suppressed.

The second wave of Trust purchase, in the late 1940s, allowed the partial consolidation of land planned for African occupation throughout the district. It thus gave rise to a determined official effort to rationalise the terms of settlement: initially on the basis of a uniformly inadequate allowance of land per household for arable and pastoral purposes; and later, after the Tomlinson Commission report of the mid-1950s, on the basis of a division of the rural population into 'farming' and 'non-farming' households. The coercive measures associated with the Trust regime provoked a stubborn refusal to co-operate with the culling of livestock and the re-allocation of arable lands. Resistance was concentrated in the Seliba reserve, and it came to a head in 1956, when many other parts of South Africa simmered with revolt against the Nationalist government's efforts to intensify its policies of control and repression. Trust areas were systematically replanned in the late 1950s, and villagisation was finally enforced at Seliba in the late 1960s (Chapter 5). All this left an enduring legacy of bitterness and resentment.

Meanwhile, several hundred thousand people—labour tenants, 'squatters' and redundant farm labourers—were pushed off white-owned farms all over the eastern and northern OFS, as a result partly of pressure from the central state and partly of a process of rapid capital intensification in 'white' agriculture. From the late 1960s, a housing freeze was imposed in Mangaung, outside Bloemfontein, and in many other African locations attached to 'white' towns in various parts of the province; and pass law restrictions were intensified. The result was a massive flow of refugees from 'white' areas, both urban and rural. Some of these refugees went to Qwaqwa, the tiny South Sotho Bantustan. Others went to Thaba Nchu, by this time incorporated within Bophuthatswana. This was the origin of the squatter slum of Kromdraai (Chapter 6). The Barolong Tribal Authority at Thaba Nchu resented the surge of newcomers who quickly became a numerical majority of non-Tswana. The people were divided into citizens of Bophuthatswana, who were able to compete for access to residence permits, jobs, schools, pensions, rudimentary services, etc., in Thaba Nchu; and citizens of Qwaqwa, who were excluded from that competition. Here as elsewhere, the politics of Separate Development gave rise to vicious inter-ethnic antagonisms.

Following Bophuthatswana's 'independence' in December 1977, the local state launched a purge of its unwanted residents. The Kromdraai squatters were expelled to the new site of Onverwacht, on the western boundary of the (new) Thaba Nchu district, within commuting distance of Bloemfontein but far from their 'own' homeland of Qwaqwa. They were quickly followed by many others. Botshabelo became a 'place of refuge' for disparate categories of 'surplus people' (Chapter 6). The place was a huge concentration of poverty and unemployment. It was also a place where many people, for the first time in their lives, could establish a home without threat of eviction.

From the mid-1970s to the late 1980s, the boundary between the (new) district of Thaba Nchu and the rest of Chief Moroka's old domain was one of considerable political significance. On one side of the line were those who had rights in Bophuthatswana but who, from the moment of 'independence' in 1977, became aliens in the rest of South Africa. On the other side of the line were those who were politically extruded from the Bantustan but who acquired, with the repeal of the pass laws in 1986, nominal freedom of movement within the rest of South Africa. By the end of 1990, it was probable that the (new) Thaba Nchu district would be re-incorporated into a unitary South Africa. But President Mangope, with the whimsical tyranny of imminent political demise, had committed himself to negotiations with the ANC only on the basis of the ANC's recognition of Bophuthatswana's 'independence'.[5] This was the sense in which the question, Whose land?, had the most pressing political relevance for the people of Thaba Nchu.

In retrospect, both within the Bantustan and outside it, what is striking is the tenuous and transient quality of rights to the land. For both white and black landowners, formal ownership was one thing; effective control of land was another. On the one hand, landlords were 'manacled hand and foot by the chains of debt' they owed to outside money-lenders.[6] When their creditors pressed, they were vulnerable to dispossession precisely because they had freehold titles. By the 1980s, the burden of agricultural debt had massively increased (Chapter 6). After decades of protective intervention by the central state on their behalf, many white farmers felt politically betrayed by a combination of galloping inflation in the cost of inputs and much higher interest rates on their mortgage bonds and their bank loans than had prevailed in the past. Faced by the vagaries of drought and interest rates of 20 per cent or more per annum, a white farmer from the Bothaville district remarked in November 1990, 'this government has begun to kill us like flies'.[7]

On the other hand, those who worked the land were locked into the tightening grip of the landlords. As Albie Sachs observed, property law in South Africa 'is one of the bastions of rightlessness'.[8] The historical consolidation of white freehold property rights, cadastrally surveyed, officially registered and judicially defended by a white supremacist state, was the prime instrument by which Africans were dispossessed of their rights to land. As share-croppers on white-owned land, they had partial independence and a rough-and-ready contractual equality. As labour tenants, they were exposed to increasing demands for labour and a recurrent squeeze on access to arable and grazing land. As wage labourers, scattered and unorganised, they were paid very low wages in cash and kind and subject to the landowner's every arbitrary imposition. Despite the inexorable pressures of dispossession, through eviction or conversion to a wage labour regime, there were nevertheless parts of South Africa in the 1980s, such as some magisterial districts of the south-eastern Transvaal, where labour tenants had survived, grimly determined to defend their access to land.[9]

Thus land ownership was rarely 'absolute' as implied in possession of the title deeds. It was qualified, in practice, by the claims either of outside bond-holders or of those who worked the land or of both. This fact poses fundamental questions about future arrangements on the land. Who will own the land? Who will control it? Who will work it? What forms of state support for agriculture will predominate in future?

Late in 1990, President De Klerk committed his government to repealing the 1913 and 1936 Land Acts, as blatantly discriminatory instruments of dispossession by which black South Africans were deprived of direct access to 87 per cent of the land area of South Africa. Mere repeal of the Acts, however, is quite insufficient. In the first place, deracialisation of the land market will serve to legitimise existing gross inequalities of land ownership. In the second place, it will do nothing to restore land rights to 'black spot' communities which were compulsorily expropriated and forcibly relocated, or to generations of share-croppers and labour tenants who were evicted from white-owned lands.

The nationalisation of land, however, is not a realistic solution, a point apparently accepted by the African National Congress. A 'new' state will not have the resources to buy out established commercial farmers at existing market values. Any threat of expropriation without compensation would induce an immediate collapse of confidence and thence of capital investment and food production. Nor is it possible to be sanguine, on the basis of comparative experience, about the prospects of establishing an efficient and competitive state-controlled agriculture. What is at issue, therefore, is the development of a framework for the practical recognition of rights to land other than those expressed in possession of title deeds; and an infrastructure of state support which is able to promote productive investment, partly on a smallholder or co-operative basis, but does not grotesquely distort the national budget.[10]

In 1990, in microcosm, the (old) Thaba Nchu district contained most of the challenges which confront a 'new' South Africa. Most of the land was owned by whites. Many of them were mortgaged to the hilt; many were bitterly disillusioned with the Nationalist government for 'selling out' white supremacy; and many were grimly determined to defend their land. Some white farmers, however, had been displaced a decade previously to accommodate the huge rural slum of Botshabelo. Sited incongruously in one of the most fertile regions of South Africa's maize triangle, Botshabelo was a vast repository of the under-employed and the under-skilled. The slum posed what is perhaps the starkest economic challenge of all: how to reconcile an over-abundance of labour with an acute shortage of skills.

The remainder of the district, slightly more than one-third of Moroka's old territory, had been returned to the Barolong, in the limited sense that it was administered as part of the 'independent' republic of Bophuthatswana. The (new) Thaba Nchu district contained its own complex hierarchy of unequal life-chances. At the top of the hierarchy were the Bantustan bureaucrats with comfortable salaries and some vested interest in the continuing 'independence' of the local state. At the bottom of the hierarchy were the occupants of Trust villages who had not survived the rigours of the 'communal' regime described in Chapter 5, but who had not been able to establish secure employment elsewhere. On various other rungs of the hierarchy, the majority of the people who lived in the 'old' Thaba Nchu locations, the 'new' town of Selosesha and the three Bultfontein 'zones' were dependent, not on agriculture, but on employment in Bloemfontein or in the local state.

Scattered fragments of the land survived in private ownership (Figure 6.2). A few African landowners, such as the Seape brothers, were successful farmers. Other African landowners, waged or salaried absentees, leased portions of their land to white farmers of Excelsior or Dewetsdorp on a share-cropping basis: a curious reversal of the pattern that predominated around the turn of the century. Otherwise, there were a very few Trust villagers who derived their livelihood entirely from agriculture.[11] They rented substantial portions of Trust (Bophuthatswana state) land from Agricor, the Bophuthatswana state agency which was responsible generally for the administration of agricultural operations on Trust (state) land and specifically for the administration of credit. Agricor was notorious for its authoritarian approach and its apparently unlimited capacity to accumulate financial losses.[12]

To what extent would white farmers in the (old) Thaba Nchu district survive a decisive shift in the balance of power in the central state? On what terms would the (new) Thaba Nchu district rejoin one South Africa? How would 'communal' lands be administered in future? How far, and in what ways, could a 'new' state accommodate the demands of half a million of its constituents in Botshabelo for security, employment and some access to land?

Whose land, indeed?

# APPENDIX: A LANDOWNER, THREE LAWYERS AND A LIBERAL

That cute lawyers so often become successful farmers is testimony to the low standards of agriculture generally.

W.M. Macmillan
*Complex South Africa* (1930), p. 76

With reference to one small patch of land in the northern part of the (old) Thaba Nchu district, this Appendix illustrates the process by which, in Macmillan's cryptic phrase, 'cute lawyers' became 'successful farmers'. The story has two separate themes, however, linked perhaps adventitiously by the fact that Jean Baptiste Van Riet, the successful farmer here described, was the elder son of Gideon Jacobus Van Riet, one of the local lawyers actively implicated in the creeping dispossession of Barolong landowners. The first theme is the professional sharp practice by which law agents of one kind or another directly profited, without necessarily behaving illegally, from the financial discomfiture of landowners, both black and white. The second theme is the progressive and unorthodox route by which one farmer achieved a lasting resolution of the labour problems of which most white farmers routinely complained. He introduced a system of incentives and of workers' particip-ation in management decisions that ensured both enthusiasm and profit-ability and also earned him social ostracism by his white neighbours in the Excelsior area.

The patch of land concerned is the original farm Mosheunyana 86 (see Figures 1.3 and 3.1). In 1886 the farm was granted to the estate of Jacob Ngakantsi, the elderly and gouty councillor who was stoned and left for dead during Samuel Lehulere's attack on Thaba Nchu in July 1884 (Chapter 1). The transactions recorded below relate to one small portion of the farm which was inherited by one of his sons, Masaele Ngakantsi. An otherwise obscure land-owner, Masaele Ngakantsi was in chronic financial difficulty in the first decade of the twentieth century. This arose largely out of the obligation of Jacob Ngakantsi's heirs—his two widows and eighteen children, nine in each 'house'—to meet the costs of administration of his estate. A long statement which Masaele Ngakantsi made in 1908 reveals the complete confusion of his affairs at the time and the extent to which he found himself preyed upon by three different legal entrepreneurs in Thaba Nchu. The statement survives in the archival record in Bloemfontein and thus—unusually—provides docu-mentary evidence of the sharp practice which prevailed.

Braby's ORC Directory for 1908 lists three 'Law Agents' in Thaba Nchu: John Hamilton Diepraem, John Henry Faustmann and Gideon Jacobus Van Riet. Diepraem's professional credentials were murky, at best. He joined the OFS civil service before the South African war, then became clerk to the Resident Magistrate at Kimberley (Cape), but 'left the service suddenly'. For a few years from 1902 he worked in an attorney's office and as a law agent himself in the small town of Lady Grey, adjoining the Herschel district (Cape). In the face of two separate allegations of embezzlement there, he 'absconded' to the ORC and set himself up as a law agent in Thaba Nchu, where in due course he became a town councillor.[1]

Faustmann (1868–1944) and Van Riet (1872–1954) were both listed as 'old colonists' of the ORC in 1906. Faustmann was born in Port Elizabeth and educated in Bloemfontein, and established his own legal practice at Thaba Nchu in 1894. Van Riet's father had been a member both of the OFS Volksraad and of the Stellaland Bestuur (Board of Management). In the latter capacity, in 1885, he had handed over this short-lived Boer republic to be incorporated as part of British Bechuanaland. Gideon Jacobus Van Riet managed his father's law business in Thaba Nchu from 1891; he formed the Thaba Nchu commando in 1900 and was sent to Bermuda as a prisoner of war; on his release he returned to Thaba Nchu and started his own business as a law agent in the town. In 1908 Van Riet was a member of the Legislative Assembly of the ORC and a former mayor of Thaba Nchu. He advertised himself as an 'Admitted Agent, Government Appraiser, Deputy Sheriff of the High Court, ORC, and Auctioneer'.[2]

Faustmann handled the Ngakantsi family's affairs from the time he came to Thaba Nchu in 1894. A portion of the original farm Mosheunyana 86 (4,460 morgen) was sold to a white farmer in that year, presumably to defray the costs of administration of Jacob Ngakantsi's estate and of registration of the heirs' titles. As a result of partial subdivision of the remainder of the farm in 1894, Masaele Ngakantsi received title to a surveyed portion registered as Driftplaats (123 morgen). Later, he acquired an undivided one-sixth share of another portion of the original farm registered as Mafikeng (1,115 morgen).[3] Here follows Masaele Ngakantsi's extended account of a series of small but complex transactions in the early 1900s, as recorded verbatim in June 1908 by the South African Constabulary at Thaba Nchu. The statement conveys his confusion and distress with remarkable precision:

> Shortly after the war I went to Mr Faustmann for the papers concerning my portion of the farm Mafikeng. Mr F. told me I must first pay the 'Boodle' money. I could not pay it, and didn't understand it, so I went to Mr Van Riet and asked him to get the papers. Mr Van Riet did so and said, 'Now you know that I pay all the monies due by you to Mr Faustmann and the farm will belong to me now'. I couldn't answer him as I didn't understand what he meant, because I didn't tell him to pay the money for

me. I went away with the papers and then boys came and ploughed for Mr
Van Riet for 2 years. I put up with it during that time, I remonstrated with
the boys but it helped nothing. I came then to Van Riet and said to him,
'Now if you say you own my farm or a piece of it take your piece and leave
me mine so that I can plough'. I was frightened about the 'Boodle' and
thought Van Riet must have some right on my farm. Van Riet said,
'Alright I will bring a surveyor'. The surveyor did not come. Later I came
to Thaba Nchu and found a letter for me at the R.M.'s; in it I read that Mr
Van Riet says that I will sell my farm. I showed it to the R.M. (Maj
Robertson) because I knew nothing about it. The R.M. advised me to go
to my farm and take no notice of anyone about my farm. So I voetsacked
all the natives who were working for Mr Van Riet. From then on I had no
more trouble with Van Riet. About a year ago I came to Diepraam, the
agent, and asked him to try and get me some money from Government.
He said, 'Yes, but if you want money you must bring me your farm
papers'. I went back and brought them. I asked for £130. D. said 'Alright
you can go back'. Next morning D. and I went to the R.M. office and Mr
Ham [Assistant R.M.] said, 'I don't think the Govt. give more money'.
We went away. D. said, 'We will get the money from young De Wet at
Aitchison's store'. I said, 'Will he give me a long time to repay it like the
Govt?'. D. replied, 'Yes, only you must pay the interest regularly'. I
agreed to that. Some days later I came to D. for the money and didn't get
it. From then onward I have continually come for it. That was about a year
ago. D. always says he hasn't got the money. I must wait a bit. On the 3rd
of this month I went to Diepraam and said, 'Where is the money?' and D.
replied, 'I haven't got the money'. I went to young De Wet (the man
Diepraam said he would raise the money from) and asked him if he had
given D. any money for me and he replied, 'Long ago I gave Mr D. the
money. You can go yourself to see Van Riet and ask him if he doesn't
know that Mr D. has got the money'. I went and asked Mr Van Riet and
he replied, 'Yes'. From there I went to Mr D. and said, 'Better you give
me the farm papers if you can't give me the money'. D. replied, 'No, I
cannot give you that, the papers are in Bloemfontein'. D. gave me
nothing. That morning I went to Mr Van Riet and asked him if he could
not get my farm papers from Mr D. Mr Van Riet agreed to. Last Saturday
(6th instant) I came to Mr Van Riet and he showed me the farm papers and
a little piece of paper which Mr Van Riet said was a letter from D. to say
that he Van Riet must not give me the farm papers before I pay him all his
trouble which he make for me. Mr Van Riet said the letter said I must pay
Mr D. £52. I said, 'What for I have got nothing from Diepraam?'. I can't
pay that money. But I know that I owe Mr D. £18.6d. which he lent me. I
got this money on the occasion I called on D. office for the big loan of
£130. I had told D. I was very short of money and D. had always said, 'I

can always help you but you must pay me back when you get the £130'. Mr
Van Riet explained that he couldn't give me the papers unless I paid the
£52 and if he gave me the papers D. might get him into trouble. So then I
came to the police to see if I can get help. I was told by the Head Constable
to go and see if young De Wet of Van Riet's office can give the a/c from Mr
Diepraam. I got it from him and now hand it to the police. The only
money I have asked D. to raise for me is the £130. When Van Riet told me
he had paid Mr Faustmann he said he was going to take away my farm. I
considered that he has been repaid by me for the money I owed Mr F.
which he Van Riet told me he had paid to Mr F. by the use of my farm for
those two years. Van Riet once said I must pay him £50. I do not know
what for. I have never spoken about the matter without the two, D. and
Van Riet together. I never received a sum of £15.10s. from D. in this or at
all. I am the owner of Driftplaats only and have not raised any money and
at any time on my farm. And this is the first time I have tried to raise
money.[4]

With the assistance of Quayle Dickson, ORC Native Affairs Adviser, the
whole matter was investigated; a police report on Diepraem was requested,
which revealed his shady past; Masaele Ngakantsi was summoned to Bloemfontein to give further evidence before the Law Society, which was prepared to
recommend that Diepraem be 'struck off the Rolls' for over-charging; meanwhile, however, Diepraem pressed for judgement against Ngakantsi in respect
of the amount allegedly owed to him; after all this, no steps were taken against
either Diepraem or Van Riet for professional misconduct. Ngakantsi had
taken out two mortgage bonds in favour of J.M. De Wet, who was also Van
Riet's brother-in-law: £100 in September 1907 on Driftplaats; and £130 in
February 1908 on his one-sixth share of Mafikeng. These credits were barely
sufficient to meet his immediate debts, but he was able for the time being to
stave off the threat of the sale of his land in execution of the court's judgement
against him. Later, he had to consolidate his debts and take out fresh bonds, so
that in 1916 his two portions of land were bonded respectively for £700 and
£450.[5]

    The details of the outcome hardly matter for my present purpose, however.
The point of reproducing Masaele Ngakantsi's statement above is to demonstrate the confusion and distress which pervaded his experience over many
years of dealing with the triumvirate of law agents who dominated the local
transaction of land transfers and mortgage bonds. His predicament must have
been typical of that of many Barolong landowners of marginal literacy, little
knowledge of the law and no political influence.

    In the end, at various dates in the 1920s and early 1930s, Gideon Jacobus
Van Riet acquired title to many different portions of the erstwhile Ngakantsi
family estate. In 1932, Van Riet's elder son, Jean Baptiste, started farming on
part of this land, after an unhappy period in his father's office. He paid rent to

his father until the property was transferred to his name in 1944. The farm became known as Barolong. In common with other farmers, Jean Baptiste Van Riet had two problems: shortage of rain and unsatisfactory labour. He solved the water shortage by building a large dam and irrigating 300 morgen of the 1,000 morgen farm. In 1937 he saw a film about the original Boys' Town in the United States, and decided to initiate an experiment on Barolong. He built 4-room houses of burnt brick and corrugated sheeting roofs for each African family he employed. He started a school on the farm and assisted the children with books. He set aside fruit and vegetable plots whose produce was consumed by workers' families. Most radically, he established a bonus scheme to provide an incentive and a workers' management committee to promote self-regulation. In addition to monthly wages in cash and kind, each worker received a cash bonus paid half-yearly from a 'pool' set aside in respect of each product of the farm: in the 1940s, the bonus on wheat was 1s.9d. per 35s. bag; on maize, 1s.1d. per 17s.6d. bag; on lucerne, 2d. for every pressed bale valued at £6 a ton. In addition, the pool was credited with 5 per cent of all sales of milk and cream. The function of the management committee was 'to engage new workers and to terminate the services of the workers who did not pull their weight'. Van Riet retained a right of veto on the decisions of this committee, but never had to exercise it.[6]

Van Riet's neighbours reacted with hostility to these innovations. They resented his benevolence to black labour: *hy bou kakhuise vir sy kaffirs!* ('He builds shit-houses for his kaffirs!'). Particularly strong antagonism came from the Excelsior Farmers' Union, some of whose members had pro-Nazi sympathies during the Second World War. The Union organised a meeting against him in the Town Hall in 1944. That episode sharpens the contrast of style and method between father and son. In 1937, in an ingenious and devious manner, Gideon Jacobus Van Riet organised a meeting of residents of Thaba Nchu to approve prospective purchase by the Trust of some of his own farms in place of the property of Charlie Morgan (Chapter 4). He deliberately excluded Morgan from the meeting. In 1944, Jean Baptiste Van Riet was deliberately excluded from a public meeting in Excelsior which had been called to censure him for improving the living conditions of his black farm workers. 1944 was also the year of John Henry Faustmann's death, unmarried at the age of 75. He owned thirteen farms in the district, valued at £31,000, and many plots in Thaba Nchu town; and he held sixteen outstanding mortgage bonds. One of the beneficiaries of his will was his nephew, Clarence Paver, a partner in his law firm at Thaba Nchu.[7]

A notorious 'liberal', Jean Baptiste Van Riet persisted with his experiment on Barolong and reported its success, in respect of the stability, commitment and enthusiasm of his labour force, in a series of articles from the 1940s to the 1980s. In 1953, he wrote: 'I have not once had labour trouble during 14 years, and my worries as an employer have disappeared. Today neither I nor anyone else manages the farm, the system is the manager, and a right good job it is doing'. He was Vice-Chairman of the Liberal Party in the late 1950s. With his son Johnny, he expanded his farming operations to the Tuli Block in Botswana. In 1990, at the age of 85, he still played a keen game of tennis.

# NOTES AND REFERENCES

### INTRODUCTION

1. Magisterial district boundaries in the area have been repeatedly redrawn. Some time after its annexation in 1884, Moroka's territory was incorporated into the OFS as a ward (*wyk*) of Bloemfontein district. In 1902 it was reconstituted as the independent district of Thaba Nchu, extended in the north-west so that it was slightly larger than Moroka's territory. The district boundaries were revised several times thereafter. With the gradual consolidation of land purchases under the 1936 Trust and Land Act (see Chapter 5), parts of Thaba Nchu were detached and added, respectively, to the districts of Dewetsdorp, Bloemfontein, Brandfort, Excelsior and Ladybrand. Thus the (new) district of Thaba Nchu (Bophuthatswana) at 'independence' in 1977 was slightly more than one-third the size of the (old) Thaba Nchu district that comprised the territory of Chief Moroka's Barolong (see Figure I.1).
2. Keegan, 1987.
3. C. Murray, 1980, 1981.
4. C. Murray, 1983a, 1983b.
5. Martin and Beittel, 1987; C. Murray, 1987a.
6. For extensive discussion of this issue, with reference to other Barolong populations, see John Comaroff, 1982, and Jean Comaroff, 1985.
7. Three very valuable studies were published in the mid-1980s: Beinart, Delius and Trapido, 1986; Keegan, 1987; and Bradford, 1988. For criticism of the 'social historians' and responses to that criticism, see Morris, 1987; M.J. Murray, 1989b; and Keegan, 1989a and 1989b. For an earlier seminal analysis see Morris, 1976.
8. Bradford, 1990. See also Williams, 1990; Keegan, 1990.
9. Wilson and Ramphele, 1989.

### 1 'DUST AND ASHES': THE COLLAPSE OF AN AFRICAN POLITY

1. Froude, 1883: 544–6.
2. Trollope, 1878: 275–85.
3. Doke, 1967: 24.
4. Trollope, 1878: 276, 284; Mitchell, 1875: 233, 239, 241–2; 'The Orange River Free State: a visit to Thaba Nchu', *The Net Cast Into Many Waters* 1 November 1874, pp. 168–74; Wales, 1985, especially Chapter V.
5. For discussion of this issue and further references, see Jean Comaroff, 1985: 74–7.
6. Molema, 1951: 37, and Chapters II, III; Edwards, 1988, Chapters V, VI; and Breutz, 1989, Chapter V.
7. Theal, 1964: 97–8; Sanders, 1975: 61–6; Thompson, 1975: 109–14.
8. *ibid.*
9. Sanders, 1975, particularly Chapters IX, XIII, XIV.
10. Sanders, 1975, Chapter V; Thompson, 1975, Chapter IV; Wales, 1985, Introduction, Chapters I, II, III.

11. Wales, 1985, Chapter IV; Shillington, 1985: 128.
12. For more than thirty years, culminating in a Supreme Court case in 1927, a bitter dispute was fought between Petrus Malefo's son and successor, as chief of this community, and the Wesleyan Methodist Society over ownership of the farm. See Molema, 1951: 140–2; and Wales, 1985: 245.
13. Molema, 1951: 203.
14. Wales, 1985, Chapter V.
15. USPG, E32, Mitchell's report 31 March 1877.
16. Watson, 1977: 403–7; Sanders, 1975: 165, 258.
17. Molema, 1951: 113–14, 129.
18. Wales, 1985: 257.
19. Wales, 1985, Chapter VI; SOAS, MMS 343, Bloemfontein District File, Schedule of Members, 1879; USPG, E34, Mitchell's report 1 January 1879.
20. SOAS, MMS 343, Report of the Thaba Nchu circuit, 1879.
21. SOAS, MMS 343, Report of the Thaba Nchu circuit, 1879. For specialist accounts of these events, see Guy, 1979; Burman, 1981; and Delius, 1983. For an overview of their political and economic significance, see Marks, 1985, especially pp. 382–99.
22. Delius, 1983, Chapter 3; Kimble, 1982; Shillington, 1985, Chapter 3.
23. SOAS, MMS 343, Report of the Thaba Nchu circuit, 1879.
24. Wales, 1985: 264–7; Burman, 1981, Chapter 10.
25. Molema, 1951: 151; Wales, 1985: 269; VAB, BOV 1/127, N1/1/3/1, 'Statement' enclosed in S.J. Setanka to NC, Thaba Nchu, 9 April 1947.
26. Molema, 1951: 152.
27. Molema, 1951: 152; Wales, 1985: 268; Watson, 1980: 362.
28. Wales, 1985: 268.
29. Wales, 1985: 269–70. See also Trollope, 1878: 278–9; and USPG, E34, Mitchell's report 1 January 1879. Molema (1951: 140) both misquoted and misconstrued Trollope's remarks about Motlhware. The date of 1874 which Molema suggests (p. 151) for Motlhware's death is also wrong, possibly reflecting the faulty memory in extreme old age of Majang, one of Molema's principal informants.
30. Wales, 1985: 272–5; CLHR, MS 15 620, Report of the Thaba Nchu circuit, 1880; USPG, E35A, Mitchell's report 30 September 1880; SOAS, MMS 326, Daniel to J. Kilner, General Secretary of the Wesleyan Mission Society, London, 22 April 1881.
31. Wales, 1985, Chapter VII.
32. CLHR, MS 15 620, Report of the Thaba Nchu circuit, 1880; Wales, 1985: 261; USPG, E35A, Mitchell's report 30 September 1880; SOAS, MMS 326, Daniel to Kilner 22 April 1881.
33. SOAS, MMS 326, Daniel to Kilner 29 August 1881; MMS 343, report on subordinate paid agents.
34. SOAS, MMS 326, Daniel to Kilner 29 August 1881, 28 November 1881.
35. SOAS, MMS 326, Daniel to Kilner 31 October 1882.
36. SOAS, MMS 326, Daniel to Kilner 31 October 1882; extracts from the Bloemfontein *Friend*, and commentaries thereon, in Boon, 1885: 154–67; Molema, 1951: 166; VAB, ORC 46 (1901), Annexure N, Gregorowski Report B.
37. Wales, 1985: 280, 281, 284; VAB, GS 1410, J.A. Cameron to Tshipinare 11 September 1883, C. Voigt to Brand 18 April 1885.
38. Baumann, 1940: 95.
39. CLHR, MS 15 620, Reports of the Thaba Nchu circuit, 1882, 1883.
40. USPG, E39A, Crisp's report 31 December 1883.
41. Wales, 1985, Chapter VIII. See also Shillington, 1985, Chapter 5.

42. USPG, D65, Chesson to Tucker 29 December 1883; D69, Moroka to Tucker 4 February 1884, Fowler to Tucker 8 February 1884, Chesson to Tucker 22 February 1884. See also Wales, 1985: 282; and Watson, 1980: 363.
43. USPG, E39B, Crisp's report 31 December 1884.
44. This and previous quotation, BPP, C. 4263, Statement of Privates Khotho and Libopuoa of the Basutoland Mounted Police, pp. 95–6. Khotho and Libopuoa were not themselves witnesses of the attack, but messengers sent by Colonel Marshall Clarke, RC Basutoland, to President Brand at Thaba Nchu on Monday 14 July. They recorded various accounts of the attack in their report.
45. BPP, C. 4263, Statement of Khotho and Libopuoa, p. 96; USPG, Crisp's report 31 December 1884.
46. VAB, GS 1407, H. de Marillac to Landdrost, Ladybrand, 10 July 1884; CLHR, MS 15 620, Report of the Thaba Nchu circuit, 1884.
47. VAB, GS 1407, O. Jensen and H. de Marillac to Landdrost, Ladybrand, 10 July 1884; *Friend* 17 July 1884; Wales, 1985: 283.
48. *Friend* 17 July 1884.
49. Molema, 1951: 35, 138; Theal, 1964: 318; Shillington, 1985: 50.
50. BPP, C. 4263, telegram Clarke to Robinson 16 July 1884, p. 92; Letsie to Clarke 16 July 1884, pp. 97–8; Clarke to Brand 20 July 1884, pp. 99–100; Brand to Clarke 22 July 1884, pp. 100–1.
51. VAB, GS 1410, Voigt to Brand 18 April 1885.
52. BPP, C. 4589, Samuel Moroka proclamation 22 January 1885, and other enclosures, pp. 56–61. See also Wales' commentary on these events, 1985: 292–3.
53. USPG, E39B, Crisp's report 31 December 1884; CLHR, MS 15 620, Report of the Thaba Nchu circuit, 1884.
54. USPG, E41A, Crisp's report 12 February 1886; CLHR, MS 15 620, Report of the Thaba Nchu circuit, 1885.
55. Molema, 1951: 167.
56. Wales, 1985: 289.
57. VAB, ORC 46 (1901), Annexures I, J; Wales, 1985: 287–8.
58. Wales, 1985: 288–90.
59. VAB, ORC 46 (1901), Annexure K. For detailed discussion of these commissions of enquiry, see also Wales, 1985, Chapter VIII.
60. Wales, 1985: 289.
61. Wales, 1985: 291–4; VAB, GS 1408, Barolong Census 1884, Schedules A and B.
62. VAB, GS 1410, Gregorowski Report A, English translation in ORC 46 (1901), Annexure M.
63. VAB, GS 1410, Gregorowski Report B, English translation in ORC 46 (1901), Annexure N.
64. *ibid.*
65. VAB, ORC 46 (1901), Annexure O.
66. VAB, Minutes of the Volksraad 23 June 1885, p. 473; GS 1410, Voigt to Brand 28 July 1885; AKT 2/1/144, Thaba Nchu Land Register, Zamenloop 56, Khabanyana 57 and Morokashoek 58.
67. Wales, 1985: 296; CLHR, MS 15 620, Report of the Thaba Nchu circuit, 1885.
68. Wales, 1985: 297; CLHR, MS 15 620, Report of the Thaba Nchu circuit, 1886.
69. *ibid.*
70. VAB, GS 1410, Daniel to Brand 14 September 1885.
71. VAB, ORC 46 (1901), Annexure R, Government Notice No. 10, 1 September 1887.
72. VAB, Minutes of the Volksraad 10 May 1887; Wales, 1985: 299; VAB, ORC 46

(1901), Annexures P, Q; CLHR, MS 15 620, Report of the Thaba Nchu circuit, 1887.
73. Shillington, 1985: 173–7.
74. BPP, C. 5363, Shippard to Robinson 30 September 1887, p. 7.
75. BPP, C. 5363, Shippard to Robinson 3 February 1888, p. 43.
76. BPP, C. 4889, Annexure A to Report of the Land Commission, p. 22; Shillington, 1985: 171. Richard Maramantsi's eleven farms on the erstwhile Stellaland border were Steilhoogte, Kromdraai, Likatlong, Mokala, Selemo, Salem, Kgoro, Zwart-laagte, Parnell, Olifantshoek and Leeuwbosch. Michael Tshabadira's large farm to the east, derived from unsurveyed Crown land, was Clober. The relevant transfer deeds are held in DRV, Division of Mafeking Land Register.
77. USPG, E44B, Bevan's report 30 September 1889.
78. DRV, Division of Mafeking Land Register, Clober 12; Molema, 1951: 169, 177–8; SAB, NTS 8141, 1/341 (1912–32), magistrate, Thaba Nchu, to SNA 24 August 1914; VAB, MHG M3161, estate Robert Tsipinare Moroka.
79. This summary is derived from a detailed study of VAB, AKT 2/1/144–6, Thaba Nchu Land Registers.
80. Keegan, 1986a: 204.
81. For detailed evidence on patterns of accumulation and speculative investment in land in other regions of South Africa in the same period, see Beinart, 1986; Delius, 1986; and Keegan, 1986b.
82. Oberholster, 1969: 50–1; Keegan, 1987: 99, 250 n.77; Keegan 1986a: 206; BPP, Cd. 627, p. 233.
83. VAB, AKT 2/1/144, Thaba Nchu Land Register.
84. The first figure is Charles Newberry's own estimate, given in a few pages of parsimonious and moralistic reminiscences of his life which he compiled for his children in 1912. I am indebted to his grandson John Moffett of Kirklington, Clocolan, for access to this brief autobiography. The second figure is taken from Turrell, 1987: 218.
85. Knight, 1903: 146; Playne, 1916: 102; David Boddam-Whetham, letter to author 23 April 1983.
86. Charles Newberry's autobiographical notes (see n. 84 above). Brief biographical notes on Charles and Libby Newberry were also compiled by their grand-daughter June Boddam-Whetham, and are held in the Albany Museum, Grahamstown, Daniel file.
87. VAB, GS 1410, Newberry to Brand 26 July 1885.
88. VAB, AKT 2/1/144, Thaba Nchu Land Register.
89. Keegan, 1987: 57–8; VAB, ORC 46 (1901), Annexure S, Report of the Com-mission; Annexure X, Government Notice No. 414–1899.
90. VAB, DLS 2 A40, enclosures with letter from Hanger to Land Settlement Board, Bloemfontein, 3 April 1902; ORC 46 (1901), Annexure S; Annexure Z, evidence of Harry Hanger.

## 2 IMPERIAL INTERVENTION: THE LAND SETTLERS

1. Pakenham, 1979.
2. For detailed accounts of these engagements, see Amery, Vol. IV, 1906: 29–50, 96–100; Vol. V, 1907: 28, 40–2, 133, 260, 401. See also Pakenham, 1979; and Churchill, 1900, Chapters VII, IX. The Sannahspos battle has been analysed in depth by a serving officer of the South African Defence Force, with a view to deriving lessons from De Wet's tactics for the conduct of modern guerilla warfare. See Rabie, 1980, the maps from which are displayed in the Sannahspos museum.

3. Warwick, 1983, Chapter 3; VAB, CO 86 358/02, G. de Lotbiniere to Goold-Adams 18 January 1902; Beak, 1906: 24–9.
4. VAB, CO 86 358/02, de Lotbiniere to Goold-Adams 18 January 1902; Beak, 1906: 164; Warwick, 1983: 157.
5. VAB, CO 86 390/02, Robert Dickie, Superintendent Native Refugee Camp Thaba Nchu, to Wilson Fox, Superintendent Native Refugee Department, 8 February 1902; Amy M. Wilson, South African Diary 1901–2, entry for 29 March 1902.
6. VAB, ORC 46 (1901), Report on the District of Moroka.
7. VAB, ORC 46 (1901), evidence of Elizabeth Nkhabele Fenyang, p. 122.
8. VAB, GS 1408, Barolong Census 1884.
9. VAB, ORC 46 (1901), evidence of Joseph Moses Masisi, p. 130; GS 1408, Barolong Census 1884.
10. VAB, ORC 46 (1901), Annexure X, and Evidence taken by the Commission, pp. 115–34.
11. VAB, ORC 46 (1901), report on Leases of Government Farms, and Annexures A, B, C.
12. VAB, ORC 46 (1901), IX, Leases of Government Farms in Thaba Nchu District, Annexures B and C, and evidence of Jan Frederik Labuschagne and Daniel Benjamin Lombaard, p. 132; DLS 7 A578, List of Burghers, late Orange Free State, registered as living on Government Farms; PRO, CO 224/12 f39781, enclosures with report of Van Iddekinge, magistrate Thaba Nchu, 7 September 1903, pp. 711–15.
13. VAB, ORC 46 (1901), IX, Leases of Government Farms, and evidence of Cornelia Dippenaar, Josina Dry and Martha Bezuidenhout, p. 129; DLS 19 A1335, report of Land Settlement Board Inspector Dumaresq, 2 February 1903.
14. VAB, DLS 8 A734, Hanger to Secretary, Land Settlement Board, Bloemfontein, 1 August 1902.
15. BPP, Cd. 1163, Milner to Chamberlain 30 December 1901, 25 January 1902, pp. 83–7, 88–94. For an illuminating account of the various schemes of social engineering launched in the Reconstruction period, see Marks and Trapido, 1979.
16. BPP, Cd. 1163, ibid.
17. BPP, Cd. 626; Cd. 627.
18. VAB, DLS 4 A230, Purchase of Farms by Land Settlement Board. These farms are identified in ORC 46 (1901), Annexure U. See also Keegan, 1987: 235–6 n. 123.
19. PRO, CO 224/7 f25144, Goold-Adams to Milner 27 May 1902, enclosure 5, p. 556.
20. Amy M. Wilson, South African Diary 1901–2, entry for 29 March 1902. Amy Wilson was a sister of H.F. Wilson, Secretary to the ORC administration.
21. PRO, CO 224/5 f1725, Milner to Chamberlain 20 December 1901, enclosure pp. 394–8.
22. These negotiations are detailed in PRO, CO 224/9 f49776, f52352; CO 224/10 f29006, f29516, f30524, f42524, f44030, f46317, f50834; CO 224/13 f3131, f8315, f9183. The eventual outcome may be traced in CO 224/21 f47984 and CO 224/29 f14796. See also VAB, ORC 191 (1903) for the new Agreement, and DLS 32 A1745, Brotherston's report to Hill for period 26 April 1902 to 1 June 1903.
23. BPP, Cd. 1163, pp. 128–34. See also Beak, 1906: 267–8, Appendix B.
24. PRO, CO 224/14 f16276, report of the Land Settlement Department, 30 September 1903, for period 1 July 1902 to 30 June 1903.
25. PRO, CO 224/13 f18075, telegram Goold-Adams to Just, Colonial Office, London, 15 May 1903; Michael Thatcher, manager of the Westminster Estate, letter to author 19 August 1984.
26. The African Review 17 October 1903.

27. W.F. Gebhardt, Diary 1902–8, entry for 6 July 1903. Gebhardt's farm was Lion's Rump 310.
28. Wales, 1985: 278, 282, 301; VAB, GS 1407, H. de Marillac to Landdrost, Ladybrand, 10 July 1884; and see the relevant map in the Africa 1:125,000 GSGS 2230 series, Thaba Nchu, sheet South H-35/I-II, 1913.
29. Hutchinson, 1905: 179.
30. Hutchinson, 1905: 179; Michael Thatcher, letters to author 19 August, 30 September 1984, citing letter from the first estate manager, Colonel Byron, to A.E. Garrett, the settler on Aldford, 23 July 1904.
31. Flemming, 1924, Chapters II to XIII; VAB, ORC 194 (1905), List of Government Farms.
32. BPP, Cd. 627, p. 243; VAB, ORC 46 (1901), Annexure C; Flemming, 1924: 85, 90, 92–3.
33. Flemming, 1924: 99.
34. See, for example, Flemming, 1910, 1916. Additional biographical details are drawn from the *Dictionary of South African Biography*, Vol. I, 1968: 294–5.
35. Evelyn Langbridge, London, letter to author 22 May 1985. Her father had encountered Winston Churchill during the march to Pretoria in 1900. Her reminiscences continue:
'W.C. was considered a pretty awful type, always out for fame and glory. Most generals would only consider him attached to their regiments and refused any special care for his life. He also used face creams and lotions and had a sort of trailer caravan to himself which caused much ribald laughter from the other chaps'.
36. Knight, 1903: 143–7.
37. *ibid.*: 145. See also n. 20 above.
38. *ibid.*: 147.
39. Marge Bairstow, Jevington, letter to author April 1985.
40. Evelyn Langbridge, London, letter to author 22 May 1985.
41. Dickinson, 1978.
42. Manuscript by Fred Nicholson entitled 'Heathfield: An autobiography of eighty-five years of my life', 1966, kindly lent to me by his daughter, Agnes Oats of Linksfield, Johannesburg. Most of this manuscript was published as Nicholson, 1977.
43. Nicholson, 1977: 207. Scully's life and writings are examined in Marquard, 1984.
44. Nicholson, 1977: 207.
45. Frederick Nicholson, Diary 1903–6, entries for 2, 3 and 20 October and 12 November 1903.
46. Nicholson, 1977: 207.
47. VAB, CO 132 2679/02, Van Iddekinge to Colonial Secretary, Bloemfontein, 23 July 1902; Acting Colonial Secretary to magistrate, Thaba Nchu, 23 August 1902.
48. VAB, DLS 7 A595.
49. PRO, CO 224/12 f21691, Van Iddekinge to Colonial Secretary, Bloemfontein, 28 April 1903.
50. PRO, CO 224/15 f28496, report of Quayle Dickson 22 June 1904. The date of Anderson's visit may have been wrongly reported by Dickson, who relied mainly on Worringham for his information. The latter's near neighbour Gebhardt, of Lion's Rump 310, recorded in his diary the passage of a cyclist on 16 December 1903, who 'had the appearance of a missionary man', and 'before he departed he read a verse out of the scripture' (see n. 27 above).
51. PRO, CO 224/16 f15076, Parliamentary Question by Hunter Craig, 27 April 1904.

52. PRO, CO 224/15 f28496, report of Quayle Dickson 22 June 1904.
53. SANAC, Vol. IV, 1904, evidence of R. Dickie, p. 307.
54. PRO, CO 224/15 f28496, report of Quayle Dickson 22 June 1904.
55. Knight, 1903: 149; VAB, DLS 19 A1335, Inspector Dumaresq to Secretary Land Settlement Board, Bloemfontein, 2 February 1903.
56. Knight, 1903: 153.
57. Interview, Jean Hipkin, Deveron farm, 20 December 1981.
58. VAB, CO 271 3453/03, Stuart MacKenzie to Colonial Secretary 5 May 1903; CO 276 3703/03, report of subcommittee of Moroka FA.
59. VAB, CO 276 3703/03, Quayle Dickson to Acting Colonial Secretary 15 May 1903; PRO, CO 224/12 f21691, correspondence and affidavits, April 1903, pp. 81–99.
60. SANAC, Vol. IV, 1904, evidence of A. Wilson, p. 311.
61. VAB, NAB 7 83/A/05.
62. VAB, NAB 11 N471/06.
63. *ibid.*
64. PRO, CO 224/27 f39863, Allason (Administrator ORC) to Crewe (Secretary of State for the Colonies) 12 October 1908, p. 233. On the 'moral panic' concerning white impoverishment, see Keegan, 1987: 180–2.
65. PRO, CO 224/27 f39863, resolution passed by Becoana Mutual Association 12 September 1908, pp. 247–8; Odendaal, 1984: 108–10; Keegan, 1987: 183.
66. See particularly VAB, CO 901 760/1–23, for files detailing these transactions.
67. PRO, CO 224/21 f28658, enclosures with Selborne to Elgin 16 July 1906, pp. 17–37. On the depression of 1904–8, see Keegan, 1987: 45–9.
68. PRO, CO 224/19 f4488, Hawkins to Lyttelton 10 February 1905; CO 224/22 f18044, Hawkins to Churchill 18 May 1906, and enclosure Marriott to Hawkins 18 April 1906.
69. PRO, CO 224/22 f21696, Hawkins to Churchill 16 June 1906, and enclosure of extracts from letter 'XYZ' to Hawkins 20 April 1906.
70. One of Hawkins' grandsons, Seymer Selby's nephew, was Roger Tancred Robert Hawkins, a founder of the Rhodesian Front and minister in Ian Smith's government.
71. PRO, CO 224/21 f35951, Hanger to Acting Director Land Settlement Board 24 July 1906.
72. PRO, CO 224/22 f16179, Apthorp to Churchill 29 August 1906.
73. PRO, CO 224/26 f32550, report of Plumptre 18 July 1908.
74. PRO, CO 224/20 f19936, Apthorp report 30 April 1906. See also CO 224/24 f24130, telegram Goold-Adams to Secretary of State for Colonies 8 July 1907; VAB, DLS 120 A4411, Apthorp report to Colonial Secretary, Bloemfontein, 30 April 1906.
75. PRO, CO 224/20 f19936, Goold-Adams to Selborne 7 May 1906, and enclosures; CO 224/20 f25585, Selborne to Elgin 25 June 1906.
76. PRO, CO 224/20 f19936, A. Hayward, Morning Star, Ficksburg, to Apthorp 6 March 1906, p. 376.
77. *Friend* 31 March 1906, enclosed in PRO CO 224/20 f19936, Selborne's despatch to Elgin, p. 382.
78. PRO, CO 224/20, f19936, report of Apthorp 1 May 1906, p. 394.
79. *Times* 18 August 1906.
80. Hyam, 1968: 165–70; PRO, CO 224/26 f21342, Goold-Adams to Crewe 25 May 1908; f32550, Goold-Adams to Crewe 5 September 1908.
81. Keegan, 1987, especially Chapter 6.
82. See Annual Report of the Land Settlement Department, PRO, CO 224/23, 1905–6,

7 January 1907; and of the Land Settlement Board, CO 224/30, 1908–9, 22 November 1909.

83. PRO, CO 224/23, Apthorp to Colonial Secretary 28 December 1906; CO 224/24, telegram Goold-Adams to Secretary of State for Colonies 8 July 1907; CO 224/30 f40222, Annual Report 1908–9; CO 551/3 f38606, Annual Report 1909–10.

84. PRO, CO 224/30 f40222, Annual Report 1908–9, and enclosure Crout to Apthorp 14 September 1909; CO 224/31 f10079, Dewdney Drew to Crewe 26 February 1909.

85. PRO, CO 224/30 f40220, Goold-Adams to Crewe 22 November 1909; CO 224/33 f11300, Goold-Adams to Crewe 28 March 1910; CO 551/3 f38606, Annual Report 1909–10.

86. On this point, generally, see Keegan, 1987: 81–95.

87. Playne, 1916: 349–60. For evidence on intensifying antagonism in the OFS countryside in this period, see M.J. Murray, 1989a.

88. Playne, 1916: 72, 354. See also Greig, 1970: 146–7.

89. Playne, 1916: 360; Agnes ('Doody') Oats, letter to author 25 September 1983.

### 3 VARIETIES OF DISPOSSESSION

1. For some valuable oral histories of this experience, see Keegan, 1988.

2. Plaatje, 1969: 113–14.

3. *ibid.*: 65–71, 79–90.

4. *ibid.*: 102–5.

5. *ibid.*: 11, 114.

6. *ibid.*: 114–16.

7. UG 22–1916, pp. 23–6.

8. *Men of the Times*, p. 566.

9. UG 22–1916, p. 22; Appendix XI, report of Thaba Nchu magistrate 25 September 1913.

10. UG 22–1916, p. 15.

11. UG 22–1918, p. 7.

12. Lacey, 1981: 128, 345 n. 29. See also her Appendix C.1, p. 397, my emphasis; and UG 22–1918, p. 4, my emphasis.

13. UG 19–1916, Appendix IV, p. 8; UG 25–1916, Annexure 2, p. 28; UG 22–1918, pp. 3–4.

14. Keegan, 1987: 200. See also UG 22–1916, Appendix XI, report of Thaba Nchu magistrate 25 September 1913.

15. Keegan, 1987, Chapter 6 and Conclusion.

16. SAB, NTS 8141, 1/341 (1912–32), RM, Thaba Nchu, to SNA 24 September 1917.

17. Molema, 1951: 162–3; Schapera, 1971: 267 n. 9; BNA, RC 4/8, W. Jones, General Manager, Tati Concessions Ltd., to RC, Mafeking, 29 July 1898; Phillips, 1976: 17–18.

18. Schapera, 1971: 225, 261; VAB, NAB 11 N360/06, petition of Samuel Moroka 6 February 1904; CO 677 3203/2, Moroka to Goold-Adams 22 September 1907, Moroka to A. Fischer, undated 1907, Prime Minister's Minutes 14 December 1907, 25 January 1908; CO 677 3202/6, I. Goldinger to S. Marks 11 September 1906, Marks to Colonial Secretary, Bloemfontein, 26 September 1906.

19. Schapera, 1971: 226; SAB, GG 1166, 50/558, W. Lack to Under Secretary of Native Affairs, Pretoria, undated 1915; BNA, RC 8/5, J.A. Ashburnham, magistrate, Bloemfontein, to SNA 22 January 1915; S 10/4/1, S. Moroka to RC, Mafeking, 23 December 1915.

20. SAB, GG 1166, 50/543, S. Moroka to RC, Mafeking, 28 June 1915; 50/551, Thaba

Nchu landowners' petition to Robertson 2 August 1915; Robertson to SNA, Pretoria, 3 August 1915; 50/558, Lack to Acting Assistant Commissioner, Francistown, 3 September 1915; RC, Mafeking, to High Commissioner, Pretoria, 9 September 1915.

21. BNA, S 10/3, Lack to E.O. Butler, Acting Assistant Commissioner, Francistown, 19 June 1916; S. Moroka to RC, Mafeking, 15 September 1916; Lack to [unknown] 4 January 1917 and reply 10 January 1917; Principal Medical Officer's report of visit to Matsiloje 15 April 1918.

22. BNA, S 10/3, Lack to Viscount Buxton, High Commissioner, Cape Town, 8 January 1918; minutes of meeting of the Moroka Land Settlement Advisory Committee, 17 April 1918; S 10/4/1, Statements taken at Moroka Stadt, October 1917; Butler to Acting Government Secretary, Mafeking, 1 November 1917; minutes of meeting of the Moroka Land Settlement Advisory Committee, 15 January 1918, and Butler's covering letter to Acting Government Secretary, Mafeking, 18 January 1918; Schapera, 1971: 227; Molema, 1951: 163. These experiences are reminiscent of the various land resettlement schemes initiated by the Griqua leader A.A.S. le Fleur in the same period. See Edgar and Saunders, 1982: 201–20.

23. Schapera, 1971: 226, 265; Molema, 1951: 163; BNA, RC 8/5, RC, Mafeking, to RM, Francistown, 9 February 1926; Assistant RC, Francistown, to Government Secretary, Mafeking, 12 July 1924, 13 October 1924, and 'attached notes' on the deputation's visit to Francistown on 15 April 1924 and the meeting at Matsiloje on 5 July 1924.

24. BNA, RC 8/5, Assistant RC, Francistown, to Government Secretary, Mafeking, 12 July 1924, and 'attached notes'; RM, Francistown, to Government Secretary, Mafeking, 16 March 1925; S. Moroka to RM, Francistown, 16 March 1925; RC, Mafeking, memo to Government Secretary 2 March 1928.

25. Schapera, 1971: 239–40; Molema, 1951: 163–5.

26. UG 19–1916, Schedule IV, pp. 37–40, and p. 45.

27. Lacey, 1981: 18–19.

28. UG 22–1918.

29. UG 22–1918, p. 6. For accounts of the Opperman family, see Ross, 1983: 91–5; and 'Frederick Opperman: Cape Slave', *Christian Express* July/August 1891, reprinted in Wilson and Perrot, 1973: 41–9.

30. UG 22–1918, pp. 4–7.

31. Davenport and Hunt, 1974: 37–8.

32. UG 22–1916, p. 20.

33. UG 19–1916, Appendix III, p. 8.

34. UG 22–1916, Appendix XI, p. 6.

35. UG 22-1916, p. 15.

36. Interview, Blanche Dinaane Tsimatsima, Thaba Nchu, 3 July 1986.

37. Plaatje, 1969: v, referring to UG 25–1916.

38. UG 25-1916, Annexure 2, p. 29. The farms only, not the owners, are identified in this list. The leases are recorded in SAB, NTS 3139, 21/306.

39. UG 22–1916, p. 48; Appendix X, Annexure 1.

40. UG 22–1916, pp. 23–6.

41. *ibid.*: 26.

42. For detailed accounts of the conflicts over Hertzog's 'four bills' of 1926, see Lacey, 1981; and Dubow, 1989, Chapters 5 and 6. The issues are briefly reviewed in Chapter 4 of this book.

43. SAB, NTS 1693, 24/276, enclosure with memo, R.S. Medford, Secretary NAC, to SNA 6 April 1922. See also UG 36-1923, p. 11.
44. SAB, NTS 1693, 24/276, Medford to SNA 6 April 1922.
45. *ibid.*, SNA to magistrate, Thaba Nchu, 5 June 1923.
46. Willan, 1984: 299.
47. Moroka Ward Land Relief Act, No. 28 of 1924.
48. Davenport and Hunt, 1974: 43; Dubow, 1989: 88–9.
49. The details of this arrangement are outlined in Chapter 5.
50. UNISA, NEC Oral Evidence, vol. 8, pp. 4896–7, 4921–3. Dr Moroka did not identify the properties or the individuals concerned in his evidence to the NEC. I have drawn upon the Thaba Nchu Land Registers in DRB to fill in these details.
51. For the methods used to trace the history of transmission of registered land titles, see Selected Sources (below), under the heading 'Deeds Registries'.
52. Crisp to his mother 13 August 1868, cited in Wales, 1985: 268. See also Molema, 1951: 34.
53. *Mochochonono* 9 April 1949. It is probable that Fenyang's mother, Elizabeth Nkhabele, was Molema's principal source on the story.
54. Wales, 1985: 290.
55. SAB, NTS 3139, 23/306 part I, Plaatje to Burton 8 November 1910; RM, Thaba Nchu, to Acting SNA 19 November 1910. See also Willan, 1984: 143–6.
56. VAB, MHG S4296, estate Ephraim Setlogelo.
57. *Setlogelo v. Setlogelo* (1914), OFS Appellate Division 121.
58. Plaatje, 1969: 112.
59. VAB, MHG S4296, estate Ephraim Setlogelo.
60. VAB, MHG 18886, estate Hessie Sealimo Setlogelo.
61. VAB, MHG 33806, estate Rebecca Ntsetsa Setlogelo.
62. SAB, NTS 3139 22/306, Petition to Governor General by Israel Setlogelo 8 July 1922, and subsequent correspondence.
63. SAB, NTS 3139, 20/306 part II.
64. Interview, Blanche Dinaane Tsimatsima, Thaba Nchu, 4 July 1986.
65. VAB, LTN 2/2 N2/7/3/47 parts I, III; MHG 34101, estate Izaak Setlogelo.
66. UNISA, NEC Oral Evidence, vol. 8, p. 4938.
67. UNISA, NEC Oral Evidence, vol. 8, pp. 4957–9. Van Riet did not identify his own or anyone else's property to the NEC. I have done so through persistent detective work in the DRB. I am very grateful to William Beinart for translation of Van Riet's and De Wet's evidence from Afrikaans.
68. *ibid.*: 4959–61.
69. *ibid.*: 4967.
70. *ibid.*: 4968–70.
71. UG 22–1932, p. 197.
72. Bradford, 1988: 60.
73. 'Mass Production of Potatoes', *Farming in South Africa*, June 1928, reprinted by Department of Agriculture, p. 2.
74. UNISA, NEC Oral Evidence, vol. 8, pp. 4971, 4882–3, 4918.
75. UG 22–1932, p. 179.
76. UNISA, NEC Oral Evidence, vol. 8, p. 4947.
77. *ibid.*: 4962–4.
78. VAB, AKT 2/1/145; UNISA, NEC Oral Evidence, vol. 8, pp. 4962–3; Plaatje, 1969: xix; UG 22-1916, p. 26; Willan, 1984: 143; VAB, MHG M3954, estate Phokoane Mokgobisi; VAB, MHG 22660, estate John Mokitlane Nyokong.
79. UNISA, NEC Oral Evidence, vol. 8, p. 4948.

80. UG 22–1932, p. 179; SAB, NTS 3154, 133/306, 'Landowners and members of the Barolong tribe' to E.G. Jansen, Minister of Native Affairs, 26 February 1930; SNA to NC, Thaba Nchu, 15 March 1930.
81. UNISA, NEC Oral Evidence, vol. 8, pp. 4929–30; SAB, NTS 3155, 143/306, report from the Director of Native Agriculture 11 December 1931; UNISA, AAS 162, 'Rights of residence on Native Reserves in Thaba Nchu District'; UG 25-1916, p. 28; UG 22-1918, p. 4; SAB, NTS 8141, 1/341 (1912–32), meeting of Thaba Nchu Reserve Board 16 August 1918.
82. SAB, NTS 3155, 143/306, report from the Director of Native Agriculture 11 December 1931; UNISA, AAS 162, 'Rights of residence on Native Reserves in Thaba Nchu District'.
83. UNISA, NEC Oral Evidence, vol. 8, p. 4900.
84. *ibid.*: 4899–902.

## 4 STRUGGLES OVER LAND

1. Lacey, 1981: 25, Table 1.1, cols. A and C.
2. Lacey, 1981: 385, Appendix A.4(a). The total given here of 79,500 morgen for the OFS is derived from the figures given in UG 22-1918, pp. 4–5, for the Thaba Nchu district, and Beaumont's figures for 'additional' Areas 17, 18 and 19, district of Thaba Nchu, UG 19-1916, Schedule IV, p. 40. The total includes the 'additional' farm Eerstesending, 500 morgen in extent and adjoining the Witzieshoek reserve (Beaumont's Area 1), whose incorporation was assumed without comment by the OFS Local Land Committee.
3. For the account that follows I have drawn mainly on Davenport, 1977, Chapter 11; Lacey, 1981, Chapter 2; and Dubow, 1989, Chapter 5.
4. UG 17–1927, pp. 10–13, and Annexure IV, pp. 50–87.
5. Dubow, 1989: 151.
6. *ibid.*: 145; Davenport and Hunt, 1974: 33.
7. Lacey, 1981; Dubow, 1989.
8. Lacey, 1981, especially Chapter 11.
9. Dubow, 1989: 172.
10. *ibid.*: Part III.
11. The Native Trust and Land Act, No. 18 of 1936.
12. Lacey, 1981: 25, Table 1.1, cols. A and C; and Appendix A.4(a), col. 3, p. 385. For argument on this point, see also pp. 22–35.
13. Compare UG 22–1918, p. 5, with the First Schedule, Part IV, to Act No. 18 of 1936.
14. UWL, AD843, B62.11. For evidence and interpretation of Rheinallt Jones' position in inter-war South African liberalism, see Rich, 1984, especially Chapter 4; and Rich, 1989; also Elphick, 1987.
15. UWL, AD843, B62.11, Edith Jones to Nehemiah Motshumi 2 September 1936, 10 June 1937; Jones (Mrs Rheinallt Jones), 1938: 3.
16. SAB, NTS 3159, 196/306 vol. I; VAB, LTN 2/2, N2/7/3/47 part I, NC, Thaba Nchu, to CNC, Northern Areas, 24 August 1937.
17. Rheinallt Jones' views on the land question were elaborated in a 'very valuable' paper presented to the European-Bantu Conference of the Federal Council of the Dutch Reformed Churches early in 1927, which formed the basis of evidence given to the Select Committee on the Native Bills in the same year. The liberal economic historian, W.M. Macmillan, also proposed a system of leasehold tenure for Africans in white areas. See 'The Land Question in South Africa', *The South African Outlook* 57, 1 March 1927, pp. 50–2; and Dubow, 1989: 157–8.

18. UWL, AD843, B62.11, Motshumi to Rheinallt Jones 15 July 1936; subsequent correspondence between Motshumi, Rheinallt Jones, Merafe and Musi, November 1936; Ralphe Bunche, South African Diary, entry for 14 November 1937.
19. SAB, NTS 3159, 196/306 vol. I, report of the NAC 20 February 1937.
20. *ibid.*; also A.E.M. Jansen, Secretary for Justice, to D.L. Smit, SNA, 30 March 1937.
21. UWL, AD843, B62.11, D.L. Smit, SNA, to Assistant Secretary, SAIRR, 2 April 1937.
22. UWL, AD843, B62.11, J.S. Moroka to Rheinallt Jones 5 August 1937; Howard Rogers for SNA to Rheinallt Jones 12 November 1937.
23. UWL, AD843, B62.11, Motshumi to Edith Jones 16 September 1937.
24. SAB, NTS 3159, 196/306 vol. I, W.A. Ross and J.M. De Wet to SNA 11 August 1938; G. Ingham to Minister of Native Affairs 14 July 1937; E.J. Heath to NC, Thaba Nchu, 3 September 1937; K. Salzmann to Minister of Native Affairs 23 September 1937.
25. Interviews, J.M. de Wet Van Riet, Ladybrand, 5 July 1986; Billy Morgan of Carnavon, Thaba Nchu, 6 September 1983.
26. SAB, NTS 3159, 196/306 vol. III, Statement by C.H. Morgan submitted to Prime Minister Hertzog, April 1937; NTS 3159, 196/306 vol. I, SNA to Morgan 9 March 1938.
27. SAB, NTS 3159, 196/306 vol. III, Statement by C.H. Morgan; MHG 31066, estate Charles Henry Morgan.
28. UNISA, NEC Oral Evidence, vol. 8, p. 4966. In this district, as in others, several attorneys had the reputation of having profited from sharp practice over land transactions and mortgage bonds. There is, however, little direct documentary evidence to support the presumption by both white and black inhabitants that they were 'crooks'. See Appendix for the experience of one Morolong landowner of a kind that must been very familiar to others. For a detailed account elsewhere of this 'ugly little legal sub-culture', which illustrates that 'the pen was as important an agent of dispossession as the sword', see Peires, 1987.
29. VAB, AKT 2/1/144–6, Thaba Nchu Land Registers; LTN 2/3, N2/7/3/57.
30. SAB, NTS 3151, 102/306, Fenyang to NC, Thaba Nchu, 13 November 1933; NTS 3159, 196/306 vol. I, Faustmann and Paver to SNA 19 April 1937; South African Association to Faustmann and Paver 18 August 1937.
31. VAB, LTN 2/3, N2/7/3/57; SAB, NTS 3165, 266/306 part I; NTS 3165, 266/306 part II, correspondence concerning Nyokong's loan from the Trust, 1941–9; DRM, Thaba Nchu Land Register; VAB, MHG 22660, estate John Mokitlane Nyokong; Rich, 1989: 187; interview, Elizabeth 'Mananga' Thubisi, Thaba Nchu, 29 August 1983.
32. VAB, LTN 2/3, N2/7/3/57, Agricultural Officer Swain to ANC, Thaba Nchu, 1 August 1939; SAB, NTS 3165, 266/306 part II; *Free State Advocate* 23 November 1940.
33. Jones, 1938: 51–2.
34. VAB, LTN 2/2, N2/7/3/47 part I, correspondence concerning Isaac Setlogelo's affairs, 1927 to 1937; Faustmann and Paver to NC, Thaba Nchu, 14 August 1937.
35. *ibid.*
36. UWL, AD843, B62.11, John Makgothi to Rheinallt Jones 15 and 27 December 1937.
37. UWL, AD843, B62.11, Smit to Rheinallt Jones 19 February 1938.
38. UWL, AD843, B62.11, Rheinallt Jones to SNA 26 January 1938.
39. For examples, see SAB, NTS 3154, 133/306, Acting NC, Thaba Nchu, to SNA 20

February 1934; VAB, LTN 2/2, N2/7/3/47 part I, NC, Thaba Nchu, to CNC, Northern Areas, 24 August 1937.

40. SAB, NTS 3159, 196/306 vol. III, Statement by C.H. Morgan.
41. UWL, AD843, B101.19, Motshumi to Rheinallt Jones 8 September 1938.
42. SAB, NTS 3159, 196/306 vol. I, CNC, Northern Areas, to SNA 5 March 1938.
43. Macmillan, 1930: 76. See also Bradford, 1988, Chapter 2; and, for an overview of South African agrarian history to the 1930s, the Introduction to Beinart, Delius and Trapido, 1986.
44. Act No. 25 of 1932. See Nicholson, 1977: 210.
45. For sources on and discussion of the intensification of mortgage indebtedness in agriculture through the early decades of the twentieth century, see Keegan, 1987, particularly Chapter 2; Bradford, 1988: 23–34, 287 n. 18; and Hall, 1923. On the importance of co-operative societies, see Morrell, 1986.
46. VAB, LTN 2/1, N1/16/5, BPA officers to magistrate, Thaba Nchu, 19 March 1928; J. Soldaat to magistrate 11 March 1929.
47. VAB, LTN 2/1, N1/16/5, Soldaat to SNA 6 March 1929; Soldaat to magistrate 2 July 1930; Women's Branch, BPA, to magistrate undated 1930.
48. UNISA, AAS 162, 'Rights of residence in Native Reserves in Thaba Nchu District'.
49. SAB, NTS 3155, 143/306, SNA to NC, Thaba Nchu, 8 January 1931; SNA to Mahabane 10 March 1930.
50. UNISA, NEC Oral Evidence, vol. 8, pp. 4925–38; UNISA, 338.968 SUP/199690, NEC Written Evidence, Orange Free State, Soldaat to Chairman NEC 20 February 1931; UG 22-1932, pp. 178–80.
51. UNISA, AAS 162, 'Report on the Thaba Nchu Chieftainship', March 1941.
52. Dubow, 1986: 230–4; Lacey, 1981: 107–11.
53. SAB, NTS 308, 4/54, magistrate to SNA 6 October 1926. According to Chief John Phetogane Moroka's obituary notice, in the *Free State Advocate* 28 December 1940, he had been employed for 'very many years of honest and devoted services' as a clerk by one of the Thaba Nchu 'law agents', J.H. Diepraem, who gave a floral tribute at his funeral. On Diepraem, see Appendix.
54. SAB, NTS 308, 4/54, NC, Thaba Nchu, to SNA 16 November 1929; SNA to NC, Thaba Nchu, 31 March 1930.
55. Interview, Moses Nkoane, Thaba Nchu, 11 July 1986.
56. Molema, 1951: 156.
57. Interview, Amos Tlale Matsheka and Solomon Ramolehe Ramagaga, Thaba Nchu, 26 August 1989.
58. VAB, LTN 2/1, N1/16/5, Matsheka to magistrate 28 November 1930; SAB, NTS 3154, 133/306, Bishop of Bloemfontein to Minister of Native Affairs 27 May 1931.
59. SAB, NTS 8141, 1/341 (1912–32), minutes of meetings of Thaba Nchu reserve board, 16 August 1918 and 18 March 1921.
60. SAB, NTS 3154, 133/306, 'Landowners and members of the Barolong tribe' to Minister of Native Affairs 26 February 1930, and accompanying memo by magistrate.
61. UWL, AD843, B62.11, Matsheka to SAIRR 15 February 1933; SAB, NTS 9495, 121/400, BPA to Bishop of Bloemfontein 15 February 1933.
62. VAB, LTN 2/1, N1/16/5, SNA to Secretary for External Affairs 7 August 1935; Chief John S. Moroka to ANC, Thaba Nchu, 9 December 1938; *Free State Advocate* 25 February, 22 April 1939.
63. SAB, NTS 3155, 143/306, CNC, Northern Areas, to SNA 20 October 1936.
64. VAB, LTN 2/1, N1/16/5, Exhibit 'O', BPA to NC, Thaba Nchu, 1 February 1940.

65. VAB, LTN 2/1, N1/16/5, Case No. 161 of 1940; 'Statement about the Pico held by the Barolong Progressive Association . . .', probably written by Fenyang, signed by councillors Bethuel Motuba and Lucas Lencoe, clerk to the magistrate's court Peter Malego Makgothi, interpreter Isaiah Tonya Makgothi, D. Tau and Timothy Tlhakung; Proceedings of an Enquiry, 29–30 October 1940; Removal Order, Governor-General to Matsheka 28 January 1941; SNA to Matsheka 4 November 1948; unreferenced press cutting, 5 July 1940; SAB, NTS 9495, 121/140, Criminal Record No. 131 of 1940.
66. VAB, LTN 2/1, N1/16/5, Exhibit 'B'.
67. VAB, LTN 2/1, N1/16/5, Rheinallt Jones to ANC, Thaba Nchu, 29 October 1940; Booysen to Rheinallt Jones 8 November 1940.
68. VAB, LTN 2/1, N1/16/5, Proceedings of an Enquiry, evidence of Daniel Ngakantsi 30 October 1940.
69. The phrase was suggested by a comparison with the 'defensive communalism' that characterised a popular movement in Herschel ten years earlier. See Beinart, 1987: 262.
70. SAB, NTS 9495, 121/400, Petition of the Barolong tribe; and see n. 60 above. Elisha Maimane Ramagaga signed both petitions and thus adopted what were already, by this time, implicitly contradictory positions.
71. Bradford, 1988: 14, 305 n. 64.
72. Interview, Amos Tlale Matsheka and Solomon Ramolehe Ramagaga, 26 August 1989.

## 5 THE MAKING OF A BANTUSTAN

1. Walker, 1948: 7–8; Desmond, 1971.
2. For general accounts of resistance to 'betterment' etc., see Hirson, 1976; Yawitch, 1981; Lodge, 1983, Chapter 11; and Chaskalson, 1987. For particular case studies see Hendricks, 1989; De Wet, 1989; and McAllister, 1989. The best firsthand accounts of resistance in the 1950s are Hooper, 1989; and Mbeki, 1984.
3. The central government's 'model' in respect of Bantustan constitutional development was the Transkei. See, particularly, Streek and Wicksteed, 1981; and Southall, 1982.
4. VAB, BOV 1/138, N2/11/2, 'Locations Reclamation Report', comments by the Controller of Native Settlements, the Director of Native Agriculture and the Senior Engineer, Pretoria, 14 November 1939, p. 4.
5. VAB, BOV 1/138, N2/11/2, 'Reclamation Survey: Thaba Nchu', forwarded to CNC, Pretoria, 30 March 1939, p. 1; CNC, Pretoria, to SNA 14 September 1939; 'Locations Reclamation Report', 14 November 1939, pp. 2–3; Acting SNA to CNC, Pretoria, 9 January 1940.
6. VAB, BOV 1/138, N2/11/2, 'Locations Reclamation Report', pp. 26–8. On the conditions of farm labour in the OFS at this time, see the *Report of the Native Farm Labour Committee 1937–9*; and SAIRR, 1939.
7. Yawitch, 1981: 9–11.
8. The above account is based on reports and correspondence in VAB, BOV 1/138, N2/11/2. For specific references see n. 5 above.
9. VAB, BOV 1/136, N2/7/2, Motshumi to NC, Thaba Nchu, 29 November 1938; ANC, Thaba Nchu, to CNC, Pretoria, 5 December 1938; UWL, AD843, B101.19, Motshumi to Rheinallt Jones 19 July 1939; Rheinallt Jones to Motshumi 12 August 1939.
10. VAB, BOV 1/136, N2/7/2, CNC, Pretoria, to SNA 7 March 1938; SNA to CNC, Pretoria, 8 November 1938.

11. SAB, NTS 8131, 362/340, telegraph Acting SNA to CNC, Pretoria, 6 February 1940, and subsequent correspondence; UWL, AD843, B101.19, Motshumi to Rheinallt Jones 27 February 1940; VAB, BOV 1/137, N2/10/2, Faustmann & Paver to magistrate, Thaba Nchu, 19 February 1940; telegraph NAD to NC, Thaba Nchu, 5 March 1940.
12. SAB, NTS 8131, 362/340, CNC, Pretoria, to SNA 4 April 1940.
13. SAB, NTS 8131, 362/340, ANC, Thaba Nchu, to CNC, Pretoria, 20 June 1940, enclosing letter from the African Farmers' Association 28 May 1940; UWL, AD843, B101.19, J. Makgothi to Rheinallt Jones 10 July 1940.
14. UWL, AD843, B62.11, Nehemiah Gabashane to Rheinallt Jones 23 November 1937, 25 January 1938, and accompanying correspondence. Nehemiah Gaba-shane's father was almost certainly Reverend Marcus Gabashane, a Wesleyan Methodist minister who was prominent in the establishment in South Africa of the African Methodist Episcopal Church in 1897. His connection with Chief Samuel Moroka, and the latter's connection with the AME Church, probably dated from 1897–8, when the AME Church was established at Khunwana (western Transvaal) in response to an invitation from the ageing Chief Moswete of the Ratlou Barolong. Samuel Moroka had sought temporary refuge at Khunwana between 1896 and 1898 (see Chapter 3); and in 1902 Marcus Gabashane was 'illegally solemnizing marriages' at Khunwana. In the eyes of the ORC authorities in 1904, therefore, it is probable that Nehemiah Gabashane was tainted by association both with Samuel Moroka's abortive effort to return to Thaba Nchu and with what was perceived as the political threat of independent Ethiopianism. See Skota, 1931: 21, 301–12, 337–44, 208–11, 213; and Campbell, 1990: 40–1, 49 n. 8.
15. UWL, AD843, B101.19, correspondence 1937–42 between E.A. Tsoai, Azael Tsoai, Rheinallt Jones and SNA.
16. VAB, BOV 1/138, N2/11/2, Acting SNA to CNC, Pretoria, 9 January 1940; CNC, Pretoria, to SNA 6 April 1940.
17. ibid.; SAB, NTS 8131, 362/340, Tables showing aggregated estimated crop yields and livestock holdings, 1941–2, for the various blocks of Trust-administered land in the district; ANC, Thaba Nchu, to SNA 7 September 1943.
18. SAB, NTS 8131, 362/340, ANC, Thaba Nchu, to SNA 17 December 1943.
19. SAB, NTS 3159, 196/306 vol. III, report of NAC to Minister of Native Affairs 22 May 1946, Annexure J; Town Clerk, Thaba Nchu, to Prime Minister Smuts 27 February 1941; SNA to magistrate, Thaba Nchu, 7 February 1945; Friend 23 April 1945.
20. SAB, NTS 3159, 196/306 vol. III, ANC, Thaba Nchu, to CNC, Pretoria, 8 April 1946; report of NAC to Minister of Native Affairs 22 May 1946, Annexure A. The ANC apparently omitted the two new northern settlements of Tiger River and Moroto from his aggregate figures.
21. SAB, NTS 3159, 196/306 vol. III, report of NAC 22 May 1946; ANC, Thaba Nchu, to SNA 24 June, 6 July 1946.
22. VAB, BOV 1/138, N2/11/2, G. Van der Merwe to CNC, Potchefstroom, 9 March 1948; Rehabilitation report, 1949.
23. VAB, BOV 1/138, N2/11/2, Rehabilitation report, 1949.
24. SAB, NTS 8131, 362/340, ANC, Thaba Nchu, to SNA 7 September 1942; NTS 7692, 387/332, 'Minutes of a meeting held at Petra Clinic, Seliba, on the 27th March 1956'; VAB, LTN 2/1, N1/1/5/6, ANC, Thaba Nchu, to SNA 9 October 1941; Setouto to magistrate, Thaba Nchu, 2 February 1942.
25. SAB, NTS 8131, 362/340, Pule to SNA 15 January 1945; Senior Agricultural

Officer, Thaba Nchu, to ANC, Thaba Nchu, 8 February 1945; ANC, Thaba Nchu, to SNA 12 February 1945.

26. VAB, BOV 1/129, N1/14/3/1, ANC, Thaba Nchu, to CNC, Pretoria, 22 August 1946; African National Congress officers, Seliba, to NC, Thaba Nchu, 12 August 1947; ANC, Thaba Nchu, to CNC, Potchefstroom, 3 July 1948.

27. VAB, BOV 1/140, N2/11/4 vol. II, A.S. Moroka and W.Z. Fenyang to ANC, Thaba Nchu, 31 October 1950; ANC, Thaba Nchu, to CNC, Potchefstroom, 8 November 1950; Fenyang to ANC, Thaba Nchu, 4 May 1951.

28. *Guardian* 11 January, 8 March 1951, for which references I am grateful to Baruch Hirson; Atwell Mopeli-Paulus manuscript, Part II, 'The Stubborn Ones', p. 208, which was kindly lent to me by Miriam Basner; SAB, NTS 7692, 387/332, W.G. Ballinger to SNA (Eiselen) 18 March 1953; ANC, Thaba Nchu, to CNC 7 May, 20 July 1953; SNA to Ballinger 15 September 1953; Ballinger to NC, Seliba, 8 December 1953.

29. VAB, BOV 1/129, N1/9/2, Israel Setlogelo to SNA 8 September 1956. On the Defiance Campaign of 1952, see Lodge, 1983, Chapter 2.

30. VAB, BOV 1/129, N1/9/2, NC, Thaba Nchu, to CNC, Potchefstroom, 1 February 1956. I am very grateful to Reinier Holst for translation from Afrikaans of material from the VAB, BOV files and the SAB, NTS files relating to 'betterment' planning and to unrest at Seliba in the 1950s and 1960s.

31. *ibid*.

32. SAB, NTS 7692, 387/332, NC, Thaba Nchu, to CNC, Potchefstroom, 24 February 1956.

33. *ibid*.

34. SAB, NTS 7692, 387/332, NC, Thaba Nchu, to SNA 17 March 1956.

35. SAB, NTS 7692, 387/332, 'Minutes of a meeting held at Petra Clinic, Seliba, on the 27th March 1956'.

36. *ibid*.

37. SAB, NTS 7692, 387/332, NC, Thaba Nchu, to CNC, Potchefstroom, 18 May, 28 May, 7 June, 2 July, 28 July, 15 December 1956; VAB, BOV 1/129, N1/9/2, NC, Thaba Nchu, to CNC, Potchefstroom, 14 October 1956.

38. Simkins, 1981.

39. Yawitch, 1981: 27–31; VAB, BOV 1/140, N2/11/6 part I, enclosure with NC, Thaba Nchu, to CNC, Bloemfontein, 18 March 1958.

40. VAB, BOV 1/139, N2/11/3(5), Herwinningsverslag: Seliba Gebied, Thaba Nchu, 22 May 1958.

41. *ibid*.

42. Simkins, 1981: 281–3; Yawitch, 1981: 28, 41–2.

43. VAB, BOV 1/139, N2/11/3, Chief Agricultural Officer, OFS, to CNC, Bloemfontein, 26 September 1958.

44. VAB, BOV 1/140, N2/11/6 part I, enclosure with NC, Thaba Nchu, to CNC, Bloemfontein, 18 March 1958.

45. This probability requires investigation through detailed oral interviews of the kind that I was unable to conduct in any Trust village. Largely through this technique, Peter Delius (1989) illustrated the importance of migrant worker linkages between the African National Congress and resistance to rural restructuring in Sekhukhuneland in the mid-1950s.

46. VAB, BOV 1/129, N1/9/2, 'Minutes of a meeting held in the office of the Bantu Affairs Commissioner, Thaba Nchu, on 26 January 1960'.

47. *ibid*.

48. VAB, BOV 1/140, N2/11/4 part III, Secretary, Barolong Regional (Tribal)

Authority, to BAC, Thaba Nchu, 13 November 1961; BOV 1/139, N2/11/3(5), BAC, Thaba Nchu, to CBAC, Bloemfontein, 24 May 1963.

49. VAB, BOV 1/140, N2/12/3(1), correspondence concerning the development of Selosesha, 1949–63.

50. VAB, BOV 1/139, N2/11/3(5), Anonymous to Secretary for Bantu Administration and Development 17 June 1965; letter from Isaiah Mihi 19 June 1967; BAC, Thaba Nchu, to CBAC, Bloemfontein, 18 July 1967; and following correspondence.

51. VAB, BOV 1/128, N1/2/2, BAC, Thaba Nchu, to CBAC, Bloemfontein, 23 November 1967, 16 January 1968; District Commandant, South African Police, Ladybrand, to CBAC, Bloemfontein, 28 December 1967; CBAC, Bloemfontein, to District Commandant, South African Police, Ladybrand, 30 January 1968.

52. Desmond, 1971: 209–10.

53. Desmond, 1971: 211.

54. VAB, BOV 1/127, N1/1/3/1, ANC, Thaba Nchu, to CNC, Potchefstroom, 17 September 1955.

55. UNISA, AAS 162, 'Report on the Thaba Nchu Chieftainship', March 1941.

56. *Friend* 25 February 1982, obituary Maria Moipone Moroka.

57. VAB, BOV 1/127, N1/1/3/1, ANC, Thaba Nchu, to CNC, Potchefstroom, 20 April 1955.

58. VAB, BOV 1/127, N1/1/3/1, ANC, Thaba Nchu, to CNC, Potchefstroom, 17 September 1955, 25 April 1956, 26 November 1956, 13 December 1956, 18 March 1957; Barolong Tribal Authority to ANC, Thaba Nchu, 3 May 1955; SNA to CNC, Potchefstroom, 24 November 1956.

59. VAB, BOV 1/127, N1/1/2, BAC, Thaba Nchu, to CBAC, Bloemfontein, 6 March, 3 November 1959, and related correspondence.

60. VAB, BOV 1/127, N1/1/3/1, Regional Authority to BAC, Thaba Nchu, 28 July 1960 and subsequent correspondence; Maria Moipone Moroka to BAC, Thaba Nchu, 6 December 1960, etc.

61. *Friend* 25 February 1982, obituary Maria Moipone Moroka; VAB, BOV 1/127, N1/1/2, Installation Programme 27 November 1964.

62. My account of this event is drawn from detailed notes taken by John Comaroff, who attended it, and who kindly made his notes available to me. Official correspondence on the planning of it may be found in VAB, BOV 1/129, N1/1/2.

63. VAB, BOV 1/127, N1/1/3/1, ANC, Thaba Nchu, to CNC, Potchefstroom, 20 April 1955.

64. Obituaries of Elizabeth Nkhabele Fenyang were published in the *Friend* 24 September 1947 and the *Free State Advocate* 4 October 1947, the latter written by her son, Israel Tlale Setlogelo.

65. VAB, BOV 1/129, N1/9/2, Israel Setlogelo to SNA 8 September 1956; NC, Thaba Nchu, to CNC, Potchefstroom, 14 October, 24 December 1956; MHG 534/58, estate Israel Tlale Setlogelo.

66. Willan, 1984: 9–17; notes of interview with Eric 'Boy' Mojanaga, Thaba Nchu, 2 June 1978, kindly made available to me by Andrew Reed; interview, Eric's widow Mmamojanaga Mojanaga, Homeward farm, 27 August 1989; DRV, Division of Mafeking Land Register. In fond recollection of the family farm, Ephraim Mojanaga called his first motor car 'Buccleugh' and his second 'Kabe'.

67. VAB, BOV 1/138, N2/10/3(25), Copy of Will of Joel David Goronyane; UWL, SAIRR-RJ (C3), file 'Request for Exchange farm Buccleuch (Mafeking District) 1940–42'.

68. MHG 2000/65, estate Ephraim Mabilo Mojanaga; interview, Mmamojanaga

Mojanaga, 27 August 1989; VAB, BOV 1/127, N1/1/3/1, BAC, Thaba Nchu, to CBAC, Bloemfontein, 7 December 1960.
69. Interview, Mmamojanaga Mojanaga, 27 August 1989.
70. VAB, MHG 21157, estate Maggie Moroka.
71. Walker, 1948: 117–28; Walshe, 1970: 281–6, 399–401; Karis and Carter, 1977: 421, 425; 'Moroka—the political years', *Friend* 22 January 1981.
72. *Friend* 22 January 1981; interviews, Dr James Moroka, Mafane farm, 16 August, 16 December 1981; Itumeleng Moroka, Thaba Nchu, 15 September 1991; family obituary notice at funeral, 16 November 1985.
73. VAB, DLS 7 A578, 'List of burghers'; ORC 46 (1901), Annexures A, B, C.
74. VAB, MHG K1489, estate Ketimetse; CO 882 617/1, Maggie Moroka's application for bond, 1909; CO 901 760/6–7, leases of undivided halves of farm Victoria; AKT 5/4/746, MB 13140.
75. VAB, MHG K1489, estate Ketimetse; AKT 2/1/145, Thaba Nchu Land Register, Middelerf 114, Bittervlei 115 and Walhoek 116; AKT 5/4/738, MB 12730; MB 19342.
76. VAB, MHG K1441, estate Hermanus Keikelame; MHG K1880, estate George Keikelame.
77. VAB, LTN 2/4, N2/7/3/77.
78. The land transactions of B.H. Keikelame and his brothers were traced through DRB, TDs 1888/32, 2729/34, 372/39, 893/39, 1079/39, 273/64; and DRM, Thaba Nchu Land Register, Rietfontein 119 and registered subdivisions.
79. Interview, Maria Keikelame, Thaba Nchu, 3 July 1986.
80. VAB, MHG 33806, estate Rebecca Ntsetsa Setlogelo.
81. M.J. Murray, 1989a: 109–10; DRB, MBs 5691/29, 4065/31, 4268/31, and TD 2610/35; interviews, Maria Keikelame, Thaba Nchu, 3 July 1986; Solomon Ramolehe Ramagaga and Amos Tlale Matsheka, Thaba Nchu, 26 August 1989.
82. MHG 702/63, estate Robert Frederick Setlogelo; VAB, BOV 1/137, N2/10/2, correspondence relating to possible sale of portions of Matlapaneng 455, 1959.
83. MHG 702/63, estate Robert Frederick Setlogelo; DRB, MB 3587/66.
84. Interviews, Cathy and Albert Mohale, Vrywoning farm, 24 August 1989; Clement Seape, Potsane farm, 3 September 1983.
85. *Golden City Press* 26 September 1982.
86. *Friend* 25 January 1982.
87. Interview, Seabata Mehlolo, Yoxford, 30 August 1983.
88. Interview, Selekisho Segoneco, Yoxford, 12 July 1986.
89. Sun International advertising leaflet.

## 6 RURAL SLUM: BOTSHABELO

1. Keenan, 1986: 362; C. Murray, 1987b; McCaul, 1987a; Sharp, 1987.
2. Figures adapted from Simkins, 1983: 53–7. See also Simkins' appendices, pp. 86–100, for discussion of the problems of comparison of census data from different years. For further analysis of the phenomenon of displaced urbanisation, see Hindson, 1987; C. Murray, 1987b; Mabin, 1989; and Sutcliffe, Todes and Walker, 1990.
3. J. Graaf, cited in Cobbett, 1986a: 121.
4. For details and analysis, see Platzky and Walker, 1985.
5. De Clerq, 1984: 272.
6. For a review of state housing policy, see Hendler, Mabin and Parnell, 1986.
7. SAIRR, *Survey 1986*, Part I (1987): 358–61; *Survey 1988/89* (1989): 188–90; *Survey 1989/90* (1990): 100. See also Hindson, 1987: 614–15.

8. SAIRR, *Survey 1984* (1985): 258–9; McCaul, 1987b.
9. Lelyveld, 1986: 122. The desperate half-life of KwaNdebele's commuters on the Putco buses is movingly described by Lelyveld, pp. 127–31 above, and by the photographer David Goldblatt in Badsha and Wilson, 1986.
10. In 1979 and for some years afterwards it was known as Onverwacht to its inhabitants, after one of the farms in a block compulsorily purchased from white owners by the government. Its official name of Botshabelo is intended to reflect its initial function as a place of refuge (*botshabelo*) for 'illegal squatters' in Thaba Nchu [see section on Kromdraai in this chapter]. The official name was only generally adopted later by the people who live there. Accordingly, I use both names in this chapter: Onverwacht, predominantly in reference to 1979 and the early 1980s; Botshabelo, predominantly in reference to the middle and late 1980s.
11. TRAC, 1988. See also Beinart, 1988.
12. For important debates on Zimbabwe in this respect, see Bush and Cliffe, 1984; Simon, 1985; and Potts and Mutambirwa, 1990.
13. Plaatje, 1969: 91.
14. Wells, 1980.
15. Wilson, 1972: 163.
16. Cobbett, 1987a: 34.
17. *Friend* 17 May 1979.
18. *Friend* 18 June 1981.
19. *Sunday Express* 21 September 1980, 9 November 1980.
20. Cobbett, 1987a: 37; NCAR, 1987: 18.
21. SPP Reports, 1983, Vol. I: 6.
22. Keenan and Sarakinsky, 1987: 581.
23. De Klerk, 1984; 1985: 18.
24. Sharp and Spiegel, 1990.
25. Cooper, 1988; De Klerk, 1990.
26. Central Statistical Services, Population Census 1970, report 02-05-10. Pretoria: Government Printer.
27. *Voice* 8 April 1978.
28. *ibid.*
29. *Rand Daily Mail* 2, 23, 30 October 1974.
30. *Friend* 25 September 1976.
31. BENBO, 1978: 22.
32. *Friend* 14 September 1976.
33. SAIRR, *Survey 1976* (1977): 254; *Survey 1979* (1980): 318. See also Streek and Wicksteed, 1981: 50–6.
34. Interview, Dr Mervyn Griffiths, Cape Town, 30 October 1985, kindly undertaken on my behalf by Andrew Spiegel. Dr Griffiths worked at the Moroka hospital, Thaba Nchu, from 1973 to 1984.
35. *Friend* 22 October 1976.
36. *Voice* 8 April 1978.
37. *Friend* 13 May 1978.
38. *World* 22 May 1977; *Friend* 19 September 1978.
39. Interview, Dr Mervyn Griffiths, 30 October 1985.
40. Interview, Mmaboraki Mmeko and others, Onverwacht, 16 May 1980.
41. Interview, Hanyane Rebecca Mofihli, Onverwacht, 16 May 1980.
42. Interview, Hanyane Rebecca Mofihli, Onverwacht, 13 June 1980.
43. *World* 22 May 1977.
44. *Star* 18 September 1980.

45. *Race Relations News 43*, 11 (December 1981), p. 4.
46. *Friend* 11 July 1980.
47. *Friend* 31 March 1981.
48. *Friend* 20 April 1981.
49. *Friend* 24 July 1981.
50. Interviews, Tozi Xaba and other members of the family, Onverwacht, various dates 1980.
51. Interviews, Motlatsi Ntomane and his wife, Onverwacht, various dates, 1980; Serialong Ntomane, Phuthaditjhaba, Qwaqwa, May/June 1980.
52. C. Murray, 1983b: 171–3.
53. Bureau of Market Research, 1985.
54. Interviews, Mmaboraki Mmeko and other members of the family, Onverwacht, various dates, 1980, 1981, 1983, 1986, 1989.
55. C. Murray, 1987b: 120–1; NCAR, 1987: 8.
56. NCAR, 1987: 8.
57. 'Place of Refuge', *SA Digest* 29 May 1987, p. 9.
58. For a critique of regional development, see Cobbett, Glaser, Hindson and Swilling, 1986.
59. See, particularly, Van Zeyl, 1985a, 1985b, 1986.
60. Cobbett, 1986b.
61. Cobbett, 1986b: 26.
62. For analysis of industrial decentralisation as one element of the strategy of regional development, see Cobbett, Glaser, Hindson and Swilling, 1986.
63. First Annual Report of the South African Development Trust Corporation (STK), 1985, p. 20; *SA Digest* 29 May 1987, p. 9.
64. Cobbett, 1987b.
65. Van Zeyl, 1985b.
66. Cobbett, Glaser, Hindson and Swilling, 1986; SAIRR, *Survey 1986* Part I (1987): 105–9; Grest, 1988.
67. SAIRR, *Survey 1986* Part I (1987): 344; Part II (1988): 603, 731. See also Budlender, 1986.
68. SAIRR, *Survey 1986* Part I (1987): 94–5; Keenan, 1988: 142–3.
69. NCAR, 1987: 33; undated police directive, May 1986; *Lengolo La Batswadi*, 12 July 1986; directive from N.P.J. Botha, Regional Director of Education and Training, 10 December 1986.
70. *Weekly Mail* 22 May 1987.
71. NCAR, 1987: 42–3.
72. Proc. R169 of 2 December 1987, *Government Gazette* 11051; *Weekly Mail* 22 January 1988; NCAR press releases, January 1988, 10 February 1988. The bill did not pass into law.
73. *Weekly Mail* 2 September 1988; SAIRR, *Survey 1988/89* (1989): 89. The case was Lefuo v. Staatspresident van die Republiek van Suid Afrika 1989 (3) SA 924 (O). See Plasket, 1990.
74. Southern Free State Council of Churches, 'Minutes of the workshop on the incorporation of Botshabelo into Qwaqwa held on the 15th April 1989 at Lefika Lutheran Church'; *Focus* No. 86, January–February 1990; *The Natal Witness* 3 March 1990.
75. Black Sash, 1988. See also O'Regan, 1990.
76. NCAR, 1987: 19.
77. *Weekly Mail* 16 November, 23 November 1990; NLC, 1990; Van Niekerk, 1990; Daphne, 1990.

7 TWO FARMS: ONE HUNDRED YEARS

1. Thaba Phatshwa, in Sesotho, refers to a mountain 'of a speckled character'. I use this form, in the modern South African orthography, to refer to the mountain, the Coloured village and more loosely the south-eastern corner of the Moroka territory. But the farm whose name derives from the mountain is formally recorded in DRB as Thaba Patchoa 106, and it generally appears in this form in written sources. I have retained this small distinction.

2. A similar orthographical problem arises. Ngoanyana is the Serolong equivalent of the Sesotho Ngoananyana (more commonly found, in this case, in the form prescribed by the old Lesotho orthography). The registration of the farm as Ngoanyana reflects the domination of Serolong political culture in the late nineteenth century. Most people who now live in the neighbourhood, who speak Sesotho, refer to the hill and its immediate environment, including the farm, as Ngoananyana. My usage of the two terms in this chapter consistently follows this small difference.

3. Pakenham, 1979, Chapter 41.

4. Arbousset and Daumas, 1968: 234–5.

5. *ibid*: 235, and map, p. 1.

6. CLHR, MS 15 620, Reports of the Thaba Nchu circuit, 1881, 1882, 1883; VAB, GS 1408, Barolong Census 1884.

7. VAB, GS 1409, Moroka Landhof Regter Gregorowski 1885; AKT 2/1/144, Thaba Nchu Land Register; Wales, 1985: 296.

8. CLHR, MS 15 620, Reports of the Thaba Nchu circuit, 1885, 1886; Wales, 1985: 296–7.

9. VAB, MHG M2073, estate Joseph Thoto Masisi; AKT 2/1/144–6, Thaba Nchu Land Registers, and supplementary information from DRB; CO 88 473/02, Makgothi to Hanger February 1902; Fuller, 1953: 152. For a brief account of Jeremiah Makgothi's life, see Kuzwayo, 1985: 59–61. The white children whom he taught included the daughter of J.M. De Wet, the then *landdrost*, and the younger children of the missionary John Daniel, one of whom—Pat O'Shaughnessy Daniel—she later married.

10. Interview, Blanche Tsimatsima, Thaba Nchu, 3 July 1986; VAB, MHG M433, estate Stephanus Koko Moroka.

11. VAB, MBs 16577/89, 18019/91, 18958/92; DRB, TDs 36831/89, 38082/90, 38087/90, 38253/90, 40673/91, 40674/91.

12. VAB, MHG M2073, estate Joseph Masisi; MBs 8749/05, 9982/06; DRB, TDs 14749–51/05.

13. Willan, 1984: 143; Odendaal, 1984: 109, 168, 178, 232–3, 235.

14. VAB, CO 669 2991/6, 901 760/4, applications for permission to lease portions of Thaba Patchoa; interview, Blanche Tsimatsima, 4 July 1986.

15. Kuzwayo, 1985: 56.

16. *ibid*.: 56, 68–9; interview, Blanche Tsimatsima, 4 July 1986.

17. Kuzwayo, 1985: 62–3.

18. VAB, AKT 31 D6/1/22(14), petition re estate of Jeremiah Makgothi; DRB, MB 2537/18.

19. VAB, AKT 31 D6/1/22(14).

20. DRB, TDs 3730–3740/24; MBs 3174/24, 3172/24, 3170/24, 3169/24.

21. Interview, Blanche Tsimatsima, 4 July 1986; Kuzwayo, 1985: 66.

22. Interview, Blanche Tsimatsima, 4 July 1986; Mancoe, 1934: 77–8.

23. Interview, Blanche Tsimatsima, 4 July 1986.

24. Interview, Blanche Tsimatsima, 4 July 1986; DRB, TDs 2981/30, 1304/32, 1418/32.
25. Interview, Blanche Tsimatsima, 4 July 1986; DRB, TDs 3738/24, 3076/29, 3077/29, 230/31, 1055/31, 875/32.
26. MHG 25135, estate Moses Masisi; DRB, TDs 2488/33, 2450/33, 400/36, 94/43.
27. *Free State Advocate* 15 January 1938.
28. Kuzwayo, 1985. The above account of Ellen Kuzwayo's career is largely drawn from this autobiographical source.
29. SAB, NTS 3159 196/306 vol. I, D.L. Smit to Controller of Native Settlements 9 March 1937.
30. Theal, 1919: 233–4. Sanders (1975: 285) identified the journal of an anonymous British officer in the Gubbins Library, Johannesburg (reference MS vol. A27), as 'the best account of this battle'.
31. This manuscript, headed 'Opskrif van die Bewoners van die Kaptein Carolus Baadjies', was kindly lent to me by John Weymers, Thaba Phatshwa. I am grateful to Joan McGregor for translation from Afrikaans.
32. Van Aswegen, 1971: 207, 212–4. I am grateful to Reinier Holst for translation from Afrikaans.
33. VAB, NAB 9, N108/06.
34. VAB, BOV 1/138, N2/11/2, 'Reclamation Survey: Thaba Nchu', March 1939; 'Locations Reclamation Report', 14 November 1939, pp. 20–3.
35. VAB, BOV 1/138, N2/11/2, ANC, Thaba Nchu, to CNC, Pretoria, 15 April, May 1940; interview, John Weymers, Thaba Phatshwa, 9 July 1986. I am grateful to John Parr, of Yaxham farm, for translation from Afrikaans.
36. SAB, TES 8745 f152/4/3, SNA to Secretary for Social Welfare 18 March 1944.
37. SAB, TES 8745 f152/4/3, Secretary for Social Welfare to Treasury 23 October 1951; NTS 3139, 19/306, explanatory memo 26 October 1953 on Proc. 239 of 1953; interview, John Weymers, 9 July 1986.
38. DRB, TD 8428/78; SAB, NTS 3139, 19/306, NC, Thaba Nchu, to CNC 1 October 1956; interviews, Lydia Masisi, Thaba Nchu, 20 December 1981, 4 July 1986; John Parr, Yaxham, 9 July 1986. The number of people removed from Sweet Home was officially recorded as 161: see *House of Assembly Debates*, Questions and Replies, 614, 619, 22 April 1980.
39. DRB, TDs 3574–5/74, 3580/78; interview, Blanche Tsimatsima, 4 July 1986.
40. Interview, John Weymers, 9 July 1986.
41. Interview, Roelf Van Wyk, Tshiamelo, 1 July 1986.
42. Keegan, 1986a: 207.
43. Marge Bairstow, letter to author, 2 April 1985.
44. VAB, DLS 4 A230, Purchase of Farms by Land Settlement Board.
45. VAB, DLS 4 A294, DLS 17 A1213, reports of Walter S. Cohen, 1902; DLS 117 A4340, memo Apthorp to Colonial Secretary 26 June 1906.
46. Interview, Lul Lurie (J.B. Lurie's elder son), Fortuinspruit, 4 September 1983.
47. I am grateful to Richard McPherson of Dawn, Tweespruit, for access to papers relating to his grandfather's will.
48. Interview, John Nieuwenhuysen, Daniel McPherson's grandson, London, 1 December 1983.
49. Interview, Mmadiphapang Thakho, Thaba Nchu, 14 July 1986.
50. Tucker and McGregor, 1961.
51. Interview, John Nieuwenhuysen, 1 December 1983.
52. *ibid*.
53. Hugh Macmillan (1991: 90) reviewed the circumstances which led 'the more

critical younger economists' including Nieuwenhuysen to leave South Africa in the early 1960s.

54. John Nieuwenhuysen, letter to author, 22 April 1987; *The Age*, Melbourne, 20 March 1986.
55. Interview, Mmadiphapang Thakho, Thaba Nchu, 14 July 1986.
56. *Commission of Enquiry into the European Occupancy of the Rural Areas*, 1959, from which the map was reproduced in Thompson and Wilson , 1971: 105.
57. Interview, John Nieuwenhuysen, 1 December 1983.
58. Papers in the possession of Richard McPherson relating to the administration of Daniel McPherson's estate.
59. Dickinson, 1978.
60. Interview, Mmadiphapang Thakho, Thaba Nchu, 14 July 1986.
61. *Sunday Tribune* 6 May 1979; *Friend* 14 May 1979; interview, Naas Du Plessis, Thaba Nchu, 9 July 1986.
62. DRB, MB 8011/80; interview, Naas Du Plessis, 9 July 1986.
63. Interview, Mmadiphapang Thakho, Onverwacht, 13 June 1980.
64. DRB, MB 6357/85.
65. Interview, Mmadiphapang Thakho, Onverwacht, 13 June 1980. The following account of the circumstances of this household through the 1980s is drawn from visits in June–July 1980, August–September 1983, June–July 1986 and August 1989.

CONCLUSION

1. Beinart, 1986: 265–9.
2. Such a tenuous equality was also characteristic of the share-cropping economy in other regions in the early part of the twentieth century. See Keegan, 1988; and Van Onselen, 1990.
3. Keegan, 1987, Chapter 6.
4. Kuzwayo, 1985: 56.
5. *Weekly Mail* 23 November 1990.
6. Bradford, 1990: 79.
7. *Weekly Mail* 30 November 1990.
8. Quoted in *Weekly Mail* 14 September 1990.
9. TRAC, 1988.
10. Cooper, 1990; 'Nationalise the laws not the land', *Weekly Mail* 14 September 1990; 'Reform and the tragic legacy of racial land laws', *Weekly Mail* 12 October 1990. See also Beinart, 1988.
11. Interviews, Stephen Matsididi, Mariasdal, 4 July 1986; Molefe Richard Kodisang, Rakhoi, 28 August 1989.
12. Interview, Thaba Nchu district manager, Agricor, 28 August 1989; Keenan and Sarakinsky, 1987.

APPENDIX

1. Braby's *ORC Directory* for 1908; *OFS Directory* for 1913, 1917, 1918; VAB, NAB 13, 2026/08, report of C. Berrange, Inspector of the Cape Mounted Police (CMP), Aliwal North, to the Commissioner of the CMP, Cape Town, 8 June 1908.
2. *Men of the Times*, pp. 543, 574–5; Braby's *ORC Directory* for 1908, p. 972.
3. VAB, AKT 2/1/144–5, Thaba Nchu Land Registers; AKT 2/1/23, Bloemfontein Land Register.
4. VAB, NAB 13, 2026/08, Statement of Masaele Ngakantsi, June 1908.

5. VAB, CO 951, 1385, correspondence 1908–9; AKT 5/4/741, MB 12,801; AKT 5/4/760, MB 13,783; UG 25–1916, Annexure 2.
6. Interview, Jean Baptiste Van Riet, Barolong farm, 20 August 1989; Van Riet, 1945: 37, 39; 'A Farm Labour System That Succeeds', *The South African Outlook*, 1 September 1953, pp. 136–7; 'The liberal farmer whose methods paid off', *Frontline*, December 1982/January 1983, pp. 35–6; Gittens, 1987: 42–4.
7. MHG 36230, estate John Henry Faustmann.

# SELECTED SOURCES

ARCHIVAL SOURCES

## Public Record Office, London (PRO)

Colonial Office (CO) series:
CO 224/4-33 Despatches, Offices and Individuals, Orange River Colony, 1901–10
CO 551/1-24 Despatches, Offices and Individuals, Orange Free State, 1910–11

## Orange Free State Archives Depot, Bloemfontein (VAB)

Government Secretary OFS (GS) series:
GS 1407 Moroka, 1884
GS 1408 Barolong Census, 1884
GS 1409 Moroka Landhof: Regter Gregorowski, 1885
GS 1410 Barolong Grondgebied: Aansprak Grondregte, 1885–6
GS 1411 Barolong Grondgebied: Lijst van Plaatsen en Eigenaren
*Bylae tot Volksraadsnotule* [Annexures to Minutes of the Volksraad] (VR) series:
VR 285 22–25 June 1885
Native Affairs Branch ORC (NAB) series: various files, 1905–8
Department of Land Settlement ORC (DLS) series: various files, 1901–8
Colonial Secretary ORC (CO) series: various files, 1902–10
*Aktes* [Deeds] (AKT) series:
AKT 2/1/144-6, Thaba Nchu Land Registers.
Mortgage Bonds (MBs) for the OFS Republic period and the ORC period are held in VAB in the AKT series. Surviving MBs for the period since 1910 are held in the Deeds Registry, Bloemfontein (DRB, see below).
*Landdrost* [magistrate] Thaba Nchu (LTN) series: various files, 1910s–1940s.
The most useful single file for my purposes was LTN 2/1, N1/16/5, relating to the Barolong Progressive Association in the late 1930s.
Master of the Supreme Court (MHG) series:
Estate records up to 1930 are held in VAB in the MHG series. From 1930 they are held in the office of the Master of the Supreme Court, elsewhere in Bloemfontein (MHG, see below). For example, estate papers relating to Ephraim Setlogelo, who died in 1918, are held in the Archives and referenced here VAB, MHG S4296; estate papers relating to John Henry Faustmann, who died in 1944, are held by the Master of the Supreme Court and referenced here MHG 36230.
Chief Bantu Affairs Commissioner OFS (BOV) series:
BOV 1/127-140 Bantu Affairs, Thaba Nchu, 1940s–1960s

## Central Archives Depot, Union Buildings, Pretoria (SAB)

Governor General (GG) series:
GG 1166, 50/543, 50/551, 50/552, 50/558 The exodus of Barolong from the OFS to the Tati district of Bechuanaland, 1916

Secretary for Finance (TES) series:

TES 8745 The relocation of the 'Coloured' community of Carolusrus (Bofulo) to Thaba Phatshwa, 1940–53

Secretary for Native Affairs (NTS) series: various files, 1910s–1960s.

The following files were particularly useful: NTS 308, 4/54; NTS 1693, 24/306; NTS 3139, 19/306; NTS 3139, 21/306; NTS 3154, 133/306; NTS 3158, 193/306; NTS 3159, 196/306; NTS 3165, 266/306; NTS 7692, 387/332; NTS 8131, 362/340; NTS 8141, 1/341.

## Botswana National Archives, Gaborone (BNA)

Resident Commissioner (RC) series:

RC 4/8 Correspondence from Tati Concessions Ltd. and minutes regarding settlement of Samuel Moroka, 1898–9

RC 8/5 Affairs of Moroka and followers, 1902–28

Secretary (S) series:

S 10/4/1 Moroka Land Settlement Scheme, 1915–18

S 10/3 Removal of Chief Moroka and followers to Tati district, 1915–18

## School of Oriental and African Studies, London (SOAS)

Archive of the Wesleyan Methodist Missionary Society (MMS):

MMS 326 South Africa, Missionary Correspondence, Bloemfontein District (1876–85), letters of John Daniel 1881–2

MMS 343-4 South Africa, Synod Minutes, Kimberley and Bloemfontein District, Thaba Nchu circuit reports 1879–83

## Rhodes House, Oxford: Archive of the United Society for the Propagation of the Gospel (USPG)

Original Letters Received (series D):

D65: 1883; D69: 1884

Missionary Reports (series E):

E32-44: 1877–89

## Cory Library for Historical Research, Grahamstown (CLHR)

MS 15 620 Wesleyan Methodist Missionary Society, Kimberley and Bloemfontein District, Thaba Nchu circuit reports 1880–1889

## University of the Witwatersrand Library, Johannesburg (UWL)

Records of the South African Institute of Race Relations (AD 843).

The following files were particularly useful:

AD 843, B62.11 Thaba Nchu 1931–8

AD 843, B101.19 Thaba Nchu 1937–42

[For the B series see Inventory 10, Records of the SAIRR Part I, 1981]

SAIRR-RJ (C3), Request for Exchange Farm Buccleugh (Mafeking District), 1940–2.

Documentation Centre for African Studies, University of South Africa (UNISA)

AAS 162  Land rights in the Thaba Nchu area [miscellaneous, 1833–1969, donor D.A. Kotze]

NEC Oral Evidence: Transcript of oral evidence given to the Native Economic Commission 1930–2 [for the Report of the Commission see UG 22–1932 below]. Volume 8, pp. 4867–4979, contains evidence given by witnesses from the Thaba Nchu district.

338.968 SUP/199690  Written Evidence, Orange Free State, given to the Native Economic Commission 1930–2

## UNPUBLISHED DIARIES

William Francis Gebhardt, Diary 1902–8, in possession of his grand-daughter, Ailsa Du Plessis of Bloemfontein.

Amy M. Wilson, South African Diary 1901–2, Royal Commonwealth Society Library, London, reference MSS 5V.

Frederick Nicholson, Diary 1903–6, in possession of his daughter Agnes Oats of Johannesburg.

Ralphe Bunche, South African Diary, late 1937, in possession of Bob Edgar of Howard University, Washington DC.

## OFFICIAL RECORDS

### Deeds Registries (DRB, DRM, DRV)

The history of the transmission of any original farm in the Orange Free State, and of its registered subdivisions, may be completely reconstructed through the records maintained by district in the Deeds Registry, Bloemfontein (DRB). In the basement are kept survey diagrams, filed by district, and transfer deeds (TDs) and mortgage bonds (MBs), filed by year of transaction. The TDs are an invaluable documentary source on testamentary dispositions, family disputes, the circumstances behind particular transactions, etc. Unfortunately, many cancelled MBs first registered in the period since 1910 were destroyed during the 1980s in order to rationalise storage space. MBs registered in the period of the OFS Republic and the Orange River Colony period are retained, however, in the basement of the OFS Archives Depot (VAB) [see VAB, AKT above]. I have used pertinent TDs and MBs to reconstruct the histories of particular farms, but most are not cited individually in the endnotes.

The pages in the Thaba Nchu Land Register relating to land enclosed within the (new) Thaba Nchu district were transferred from Bloemfontein to Bophuthatswana at 'independence' in December 1977. I have therefore drawn upon the Deeds Registry, Mmabatho (DRM), as a supplementary source on the history of some of these farms. Similarly, I have drawn upon the Deeds Registry, Vryburg (DRV), attached to the Department of Public Works and Land Affairs, for the early history of farms in the Mafeking Division of the northern Cape which were bought by some of the senior Barolong exiles from Thaba Nchu in the late 1880s and early 1890s (see Chapter 1).

### Master of the High Court (MHG)

Estate papers in respect of property-owning individuals who died in the OFS in the period since 1930 are held in the office of the Master of the High Court, Bloemfontein (MHG). [See VAB, MHG above for estates of people who died before 1930 or in that year].

## PUBLISHED GOVERNMENT PAPERS

### Orange Free State

*Notulen der Verrichtingen van den Hoogedelen Volksraad* [Minutes of the Volksraad, annual], 1884–5, 1887

### British Parliamentary Papers (BPP)

C. 4263 (December 1884), C. 4589 (August 1885), *Further Correspondence respecting the Cape Colony and Adjacent Territories.*

C. 4889 (1886), *Report of the Commissioners appointed to determine land claims and to effect a land settlement in British Bechuanaland.*

C. 5363 (April 1888), *Further Correspondence respecting the Affairs of British Bechuanaland and Adjacent Territories.*

Cd. 626 (June 1901), *Report of the Land Settlement Commission, South Africa, November 1900*; Cd. 627, *Documents, Evidence, etc.*

Cd. 1163 (July 1902), *Further Correspondence relating to Affairs in South Africa.*

### Orange River Colony

ORC 46 (1901), *Report of a Commission of Enquiry into the leasing of government farms and the conditions of land tenure in the district of Moroka (now Thaba Nchu)*, with Annexures A to Z.

ORC 191 (1903), *Agreement between Colonel T.A. Hill and the Crown Agents, London, relating to the purchase of lands in the ORC.*

ORC 192–4 (1903–5), *Lists of farms administered by the Land Settlement Department, ORC.*

### South Africa

SANAC, South African Native Affairs Commission 1903–5, Volume IV, *Minutes of Evidence taken in . . . ORC . . .*, (Cape Town, 1904).

UG 19–1916 *Report of the Natives Land Commission.*

UG 22–1916 Natives Land Commission, *Evidence.*

UG 25–1916 *Minute addressed to the Honourable the Minister of Native Affairs by the Honourable Sir W.H. Beaumont (Chairman of the Natives Land Commission).*

UG 22–1918 *Report of the Orange Free State Local Natives Land Committee.*

*Reports of the Native Affairs Commission:* UG 15–1922 (1921); UG 36–1923 (1922); UG 47–1923 (1923); UG 40–1925 (1924); UG 17–1927 (1925–6); UG 48–1937 (1936); UG 54–1939 (1937–8).

UG 22–1932 *Report of the Native Economic Commission 1930–32.*

*Report of the Native Farm Labour Committee, 1937–9.* Pretoria, 1939.

*Report of the Commission of Inquiry into European Occupancy of the Rural Areas* [the Du Toit Commission]. Pretoria, 1959–60.

*House of Assembly Debates*, 1980.

## NEWSPAPERS AND PERIODICALS

*The Net Cast Into Many Waters*
*Mission Field*
*The African Review*
*Christian Express / South African Outlook*
*Mochochonono / Free State Advocate*
*Farming in South Africa*

*Race Relations* / *Race Relations News*
*Friend* (Bloemfontein)
*Guardian*
*Times* (London)
*Farmer's Weekly*
*South African Advertising and Selling*
*Frontline*
*SA Digest*
*Focus*
*Golden City Press*
*Weekly Mail*
*Sunday Express*
*Sunday Tribune*
*Voice*
*Rand Daily Mail*
*World*
*Star*
*Natal Witness*
*The Age* (Melbourne)
*New Ground*

ILLUSTRATIONS

Figures (Maps)

Figures I.1, 1.3, 3.1, 4.1, 5.1 and 6.2 were drawn from the South Africa 1:250,000 topo-cadastral series, sheets 2826 WINBURG and 2926 BLOEMFONTEIN (1958 edition). The farm boundaries in 1886 [Figure 1.3], the year most land grants were made by the OFS government, were reconstructed on the basis of the original survey diagrams for Thaba Nchu in the DRB basement. African-owned land in 1913 [Figure 3.1] was identified as 'additional' land in UG 19–1916, Schedule IV, which source was checked through VAB, AKT 2/1/144-6. The Released Areas [Figure 4.1] were defined in Part IV of the First Schedule to the Native Trust and Land Act, No. 18 of 1936. Revisions to the boundaries of the Released Areas were traced through correspondence and reports in SAB, NTS 3159, 196/306. Purchases of land by the South African Native Trust [Figure 5.1], with the dates of each transaction, were derived from a 'List of titles transferred to Bophuthatswana' in December 1977, at the time of 'independence'. This list is held in DRB, Thaba Nchu Land Register. Land still owned by Africans within the (new) Thaba Nchu district in 1977 [Figure 6.2] was identified by reference to the same list. The modern boundaries between registered subdivisions of privately-owned land were clarified by reference to the 1:25,000 compilation plans (FP series) held in the office of the Surveyor General, Bloemfontein. The sites of Trust villages and of the three Bultfonteins were drawn from the 1977-9 edition of the 1:250,000 topo-cadastral sheets above.

Figures 1.1 and 6.1 were drawn from the 1:2,500,000 map, 'Southern Africa— Political' (Buckley Map Productions, reference 6745/E/78/C, c. 1978). Information on 19th century sites and political boundaries [Figure 1.1] was derived from the maps in Breutz (1989) and from the 1:2,530,000 Map of South Africa incorporated with Amery, Vol. I, 1900, the earliest reasonably accurate map of the region that I was able to trace. It should be noted that the boundaries of Bophuthatswana shown in Figure 6.2 are not definitively accurate for any one point in time. Rather, they reflect the officially-projected outcomes of a series of proposals for land consolidation, integration and exclusion that were implemented, to a greater or lesser extent, in the 1970s and 1980s.

Figures 3.3 and 7.2 were drawn from the South Africa 1:50,000 topographical series, sheets 2926 BB Thaba Nchu (1982), 2927 AA Tweespruit (1984) and 2927 AC Thaba Phatshwa (1982). Figures 7.3 and 7.4 were drawn from the Africa 1:125,000 GSGS 2230 topographical series, Thaba Nchu, sheet South H-35/I-II, and Ladybrand, sheet South H-35/J-I & II (1913).

Figure 6.4 was drawn from an official plan of Botshabelo, with reference to a set of aerial photographs of Botshabelo taken in July 1987 by Stamway Edwards and Associates, of Pretoria, for the Department of Development Aid. It was not drawn from the *Meesterplan* of 1985 (see p. 237).

## Figures (Genealogies)

Figure 1.2 [the Moroka genealogy] is derived mainly from Molema's (1951) biography of Chief Moroka, but supplemented and in some points qualified by unpublished notes kindly lent to me by Paul-Lenert Breutz. Breutz was a government ethnologist from 1948 to 1977, primarily responsible for Tswana-speaking areas of South Africa. Breutz's notes, in turn, were based to a large extent on genealogical information compiled by N.J. van Warmelo, another government ethnologist, at the time of the 1941 enquiry into succession to the Thaba Nchu chieftainship (see Notes to Chapter 5, n. 55). It is clear that for this purpose, as for others, both van Warmelo and Breutz relied heavily on W.Z. Fenyang, whose mother Elizabeth Nkhabele Fenyang was one of Molema's prime informants.

The main sources for Figures 1.3, 1.4 and 1.5 are VAB, AKT 2/1/144, and VAB, GS 1409, supplemented by genealogical information from Molema (1951) and Breutz (as above), and other detail from VAB, ORC 46 (1901).

Figures 3.2 [the Setlogelo genealogy] and 7.1 [the Makgothi/Masisi genealogy] are based primarily on the evidence of attachments to TDs and MBs relating to the farms Moroto 68, Somerset 55 and Thaba Patchoa 106, and their respective subdivisions. These records are held in DRB.

Figure 5.2 [the Barolong elite] is drawn largely from Figures 1.2, 3.2 and 7.1, supplemented by oral information from members of the families concerned. Figure 7.5 [the McPherson genealogy] is drawn from interviews with various members of the McPherson family and from papers relating to Daniel McPherson's will in the possession of his grandson, Richard McPherson.

Figures 6.3 [Mmaboraki Mmeko] and 7.6 [Mmadiphapang Thakho] are drawn from my field notes through the 1980s.

## Photographs

1. Kirby, 1940.
2. Backhouse, 1844, p. 411, reproduced in Collins, 1965, p. 171, from which source this photograph was taken.
3. Molema, 1951: 157.
4. *Free State Advocate* 11 November 1939.
5. Plaatje, 1916 (courtesy of Brian Willan).
6. Kuzwayo, 1985: 106.
9. Original in possession of Evelyn Langbridge.
10. Original in possession of Richard McPherson.
11. *Men of the Times*, p. 543.
12. Original in possession of Jean Baptiste Van Riet.
13. Original in possession of P-L. Breutz.

14. Original in possession of J. S. Moroka's widow.
15. From aerial photograph 11/4637, Job No. 749, 20 March 1975, Director-General of Surveys, Mowbray, Cape.
16. From a set of aerial photographs of Botshabelo taken in July 1987 by Stamway Edwards and Associates, of Pretoria, for the Department of Development Aid.
Other photographs were taken by the author.

BOOKS, ARTICLES AND UNPUBLISHED THESES

Amery, L.S. (gen. ed.), *The Times History of the War in South Africa 1899–1902*. Volumes I, 1900; IV, 1906; and V, 1907. London: Sampson Low, Marston & Co.

Arbousset, T. and Daumas, F., 1968. *Narrative of an Exploratory Tour to the North-East of the Colony of the Cape of Good Hope*. Cape Town: Struik [facsimile reprint of the 1846 edition].

Backhouse, J., 1844. *A Narrative of a Visit to the Mauritius and South Africa*. London: Hamilton, Adams & Co.

Badsha, O. and Wilson, F. (eds.), 1986. *South Africa: The Cordoned Heart*. Cape Town: Gallery Press.

Baumann, G. with Bright, E., 1940. *The Lost Republic*. London: Faber and Faber.

Beak, G.B., 1906. *The Aftermath of War: An Account of the Repatriation of Boers and Natives in the Orange River Colony 1902–1904*. London: Edward Arnold.

Beinart, W., 1986. 'Settler accumulation in East Griqualand from the demise of the Griqua to the Natives Land Act', in Beinart, Delius and Trapido, 1986, pp. 259–310.

Beinart, W., 1987. '*Amafelandawonye* (the Die-hards): popular protest and women's movements in Herschel district in the 1920s', in W. Beinart and C. Bundy, *Hidden Struggles in Rural South Africa: Politics and Popular Movements in the Transkei and Eastern Cape 1890–1930*, pp. 222–69. London: James Currey; Berkeley and Los Angeles: University of California Press; Johannesburg: Ravan Press.

Beinart, W., 1988. 'Agrarian historiography and agrarian reconstruction', in J. Lonsdale (ed.), *South Africa in Question*, pp. 134–53. Cambridge: Cambridge University Press in association with the Centre for African Studies, Cambridge.

Beinart, W., Delius, P. and Trapido, S. (eds.), 1986. *Putting a Plough to the Ground: Accumulation and Dispossession in Rural South Africa 1850–1930*. Johannesburg: Ravan Press.

BENBO, 1978. *Qwaqwa ekonomiese-economic revue*. Pretoria: Bureau for Economic Research, Bantu Development.

Black Sash, 1988. 'Of squatters, slums, group areas and homelessness', Johannesburg: Black Sash.

Boon, M.J., 1885. *The History of the Orange Free State*. London: William Reeves.

Braby's *Orange River Colony Directory* for 1908; *Orange Free State Directory* for 1913, 1917, 1918. Bloemfontein.

Bradford, H., 1988. *A Taste of Freedom: The ICU in Rural South Africa, 1924–1930*. Johannesburg: Ravan Press.

Bradford, H., 1990. 'Highways, byways and culs-de-sacs: the transition to agrarian capitalism in revisionist South African history', *Radical History Review* 46 (7): 59–88.

Breutz, P-L., 1989. *A History of the Batswana*. Margate (Natal).

Budlender, G., 1986. 'Influx control in the Western Cape: from pass laws to passports', *South African Labour Bulletin* 11 (8): 34–41.

Bureau of Market Research, 1985. 'Income and expenditure patterns of households in Botshabelo, 1984', Research Report No. 121. Pretoria: University of South Africa.

Burman, S., 1981. *Chiefdom Politics and Alien Law*. London: Macmillan.

Bush, R. and Cliffe, L., 1984. 'Agrarian policy in migrant labour societies: reform or transformation in Zimbabwe?', *Review of African Political Economy* 29: 77–94.

Campbell, J., 1990. 'Chiefly authority and the AME Church, 1896–1910', *Collected Seminar Papers* 38, pp. 40–50. London University: Institute of Commonwealth Studies.

Chaskalson, M., 1987. 'Rural resistance in the 1940s and 1950s', *Africa Perspective* New Series 1 (5 & 6): 47–59.

Churchill, W.S., 1900. *Ian Hamilton's March*. London: Longmans, Green & Co.

Cobbett, W., 1986a. '"Orderly urbanisation": continuity and change in influx control', *South African Labour Bulletin* 11 (8): 106–21.

Cobbett, W., 1986b. 'A test case for "planned urbanisation"', *Work in Progress* 42: 25–30.

Cobbett, W., 1987a (with Brian Nakedi). 'Behind the "curtain" at Botshabelo: redefining the urban labour market in South Africa', *Review of African Political Economy* 40: 32–46.

Cobbett, W., 1987b. 'Industrial decentralisation and exploitation: the case of Botshabelo', *South African Labour Bulletin* 12 (3): 95–109.

Cobbett, W., Glaser, D., Hindson, D. and Swilling, M., 1986. 'South Africa's regional political economy: a critical analysis of reform strategy in the 1980s', in South African Research Service (eds.), *South African Review* 3, pp. 137–68. Johannesburg: Ravan Press.

Collins, W.W., 1965. *Free Statia: Reminiscences of a Lifetime in the Orange Free State*. Cape Town: Struik [copy of the original 1907 edition published in Bloemfontein].

Comaroff, Jean, 1985. *Body of Power, Spirit of Resistance: The Culture and History of a South African People*. Chicago and London: Chicago University Press.

Comaroff, John, 1982. 'Dialectical systems, history and anthropology: units of study and questions of theory', *Journal of Southern African Studies* 8 (2): 143–72.

Cooper, D., 1988. 'Ownership and control of agriculture in South Africa', in J. Suckling and L. White (eds.), *After Apartheid: Renewal of the South African Economy*, pp. 47–65. London: James Currey.

Cooper, D., 1990. 'Claiming the land', *New Ground* 1 (1): 3–5.

Daphne, P., 1990. 'The last outpost of grand apartheid', *New Ground* 1 (1): 12–14.

Davenport, T.R.H., 1977. *A Modern History of South Africa*. London: Macmillan.

Davenport, T.R.H. and Hunt, K.S. (eds.), 1974. *The Right to the Land*. Cape Town: David Philip.

De Clerq, F., 1984. 'Some recent trends in Bophuthatswana: commuters and restructuring in education', in South African Research Service (ed.), *South African Review* II, pp. 271–83. Johannesburg: Ravan Press.

De Klerk, M., 1984. 'Seasons that will never return: the impact of farm mechanisation on employment, incomes and population distribution in the western Transvaal', *Journal of Southern African Studies* 11 (1): 84–105.

De Klerk, M., 1985. 'The labour process in agriculture: changes in maize farming in South Africa during the 1970s', *Social Dynamics* 11 (1): 7–31.

De Klerk, M., 1990. 'The accumulation crisis in agriculture', paper presented at the Johannesburg History Workshop on Structure and Experience in the Making of Apartheid, 6–10 February.

Delius, P., 1983. *The Land Belongs to Us*. Johannesburg: Ravan Press.

Delius, P., 1986. 'Abel Erasmus: power and profit in the Eastern Transvaal', in Beinart, Delius and Trapido, 1986, pp. 176–217.

Delius, P., 1989. 'Sebatakgomo: migrant organization, the ANC and the Sekhukhuneland revolt', *Journal of Southern African Studies* 15 (4): 581–615.

Desmond, C., 1971. *The Discarded People: An Account of African Resettlement in South Africa*. London: Penguin Books.

De Wet, C., 1989. 'Betterment planning in a rural village in Keiskammahoek, Ciskei', *Journal of Southern African Studies* 15 (2): 326–45.

Dickinson, E.B., 1978. 'Wheat development in the Orange Free State: some recollections', *Fertilizer Society of South Africa* 2: 73–8.

*Dictionary of South African Biography*, Volume I, 1968. Pretoria: National Council for Social Research.

Doke, C.M., 1967. *The Southern Bantu Languages*. London: Dawsons.

Dubow, S., 1986. 'Holding "a just balance between white and black": the Native Affairs Department in South Africa c.1920–33', *Journal of Southern African Studies* 12 (2): 217–39.

Dubow, S., 1989. *Racial Segregation and the Origins of Apartheid in South Africa, 1919–36*. London: Macmillan.

Edgar, R. and Saunders, C., 1982. 'A.A.S. le Fleur and the Griqua trek of 1917: segregation, self-help, and ethnic identity', *International Journal of African Historical Studies* 15 (2): 201–20.

Edwards, J., 1988. *Fifty Years of Mission Life in South Africa, 1832–1882*. Graaff-Reinet: John Edwards Memorial Committee [reprinted from the second edition, 1886].

Elphick, R., 1987. 'Mission Christianity and interwar liberalism', in J. Butler, R. Elphick and D. Welsh (eds.), *Democratic Liberalism in South Africa: Its History and Impact*, pp. 64–80. Connecticut: Wesleyan University Press.

Flemming, L., 1910. *A Settler's Scribblings in South Africa*. London: Stephen T. Green.

Flemming, L., 1916. *A Fool on the Veld*. Cape Town: Argus Co.

Flemming, L., 1924. *The Call of the Veld*. London: Hutchinson & Co.

Froude, J.A., 1883. 'Leaves from a South African journal', in *Short Stories on Great Subjects*, Third Series. London: Longmans, Green & Co.

Fuller, B., 1953. *Call Back Yesterday*. Cape Town and Pretoria: J.H. de Bussy.

Gittens, C., 1987. 'What labour problems?', *Farmer's Weekly* 5 June, pp. 42–4.

Greig, Doreen E., 1970. *Herbert Baker in South Africa*. Cape Town: Purnell.

Grest, J. 1988. 'The crisis of local government in South Africa', in P. Frankel, N. Pines and M. Swilling (eds.), *State, Resistance and Change in South Africa*, pp. 101–9. London: Croom Helm.

Guy, J., 1979. *The Destruction of the Zulu Kingdom*. London: Longman.

Hall, C., 1923. 'An analysis of the sources of agricultural credit in S.A.', *Journal of the Institute of Bankers in South Africa* XIX (February): 494–502; (March): 553–60.

Hendler, P., Mabin, A. and Parnell, S., 1986. 'Rethinking housing questions in South Africa', in South African Research Service (eds.), *South African Review* 3, pp. 195–207. Johannesburg: Ravan Press.

Hendricks, F., 1989. 'Loose planning and rapid resettlement: the politics of conservation and control in Transkei, South Africa, 1950–1970', *Journal of Southern African Studies* 15 (2): 306–25.

Hindson, D., 1987. 'Alternative urbanisation strategies in South Africa: a critical evaluation', *Third World Quarterly* 9 (2): 583–621.

Hirson, B., 1976. 'Rural revolts in South Africa, 1937–1951', *Collected Seminar Papers* 22, pp. 115–32. London University: Institute of Commonwealth Studies.

Hooper, C., 1989. *Brief Authority*. Cape Town: David Philip [originally published London: Collins, 1960].

Hutchinson, G.T., 1905. *From the Cape to the Zambezi*. London: John Murray.

Hyam, R., 1968. *Elgin and Churchill at the Colonial Office 1905–1908*. London: Macmillan.

Jones, E. (Mrs Rheinallt Jones), 1938. 'Some considerations which arise from the administration of the Native Trust and Land Act, 1936', *Race Relations* 5 (August): 51–60.

Karis, T. and Carter, G.M., 1977. *From Protest to Challenge: A Documentary History of African Politics in South Africa, 1882–1964*, Volume 4: Political Profiles. Stanford: Hoover Institution Press.

Keegan, T., 1986a. 'Trade, accumulation and impoverishment: mercantile capital and the economic transformation of Lesotho and the conquered territory, 1870–1920', *Journal of Southern African Studies* 12 (2): 196–216.

Keegan, T., 1986b. 'White settlement and black subjugation on the South African highveld: the Tlokoa heartland in the north eastern Orange Free State, ca.1850–1914', in Beinart, Delius and Trapido, 1986, pp. 218–58.

Keegan, T., 1987. *Rural Transformations in Industrializing South Africa: The Southern Highveld to 1914*. London: Macmillan; Johannesburg: Ravan Press.

Keegan, T., 1988. *Facing the Storm: Portraits of Black Lives in Rural South Africa*. Cape Town: David Philip.

Keegan, T., 1989a. 'Mike Morris and the social historians: a response and a critique', *Africa Perspective* New Series 1 (7 & 8): 1–14.

Keegan, T., 1989b. 'The origins of agrarian capitalism in South Africa: a reply', *Journal of Southern African Studies* 15 (4): 666–84.

Keegan, T., 1990. 'Primitive accumulation and class formation in the making of agrarian capitalism in South Africa', *Collected Seminar Papers* 40, pp. 198–211. London University: Institute of Commonwealth Studies.

Keenan, J., 1986. 'Pandora's box: the private accounts of a Bantustan community authority', in South African Research Service (eds.), *South African Review* 3, pp. 361–71. Johannesburg: Ravan Press.

Keenan, J., 1988. 'Counter-revolution as reform: struggle in the Bantustans', in W. Cobbett and R. Cohen (eds.), *Popular Struggles in South Africa*, pp. 136–54. London: James Currey.

Keenan, J. and Sarakinsky, M., 1987. 'Reaping the benefits: working conditions in agriculture and the Bantustans', in G. Moss and I. Obery (eds.), *South African Review* 4, pp. 581–99.

Kimble, J., 1982. 'Labour migration in Basutoland, c. 1870–1885', in S. Marks and R. Rathbone (eds.), *Industrialisation and Social Change in South Africa: African Class Formation, Culture and Consciousness 1870–1930*, pp. 119–41. London: Longman.

Kirby, P.R. (ed.), 1940. *The Diary of Dr Andrew Smith*, director of the 'Expedition for Exploring Central Africa', 1834–1836, Volume I. Cape Town: The Van Riebeeck Society.

Knight, E.F., 1903. *South Africa After the War: A Narrative of Recent Travel*. London: Longmans, Green & Co.

Kuzwayo, E., 1985. *Call Me Woman*. London: The Women's Press.

Lacey, M., 1981. *Working for Boroko: The Origins of a Coercive Labour System in South Africa*. Johannesburg: Ravan Press.

Lelyveld, J., 1986. *Move Your Shadow: South Africa Black and White*. London: Michael Joseph.

Lodge, T., 1983. *Black Politics in South Africa since 1945*. London: Longman.

McAllister, P.A., 1989. 'Resistance to "betterment" in the Transkei: a case study from Willowvale district', *Journal of Southern African Studies* 15 (2): 346–68.

McCaul, C., 1987a. *KwaNdebele*. Johannesburg: South African Institute of Race Relations.

McCaul, C., 1987b. 'Crisis and restructuring in the passenger transport sector', in G. Moss and I. Obery (eds.), *South African Review* 4, pp. 433–50.

Mabin, A., 1989. 'Struggle for the city: urbanisation and political strategies of the South African state', *Social Dynamics* 15 (1): 1–28.

Macmillan, H., 1991. 'Economists, apartheid and the "common society"', *Social Dynamics* 17 (1): 78–100.

Macmillan, W.M., 1930. *Complex South Africa*. London: Faber & Faber.

Mancoe, J., 1934. *First Edition of the Bloemfontein Bantu and Coloured People's Directory*. Bloemfontein: A.C. White.

Marks, S., 1985. 'Southern Africa, 1867–1886', in R. Oliver and G.N. Sanderson (eds.), *The Cambridge History of Africa*, Volume 6: From 1870 to 1905, pp. 359–421. Cambridge: Cambridge University Press.

Marks, S. and Trapido, S., 1979. 'Lord Milner and the South African state', *History Workshop Journal* 8: 50–80.

Marquard, J., 1984. 'A neglected pioneer in South African literature: W.C. Scully'. Unpublished Ph.D. thesis, University of the Witwatersrand.

Martin, W.G. and Beittel, M., 1987. 'The hidden abode of reproduction: conceptualising households in Southern Africa', *Development and Change* 18 (2): 215–34.

Mbeki, G., 1984. *South Africa: The Peasants' Revolt*. London: International Defence and Aid Fund [originally published by Penguin Books, 1964].

*Men of the Times: Old Colonists of the Cape Colony and Orange River Colony*, 1906. Johannesburg: Transvaal Publishing Co.

Mitchell, G., 1875, 'Some account of the Barolong—a South African tribe', Part I, *Mission Field* 2 August: 233–42.

Molema, S.M., 1951. *Chief Moroka: His Life, His Times, His Country and His People*. Cape Town: Methodist Publishing House.

Morrell, R., 1986. 'Competition and co-operation in Middelburg, 1900–1930', in Beinart, Delius and Trapido, 1986, pp. 373–419.

Morris, M., 1976. 'The development of capitalism in South African agriculture: class struggle in the countryside', *Economy and Society* 5 (3): 292–343.

Morris, M., 1987. 'Social history and the transition to capitalism in the South African countryside', *Africa Perspective* New Series 1 (5 & 6): 7–24.

Murray, Christina, and O'Regan, C., 1990. *No Place to Rest: Forced Removals and the Law in South Africa*. Cape Town: Oxford University Press in association with the Labour Law Unit, University of Cape Town.

Murray, C., 1980. '"Stabilization" and structural unemployment', *South African Labour Bulletin* 6 (4): 58–61.

Murray, C., 1981. *Families Divided: The Impact of Migrant Labour in Lesotho*. Cambridge: Cambridge University Press; Johannesburg: Ravan Press.

Murray, C., 1983a. 'Struggle from the margins: rural slums in the Orange Free State', in F. Cooper (ed.), *Struggle for the City: Migrant Labor, Capital and the State in Urban Africa*. California: Sage Publications.

Murray, C., 1983b. 'The Orange Free State', in SPP Reports, 1983, Volume 3, pp. 143–81.

Murray, C., 1987a. 'Class, gender and the household: the developmental cycle in Southern Africa', *Development and Change* 18 (2): 235–49.

Murray, C., 1987b. 'Displaced urbanisation: South Africa's rural slums', *African Affairs* 86 (344): 311–29. Also published in J. Lonsdale (ed.), *South Africa in Question*, pp. 110–33. Cambridge: Cambridge University Press in association with the Centre for African Studies, Cambridge.

Murray, M.J., 1989a. '"The natives are always stealing": white vigilantes and the "reign of terror" in the Orange Free State, 1918–24', *Journal of African History* 30 (1): 107–23.

Murray, M.J., 1989b. 'The origins of agrarian capitalism in South Africa: a critique of the "social history" perspective', *Journal of Southern African Studies* 15 (4): 645–65.

NCAR, 1987. *Botshabelo: Incorporation Now, Independence Next?* Cape Town: National Committee Against Removals.

Nicholson, F., 1977. 'Frederick Nicholson of Heathfield', *Africana Notes and News* 22 (5); 201–11 [based on his unpublished manuscript, 1966, 'Heathfield: an autobiography of eighty-five years of my life'].

NLC, 1990. *The Bantustans in Crisis*. Johannesburg: National Land Committee.

Oberholster, J.J., 1969. *Wepener 1869–1969*. Wepener: Stadsraad.

Odendaal, A., 1984. *Vukani Bantu! The Beginnings of Black Protest Politics in South Africa to 1912*. Cape Town: David Philip.

O'Regan, C., 1990. 'The Prevention of Illegal Squatting Act', in Christina Murray and C. O'Regan, 1990, pp. 162–79.

Pakenham, T., 1979. *The Boer War*. London: Weidenfeld and Nicolson.

Peires, J., 1987. 'The legend of Fenner-Solomon', in B. Bozzoli (ed.), *Class, Community and Conflict: South African Perspectives*, pp. 65–92. Johannesburg: Ravan Press.

Phillips, H.Y., 1976. 'The Bagaseleka Barolong's search for a homeland', unpublished B.A. dissertation, University of Botswana, Lesotho and Swaziland (Gaborone).

Plaatje, S., 1916. *Sechuana Proverbs*. London: Kegan Paul & Co.

Plaatje, S., 1969. *Native Life in South Africa*. New York: Negro Universities Press [originally published London: P.S. King & Son, 1916].

Plasket, C., 1990. 'Homeland incorporation: the new forced removals', in Christina Murray and C. O'Regan, 1990, pp. 214–21.

Platzky, L. and Walker, C., 1985. *The Surplus People*. Johannesburg: Ravan Press.

Playne, S. (comp.), 1916. *The Orange Free State: Its Pastoral, Agricultural and Industrial Resources*. London: Foreign and Colonial Compiling and Publishing Co.

Potts, D. and Mutambirwa, C., 1990. 'Rural-urban linkages in contemporary Harare: why migrants need their land', *Journal of Southern African Studies* 16 (4): 677–98.

Rabie, J.E., 1980. *Generaal C.R. de Wet se Krygsleiding by Sannahspos en Groenkop*. Publication No. 6, Pretoria: Documentation Service, South African Defence Force.

Rich, P., 1984. *White Power and the Liberal Conscience: Racial Segregation and South African Liberalism 1921–60*. Manchester: Manchester University Press.

Rich, P., 1989. 'Managing black leadership: the Joint Councils, urban trading and political conflict in the Orange Free State, 1925–1942', in P. Bonner, I. Hofmeyr, D. James and T. Lodge (eds.), *Holding Their Ground: Class, Locality and Culture in 19th and 20th Century South Africa*, pp. 177–200. Johannesburg: Witwatersrand University Press and Ravan Press.

Ross, R., 1983. *Cape of Torments*. London: Routledge & Kegan Paul.

SAIRR, 1939. *Farm Labour in the Orange Free State*. Monograph Series No. 2, Johannesburg: South African Institute of Race Relations.

SAIRR, Annual *Survey of Race Relations in South Africa*: 1976 (1977); 1979 (1980); 1984 (1985); 1986 Part I (1987), Part II (1988); 1988/89 (1989); 1989/90 (1990). Johannesburg: South African Institute of Race Relations.

Sanders, P., 1975. *Moshoeshoe: Chief of the Sotho*. London: Heinemann.

Schapera, I., 1971. 'The native land problem in the Tati district', *Botswana Notes and Records* 3: 219–68. [This report was published in 1971 as originally written in 1943].

Sharp, J., 1987. 'Relocation, labour migration and the domestic predicament: Qwaqwa in the 1980s', in J. Eades (ed.), *Migrants, Workers and the Social Order*, pp. 130–47. London: Tavistock.

Sharp, J. and Spiegel, A., 1990. 'Women and wages: gender and the control of income in farm and Bantustan households', *Journal of Southern African Studies* 16 (3): 527–49.

Shillington, K., 1985. *The Colonisation of the Southern Tswana 1870–1900*. Johannesburg: Ravan Press.

Simkins, C., 1981. 'Agricultural production in the African reserves of South Africa, 1919–1969', *Journal of Southern African Studies* 7 (2): 256–83.

Simkins, C., 1983. *Four Essays on the Past, Present and Possible Future of the Distribution of the Black Population of South Africa*. Cape Town: Southern Africa Labour and Development Research Unit.

Simon, D., 1985. 'Agrarian policy and migration in Zimbabwe and Southern Africa: reform or transportation?', *Review of African Political Economy* 34: 82–9.

Skota, T.D. Mweli, (ed.), 1931. *The African Yearly Register*. Johannesburg: R.L. Esson & Co.

Southall, R., 1982. *South Africa's Transkei: The Political Economy of an 'Independent' Bantustan*. London: Heinemann.

SPP Reports, 1983. *Forced Removals in South Africa*, Volumes 1–5. Cape Town: The Surplus People Project.

Streek, B. and Wicksteed, R., 1981. *Render unto Kaiser: A Transkei Dossier*. Johannesburg: Ravan Press.

Sutcliffe, M., Todes, A. and Walker, N., 1990. 'Managing the cities: An examination of state urbanization policies since 1986', in Christina Murray and C. O'Regan, 1990, pp. 86–106.

Theal, G.W. (comp.), 1919. *History of South Africa from 1795 to 1872*, Volume IV, 4th edition. London: George Allen & Unwin [originally published 1889].

Theal, G.W., 1964. *Basutoland Records, 1862–65*, Volume IIIA. Cape Town: Struik [facsimile reproduction of the 1883 edition].

Thompson, L. 1975. *Survival in Two Worlds: Moshoeshoe of Lesotho 1786–1870*. Oxford: Clarendon Press.

Thompson, L. and Wilson, M. (eds.), 1971. *The Oxford History of South Africa*, Volume II. Oxford: Oxford University Press.

TRAC, 1988. 'A toehold on the land: labour tenancy in the south-eastern Transvaal', Johannesburg: Transvaal Rural Action Committee.

Trollope, A., 1878. *South Africa*, Volume II. London: Chapman and Hall.

Tucker, E.M. and McGregor, P.M.J., 1961. *Per Noctem Per Diem: The Story of 24 Squadron, South African Airforce*. Cape Town: 24 Squadron Album Committee.

Turrell, R., 1987. *Capital and Labour in the Kimberley Diamond Fields 1871–1890*. Cambridge: Cambridge University Press.

Van Aswegen, H.J., 1971. 'Die Verhouding tussen Blank en Nie-Blank in die Oranje-. Vrystaat, 1854–1902', *Archives Yearbook for South African History* I. Pretoria.

Van Niekerk, P., 1990. 'Bantustan politics', *New Ground* 1 (1): 12–14.

Van Onselen, C., 1990. 'Race and class in the South African countryside: cultural osmosis and social relations in the sharecropping economy of the south-western Transvaal, 1900–1950', *American Historical Review* 95 (1): 99–123.

Van Riet, J.B., 1945. ' "Boys' town" system for farm labour', *South African Advertising and Selling*, February: 37–9.

Van Zeyl, P., 1985a. 'An evolving development axis', *Growth*, Autumn.

Van Zeyl, P., 1985b. 'IDPs on the development axis', *Growth*, Winter.

Van Zeyl, P., 1986. 'Botshabelo: increasing emphasis on regional co-operation set to bolster development impetus further', *Growth*, Summer.

Wales, J., 1985. 'The relationship between the Orange Free State and the Rolong of Thaba Nchu during the Presidency of J.H. Brand, 1864–1888', *Archives Yearbook for South African History* I. Pretoria.

Walker, O., 1948. *Kaffirs Are Lively: Being Some Backstage Impressions of the South African Democracy*. London: Victor Gollancz.

Walshe, P., 1970. *The Rise of African Nationalism in South Africa: The African National Congress 1912–1952*. London: Hurst.

Warwick, P., 1983. *Black People and the South African War 1899–1902*. Johannesburg: Ravan Press.

Watson, R.L., 1977. 'Missionary influence at Thaba Nchu, 1833–1854: a reassessment', *International Journal of African Historical Studies* 10 (3): 394–407.

Watson, R.L., 1980. 'The subjection of a South African state: Thaba Nchu, 1880–1884', *Journal of African History* 21: 357–73.

Wells, J., 1980. 'Women's resistance to passes in Bloemfontein during the inter-war period', *Africa Perspective* 15: 16–35.

Willan, B., 1984. *Sol Plaatje: South African Nationalist, 1876–1932*. London: Heinemann.

Williams, G., 1990. 'Capitalism and agriculture: the South African case', *Collected Seminar Papers* 40, pp. 141–8. London University: Institute of Commonwealth Studies.

Wilson, F., 1972. *Migrant Labour in South Africa*. Johannesburg: South African Council of Churches and Spro-Cas.

Wilson, F. and Perrot, D. (eds.), 1973. *Outlook on a Century: South Africa 1870–1970*. Lovedale: Lovedale Press; Johannesburg: Spro-Cas.

Wilson, F. and Ramphele, M., 1989. *Uprooting Poverty: The South African Challenge*. Cape Town: David Philip.

Yawitch, J., 1981. *Betterment: The Myth of Homeland Agriculture*. Johannesburg: South African Institute of Race Relations.

# INDEX

*Note:* The categories Barolong, Basotho, Bloemfontein and Orange Free State [Orange River Colony, 1900–10] are ubiquitous throughout the text and are not indexed separately, except (in the case of Barolong) where specific sub-entries are appropriate. Likewise, the old and new Thaba Nchu districts, Thaba Nchu town and the Black Mountain itself are not listed. The Thaba Nchu reserve is listed because of its distinctive political status within the district, analogous to that of the Seliba reserve, throughout the period from 1885 to the 'second wave' of land purchase by the South African Native Trust in the late 1940s.

Square brackets indicate alternative names; round brackets indicate titles or official positions; references in italics are to figures.